W9-CAA-863

Southern Living®
All-Time Favorites

Southern Living®
All-Time Favorites

Compiled and Edited by
Susan Hernandez Ray

Oxmoor
House®

©2009 by Oxmoor House, Inc.

Southern Living® is a registered trademark of Time Inc. Lifestyle Group. Oxmoor House is an imprint of Time Home Entertainment, Inc. All rights reserved. No part of this book may be reproduced in any form or by any means without the prior written permission of the publisher, excepting brief quotations in connection with reviews written specifically for inclusion in magazines or newspapers, or limited excerpts strictly for personal use.

ISBN-13: 978-0-8487-3277-6
ISBN-10: 0-8487-3277-4
Library of Congress Control Number: 2008930183

Printed in the United States of America
Fourth Printing 2011

To order additional publications, call 1-800-765-6400

For more books to enrich your life, visit **oxmoorhouse.com**

To search, savor, and share thousands of recipes, visit **myrecipes.com**

Cover: White-Chocolate Raspberry Cheesecake (page 386); (top, left to right) Feta-Stuffed Tomatoes (page 342), Three-Cheese Pasta Bake (page 275), Steaks With Caramel-Brandy Sauce (page 211), Dark Chocolate Bundt Cake with Wintry-White Icing (page 371)

Back Cover: Linguine With Fresh Tomato Sauce (page 136); (bottom, left to right) Orange Thing (page 43); Saucy Pork Chops With Orange Slices (page 222); Heavenly Angel Food Cake (page 382); Turkey, Bacon, and Havarti Sandwich (page 360)

Page 1: Tomato-and-Watermelon Salad (page 301)

Page 2: Praline Chicken (page 170)

***Southern Living*®**
Executive Editor: Scott Jones
Food Editor: Shannon Sliter Satterwhite
Senior Writer: Donna Florio
Associate Food Editors: Charla Draper, Shirley Harrington, Mary Allen Perry
Assistant Food Editors: Natalie Kelly Brown, Marion McGahey
Assistant Recipe Editors: Ashley Arthur, Ashley Leath
Test Kitchens Director: Lyda Jones Burnette
Assistant Test Kitchens Director: Rebecca Kracke Gordon
Test Kitchens Specialist/Food Styling: Vanessa McNeil Rocchio
Test Kitchens Professionals: Marian Cooper Cairns, Kristi Michele Crowe, Norman King, Pam Lolley, Angela Sellers
Editorial Assistant: Pat York
Senior Foods Photographer: Jennifer Davick
Photographer: Beth Dreiling Hontzas
Senior Photo Stylist: Buffy Hargett

Oxmoor House, Inc.
VP, Publishing Director: Jim Childs
Executive Editor: Susan Payne Dobbs
Brand Manager: Daniel Fagan
Managing Editor: L. Amanda Owens

Southern Living*® *All-Time Favorites
Editor: Susan Hernandez Ray
Project Editor: Vanessa Lynn Rusch
Senior Designer: Emily Albright Parrish
Director, Test Kitchens: Elizabeth Tyler Austin
Assistant Director, Test Kitchens: Julie Christopher
Test Kitchens Professionals: Catherine Crowell Steele, Kathleen Royal Phillips, Ashley T. Strickland, Deborah Wise
Photography Director: Jim Bathie
Senior Photo Stylist: Kay E. Clarke
Associate Photo Stylist: Katherine Eckert Coyne
Production Manager: Greg Amason

Contributors:
Designer: Nancy Johnson
Proofreader: Jasmine Hodges
Indexer: Mary Ann Laurens
Interns: Emily Chappell, Anne-Harris Jones, Angela Valente, Lauren Wiygul

contents

welcome

Dear Friends,

We're convinced that the best smells in the world waft out of the *Southern Living* Test Kitchens. On any given day there will be a pot of chicken and dumplings stewing on the stove, ribs fresh from the smoker, a Dutch oven full of simmering spaghetti sauce, baking sweet potatoes, or a dozen peaches waiting to be sliced for a cobbler. And it's a rare day when we're not tempted by the scent of cakes, cookies, or biscuits. Our readers love to bake, and we are happy to oblige by providing them innovative layer, loaf, and pound cake formulas, as well as the classics that we can't live without.

Luscious as the aromas are, they can't compete with the pleasure of tasting each and every one of the recipes that go into the magazine. We test some 5,000 a year, that is a whole lot of food. A recipe has really got to be top-notch to stand out. But all of us have choices so memorable that we talk about them in glowing terms (often with a faraway look in our eyes) and that we rely on for daily meals and entertaining. Most of those recipes are in this volume.

While each recipe is someone's favorite (or it likely wouldn't have made the cut), others strike a chord with the entire group. All of us are fans of Chicken Cakes With Rémoulade Sauce on page 32. The dish became an instant classic the moment it appeared in 2000. If you love Louisville's famous Hot Brown sandwich, try the baby version on page 29. This knife-and-fork appetizer has all the terrific flavor of the original. Pimiento Cheese lovers can't go wrong with our best-ever version on page 16. Be sure to check out the variations. Naturally, we couldn't publish this book without our best biscuits, so we offer several for you to choose from. The Buttermilk Biscuits on page 46 are amazingly light and flaky, thanks to a unique method of handling the dough. Truly, they are some of the best we've ever tasted. Try them yourself to see if you agree.

We hope you enjoy reading and cooking from every delicious page of this book as much as we've enjoyed compiling it for you.

The Editors
Southern Living

Rebecca Kracke Gordon, Assistant Test Kitchens Director, says about Italian Meatballs (page 217):

I like to make a large batch of these, and freeze them in meal-size portions to cook during the week.

Shannon Sliter Satterwhite, Food Editor, says about Banana Pudding (page 200):

As a dietitian, I hear angels sing whenever I taste a lightened recipe that's just as rich and sumptuous as its traditional version—this light dessert is truly divine.

Marian Cooper Cairns, Test Kitchens Professional, says about Mediterranean Chicken Couscous (page 182):

I love this easy, no-mess recipe because no pots and pans are required.

Marinated Southwestern
Cheese, page 15

party
starters

Party Mix
PREP: 10 MIN., COOK: 1 HR.

½ cup butter, melted
2 tablespoons Worcestershire sauce
1 teaspoon hot sauce
1½ teaspoons garlic salt
6 cups crisp rice cereal squares
2 cups toasted oat O-shaped cereal
1 cup mixed nuts
1 cup pretzel sticks

1. Stir together first 4 ingredients in a roasting pan. Add remaining ingredients, stirring to coat.
2. Bake mixture at 200° for 1 hour or until toasted, stirring every 15 minutes. Cool. **Makes** 10 cups.
Note: For testing purposes only, we used Rice Chex Cereal Squares.

Swedish Nuts
PREP: 15 MIN., COOK: 50 MIN.

1 cup whole blanched almonds
½ cup butter
2 egg whites
¾ cup sugar
Dash of salt
1 cup walnut halves
1 cup pecan halves

1. Spread almonds evenly on an ungreased baking sheet. Roast at 325° for 15 minutes or until lightly browned, stirring occasionally; remove from oven, and cool. Place butter in a 13- x 9-inch pan; place in oven to melt butter.
2. Beat egg whites in a large mixing bowl at high speed with an electric mixer until stiff peaks form. Gradually add sugar and salt, beating until mixture is stiff (2 to 4 minutes). Gently fold in almonds, walnuts, and pecans; spread nut mixture evenly over melted butter in pan.
3. Bake at 325° for 35 minutes or until mixture is browned and butter is absorbed, stirring every 10 minutes. Cool completely. Store in an airtight container. **Makes** 5 cups.

Sugar-and-Spice Nuts
PREP: 15 MIN., COOK: 55 MIN.

¾ cup sugar
1 tablespoon Sweet Spice Blend
¾ teaspoon salt
1 egg white
1 tablespoon water
1 pound pecan halves*

1. Combine first 3 ingredients in a bowl; set aside.
2. Beat egg white and 1 tablespoon water in a medium bowl using a handheld egg beater or a wire whisk until foamy. (No liquid should remain.) Add pecans, stirring until evenly coated.
3. Add pecans to sugar mixture, stirring until coated. Place in a single layer on a buttered 15- x 10-inch jelly-roll pan.
4. Bake at 275° for 50 to 55 minutes, stirring every 15 minutes. Spread immediately in a single layer on wax paper; cool completely. Store in an airtight container. **Makes** about 5 cups.
*Substitute whole almonds or walnut halves, if desired.

Sweet Spice Blend
PREP: 5 MIN

2 tablespoons light brown sugar
2 tablespoons ground cinnamon
4 teaspoons dried ground ginger
1 teaspoon ground nutmeg
½ teaspoon ground cloves
½ teaspoon ground cardamom

1. Combine all ingredients in a small bowl. Store in an airtight container. **Makes** 6 tablespoons.

> **These have a spicy sweet and salty taste that's truly addictive. I served them over the holidays and guests couldn't get enough.**
> NATALIE KELLY BROWN, ASSISTANT FOODS EDITOR

Marinated Olives

Look for kalamata olives in bulk at your grocery deli or local Greek market.

PREP: 10 MIN., OTHER: 8 HR.

1 pound drained kalamata olives
12 drained pimiento-stuffed Spanish olives
12 drained pickled jalapeño peppers
¼ cup tequila
¼ cup lime juice
2 tablespoons orange liqueur
¼ cup minced fresh cilantro
1 teaspoon orange zest
1 teaspoon olive oil

1. Stir together all ingredients. Chill 8 hours. **Makes** 8 servings.

Blue Cheese-Walnut Wafers

*Don't substitute margarine for butter in this recipe.
The butter makes the dough easier to handle and
results in wonderfully tender wafers.*

PREP: 10 MIN.; COOK: 12 MIN.; OTHER: 1 HR., 5 MIN.

1 (4-ounce) package blue cheese, softened
½ cup butter, softened
1¼ cups all-purpose flour
⅓ cup finely chopped walnuts

1. Process first 3 ingredients in a food processor until smooth, stopping to scrape down sides. (Mixture will be sticky.) Spoon mixture into a bowl; stir in walnuts. Cover and chill 5 minutes.
2. Divide dough in half. Shape each portion into an 8-inch log. Wrap in heavy-duty plastic wrap; chill 1 hour.
3. Slice dough into ¼-inch-thick slices; place on ungreased baking sheets.
4. Bake at 350° for 12 minutes or until lightly browned. Store in an airtight container up to 1 week. **Makes** 4 dozen.

Cheddar Cheese Straws

*If you don't have a heavy-duty stand mixer, you
can use a handheld mixer. Just divide the ingredients
in half, and work with two batches.*

PREP: 30 MIN., COOK: 12 MIN. PER BATCH

1½ cups butter, softened
1 (1-pound) block sharp Cheddar cheese, shredded
1½ teaspoons salt
1 to 2 teaspoons ground red pepper
½ teaspoon paprika
4 cups all-purpose flour

1. Beat first 5 ingredients at medium speed with a
heavy-duty stand mixer until blended. Gradually add
flour, beating just until combined.
2. Use a cookie press with a star-shaped disk to shape
mixture into long ribbons, following manufacturer's
instructions, on parchment paper-lined baking sheets.
Cut ribbons into 2-inch pieces.
3. Bake at 350° for 12 minutes or until lightly browned.
Remove to wire racks to cool. **Makes** about 10 dozen.

Cheese Wafers: Combine ingredients as directed;
chill dough 2 hours. Shape dough into 4 (8-inch-long)
logs; wrap each in plastic wrap, and chill 8 hours. Cut
each log into ¼-inch-thick slices; place on parchment paper-lined baking sheets. Bake at 350° for 13 to
15 minutes or until lightly browned. Remove to wire
racks to cool. Store in an airtight container 1 week.

Our Best Cheese Straw Tips:

- Shred your own cheese; it's stickier and blends bet-
  ter than preshredded cheese.
- Refrigerate unbaked dough between batches to
  keep cheese straws from spreading too thin when
  baked.
- Store unbaked dough in the fridge for 1 week or in
  the freezer for 1 month. Store baked cheese straws
  in an airtight container for 1 week.
- Bake on parchment paper to yield the best results;
  1 sheet can be used multiple times.
- Bake stored cheese straws in the oven at 350° for
  3 to 4 minutes to make them crispy again.

Blue Cheese Thumbprints

PREP: 15 MIN., COOK: 15 MIN. PER BATCH, OTHER: 2 HR.

2 (4-ounce) packages crumbled blue cheese
½ cup butter, softened
1⅓ cups all-purpose flour
3 tablespoons poppy seeds
¼ teaspoon ground red pepper
⅓ cup cherry preserves

1. Beat blue cheese and butter at medium speed with
an electric mixer until fluffy. Add flour, poppy seeds,
and red pepper, beating just until combined.
Roll dough into ¾-inch balls; cover and chill
2 hours.
2. Arrange balls on ungreased baking sheets, and press
thumb into each ball of dough, leaving an indentation.
3. Bake at 350° for 15 minutes or until golden.
Transfer to wire racks to cool completely. Place about
¼ teaspoon preserves in each indentation. **Makes**
about 5 dozen.

Blue Cheese Crisps

PREP: 8 MIN., COOK: 10 MIN. PER BATCH

½ cup butter, softened
1 (4-ounce) package crumbled blue cheese, softened
½ cup finely chopped pecans or walnuts
1 French baguette, sliced
Garnish: fresh parsley

1. Stir together softened butter and blue cheese until
blended; stir in chopped nuts. Set mixture aside.
2. Place baguette slices in a single layer on baking
sheets.
3. Bake at 350° for 3 to 5 minutes. Turn slices, and
spread evenly with blue cheese mixture. Bake 5 more
minutes. Garnish, if desired. Serve crisps immediately.
Makes 32 crisps.

Roasted Pepper-Tomato Bruschetta
Seeding the tomatoes will enhance the appearance of these appetizers.

PREP: 15 MIN.

1 (7-ounce) jar roasted red bell peppers, drained and chopped
6 ripe tomatoes, seeded and diced
3 tablespoons shredded Parmesan cheese
2 tablespoons chopped fresh basil
1 garlic clove, minced
½ teaspoon coarse-grained sea salt or kosher salt
¼ teaspoon freshly ground pepper
24 French bread slices, toasted

1. Combine first 7 ingredients; spoon 1 heaping table-spoon over each toasted bread slice. **Makes** 2 dozen.

Deviled Eggs

PREP: 10 MIN.

5 hard-cooked eggs, peeled
1½ tablespoons Dijon mustard
1½ tablespoons mayonnaise
5 pimiento-stuffed olives, halved
1 teaspoon Cajun seasoning

1. Cut eggs in half lengthwise; carefully remove yolks.
2. Mash yolks, and stir in mustard and mayonnaise; blend well.
3. Spoon yolk mixture evenly into egg whites. Place an olive half in the center of each; sprinkle with Cajun seasoning. **Makes** 10 eggs.

Date-Filled Cheese Pastries
PREP: 30 MIN., COOK: 25 MIN., OTHER: 45 MIN.

1½ cups (6 ounces) shredded Cheddar cheese
1 cup all-purpose flour
1 teaspoon salt
¼ teaspoon ground red pepper
⅓ cup butter, melted
24 pitted dates
24 pecan halves, toasted

1. Combine first 4 ingredients in a bowl, stirring well. Add butter, stirring just until dry ingredients are moistened. (Dough will be crumbly). Shape dough into a ball.
2. Make a lengthwise slit in each date, and stuff each date with a pecan half. Press 1 generous tablespoon cheese mixture around each date, covering completely. Cover and chill 45 minutes. (You can cover and freeze pastries up to 1 month. Thaw in refrigerator before baking.)
3. Place pastries on a greased baking sheet. Bake at 350° for 25 minutes. Remove pastries to a wire rack to cool. Serve warm or at room temperature. **Makes** 2 dozen.

Nutty Stuffed Celery
This healthy recipe is perfect for a dinner party.

PREP: 15 MIN.

3 ounces ⅓-less-fat cream cheese, softened
1 tablespoon half-and-half
½ teaspoon onion powder
½ teaspoon seasoned salt
¼ teaspoon curry powder
4 celery ribs, cut into 4-inch pieces
¼ cup coarsely chopped honey-roasted peanuts

1. Stir together first 5 ingredients. Cover and chill mixture until ready to serve.
2. Spread mixture on celery pieces, and sprinkle with peanuts. **Makes** 4 appetizer servings.

Marinated Southwestern Cheese

The first version of this appetizer ran in the late 1980s. As interest in Southwestern fare increased,
our Test Kitchens offered this variation. Serve on skewers for easy party pickups.

PREP: 30 MIN., OTHER: 8 HR.

½ cup olive oil
½ cup white wine vinegar
¼ cup fresh lime juice
½ (7.5-ounce) jar roasted sweet red peppers,
    drained and diced
3 green onions, minced
3 tablespoons chopped fresh parsley
3 tablespoons chopped fresh cilantro
1 teaspoon sugar
½ teaspoon salt
½ teaspoon freshly ground black pepper
1 (8-ounce) block sharp Cheddar cheese, chilled
1 (8-ounce) block Monterey Jack cheese with
    peppers, chilled
1 (8-ounce) package cream cheese, chilled

❝ I've made this appetizer for a long time, even before I came to work at *Southern Living*. Back when I was a *Southern Living* subscriber and stay-at-home mom, I loved the make-ahead aspect. It's so easy to prepare the night before. Here's a tip: To cube the cream cheese, use dental floss. ❞

VICKI POELLNITZ, ASSOCIATE FOOD EDITOR

1. Whisk together first 3 ingredients until blended; stir in diced red peppers and next 6 ingredients.
2. Cube cheeses, and place in a shallow dish; pour marinade over cheeses. Cover and chill 8 hours.
3. Transfer marinated cheese to a large glass jar or serving dish, and spoon marinade over top. Serve with assorted crackers. **Makes** 16 appetizer servings.

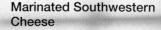

Marinated Southwestern Cheese

Pimiento Cheese

Pimiento Cheese

PREP: 15 MIN.

1¼ cups mayonnaise
1 (4-ounce) jar diced pimiento, drained
1 teaspoon Worcestershire sauce
1 teaspoon finely grated onion
¼ teaspoon ground red pepper
1 (8-ounce) block extra-sharp Cheddar cheese,
    finely shredded
1 (8-ounce) block sharp Cheddar cheese, shredded
Celery sticks or assorted crackers

1. Stir together first 5 ingredients in a large bowl; stir in cheeses. Store in refrigerator up to 1 week. Serve with celery sticks or assorted crackers. **Makes** 4 cups.

Jalapeño Pimiento Cheese: Prepare recipe as directed, adding 2 seeded and minced jalapeño peppers.

Cream Cheese-and-Olive Pimiento Cheese: Reduce mayonnaise to ¾ cup. Stir together first 5 ingredients, 1 (8-ounce) package softened cream cheese, and 1 (5¾-ounce) jar drained sliced pimiento-stuffed Spanish olives. Proceed with recipe as directed.

Pecan Pimiento Cheese: Prepare recipe as directed, stirring in ¾ cup toasted chopped pecans.

❝ You can also bake this irresistible dip in a lightly greased 2-quart baking dish at 350° for 20 minutes or until golden and bubbly.❞

MARY ALLEN PERRY, ASSOCIATE FOOD EDITOR

Simple Blue Cheese Spread

*The serious blue cheese fan will enjoy
this three-ingredient spread.*

PREP: 10 MIN.

1 (4-ounce) package blue cheese
1 (3-ounce) package cream cheese, softened
3 tablespoons brandy

1. Crumble and mash blue cheese in a bowl. Add cream cheese; beat at medium speed with an electric mixer until smooth. Add brandy, beating until mixture is blended. Cover and chill. Serve with assorted crackers, pumpernickel or rye party rounds, or apple and pear slices. **Makes** 1 cup.

Baked Hearts of Palm Spread

PREP: 10 MIN., COOK: 20 MIN.

1 (14.4-ounce) can hearts of palm, drained and
    chopped
1 cup (4 ounces) shredded mozzarella cheese
¾ cup mayonnaise
½ cup grated Parmesan cheese
¼ cup sour cream
1 green onion, minced

1. Combine all ingredients; spoon mixture into a lightly greased 9-inch quiche dish or pie plate. Bake, uncovered, at 350° for 20 minutes or until hot and bubbly. Serve with crackers or Melba rounds. **Makes** 2 cups.

Fresh Basil-Cheese Spread

PREP: 10 MIN, COOK: 10 MIN., OTHER: 1 HR.

¾ cup chopped walnuts
¼ cup fresh basil leaves, coarsely chopped
1 green onion, chopped
1 garlic clove, halved
2 (8-ounce) packages cream cheese, softened
1 cup freshly grated Parmesan cheese
½ cup olive oil

1. Bake walnuts in a shallow pan at 350° for 5 to 10 minutes or until toasted, stirring occasionally. Cool.
2. Pulse basil, green onion, and garlic in a food processor until minced. Add walnuts, cream cheese, Parmesan cheese, and oil; process until smooth. Cover and chill 1 hour. Serve spread with crackers or toasted pita wedges. **Makes** 3 cups.

Mexican Cheese Spread

PREP: 10 MIN.

2 cups (8 ounces) shredded sharp Cheddar cheese
½ cup sour cream
¼ cup butter, softened
2 green onions, chopped
1 (2-ounce) jar diced pimiento, drained
2 tablespoons chopped green chiles

1. Combine first 3 ingredients in a mixing bowl; beat at medium speed with an electric mixer until blended.
2. Stir in green onions, pimiento, and chiles. Cover and chill, if desired. Serve with crackers. **Makes** 2 cups.

Layered Cheese Torta

Be sure to layer the cheese mixtures according to directions so you'll have three even ribbons of color. Then give the mold plenty of time to chill.

PREP: 25 MIN., OTHER: 9 HR.

1 (8-ounce) package cream cheese, softened
¼ cup crumbled blue cheese
1 (8-ounce) can crushed pineapple, drained
⅛ teaspoon dried ground ginger
½ cup chopped pecans
1 (3-ounce) package cream cheese, softened
⅓ cup milk
2 cups (8 ounces) shredded Cheddar cheese
6 bacon slices, cooked and crumbled
1 teaspoon grated onion
¼ teaspoon hot sauce
Garnishes: chopped pecans, fresh parsley sprigs

1. Combine first 4 ingredients in a bowl. Beat at medium speed with an electric mixer until blended; stir in pecans.

2. Line a lightly greased 4-cup fluted mold or a $7\frac{3}{8}$- x $3\frac{5}{8}$-inch loafpan with plastic wrap, allowing edges to extend over sides of pan. Spread one-third of blue cheese mixture into mold; chill 1 hour.

3. Combine 3-ounce package cream cheese and milk, beating well. Add Cheddar cheese and next 3 ingredients, mixing well. Spread over chilled blue cheese mixture in mold. Top with remaining two-thirds blue cheese mixture, spreading evenly. Cover with plastic wrap; chill at least 8 hours or up to 3 days. Unmold onto a serving platter. Remove plastic wrap. Garnish, if desired. Serve with gingersnaps or assorted crackers. **Makes** 3 cups.

Layered Cheese Torta

Four-Cheese Pâté

Four-Cheese Pâté

This snowy white pâté makes an impressive appetizer. Toasty pecans enhance the mild blend of cheeses.

PREP: 30 MIN., OTHER: 4 HR.

1 (8-ounce) package cream cheese, softened
2 tablespoons milk
1 cup chopped pecans, toasted
2 (8-ounce) packages cream cheese, softened
1 (4½-ounce) package Camembert cheese, softened
1 (4-ounce) package blue cheese
1 cup (4 ounces) shredded Swiss cheese
Garnishes: red and green grapes

1. Line a lightly greased 8-inch round cake pan with plastic wrap; set aside. Combine 1 package cream cheese and milk in a medium mixing bowl; beat at medium speed with an electric mixer until smooth. Spread mixture into prepared pan; sprinkle evenly with chopped pecans. Cover and chill.

2. Combine remaining 2 packages cream cheese, Camembert cheese (including rind), blue cheese, and Swiss cheese in a bowl; beat until blended. Spoon mixture over pecan layer, spreading to edge of pan. Cover and chill at least 4 hours or up to 1 week.

3. To serve, invert pâté onto a serving plate; carefully remove plastic wrap. Garnish pâté, if desired. Serve with apple wedges, gingersnaps, or assorted crackers. **Makes** 4½ cups.

Pumpkin Cheese Ball

This spread is not actually pumpkin-flavored, but shaping it into a ball, carving vertical grooves, and crowning the creation with a small broccoli stalk will dress it for a costume party.

PREP: 30 MIN., OTHER: 4 HR.

2 (8-ounce) blocks extra-sharp Cheddar cheese,
    shredded
1 (8-ounce) package cream cheese, softened
1 (8-ounce) container chive-and-onion cream cheese
2 teaspoons paprika
½ teaspoon ground red pepper
1 broccoli stalk

1. Combine Cheddar cheese and next 4 ingredients in a bowl until blended. Cover and chill 4 hours or until mixture is firm enough to be shaped.
2. Shape mixture into a ball to resemble a pumpkin. Smooth entire outer surface with a frosting spatula or table knife. Make vertical grooves in ball, if desired, using fingertips.
3. Cut florets from broccoli stalk, and reserve for another use. Cut stalk to resemble a pumpkin stem, and press into top of cheese ball. Serve cheese ball with red and green apple wedges. **Makes** 16 appetizer servings.
Note: To make ahead, wrap cheese ball in plastic wrap without stalk; store in refrigerator up to 2 days. Attach stalk before serving.

Pesto Goat Cheese

There's just the right balance of herbs and cheese in this recipe.

PREP: 25 MIN., OTHER: 2 HR.

2 (3-ounce) logs goat cheese, softened
1 (8-ounce) package cream cheese, softened
1 (7-ounce) jar basil pesto, drained
1 tablespoon fresh lemon juice
1 tablespoon chopped fresh parsley
1 (¾-ounce) package fresh thyme sprigs

1. Stir together first 5 ingredients until well blended. Remove ¼ cup mixture, and wrap in plastic wrap; chill. Press remaining cheese mixture into a 6-cup or 1.5-liter plastic wrap-lined bowl. Cover and chill 2 hours.
2. Remove plastic wrap from chilled ¼ cup cheese mixture. Shape heaping teaspoonfuls of cheese mixture into egg shapes. Chill until ready to serve.
3. Unmold cheese mixture; remove plastic wrap, and place on a serving platter. Press a 2-inch indention into center of cheese mold. Press thyme sprigs around top edge and sides of mold to resemble a nest. Arrange eggs in center of nest. Serve with crackers. **Makes** 8 appetizer servings.

Goat Cheese Spread

To garnish, cut one dried tomato into slivers. Gently press tomato slivers and fresh oregano sprigs in a decorative pattern over the top of the cheese after it is inverted.

PREP: 30 MIN., OTHER: 8 HR.

2 (8-ounce) packages cream cheese, softened
8 ounces goat cheese
2 garlic cloves, minced
4 teaspoons chopped fresh or 1¼ teaspoons dried
    oregano
⅛ teaspoon freshly ground pepper
¼ cup basil pesto
½ cup dried tomatoes in oil, drained and chopped
Garnishes: dried tomato slivers, fresh oregano sprigs

1. Process first 5 ingredients in a food processor until smooth. Spread one-third of cheese mixture in bottom of a plastic wrap-lined 8- x 4-inch loafpan. Top with pesto; spread one-third of cheese mixture over pesto. Sprinkle with dried tomatoes, and top with remaining cheese mixture. Cover and chill 8 hours.
2. Invert spread onto a serving plate, discarding plastic wrap. Garnish, if desired. Serve with French bread slices or crackers. **Makes** 12 to 16 appetizer servings.

Goat Cheese Spread

Warmed Cranberry Brie

You can easily double this recipe for a large crowd.

PREP: 10 MIN., COOK: 5 MIN.

1 (15-ounce) round Brie
1 (16-ounce) can whole-berry cranberry
    sauce
¼ cup firmly packed brown sugar
2 tablespoons spiced rum*
½ teaspoon ground nutmeg
¼ cup chopped pecans, toasted

1. Trim rind from top of Brie, leaving a ⅓-inch border on top. Place Brie on a baking sheet.
2. Stir together cranberry sauce and next 3 ingredients; spread mixture evenly over top of Brie. Sprinkle evenly with pecans.
3. Bake Brie at 500° for 5 minutes. Serve with assorted crackers and apple and pear slices. **Makes** 8 appetizer servings.
*Substitute 2 tablespoons orange juice for spiced rum, if desired.

Stuffed Brie en Croûte

PREP: 20 MIN., COOK: 40 MIN., OTHER: 20 MIN.

1 small red pepper
1 (8-ounce) round Brie, chilled
¼ cup coarsely chopped ripe olives
½ (17¼-ounce) package frozen puff pastry
    sheets, thawed
2 egg yolks, lightly beaten
2 tablespoons water

1. Place pepper on an aluminum foil-lined baking sheet. Broil pepper 5 ½ inches from heat 5 minutes or until pepper looks blistered, turning twice.
2. Place pepper in a heavy-duty zip-top plastic freezer bag; seal and let stand 10 minutes. Peel pepper; remove core and seeds. Coarsely chop pepper.
3. Cut Brie in half horizontally with a serrated knife. Place pepper and olives on bottom half of Brie; replace top half, and set aside.
4. Unfold puff pastry on a lightly floured surface. Fold corners 2 inches toward center; roll into a 14-inch circle.
5. Place Brie in center of pastry circle; bring pastry together, pinching seams, to resemble a bundle. Tie with kitchen string. Cover and chill up to 8 hours, if desired.
6. Place pastry-wrapped Brie on a lightly greased baking sheet. Combine egg yolks and water; brush over pastry.
7. Bake at 400° for 30 to 35 minutes or until golden brown. Cool 10 minutes; remove string. Transfer to a small cutting board; cut into wedges. Serve warm. **Makes** 4 appetizer servings.

Layered Crabmeat Spread

Layered Crabmeat Spread

PREP: 20 MIN., OTHER: 20 MIN.

1 (8-ounce) package cream cheese, softened
2 tablespoons lemon juice
1 tablespoon mayonnaise
½ teaspoon seasoned salt
½ teaspoon lemon pepper
¼ teaspoon Worcestershire sauce
¾ cup cocktail sauce
1 (16-ounce) container lump crabmeat, drained
2 cups (8 ounces) shredded Monterey Jack cheese
3 green onions, chopped
½ green bell pepper, chopped
½ cup sliced ripe olives

1. Beat cream cheese at medium speed with an electric mixer until smooth; add lemon juice and next 4 ingredients, beating until blended. Spoon mixture into a 9-inch serving dish. Cover and chill at least 20 minutes.
2. Spread cocktail sauce evenly over cream cheese mixture. Top with crabmeat; sprinkle with cheese, green onions, bell pepper, and ripe olives. Serve spread with crackers and fresh vegetables. **Makes** 12 to 15 appetizer servings.

To lighten: Substitute ⅓-less-fat cream cheese, light mayonnaise, and 2% reduced-fat Monterey Jack cheese.

spreads **23**

Hot Crab Dip

Hot Crab Dip

PREP: 15 MIN., COOK: 35 MIN.

2 (8-ounce) packages cream cheese, softened
1 (8-ounce) container sour cream
¼ cup mayonnaise
1 tablespoon Worcestershire sauce
1 tablespoon lemon juice
1 teaspoon dry mustard
¼ teaspoon garlic salt
1 pound fresh crabmeat, drained and picked
1 cup (4 ounces) shredded Cheddar cheese
Garnish: chopped fresh parsley

1. Combine first 7 ingredients, stirring until blended. Fold in crabmeat.
2. Spoon mixture into an 11- x 7-inch baking dish; sprinkle evenly with Cheddar cheese.
3. Bake at 350° for 35 minutes or until bubbly. Garnish, if desired. Serve immediately with crackers or toasted French bread rounds. **Makes** 10 appetizer servings.

To lighten: Substitute reduced-fat cream cheese, light sour cream, 2% reduced-fat Cheddar cheese, and light mayonnaise.

Black-Eyed Pea Dip

You can chill this dip overnight. Then just microwave briefly until thoroughly heated.

PREP: 12 MIN.

¼ cup butter
2 (15.8-ounce) cans black-eyed peas, undrained
1 cup (4 ounces) shredded Cheddar cheese
½ cup (2 ounces) shredded mozzarella cheese
2 tablespoons blackened seasoning
3 green onions, chopped
¼ cup chopped green pepper
¾ cup chopped cooked ham

1. Microwave butter in a 2-quart microwave-safe bowl at HIGH 30 seconds or until melted. Stir in peas and next 5 ingredients; microwave at HIGH 7 to 8 minutes or until cheese melts, stirring every 2 minutes.
2. Add ham; spoon dip into a chafing dish. Serve warm with tortilla chips. **Makes** 12 to 15 appetizer servings.
Note: For testing purposes only, we used Paul Prudhomme's Magic Seasoning.

Warm Nacho Dip

PREP: 20 MIN., COOK: 25 MIN.

2 (16-ounce) cans refried beans
1 (4.5-ounce) can chopped green chiles, drained
1 (1.25-ounce) package taco seasoning
2 cups (8 ounces) shredded Monterey Jack cheese
    with jalapeño peppers
1 (6-ounce) can frozen avocado dip, thawed
1 (8-ounce) container sour cream
1 cup chopped tomato
6 green onions, thinly sliced
1 (4.5-ounce) can sliced ripe olives, drained

1. Combine first 3 ingredients; spread mixture in a lightly greased 11- x 7-inch baking dish. Bake, uncovered, at 350° for 20 minutes or until thoroughly heated. Sprinkle with cheese; bake 5 more minutes or until cheese melts.

2. Spread avocado dip over warm bean mixture; spread sour cream over avocado dip. Top with tomato, green onions, and olives. Serve warm with tortilla chips or corn chips. **Makes** 12 appetizer servings.

Baked Vidalia Onion Dip

PREP: 15 MIN., COOK: 25 MIN., OTHER: 10 MIN.

2 tablespoons butter
3 large Vidalia onions, coarsely chopped
2 cups (8 ounces) shredded Swiss cheese
2 cups mayonnaise
1 (8-ounce) can sliced water chestnuts, drained
    and chopped
¼ cup dry white wine
1 garlic clove, minced
½ teaspoon hot sauce

1. Melt butter in a large skillet over medium-high heat; add onion, and sauté 10 minutes or until tender.
2. Stir together shredded Swiss cheese and next 5 ingredients; stir in onion, blending well. Spoon mixture into a lightly greased 2-quart baking dish.
3. Bake at 375° for 25 minutes, and let stand 10 minutes. Serve with tortilla chips or crackers. **Makes** 18 to 20 appetizer servings.

To lighten: Substitute vegetable cooking spray for butter; substitute reduced-fat Swiss cheese and light mayonnaise.

Tomato Tart

Tomato Tart

PREP: 45 MIN.; COOK: 1 HR., 24 MIN.; OTHER: 10 MIN.

½ (15-ounce) package refrigerated piecrusts
1 garlic bulb
½ teaspoon olive oil
1½ cups (6 ounces) shredded fontina cheese, divided
4 large tomatoes
½ teaspoon salt
¼ teaspoon pepper

1. Press refrigerated piecrust on bottom and up sides of a square 9-inch tart pan. Bake at 450° for 9 minutes or until piecrust is lightly browned; set aside.
2. Cut off pointed end of garlic bulb; place garlic on a piece of aluminum foil, and drizzle with olive oil. Fold foil to seal.
3. Bake garlic at 425° for 30 minutes; cool. Squeeze pulp from garlic cloves into bottom of baked piecrust.
4. Sprinkle ½ cup fontina cheese over garlic.
5. Slice tomatoes, and sprinkle evenly with salt and pepper. Place on folded paper towels, and let stand 10 minutes. Arrange tomato slices over shredded cheese. Sprinkle with remaining 1 cup cheese.
6. Bake at 350° for 45 minutes or until tart is lightly browned. **Makes** 4 to 6 appetizer servings.

QUICK
Swiss Cheese Crostini

PREP: 12 MIN., COOK: 10 MIN.

1 French baguette
4 cups (16 ounces) shredded Swiss cheese
¼ cup beer
2 tablespoons tomato paste
1 tablespoon spicy brown mustard
¼ teaspoon garlic powder
⅛ teaspoon hot sauce

1. Cut baguette into ¼-inch-thick slices, and place on an aluminum foil-lined baking sheet.
2. Bake at 400° for 5 minutes or until lightly browned.
3. Combine cheese and next 5 ingredients; spread on bread slices.
4. Bake at 400° for 5 minutes or until cheese melts. Serve immediately. **Makes** 3 dozen.

Hot Mushroom Turnovers

Tender cream cheese pastry surrounds a rich, flavorful filling.

PREP: 45 MIN., COOK: 10 MIN., OTHER: 1 HR.

1 (8-ounce) package cream cheese, softened
½ cup butter, softened
1¾ cups all-purpose flour
3 tablespoons butter
1 (8-ounce) package fresh mushrooms, minced
1 large onion, minced
½ cup sour cream
2 tablespoons all-purpose flour
1 teaspoon salt
¼ teaspoon dried thyme
1 large egg, lightly beaten

1. Beat cream cheese and ½ cup butter at medium speed with an electric mixer until creamy; gradually add 1¾ cup flour, beating well.
2. Divide dough in half, and shape each portion into a ball; cover and chill 1 hour.
3. Melt 3 tablespoons butter in a large skillet. Add mushrooms and onion; sauté until tender. Stir in sour cream and next 3 ingredients; set aside.
4. Roll 1 dough portion to ⅛-inch thickness on a lightly floured surface; cut with a 2½-inch round cutter, and place on greased baking sheets. Repeat procedure with remaining dough.
5. Spoon 1 teaspoon mushroom mixture onto half of each dough circle. Moisten edges with beaten egg, and fold dough over filling. Press edges with a fork to seal; prick tops. Brush turnovers with beaten egg.
6. Bake at 450° for 8 to 10 minutes or until golden. Serve hot. **Makes** 3½ dozen.

Miniature Cheese Quiches

Serve these little pastries for almost any occasion—a breakfast or brunch, bridal shower, baby shower, or perhaps a picnic.

PREP: 5 MIN., COOK: 25 MIN.

2 large eggs, lightly beaten
½ cup milk
1½ tablespoons butter, melted
1 cup (4 ounces) shredded Cheddar cheese or
    Monterey Jack cheese with peppers
Pastry shells
Ground red pepper or paprika (optional)

1. Combine first 4 ingredients, stirring well. Spoon filling into pastry shells. Sprinkle with red pepper, if desired. Bake at 350° for 25 minutes or until set and golden. **Makes** 2 dozen.

Pastry Shells

PREP: 20 MIN.

1¼ cups all-purpose flour
1 teaspoon salt
3 tablespoons butter, melted
1 egg yolk
3 to 4 tablespoons ice water

1. Combine flour and salt, stirring well; add butter, mixing well. Add egg yolk and ice water; stir with a fork just until dry ingredients are moistened.
2. Shape dough into 24 (1-inch) balls. Place in lightly greased 1¾-inch miniature muffin pans, shaping each into a shell. Chill until ready to bake. **Makes** 2 dozen.

FREEZER FRIENDLY, MAKE AHEAD
Spinach Quiches

PREP: 15 MIN., COOK: 45 MIN.

1 (15-ounce) package refrigerated piecrusts
2 tablespoons butter
1 small onion, chopped
2 green onions, chopped
¼ cup chopped fresh parsley
1 (10-ounce) package frozen chopped spinach,
    thawed and well drained
1 tablespoon Worcestershire sauce
1 teaspoon salt
½ teaspoon pepper
3 large eggs
¼ cup milk
1 cup (4 ounces) shredded Swiss cheese

1. Roll each piecrust into a 12-inch square; cut each square into 24 pieces. Shape into balls, and press into lightly greased miniature muffin pans.
2. Melt butter in a large skillet over medium heat. Add onions and parsley; sauté until onions are tender. Add spinach; cook 2 minutes. Stir in Worcestershire sauce, salt, and pepper. Remove from heat.
3. Whisk together eggs and milk until blended; stir in cheese. Add egg mixture to spinach mixture; spoon evenly into prepared pans.
4. Bake at 350° for 30 to 35 minutes. Remove immediately from pans, and cool on wire racks. Freeze baked quiches up to 2 months, if desired. **Makes** 4 dozen.
Note: Thaw frozen quiches in refrigerator; bake at 300° for 10 minutes or until thoroughly heated.

Baby Hot Brown

Baby Hot Browns

Here we offer hors d'oeuvre-size servings of this famous Kentucky sandwich.

PREP: 35 MIN., COOK: 19 MIN.

16 pumpernickel rye party bread slices
2 tablespoons butter
2 tablespoons all-purpose flour
½ cup (2 ounces) shredded sharp Cheddar
    cheese
1½ cups milk
¼ teaspoon salt
¼ teaspoon ground red pepper
2 pounds thinly sliced turkey
½ cup freshly grated Parmesan cheese
6 bacon slices, cooked and crumbled

1. Arrange bread slices on a lightly greased baking sheet. Bake at 500° for 3 to 4 minutes.
2. Melt butter in a saucepan over low heat; add flour, and cook, whisking constantly, until smooth. Add Cheddar cheese, whisking until cheese melts. Gradually whisk in milk; cook over medium heat, whisking constantly, until mixture is thick and bubbly. Stir in salt and red pepper. If desired, chill until ready to bake.
3. Top bread slices evenly with turkey. Top each with about 1½ tablespoons cheese sauce. Sprinkle evenly with Parmesan cheese and bacon.
4. Bake at 500° for 7 minutes or until Parmesan is melted. **Makes** 16 appetizers.

Spicy Party Meatballs

Serve these meatballs from a slow cooker or chafing dish.

PREP: 5 MIN., COOK: 45 MIN.

1 (12-ounce) jar cocktail sauce
1 (10.5-ounce) jar jalapeño pepper jelly
½ small sweet onion, minced
½ (3-pound) package frozen cooked meatballs

1. Cook first 3 ingredients in a Dutch oven over medium heat, stirring until jelly melts and mixture is smooth.
2. Stir in meatballs. Reduce heat, and simmer, stirring occasionally, 35 to 40 minutes or until thoroughly heated. **Makes** 8 dozen.

Shanghai Spring Rolls With Sweet Chili Sauce

PREP: 30 MIN., COOK: 6 MIN. PER BATCH

½ pound unpeeled raw shrimp
2 large eggs, divided and lightly beaten
½ pound ground pork
1 (8-ounce) can sliced water chestnuts, drained and minced
1 (8-ounce) can bamboo shoots, drained and minced
3 garlic cloves, minced
2 green onions, diced
2 tablespoons minced fresh ginger
1 tablespoon soy sauce
⅛ teaspoon salt
⅛ teaspoon pepper
1 (12-ounce) package spring roll wrappers
Vegetable oil
Sweet Chili Sauce
Lettuce leaves (optional)

1. Peel shrimp, and devein, if desired; finely chop.
2. Stir together shrimp, 1 egg, pork, and next 8 ingredients. Spoon 1 tablespoon mixture in center of each spring roll wrapper. Fold top corner of each wrapper over filling, tucking tip of corner under filling, and fold left and right corners over filling. Lightly brush remaining corner with remaining egg; tightly roll filled end toward remaining corner, and gently press to seal.
3. Pour vegetable oil to a depth of 2 inches into a medium saucepan, and heat to 350°. Fry spring rolls, a few at a time, 6 minutes or until golden. Drain on paper towels. Serve spring rolls with Sweet Chili Sauce and over lettuce leaves, if desired. **Makes** 15 spring rolls.

Sweet Chili Sauce

PREP: 5 MIN.

1 (7-ounce) bottle hot chili sauce with garlic
½ cup water
½ cup rice wine vinegar
¼ cup sugar
¼ cup lemon juice
2 tablespoons chili paste

1. Stir together all ingredients until blended. Chill until ready to serve. **Makes** 2 cups.

(EDITOR'S CHOICE)

Texas Rockets

You'll want to make more than one batch of these yummy appetizers. For less heat, look for jalapeño peppers with rounded tips.

PREP: 30 MIN., COOK: 35 MIN., OTHER: 30 MIN.

½ pound chicken breast strips
¾ cup Italian dressing, divided
½ (8-ounce) package cream cheese, softened
⅛ teaspoon salt
⅛ teaspoon black pepper
12 jalapeño peppers (about 3½ to 4 inches long)
12 thin bacon slices

1. Place chicken and ½ cup Italian dressing in a shallow dish or zip-top plastic freezer bag; cover or seal, and chill 30 minutes.
2. Remove chicken from marinade, discarding marinade. Grill chicken, covered with grill lid, over medium heat (300° to 350°) 4 to 5 minutes on each side or until done, basting with remaining ¼ cup Italian dressing. Let chicken cool slightly, and finely chop.
3. Stir together chicken, cream cheese, salt, and black pepper in a bowl.
4. Cut jalapeño peppers lengthwise down 1 side, leaving other side intact; remove seeds. Spoon 1½ to 2 tablespoons chicken mixture into cavity of each pepper. Wrap each pepper with 1 bacon slice, securing with 2 wooden picks.
5. Grill stuffed jalapeños, without grill lid, turning frequently, over medium heat 20 to 25 minutes or until bacon is crisp. **Makes** 1 dozen.

"I always have to make a double recipe of these—guests just stand around the grill waiting for them to come off."

PAM LOLLEY, TEST KITCHENS PROFESSIONAL

Chicken Cake With
Rémoulade Sauce

Chicken Cakes With Rémoulade Sauce

We love this recipe because it delivers the quality of crab cakes at a much friendlier price, and the chicken cakes are easy to make ahead. You can also make smaller, bite-size portions by simply forming 16 patties instead of 8.

PREP: 20 MIN., COOK: 15 MIN.

2 tablespoons butter
½ medium-size red bell pepper, diced
4 green onions, thinly sliced
1 garlic clove, pressed
3 cups chopped cooked chicken
1 cup soft breadcrumbs
1 large egg, lightly beaten
2 tablespoons mayonnaise
1 tablespoon Creole mustard
2 teaspoons Creole seasoning
¼ cup vegetable oil, divided
Garnish: parsley sprig
Rémoulade Sauce (opposite page)

1. Melt butter in a large skillet over medium heat. Add bell pepper, green onions, and garlic, and sauté 3 to 4 minutes or until vegetables are tender.
2. Stir together bell pepper mixture, chicken, and next 5 ingredients. Shape mixture into 8 (3½-inch) patties.
3. Fry 4 patties in 2 tablespoons hot oil in a large skillet over medium heat 3 minutes on each side or until golden brown. Drain on paper towels. Repeat procedure with remaining 2 tablespoons oil and patties. Garnish, if desired. Serve immediately with Rémoulade Sauce. **Makes** 8 appetizer cakes.

Rémoulade Sauce

PREP: 10 MIN.

1 cup mayonnaise
3 green onions, sliced
2 tablespoons Creole mustard
2 garlic cloves, pressed
1 tablespoon chopped fresh parsley
¼ teaspoon ground red pepper
Garnish: sliced green onions

1. Stir together first 6 ingredients in a small bowl until well blended. Garnish, if desired. **Makes** about 1¼ cups.

FAMILY FAVORITE, MAKE AHEAD
Southwestern Chicken Salad Spirals

PREP: 15 MIN., OTHER: 2 HR.

1 (7-ounce) jar roasted red bell peppers
2 cups chopped cooked chicken
1 (8-ounce) package cream cheese, softened
1 (0.4-ounce) envelope Ranch-style buttermilk
    dressing mix
¼ cup chopped ripe olives
½ small onion, diced
1 (4.5-ounce) can chopped green chiles, drained
2 tablespoons chopped fresh cilantro
½ teaspoon pepper
¼ cup pine nuts (optional)
8 (6-inch) flour tortillas
Garnish: fresh cilantro

1. Drain roasted peppers well, pressing between layers of paper towels; chop.
2. Stir together roasted peppers, chicken, and next 7 ingredients. Cover and chill at least 2 hours.
3. Stir pine nuts, if desired, into chicken mixture. Spoon evenly over tortillas, and roll up. Cut each roll into 5 slices, securing with wooden picks, if necessary. Garnish, if desired. **Makes** 40 appetizers.

Chicken-and-Brie Quesadillas With Chipotle Salsa

PREP: 15 MIN., COOK: 10 MIN., OTHER: 1 HR.

2 cups chopped plum tomato
1 small onion, chopped
3 garlic cloves, minced
3 tablespoons fresh lime juice
2 teaspoons minced canned chipotle chiles in
    adobo sauce
½ teaspoon salt
5 green onions, minced and divided
½ cup chopped fresh cilantro, divided
1 cup finely chopped cooked chicken
1 (4.5-ounce) can diced green chiles, drained
8 (7-inch) flour tortillas
8 ounces Brie, trimmed and diced

1. Stir together first 6 ingredients, ¼ cup green onions, and ¼ cup cilantro. Let salsa stand 1 hour.
2. Stir together remaining green onions, remaining ¼ cup cilantro, chicken, and diced green chiles.
3. Arrange 4 tortillas on a large lightly greased baking sheet. Top evenly with cheese, chicken mixture, and remaining tortillas, pressing down slightly.
4. Bake at 425° for 8 to 10 minutes or until cheese melts. Cut into wedges, and serve immediately with salsa. **Makes** 12 appetizer servings.
Note: Freeze remaining chipotle chiles in adobo sauce, if desired.

Shrimp Tarts

Shrimp Tarts

Asiago cheese updates the pastry in these rich appetizer tarts meant for a party.

PREP: 12 MIN., COOK: 10 MIN., OTHER: 2 HR.

2 pounds unpeeled large fresh shrimp
²⁄₃ cup finely chopped green onions
½ cup finely chopped fresh parsley
²⁄₃ cup mayonnaise
2 tablespoons capers
1 teaspoon lemon juice
½ teaspoon salt
¼ teaspoon ground red pepper
1 garlic clove, minced
Tart Shells
Garnish: thin diagonal slices of green onion

1. Bring 6 cups of water to a boil; add shrimp, and cook 3 to 5 minutes or until shrimp turn pink. Drain; rinse with cold water. Cover and chill. Peel, devein, and coarsely chop shrimp.
2. Combine chopped shrimp, green onions, and next 7 ingredients in a large bowl. Spoon mixture evenly into baked Tart Shells. Garnish, if desired. **Makes** 3 dozen.

Tart Shells

PREP: 12 MIN., COOK: 17 MIN., OTHER: 1 HR.

½ cup butter, softened
½ (8-ounce) package cream cheese, softened
1¼ cups all-purpose flour
¼ cup grated Asiago cheese
¼ teaspoon salt

1. Combine butter and cream cheese; stir until blended. Add flour, cheese, and salt, blending well. Cover and chill dough 1 hour. Divide dough into 3 portions. Shape each portion into 12 balls.
2. Press dough onto bottom and up sides of lightly greased 1¾-inch miniature muffin pans. Bake at 350° for 15 to 17 minutes or until golden. Cool. Remove from pans. **Makes** 3 dozen.

Apricot-Apple Cider Sipper

PREP: 10 MIN., COOK: 10 MIN.

1 gallon apple cider
1 (11.5-ounce) can apricot nectar
2 cups sugar
2 cups orange juice
¾ cup lemon juice
4 (3-inch) cinnamon sticks
2 teaspoons ground allspice
1 teaspoon ground cloves
½ teaspoon ground nutmeg

1. Bring all ingredients to a boil in a Dutch oven; reduce heat, and simmer 10 minutes. Remove cinnamon sticks. Serve hot. **Makes** 21 cups.

Apple Cider Sipper: Omit nectar. **Makes** 19 cups.

Pineapple Wassail

PREP: 5 MIN., COOK: 20 MIN.

4 cups unsweetened pineapple juice
1 (11.5-ounce) can apricot nectar
2 cups apple cider
1 cup orange juice
1 teaspoon whole cloves
3 (6-inch) cinnamon sticks, broken
Garnishes: orange wedges, whole cinnamon sticks

1. Bring first 6 ingredients to a boil in a Dutch oven; reduce heat, and simmer 20 minutes. Pour through a wire-mesh strainer, discarding spices. Serve hot. Garnish, if desired. **Makes** 2 quarts.

Coconut Coffee

PREP: 5 MIN., COOK: 5 MIN.

2 cups half-and-half
1 (15-ounce) can cream of coconut
4 cups freshly brewed coffee
Sweetened whipped cream

1. Bring half-and-half and cream of coconut to a boil in a saucepan over medium heat, stirring constantly.
2. Stir in coffee. Serve with sweetened whipped cream. **Makes** 8 cups.

Praline Coffee

PREP: 5 MIN., COOK: 5 MIN.

3 cups hot brewed coffee
¾ cup half-and-half
¾ cup firmly packed light brown sugar
2 tablespoons butter
¾ cup praline liqueur
Sweetened whipped cream

1. Cook first 4 ingredients in a large saucepan over medium heat, stirring constantly, until thoroughly heated (do not boil). Stir in liqueur; serve with sweetened whipped cream. **Makes** 5¼ cups.

Strawberry-Lemonade Slush

Fresh lemon juice offers a tart tang to this beverage.

PREP: 20 MIN., OTHER: 30 MIN.

2 (16-ounce) containers fresh strawberries, sliced
1½ cups sugar
2 cups water, divided
1½ cups fresh lemon juice (about 6 to 9 medium lemons), divided
4 cups ice cubes, divided

1. Stir together sliced strawberries and sugar; let stand 30 minutes.
2. Process half of strawberry mixture, 1 cup water, ¾ cup lemon juice, and 2 cups ice in a blender until smooth. Repeat procedure with remaining ingredients, and serve immediately. **Makes** about 8 cups.

Eggnog-Coffee Punch

PREP: 10 MIN.

1 quart coffee ice cream
1 quart vanilla ice cream
1 quart eggnog
2 cups hot brewed coffee
½ cup coffee liqueur or strong brewed coffee
½ cup bourbon (optional)
Frozen whipped topping, thawed
Ground nutmeg

1. Scoop ice cream into a punch bowl. Add eggnog, coffee, liqueur, and, if desired, bourbon, stirring until ice cream melts slightly. Serve in glass mugs. Dollop punch with whipped topping; sprinkle with nutmeg. Serve immediately. **Makes** 10 to 12 servings.

Note: For testing purposes only, we used Kahlúa coffee liqueur.

Eggnog-Coffee Punch

Cherry Cordial Hot Chocolate
PREP: 10 MIN., COOK: 10 MIN.

5½ cups milk
1½ cups half-and-half
1½ cups chocolate syrup
½ cup maraschino cherry juice, divided
1¾ cups whipping cream
1 tablespoon powdered sugar
Maraschino cherries with stems (optional)

1. Heat first 3 ingredients and 7 tablespoons cherry juice in a Dutch oven over medium-low heat, stirring often.
2. Beat whipping cream at medium speed with an electric mixer until foamy; gradually add powdered sugar and remaining cherry juice, beating until soft peaks form. Serve with hot chocolate; top each serving with a cherry, if desired. **Makes** 8½ cups.

Champagne Punch
PREP: 15 MIN., OTHER: 8 HR.

2 cups cranberry juice cocktail
1 (12-ounce) can frozen orange juice concentrate, thawed
1 cup lemon juice
1 cup sugar
1 (375-milliliter) bottle Sauterne or dessert wine*
2 (750-milliliter) bottles Champagne, chilled
Ice Ring

1. Combine first 4 ingredients, stirring well; chill at least 8 hours.
2. Pour juice mixture into a chilled punch bowl. Gently stir in Sauterne and Champagne just before serving. Float Ice Ring, fruit side up, in punch. **Makes** 20 servings.
*Substitute either (375 ml) Bonny Doon Muscat Vin de Glacière or (375 ml) Quady Electra for Sauterne, if desired.

Ice Ring
PREP: 10 MIN., OTHER: 10 HR.

1½ to 2 cups orange juice
½ cup cranberry juice
6 to 8 seedless red grape clusters, divided
10 to 12 orange slices, seeded
8 to 10 whole strawberries
Fresh mint sprigs

1. Combine juices. Line bottom of 6-cup ring mold with grape clusters and half of orange slices, using grapes to stand orange slices vertically. Pour a thin layer of juices into mold, and freeze until firm, about 2 hours. Arrange remaining orange slices, strawberries, and mint sprigs around grapes. Pour remaining juices around fruit almost to top of mold. Freeze 8 hours.
2. Unmold by dipping bottom half of mold in several inches of warm water 5 to 10 seconds to loosen, repeating as necessary to release ring (do not immerse entire mold in water). Invert ring onto plate. **Makes** 1 ice ring.

Easy Ice Ring: Combine juices. Fill bottom of 6-cup ring mold with 2 cups crushed ice. Lay grape clusters over ice. Arrange orange slices, strawberries, and mint sprigs around grapes. Pour juices around fruit almost to top of mold. Freeze 8 hours or until firm.

Orange Thing

Orange Thing

This drink is the house specialty at Frank Stitt's Bottega Restaurant in our hometown of Birmingham. Now you can serve it in your home as well. (also pictured on back cover)

PREP: 5 MIN.

2 cups ice cubes
¼ cup vodka
2 tablespoons orange liqueur
¼ cup fresh orange juice

1. Combine all ingredients in a martini shaker. Cover with lid, and shake until thoroughly chilled. Remove lid, and strain into a chilled martini glass. Serve immediately. **Makes** 1 serving.
Note: For testing purposes only, we used Grand Marnier for orange liqueur.

QUICK
Classic Mint Julep

PREP: 10 MIN.

3 fresh mint leaves
1 tablespoon Mint Simple Syrup
Crushed ice
1½ to 2 tablespoons (1 ounce) bourbon
1 (4-inch) cocktail straw or coffee stirrer
1 fresh mint sprig
Powdered sugar (optional)

1. Place mint leaves and Mint Simple Syrup in a chilled julep cup. Gently press leaves against cup with back of spoon to release flavors. Pack cup tightly with crushed ice; pour bourbon over ice. Insert straw; place mint sprig directly next to straw, and, if desired, sprinkle with powdered sugar. Serve immediately. **Makes** 1 serving.
Note: For testing purposes only, we used Woodford Reserve Distiller's Select Bourbon.

Mint Simple Syrup

PREP: 5 MIN., COOK: 10 MIN., OTHER: 24 HR.

1 cup granulated sugar
1 cup water
10 to 12 fresh mint sprigs

1. Bring sugar and water to a boil in a medium saucepan. Boil, stirring often, 5 minutes or until sugar dissolves. Remove from heat; add mint, and let cool completely. Pour into a glass jar; cover and chill 24 hours. Remove and discard mint. **Makes** 2 cups.

MAKE AHEAD
Orange Brandy Smash

PREP: 5 MIN., OTHER: 8 HR.

9 cups water
2 cups brandy
1 (12-ounce) can frozen lemonade concentrate
1 (12-ounce) can frozen orange juice concentrate
Garnish: fresh mint sprigs

1. Stir together first 4 ingredients in a 1-gallon container until concentrates thaw. Cover mixture, and freeze 8 hours, stirring occasionally. Spoon frozen mixture into glasses. Garnish, if desired. Serve immediately. **Makes** 14 cups.

QUICK
Brandy Cream

PREP: 5 MIN.

2 pints vanilla ice cream, softened
½ cup brandy
⅓ cup crème de cacao
¼ cup hazelnut liqueur
¼ teaspoon ground nutmeg

1. Process first 4 ingredients in a blender until smooth. Sprinkle each serving with nutmeg, and serve beverage immediately. **Makes** 5 cups.

Buttermilk Biscuits, page 46

bread
basket

Buttermilk Biscuits
Pictured on page 44.

PREP: 20 MIN., CHILL: 10 MIN., BAKE: 15 MIN.

½ cup cold butter
2¼ cups self-rising soft-wheat flour
1¼ cups buttermilk
Self-rising soft-wheat flour
2 tablespoons melted butter

1. Cut butter with a sharp knife or pastry blender into ¼-inch-thick slices. Sprinkle butter slices over flour in a large bowl. Toss butter with flour. Cut butter into flour with a pastry blender until crumbly and mixture resembles small peas. Cover and chill 10 minutes. Add buttermilk, stirring just until dry ingredients are moistened.

2. Turn dough out onto a lightly floured surface; knead 3 or 4 times, gradually adding additional flour as needed. With floured hands, press or pat dough into a ¾-inch-thick rectangle (about 9 x 5 inches). Sprinkle top of dough with additional flour. Fold dough over onto itself in 3 sections, starting with 1 short end. (Fold dough rectangle as if folding a letter-size piece of paper.) Repeat entire process 2 more times, beginning with pressing into a ¾-inch-thick dough rectangle (about 9 x 5 inches).

3. Press or pat dough to ½-inch thickness on a lightly floured surface; cut with a 2-inch round cutter, and place, side by side, on a parchment paper-lined or lightly greased jelly-roll pan. (Dough rounds should touch.)

4. Bake at 450° for 13 to 15 minutes or until lightly browned. Remove from oven; brush with 2 tablespoons melted butter. **Makes** 2 dozen.

Note: For testing purposes only, we used White Lily Self-Rising Soft Wheat Flour.

Cinnamon-Raisin Biscuits: Omit 2 tablespoons melted butter. Combine ½ cup golden raisins, ½ teaspoon ground cinnamon, and ⅓ cup chopped pecans with flour in a large bowl. Proceed with recipe as directed. Stir together ½ cup powdered sugar and 2 tablespoons buttermilk until smooth. Drizzle over warm biscuits. **Makes** 2½ dozen.

Black Pepper-Bacon Biscuits: Combine ⅓ cup cooked and crumbled bacon slices (about 5 slices) and 1 teaspoon black pepper with flour in a large bowl. Proceed with recipe as directed. **Makes** 2½ dozen.

Feta-Oregano Biscuits: Combine 1 (4-ounce) package crumbled feta cheese and ½ teaspoon dried oregano with flour in a large bowl. Proceed with recipe as directed. **Makes** 2½ dozen.

Pimiento Cheese Biscuits: Combine 1 cup (4 ounces) shredded sharp Cheddar cheese with flour in a large bowl. Reduce buttermilk to 1 cup. Stir together buttermilk and 1 (4-ounce) jar diced pimiento, undrained. Proceed with recipe as directed. **Makes** 2½ dozen.

"I've spent countless Sunday mornings in a flour-covered kitchen trying to perfect this delicacy. Like you, I'm careful to use a light hand when working the dough, but Test Kitchens Professional Vanessa McNeil Rocchio and I discovered a secret that makes these biscuits our best ever. The trick is in the dough-folding method, the same one used to make puff pastries and croissants. Folding creates multiple layers of dough and fat, giving rise to a tender, puffy biscuit. Combine the dry ingredients the night before, and refrigerate for an easy breakfast in the morning."

MARION MCGAHEY, ASSOCIATE FOOD EDITOR

Old Southern Biscuits

PREP: 10 MIN., COOK: 14 MIN.

¼ cup shortening
2 cups self-rising flour
1 cup buttermilk
Melted butter (optional)

1. Cut shortening into flour with a pastry blender or fork until crumbly. Add buttermilk, stirring the mixture just until moistened.
2. Pat dough to ½-inch thickness; cut with a 2-inch round cutter. Place on a lightly greased baking sheet.
3. Bake at 425° for 14 minutes or until golden. Brush hot biscuits with melted butter, if desired. **Makes** 1 dozen.

Sour Cream Biscuits

PREP: 15 MIN., COOK: 9 MIN.

3 cups all-purpose flour
2 tablespoons baking powder
1 teaspoon salt
½ cup cold butter, cut up
½ cup milk
½ cup buttermilk
⅓ cup sour cream
⅛ teaspoon sugar
⅛ teaspoon vanilla extract

1. Combine first 3 ingredients; cut in butter with a pastry blender until mixture is crumbly.
2. Combine milk and next 4 ingredients; add to dry ingredients, stirring with a fork just until dry ingredients are moistened.
3. Turn dough out onto a floured surface; knead 3 or 4 times. Roll to ½-inch thickness; cut with a 1½-inch biscuit cutter, and place on lightly greased baking sheets.
4. Bake at 450° for 7 to 9 minutes. **Makes** about 3 dozen.

Sweet Potato Biscuits

Enhance these sweet potato gems on the savory side by sandwiching in slices of country ham. Serve them on the sweet side with Gingered Pear Honey.

PREP: 20 MIN., COOK: 15 MIN., OTHER: 30 MIN.

1 large sweet potato
2 cups self-rising flour
¼ cup sugar
3 tablespoons shortening
2 tablespoons butter, cut up
⅓ cup milk
Country ham or Gingered Pear Honey (optional)

1. Bake sweet potato at 350° for 1 hour or until tender; cool slightly. Peel and mash; cool.
2. Combine flour and sugar in a medium bowl. Cut shortening and butter into flour mixture with a pastry blender until crumbly; add mashed sweet potato and milk, stirring just until dry ingredients are moistened.
3. Turn dough out onto a lightly floured surface, and knead 3 to 4 times. Roll dough to ½-inch thickness; cut with a 2-inch biscuit cutter. Place on a lightly greased baking sheet.
4. Bake at 400° for 15 minutes or until golden brown. Serve with ham or honey, if desired. **Makes** 10 biscuits.

(EDITOR'S CHOICE)
Gingered Pear Honey

Associate Food Editor Mary Allen Perry says, "I make this recipe almost every fall. It's made with fresh pears, and it's so versatile. Not to mention that it's killer on sweet potato biscuits."

PREP: 15 MIN., COOK: 47 MIN, OTHER: 2 HR.

6 large pears, peeled and chopped
3 cups sugar
1½ tablespoons grated fresh ginger
1 lemon, thinly sliced

1. Cook all ingredients in a heavy 3-quart saucepan over medium heat 5 to 7 minutes or until sugar dissolves, stirring often.
2. Increase heat to medium-high, and cook 40 minutes or until mixture is thickened and golden, stirring occasionally. Cool. Store honey in airtight containers in the refrigerator up to 1 month. **Makes** 3½ cups.

Drop Scones
PREP: 8 MIN., COOK: 14 MIN.

½ cup milk
1½ teaspoons white vinegar
½ cup butter, softened
½ cup sugar
2 cups all-purpose flour
1 teaspoon baking soda
2 teaspoons cream of tartar
¼ teaspoon salt
Sugar

1. Stir together milk and vinegar; set aside.
2. Stir together butter and ½ cup sugar in a large bowl.
3. Combine flour and next 3 ingredients; stir into butter mixture alternately with milk mixture, beginning and ending with flour mixture, until dry ingredients are moistened. Drop by rounded 2 tablespoonfuls onto an ungreased baking sheet; sprinkle with additional sugar.
4. Bake at 450° for 12 to 14 minutes or until golden.
Makes 10 scones.

Scone Secrets:

• Scone dough should be "shaggy" or rough; mix it quickly using cold butter, keeping mixing to a minimum.
• Don't touch the cut edges of the scone. They won't rise as nicely if the edges are pressed.
• Over-baking for even a minute can dry out scones.

Orange-Currant Scones
PREP: 12 MIN., COOK: 18 MIN.

⅓ cup currants
¾ cup buttermilk
2 cups all-purpose flour
2 tablespoons sugar
2 teaspoons baking powder
¼ teaspoon baking soda
¼ teaspoon salt
1 tablespoon orange zest
⅓ cup cold butter, cut up
Milk
Sugar

1. Combine currants and buttermilk in a small bowl.
2. Combine flour and next 5 ingredients, stirring well. Cut in butter with a pastry blender until mixture is crumbly. Gradually add currants and buttermilk, stirring just until dry ingredients are moistened.
3. Turn dough out onto a lightly floured surface, and knead 4 or 5 times. Pat dough to ¾-inch thickness; cut with a 3-inch biscuit cutter. Place scones on lightly greased baking sheet. Brush scones with milk, and sprinkle with sugar.
4. Bake at 400° for 18 minutes or until golden.
Makes 6 scones.

Ginger Scones

Ginger Scones

Top these slightly sweet scones with sweetened whipped cream, if you'd like. Crystallized ginger, which has been cooked in a sugar syrup and coated with sugar, spices them up. Before you begin to chop the ginger, coat the knife blade with vegetable cooking spray to prevent the task from becoming unmanageably sticky.

PREP: 20 MIN., COOK: 22 MIN., OTHER: 10 MIN.

2¾ cups all-purpose flour
2 teaspoons baking powder
½ teaspoon salt
½ cup sugar
¾ cup butter
⅓ cup chopped crystallized ginger
1 cup milk

1. Combine first 4 ingredients in a large bowl; cut butter into flour mixture with a pastry blender until crumbly. Stir in ginger. Add milk, stirring just until dry ingredients are moistened. Turn dough out onto a lightly floured surface, and knead 10 to 15 times. Pat or roll dough to ¾-inch thickness; shape into a round, and cut dough into 8 wedges. Place wedges on a lightly greased baking sheet.

2. Bake at 400° for 18 to 22 minutes or until scones are barely golden. Cool slightly on a wire rack.

Makes 8 scones.

Ham-and-Cheddar Muffins

These are excellent for breakfast or brunch—nice and moist with a good flavor.

PREP: 15 MIN., COOK: 23 MIN., OTHER: 3 MIN.

3 tablespoons butter
1 medium-size sweet onion, finely chopped
1½ cups all-purpose baking mix
2 cups (8 ounces) shredded Cheddar cheese, divided
½ cup milk
1 large egg
1 cup finely chopped cooked ham
Poppy seeds (optional)

1. Melt butter in a skillet over medium-high heat; add onion, and sauté 3 to 5 minutes or until tender.
2. Combine baking mix and 1 cup cheese in a large bowl; make a well in center of mixture.
3. Stir together milk and egg, blending well; add to cheese mixture, stirring until moistened. Stir in onion and ham. Spoon into lightly greased muffin pans, filling two-thirds full. Sprinkle with remaining 1 cup cheese. Sprinkle with poppy seeds, if desired.
4. Bake at 425° for 18 minutes or until golden. Let stand 2 to 3 minutes before removing from pans.
Makes 1 dozen.

Note: Substitute mini muffin pans for regular pans, if desired. Bake at 425° for 14 minutes or until golden. **Makes** 2½ dozen mini muffins.

Reduced-Fat Ham-and-Cheddar Muffins: Substitute low-fat baking mix, fat-free or low-fat shredded Cheddar cheese, and fat-free milk. Reduce butter to 1 tablespoon; proceed with recipe as directed.

Ham-and-Swiss Muffins: Substitute shredded Swiss cheese for Cheddar; whisk in 2 tablespoons Dijon mustard with milk and egg. Proceed with recipe as directed.

Sausage-and-Cheese Muffins: Substitute 1 cup hot or mild ground pork sausage, cooked and crumbled, for chopped ham. Proceed with recipe as directed.

Chicken-and-Green Chile Muffins: Substitute 1 cup finely chopped cooked chicken for ham and 2 cups shredded Mexican four-cheese blend for Cheddar; add 1 (4.5-ounce) can chopped green chiles. Proceed with recipe as directed.

Ham-and-Cheddar Muffin and
Chicken-and-Green Chile Muffins

Broccoli Cornbread Muffins

PREP: 10 MIN., COOK: 20 MIN., OTHER: 3 MIN.

1 (8½-ounce) package corn muffin mix
1 (10-ounce) package frozen chopped broccoli, thawed
1 cup (4 ounces) shredded Cheddar cheese
1 small onion, chopped
2 large eggs
½ cup butter, melted

1. Combine first 4 ingredients in a large bowl; make a well in center of mixture.
2. Stir together eggs and butter, blending well; add to broccoli mixture, stirring just until dry ingredients are moistened. Spoon into lightly greased mini muffin pans, filling three-fourths full.
3. Bake at 325° for 15 to 20 minutes or until golden. Let stand 2 to 3 minutes before removing from pans. **Makes** 2 dozen mini muffins.

Date Muffins

PREP: 10 MIN., COOK: 30 MIN., OTHER: 1 HR.

1 cup finely chopped dates
1 cup boiling water
1 tablespoon shortening
1 large egg, lightly beaten
1 teaspoon vanilla extract
1½ cups all-purpose flour
1 cup sugar
1 teaspoon baking powder
½ teaspoon salt
1 cup chopped pecans

1. Combine first 3 ingredients, and let stand 1 hour. Stir in egg and vanilla.
2. Combine flour and next 4 ingredients in a bowl; make a well in center of mixture. Add date mixture, stirring just until moistened. Spoon into greased muffin pans, filling three-fourths full.
3. Bake at 350° for 25 to 30 minutes. Remove from pans immediately. **Makes** 1 dozen.

Sesame-Cheese Muffins

PREP: 10 MIN., COOK: 23 MIN.

1 tablespoon butter
1 small sweet onion, finely chopped
1½ cups all-purpose baking mix
1 cup (4 ounces) shredded sharp Cheddar cheese*, divided
1 large egg
½ cup milk
1 teaspoon sesame seeds, toasted
2 tablespoons butter, melted

1. Melt 1 tablespoon butter in a small skillet over medium-high heat. Add onion, and sauté 2 minutes or until tender; set aside.
2. Combine baking mix and half of cheese in a large bowl; make a well in center of mixture.
3. Stir together onion, egg, and milk, blending well; add to cheese mixture, stirring just until dry ingredients are moistened. Spoon into lightly greased muffin pans, filling two-thirds full. Sprinkle evenly with remaining cheese and sesame seeds; drizzle with butter.
4. Bake at 400° for 15 to 20 minutes or until golden. **Makes** 8 muffins.
Note: Substitute mini muffin pans for regular pans, if desired. Bake at 400° for 12 to 14 minutes or until golden. **Makes** 1½ dozen mini muffins
*1 cup (4 ounces) shredded Monterey Jack cheese with peppers may be substituted for Cheddar cheese.

Blueberry-Streusel Muffin

Blueberry-Streusel Muffins

PREP: 10 MIN., COOK: 20 MIN.

¼ cup pecan halves
¼ cup firmly packed brown sugar
1 tablespoon all-purpose flour
2 tablespoons butter
½ cup uncooked regular oats
2 cups all-purpose flour
½ cup sugar
2 teaspoons baking powder
¼ teaspoon baking soda
¼ teaspoon salt
2 teaspoons lemon zest
1¼ cups fresh or frozen blueberries
1 large egg, lightly beaten
¾ cup buttermilk
¼ cup vegetable oil

1. Process pecans in a food processor 2 or 3 times or until chopped. Add brown sugar and 1 tablespoon flour; process 5 seconds. Add butter; pulse 5 times or until mixture is crumbly. Stir in oats; set aside.

2. Combine 2 cups flour and next 5 ingredients in a large bowl; add blueberries, tossing gently. Make a well in center of mixture.

3. Combine egg, buttermilk, and oil; add to flour mixture, stirring just until moistened. Spoon batter into lightly greased muffin pans, filling two-thirds full, and sprinkle with oat mixture.

4. Bake at 400° for 15 to 20 minutes or until golden. Remove from pans immediately; cool on wire racks. **Makes** 1 dozen.

Lemon Muffins

These tender muffins are best served warm from the oven. If you have leftovers, split and toast them, and add a drizzle of honey.

PREP: 10 MIN., COOK: 19 MIN.

1 cup shortening
1 cup sugar
4 large eggs, separated
2 cups all-purpose flour
2 teaspoons baking powder
1 teaspoon salt
½ cup fresh lemon juice
2 teaspoons lemon zest

1. Beat shortening at medium speed with an electric mixer until fluffy; gradually add sugar, beating well. Add egg yolks, 1 at a time, beating after each addition.
2. Combine flour, baking powder, and salt; add to shortening mixture alternately with lemon juice, beginning and ending with flour mixture. Beat at low speed after each addition until blended. Stir in lemon zest.
3. Beat egg whites at high speed until stiff peaks form. Gently fold beaten egg whites into batter. Spoon into lightly greased muffin pans, filling three-fourths full.
4. Bake at 375° for 18 to 19 minutes. Remove from pans immediately. Serve warm. **Makes** 1½ dozen.

Pecan-Pie Muffins

PREP: 5 MIN., COOK: 25 MIN., OTHER: 10 MIN.

1 cup chopped pecans
1 cup firmly packed brown sugar
½ cup all-purpose flour
2 large eggs
½ cup butter, melted
Vegetable cooking spray

1. Combine first 3 ingredients in a large bowl; make a well in center of mixture.
2. Beat eggs until foamy. Stir together eggs and butter; add to dry ingredients, stirring just until moistened.

3. Place foil baking cups in muffin pans, and coat with cooking spray; spoon batter into cups, filling two-thirds full.
4. Bake at 350° for 20 to 25 minutes or until done. Remove from pans immediately, and cool on wire racks. **Makes** 9 muffins.

Coffee Cake Muffins

Cinnamon streusel runs throughout and crowns the top of these sweet muffins that are perfect for breakfast or brunch.

PREP: 10 MIN., COOK: 24 MIN., OTHER: 10 MIN.

¼ cup firmly packed light brown sugar
¼ cup chopped pecans
1 teaspoon ground cinnamon
1½ cups all-purpose flour
2 teaspoons baking powder
¼ teaspoon baking soda
½ cup sugar
¼ teaspoon salt
1 large egg
¾ cup milk
⅓ cup vegetable oil
Vegetable cooking spray

1. Combine first 3 ingredients. Set aside.
2. Stir together flour and next 4 ingredients in a large bowl; make a well in the center of mixture.
3. Stir together egg, milk, and oil; add to flour mixture, stirring just until moistened.
4. Place paper baking cups in muffin pans, and lightly coat with cooking spray.
5. Spoon about 1 tablespoon batter into each of 12 cups; sprinkle evenly with half of brown sugar mixture. Top evenly with remaining batter, and sprinkle with remaining brown sugar mixture.
6. Bake at 400° for 22 to 24 minutes or until lightly browned. Remove from pan immediately; cool on a wire rack. **Makes** 1 dozen.

Orange-Glazed Tea Rolls

PREP: 10 MIN., COOK: 13 MIN.

1 (8-ounce) package refrigerated crescent
    dinner rolls
1 tablespoon butter, melted
⅓ cup sugar
¼ teaspoon ground cinnamon
Orange Glaze

1. Unroll crescent dough onto lightly floured wax paper; press perforations to seal. Brush dough with melted butter. Combine sugar and cinnamon; sprinkle over dough.
2. Roll dough up, jelly-roll fashion, starting at long side, and cut into 1-inch slices. Place slices, cut side down, in lightly greased miniature (1¾-inch) muffin pans.
3. Bake at 375° for 11 to 13 minutes or until golden. Remove from pans immediately, and drizzle with Orange Glaze. **Makes** 1 dozen.

Orange Glaze

PREP: 5 MIN.

⅔ cup sifted powdered sugar
2 tablespoons frozen orange juice concentrate,
    thawed and undiluted
2 teaspoons water

1. Combine all ingredients in a small bowl, stirring until smooth. **Makes** ¼ cup.

Beer Bread

PREP: 5 MIN., COOK: 1 HR., OTHER: 15 MIN.

3 cups self-rising flour
¼ cup sugar
1 (12-ounce) bottle light or dark beer

1. Stir together all ingredients; spoon dough into a lightly greased 8½- x 4½-inch loafpan.
2. Bake at 375° for 55 to 60 minutes or until golden brown. Cool in pan on a wire rack 5 minutes. Remove from pan, and cool on wire rack. **Makes** 1 loaf.
Note: For testing purposes only, we used Honey Brown beer.

Cheddar-Chive Beer Bread

This recipe is simple enough to make for easy midweek meals, and also delicious enough to take to a potluck to impress your friends.

PREP: 5 MIN., COOK: 55 MIN., OTHER: 15 MIN.

3 cups self-rising flour
½ cup sugar
¾ cup (3 ounces) shredded sharp Cheddar cheese
1 (12-ounce) bottle beer*
2 tablespoons chopped fresh chives
¼ cup butter, melted
Garnish: fresh chive sprigs

1. Stir together first 5 ingredients; pour into a lightly greased 9- x 5-inch loafpan.
2. Bake at 350° for 45 minutes. Pour melted butter over top. Bake 10 more minutes. Let cool in pan on a wire rack 5 minutes. Remove from pan, and let cool on wire rack. Garnish with chive sprigs, if desired. **Makes** 1 loaf.
*Substitute nonalcoholic or light beer for regular beer, if desired.

Cheddar-Chive Beer Bread

"This is now my standard when it comes to great banana-nut bread."

PAM LOLLEY, TEST KITCHENS PROFESSIONAL

Cream Cheese-
Banana-Nut Bread

(EDITOR'S CHOICE)
Cream Cheese-Banana-Nut Bread
PREP: 15 MIN., COOK: 1 HR., OTHER: 40 MIN.

¾ cup butter, softened
1 (8-ounce) package cream cheese, softened
2 cups sugar
2 large eggs
3 cups all-purpose flour
½ teaspoon baking powder
½ teaspoon baking soda
½ teaspoon salt
1½ cups mashed bananas (1¼ pounds unpeeled
    bananas, about 4 medium)
1 cup chopped pecans, toasted
½ teaspoon vanilla extract

1. Beat butter and cream cheese at medium speed with an electric mixer until creamy. Gradually add sugar, beating until light and fluffy. Add eggs, 1 at a time, beating just until blended after each addition.
2. Combine flour and next 3 ingredients; gradually add to butter mixture, beating at low speed just until blended. Stir in bananas, pecans, and vanilla. Spoon batter into 2 greased and floured 8- x 4-inch loafpans.
3. Bake at 350° for 1 hour or until a long wooden pick inserted in center comes out clean and sides pull away from pan, shielding with aluminum foil last 15 minutes to prevent browning, if necessary. Cool bread in pans on wire racks 10 minutes. Remove from pans, and cool 30 minutes on wire racks before slicing.
Makes 2 loaves.

Orange-Pecan-Topped Cream Cheese-Banana-Nut Bread: Prepare bread batter as directed, and spoon into desired pans. Sprinkle 1 cup coarsely chopped, toasted pecans evenly over batter in pans. Bake as directed. Cool bread in pans 10 minutes; remove from pans to wire racks. Stir together 1 cup powdered sugar, 3 tablespoons fresh orange juice, and 1 teaspoon grated orange zest until blended. Drizzle evenly over warm bread, and cool 30 minutes on wire racks.

Toasted Coconut-Topped Cream Cheese-Banana-Nut Bread: Prepare and bake bread in desired pans. While bread is baking, stir together ¼ cup butter, ¼ cup granulated sugar, ¼ cup firmly packed brown sugar, and ¼ cup milk in a small saucepan over medium-high heat; bring to a boil, stirring constantly. Remove from heat. Stir in 1 cup sweetened flaked coconut; 1 cup chopped, toasted pecans; and 2 teaspoons vanilla extract. Remove baked bread from oven, and immediately spread tops with coconut mixture. Broil 5½ inches from heat 2 to 3 minutes or just until topping starts to lightly brown. Cool in pans on wire racks 20 minutes. Remove from pans, and cool 30 minutes on wire racks before slicing.

Cinnamon Crisp-Topped Cream Cheese-Banana-Nut Bread: Prepare bread batter as directed, and spoon into desired pans. Stir together ½ cup firmly packed brown sugar; ½ cup chopped, toasted pecans; 1 tablespoon all-purpose flour; 1 tablespoon melted butter; and ⅛ teaspoon ground cinnamon. Sprinkle mixture evenly over batter. Bake and cool as directed.

Peanut Butter Streusel-Topped Cream Cheese-Banana-Nut Bread: Prepare bread batter as directed, and spoon into desired pans. Combine ½ cup plus 1 tablespoon all-purpose flour and ½ cup firmly packed brown sugar in a small bowl. Cut in ¼ cup butter and 3 tablespoons creamy peanut butter with a pastry blender or fork until mixture resembles small peas. Sprinkle mixture evenly over batter in pans. Bake and cool as directed.

Banana Basics:

The perfect bananas for this bread don't look so perfect. Let them get ripe—almost black or very speckled. It takes a week to go from green to ready. To hasten ripening, place in a paper bag with a bruised apple. Once ripe, refrigerate or freeze unpeeled bananas in zip-top plastic freezer bags; thaw before mashing. We tried to freeze mashed bananas, but once thawed, they were watery and not suitable to use. A 6-ounce unpeeled banana yields about ⅓ cup mashed banana.

Blueberry-Orange Bread

PREP: 20 MIN., COOK: 1 HR., OTHER: 15 MIN.

1 cup wheat bran cereal, crushed
¾ cup water
1 tablespoon orange zest
¼ cup fresh orange juice
½ teaspoon vanilla extract
2 cups all-purpose flour
1 cup sugar
1½ teaspoons baking powder
½ teaspoon baking soda
½ teaspoon salt
1 large egg
2 tablespoons vegetable oil
1 cup frozen blueberries, thawed

1. Stir together first 5 ingredients in a large bowl; let stand 10 minutes or until cereal softens.
2. Stir in flour and next 6 ingredients just until dry ingredients are moistened. Gently fold in blueberries. Pour batter into a greased 9- x 5-inch loafpan.
3. Bake at 350° for 1 hour or until a long wooden pick inserted in center comes out clean. Cool on a wire rack 10 to 15 minutes; remove from pan, and cool completely on wire rack. **Makes** 1 loaf.

FREEZER FRIENDLY, MAKE AHEAD
Pumpkin-Pecan Bread

PREP: 12 MIN.; COOK: 1 HR., 15 MIN.; OTHER: 10 MIN.

3 cups sugar
1 cup vegetable oil
4 large eggs
1 (15-ounce) can pumpkin
3½ cups all-purpose flour
2 teaspoons baking soda
2 teaspoons salt
1 teaspoon ground cinnamon
1 teaspoon ground allspice
1 teaspoon ground nutmeg
½ teaspoon ground cloves
⅔ cup water
1 to 1½ cups chopped pecans, toasted

1. Beat first 11 ingredients at low speed with an electric mixer 3 minutes or until blended. Add ⅔ cup water, beating until blended. Stir in pecans. Pour batter into 2 greased and floured 9- x 5-inch loafpans.
2. Bake at 350° for 1 hour and 15 minutes or until a wooden pick inserted in center comes out clean. Cool in pans on a wire rack 10 minutes; remove from pans, and cool completely on wire rack. **Makes** 2 loaves.
Note: Bread may be frozen up to 3 months.

FAMILY FAVORITE, FREEZER FRIENDLY
Zucchini Bread

Zucchini bread is great for breakfast, lunch, or snacking any time of day. This recipe makes two loaves, so you can enjoy one right away and freeze the other one or share it with a friend.

PREP: 15 MIN., COOK: 50 MIN., OTHER: 10 MIN.

3 cups all-purpose flour
1 tablespoon baking powder
½ teaspoon baking soda
¾ teaspoon salt
1 teaspoon ground cinnamon
1 teaspoon ground nutmeg
2 cups sugar
¾ cup vegetable oil
3 large eggs, lightly beaten
2 teaspoons vanilla extract
3 cups shredded zucchini (about 2 large)
1 cup chopped pecans or walnuts

1. Combine first 6 ingredients in a large bowl; make a well in center of mixture.
2. Combine sugar, oil, eggs, and vanilla; stir well. Add to dry ingredients, stirring just until moistened. Stir in zucchini and pecans.
3. Spoon batter into 2 lightly greased 8 ½- x 4 ½-inch loafpans.
4. Bake at 350° for 50 minutes or until a wooden pick inserted in center comes out clean. Cool in pans on wire racks 10 minutes; remove from pans, and cool completely on wire racks. **Makes** 2 loaves.

Lemon Tea Bread

PREP: 15 MIN., COOK: 1 HR., OTHER: 10 MIN.

½ cup butter, softened
1 cup granulated sugar
2 large eggs
1½ cups all-purpose flour
1 teaspoon baking powder
½ teaspoon salt
½ cup milk
2 tablespoons lemon zest, divided
1 cup powdered sugar
2 tablespoons fresh lemon juice
1 tablespoon granulated sugar

1. Beat softened butter at medium speed with an electric mixer until creamy. Gradually add 1 cup granulated sugar, beating until light and fluffy. Add eggs, 1 at a time, beating just until blended after each addition.
2. Stir together flour, baking powder, and salt; add to butter mixture alternately with milk, beating at low speed just until blended, beginning and ending with flour mixture. Stir in 1 tablespoon lemon zest. Spoon batter into greased and floured 8- x 4-inch loafpan.
3. Bake at 350° for 1 hour or until a wooden pick inserted in center of bread comes out clean. Let cool in pan 10 minutes. Remove bread from pan, and cool completely on a wire rack.
4. Stir together powdered sugar and lemon juice until smooth; spoon evenly over top of bread, letting excess drip down sides. Stir together remaining 1 tablespoon lemon zest and 1 tablespoon granulated sugar; sprinkle on top of bread. **Makes** 1 loaf.

Chocolate Chip Mandelbread

Chocolate Chip Mandelbread

PREP: 10 MIN., COOK: 35 MIN., OTHER: 45 MIN.

2 cups sugar, divided
3 large eggs
1 cup vegetable oil
3¾ cups all-purpose flour
2 teaspoons baking powder
½ teaspoon salt
1 teaspoon vanilla extract
1 (6-ounce) package semisweet chocolate
 mini-morsels
1½ teaspoons ground cinnamon

1. Beat 1½ cups sugar and eggs at medium speed with an electric mixer until blended. Add oil and next 4 ingredients; beat until blended. Stir in mini-morsels.
2. Divide dough in half; shape each portion into a 10- x 3-inch log on lightly greased baking sheets. (Dough will be sticky. Shape dough with floured hands, if necessary.)
3. Bake at 350° for 25 to 30 minutes or until lightly browned. Cool slightly; cut diagonally into ¾-inch-thick slices.
4. Combine remaining ½ cup sugar and cinnamon; sprinkle over slices. Bake 5 more minutes; cool completely on wire racks. **Makes** 36 servings.

FAMILY FAVORITE, QUICK
Sour Cream Corn Sticks

PREP: 5 MIN., COOK: 23 MIN.

3 large eggs, lightly beaten
1 cup self-rising cornmeal
1 (8¾-ounce) can cream-style corn
1 (8-ounce) carton sour cream
¼ cup vegetable oil

1. Heat lightly greased cast-iron corn stick pans in a 400° oven for 5 minutes.
2. Combine all ingredients, stirring just until cornmeal is moistened.
3. Remove cast-iron pans from oven, and spoon batter into hot pans.
4. Bake at 400° for 16 to 18 minutes or until golden. **Makes** 16 corn sticks.

Mexican Cornbread

PREP: 5 MIN., COOK: 30 MIN., OTHER: 5 MIN.

1 tablespoon shortening
1 cup yellow cornmeal
1 teaspoon baking powder
½ teaspoon baking soda
½ teaspoon salt
1 (8-ounce) carton sour cream
1 (8½-ounce) can cream-style corn
2 large eggs, lightly beaten
1 cup (4 ounces) shredded Cheddar cheese
1 (4.5-ounce) can chopped green chiles,
 drained

1. Place shortening in a 9-inch cast-iron skillet, and heat in a 450° oven for 3 to 5 minutes or until fat smokes.
2. Combine cornmeal, baking powder, soda, and salt; blend well. Combine sour cream, corn, and eggs, mixing well. Add to dry ingredients, stirring just until moistened.
3. Spoon half of batter into hot skillet. Sprinkle with cheese and chiles; top with remaining batter.
4. Bake at 450° for 23 to 25 minutes or until brown. Let stand 5 minutes before serving. **Makes** 8 servings.

QUICK
Southern Corncakes

PREP: 5 MIN., COOK: 6 MIN. PER BATCH

1½ cups self-rising cornmeal
1¼ cups buttermilk
1 tablespoon sugar
1 tablespoon vegetable oil
1 large egg, lightly beaten
Vegetable oil

1. Combine first 5 ingredients in a large bowl, stirring just until dry ingredients are moistened.
2. Pour oil to depth of ¼ inch into a large heavy skillet. For each corncake, pour ¼ cup batter into skillet. Fry corncakes in hot oil over medium-high heat 3 minutes on each side or until golden. Serve immediately. **Makes** 8 corncakes.

Sopaipillas

Sopaipillas

Your family will enjoy this Southwestern bread that looks like puffy little pillows. To guarantee their "puff," it's important to maintain the oil's heat at 375°. Clip a candy thermometer to the side of the pan to help regulate the heat.

PREP: 15 MIN., COOK: 18 MIN., OTHER: 1 HR.

1¾ cups all-purpose flour
1 tablespoon sugar
2 teaspoons baking powder
1 teaspoon salt
2 tablespoons shortening
⅔ cup milk
Vegetable oil
Honey
Cinnamon sugar

1. Combine first 4 ingredients; cut in shortening with a pastry blender until mixture is crumbly. Add milk, stirring with a fork just until dry ingredients are moistened; shape into a ball.

2. Turn dough out onto a lightly floured surface, and knead gently until smooth (about 1 minute). Cover dough, and let rest 1 hour.

3. Roll dough to ¹⁄₁₆-inch thickness with a floured rolling pin. Using a pizza cutter, cut dough into 3-inch squares. Cover dough with a damp towel or cloth.

4. Pour oil to depth of 2 inches in a Dutch oven; heat to 375°. Drop dough, a few squares at a time, into hot oil, turning immediately to allow even puffing; turn back over, and cook until both sides are lightly browned. Drain on paper towels. Repeat with remaining dough squares. Serve immediately with honey and cinnamon sugar. **Makes** 22 sopaipillas.

Note: Make your own cinnamon sugar, if desired, by combining ½ cup sugar and 1 tablespoon ground cinnamon.

Belgian Waffles

These waffles are baked in a Belgian waffle iron which has larger, deeper grids than the traditional appliance. You can use a regular waffle iron if you prefer. Either way, heap fresh strawberries and whipped cream on waffles to maintain the Belgian influence.

PREP: 10 MIN., COOK: 10 MIN.

4 large eggs, separated
3 tablespoons butter, melted
½ teaspoon vanilla extract
1 cup all-purpose flour
½ teaspoon salt
1 cup milk
Sweetened whipped cream
Sliced fresh strawberries

1. Beat egg yolks at medium speed with an electric mixer until thick and pale. Add butter and vanilla, beating until blended. Set aside.
2. Combine flour and salt. Add flour mixture and milk to egg mixture, beating until smooth. Set aside.
3. Beat egg whites until stiff peaks form, and gently fold into batter.
4. Bake waffles in batches in a preheated, oiled Belgian waffle iron until golden. Serve with sweetened whipped cream and strawberries. **Makes** 8 (4-inch) waffles.

MAKE AHEAD
Amaretto French Toast

PREP: 12 MIN.; COOK: 25 MIN.; OTHER: 8 HR., 5 MIN.

6 (1-inch-thick) French bread slices
4 large eggs
½ cup milk
1 tablespoon dark brown sugar
1 teaspoon almond extract
½ teaspoon ground nutmeg
2 tablespoons almond liqueur (optional)
3 tablespoons butter
¼ cup sliced almonds, toasted
Powdered sugar
Maple syrup, warmed

1. Arrange bread slices in a 13- x 9-inch baking dish.
2. Whisk together eggs, next 4 ingredients, and, if desired, liqueur; pour over bread. Let stand 5 minutes, turning once. Cover and chill 8 hours, if desired.
3. Melt butter at 400° in a 15- x 10-inch jelly-roll pan; add French bread slices. Bake at 400° for 15 minutes; turn and bake 8 to 10 more minutes or until golden. Sprinkle with almonds and powdered sugar. Serve with maple syrup. **Makes** 3 servings.

QUICK, FAMILY FAVORITE
Apple Pancakes

PREP: 10 MIN., COOK: ABOUT 16 MIN.

2 cups all-purpose flour
¼ cup sugar
1 teaspoon baking soda
¼ teaspoon salt
2 cups buttermilk
2 large eggs
2 tablespoons butter, melted
1 large Granny Smith apple, peeled
    and chopped

1. Combine first 4 ingredients in a large bowl; make a well in center of mixture.
2. Stir together buttermilk, eggs, and butter. Add to dry ingredients, stirring just until moistened. Fold in apple.
3. Pour ¼ cup batter for each pancake onto a hot lightly greased griddle. Cook until tops are covered with bubbles and edges look cooked; turn and cook other side. **Makes** 16 (4-inch) pancakes.

Buttermilk Pancakes

FAMILY FAVORITE, QUICK
Buttermilk Pancakes

PREP: 5 MIN., COOK: ABOUT 12 MIN.

1¼ cups all-purpose flour
2 tablespoons sugar
2 teaspoons baking powder
½ teaspoon baking soda
¾ teaspoon salt
1 large egg, lightly beaten
1¼ cups buttermilk
3 tablespoons vegetable oil
1 cup chopped pecans, toasted (optional)

1. Stir together first 5 ingredients in a large bowl; make a well in center of mixture.

2. Stir together egg, buttermilk, and oil; add to dry ingredients, stirring just until moistened. Add pecans, if desired.

3. For each pancake, pour about ¼ cup batter onto a hot, lightly greased griddle.

4. Cook pancakes until tops are covered with bubbles and edges look cooked; turn and cook other side. Serve with butter, warm maple syrup, and fresh berries. **Makes** 9 (4-inch) pancakes.

Brunch Popover Pancake

PREP: 10 MIN., COOK: 25 MIN.

4 large eggs, lightly beaten
1 cup milk
1 cup all-purpose flour
¼ teaspoon salt
⅓ cup butter, melted
3 tablespoons orange marmalade
3 tablespoons butter
1 tablespoon lemon juice
1 (16-ounce) package frozen sliced peaches, thawed
    and drained
1 cup frozen blueberries, thawed

1. Place a well-greased 12-inch cast-iron skillet in a 425° oven for 5 minutes.
2. Combine first 5 ingredients, stirring with a wire whisk until blended.
3. Remove skillet from oven. Pour batter into hot skillet. Return skillet to oven.
4. Bake at 425° for 20 to 25 minutes. (Pancake will resemble a giant popover and will fall quickly after removing from oven.)
5. Meanwhile, combine marmalade, 3 tablespoons butter, and lemon juice in a saucepan; bring to a boil. Add peaches, and cook over medium heat, stirring constantly, 2 to 3 minutes. Spoon on top of baked pancake. Sprinkle with blueberries. **Makes** 4 servings.

Orange Rolls

*Drizzle a simple sour cream glaze over these
heavenly rolls while they're still warm.*

PREP: 20 MIN.; COOK: 22 MIN.; OTHER: 1 HR., 45 MIN.

1 package active dry yeast
¼ cup warm water (100° to 110°)
1 cup sugar, divided
½ cup butter, melted and divided
2 large eggs, lightly beaten
½ cup sour cream
1 teaspoon salt
3¾ cups all-purpose flour, divided
2 tablespoons orange zest
Glaze

1. Combine yeast and warm water in a 1-cup liquid measuring cup; let stand 5 minutes. Combine yeast mixture, ¼ cup sugar, 6 tablespoons butter, eggs, sour cream, and salt in a large mixing bowl. Gradually add 2 cups flour, and beat at medium speed with an electric mixer until smooth. Stir in enough remaining flour to make a soft dough.
2. Turn dough out onto a well-floured surface, and knead until smooth and elastic (about 5 minutes). Place in a well-greased bowl, turning to grease top. Cover and let rise in a warm place (85°), free from drafts, 1 hour and 15 minutes or until doubled in bulk.
3. Punch dough down, and divide in half; roll each portion into a 12-inch circle. Combine remaining ¾ cup sugar and orange zest. Brush each circle with 1 tablespoon melted butter, and sprinkle each with half of orange-sugar mixture.
4. Cut each round of dough into 12 wedges. Roll up each wedge, beginning with wide end and rolling toward point.
5. Place rolls, point side down, in 3 rows in a lightly greased 13- x 9-inch pan. Cover and let rise in a warm place, free from drafts, 30 minutes or until rolls are doubled in bulk.
6. Bake at 350° for 22 minutes or until golden. Drizzle Glaze over warm rolls. **Makes** 2 dozen.

Glaze

COOK: 3 MIN.

¾ cup sugar
½ cup sour cream
½ cup butter
2 tablespoons orange juice

1. Combine all ingredients in a saucepan; bring to a boil over medium heat. Boil 3 minutes, stirring constantly. Remove from heat. **Makes** 1½ cups.

Spoon Rolls

> I love these homemade rolls because they taste like traditional yeast rolls but are as easy to prepare as from a cake mix.

LYDA JONES BURNETTE, TEST KITCHENS DIRECTOR

(EDITOR'S CHOICE)
Spoon Rolls

PREP: 10 MIN., COOK: 20 MIN., OTHER: 5 MIN.

1 (¼-ounce) envelope active dry yeast
2 cups warm water (100° to 110°)
4 cups self-rising flour
¼ cup sugar
¾ cup butter, melted
1 large egg, lightly beaten

1. Combine yeast and 2 cups warm water in a large bowl; let mixture stand 5 minutes.
2. Stir in flour and remaining ingredients until blended. Spoon into well-greased cast-iron muffin pans, filling two-thirds full, or into well-greased cast-iron drop biscuit pans, filling half full.
3. Bake at 400° for 20 minutes or until rolls are golden brown. **Makes** 14 rolls.
Note: Unused batter may be stored in an airtight container in the refrigerator for up to 1 week.

Crescent Rolls

PREP: 20 MIN.; OTHER: 1 HR., 5 MIN.; COOK: 12 MIN.

1 package rapid-rise yeast
1 teaspoon sugar
¼ cup warm water (100° to 110°)
½ cup shortening or butter, melted
¼ cup sugar
2 large eggs, lightly beaten
1 cup warm water (100° to 110°)
1 teaspoon salt
4½ to 4¾ cups all-purpose flour, divided
¼ cup butter, melted

1. Combine yeast, 1 teaspoon sugar, and ¼ cup warm water in a 1-cup liquid measuring cup; let stand 5 minutes.
2. Combine yeast mixture, shortening, and next 4 ingredients in a large mixing bowl; stir in 2 cups flour. Beat at medium speed with an electric mixer 1 minute. Gradually stir in enough remaining flour to make a soft dough.
3. Turn dough out onto a floured surface, and knead until smooth and elastic (about 5 minutes). Place in a well-greased bowl, turning to grease top. Cover and let rise in a warm place (85°), free from drafts, 45 minutes or until doubled in bulk.
4. Punch dough down, and divide into fourths. Roll each portion into an 11-inch circle. Cut each circle into 8 wedges; roll up each wedge, beginning at wide end. Place on lightly greased baking sheets, point sides down, and curve slightly. Brush with ¼ cup melted butter. Cover and let rise in a warm place, free from drafts, 20 minutes or until doubled in bulk.
5. Bake at 375° for 10 to 12 minutes. **Makes** 32 rolls.

Oatmeal Dinner Rolls
*Brown sugar gives these dinnertime delights
a lightly sweet flavor.*

PREP: 15 MIN.; COOK: 15 MIN.; OTHER: 1 HR., 35 MIN.

2 cups water
1 cup quick-cooking oats
3 tablespoons butter
2 (¼-ounce) envelopes active dry yeast
½ cup warm water (100° to 110°)
1 tablespoon granulated sugar
4 cups all-purpose flour
1½ teaspoons salt
⅓ cup firmly packed brown sugar

1. Bring 2 cups water to a boil in a medium saucepan; stir in oats and butter. Boil, stirring constantly, 1 minute. Remove from heat; let cool to 110°.
2. Stir together yeast, ½ cup warm water, and 1 tablespoon granulated sugar in a 2-cup measuring cup; let stand 5 minutes.
3. Beat oat mixture, yeast mixture, flour, salt, and brown sugar at medium speed with an electric mixer until smooth.
4. Turn dough out onto a lightly floured surface; knead until smooth and elastic (about 5 minutes). Place in a well-greased bowl, turning to grease top.
5. Cover and let rise in a warm place (85°), free from drafts, 1 hour or until doubled in bulk.
6. Punch dough down, and divide in half; shape each portion into 16 (1½-inch) balls. Divide balls evenly into 2 lightly greased 9- x 1¾-inch round cakepans.
7. Cover and let rise in a warm place, free from drafts, 30 minutes or until doubled in bulk.
8. Bake at 375° for 15 minutes or until golden brown. **Makes** 32 rolls.

Homemade Butter Rolls

PREP: 20 MIN.; COOK: 10 MIN.; OTHER: 10 HR., 5 MIN.

2 (¼-ounce) envelopes active dry yeast
1 cup sugar, divided
2 cups warm water (100° to 110°)
1 cup butter, melted
6 large eggs, lightly beaten
1½ teaspoons salt
8½ to 9½ cups all-purpose flour

1. Stir together yeast, 2 tablespoons sugar, and 2 cups warm water in a 4-cup glass measuring cup; let stand 5 minutes.

2. Stir together yeast mixture, remaining sugar, and butter in a large bowl; stir in egg and salt. Gradually stir in enough flour to make a soft dough. Cover and chill 8 hours.

3. Divide dough into 4 equal portions. Turn each portion out onto a lightly floured surface, and roll each into a 12-inch circle. Cut each circle into 12 wedges. Roll up each wedge, starting at wide end; place on greased baking sheets. (Rolls may be frozen at this point.) Cover and let rise in a warm place (85°), free from drafts, 2 hours or until doubled in bulk.

4. Bake at 400° for 10 minutes or until golden.

Makes 4 dozen.

Note: If unbaked rolls are frozen, place frozen rolls on ungreased baking sheets. Cover and let rise in a warm place (85°), free from drafts, 2 hours or until doubled in bulk. Bake as directed.

English Muffins

While English muffins are traditionally baked on a griddle, these are simply browned in the oven. The airy muffins are great split and toasted. Fill their pockets with your favorite jam.

PREP: 15 MIN.; COOK: 16 MIN.; OTHER: 2 HR., 20 MIN.

1 package active dry yeast
¼ cup warm water (100° to 110°)
1 cup milk
3 tablespoons shortening
3 tablespoons sugar
1½ teaspoons salt
1 large egg, lightly beaten
4 cups all-purpose flour, divided
Cornmeal

1. Combine yeast and warm water in a 1-cup liquid measuring cup; let stand 5 minutes.

2. Combine milk and next 3 ingredients in a small saucepan over medium heat until shortening melts; remove from heat, and cool to 100° to 110°. Stir in yeast mixture. Add egg and 2½ cups flour; beat at medium speed with an electric mixer until smooth. Add 1 cup flour, beating until mixture forms a soft dough.

3. Turn dough out onto a lightly floured surface, and knead until smooth and elastic (about 5 minutes). Add remaining flour as needed to surface to keep dough from sticking.

4. Place dough in a well-greased bowl, turning to grease top. Cover and let rise in a warm place (85°), free from drafts, 1½ hours or until doubled in bulk.

5. Sprinkle two ungreased baking sheets with cornmeal; set aside. Punch dough down; turn out onto a lightly floured surface. Pat dough into a ¼-inch-thick circle; cut dough into rounds with a 3¾-inch biscuit cutter, and place on prepared baking sheets. Let rise, uncovered, in a warm place, free from drafts, 45 minutes or until doubled in bulk.

6. Bake at 325° for 8 minutes; turn muffins over, and bake 8 more minutes. Transfer to wire racks to cool.

Makes 1 dozen.

Dried Fruit
Galette

Dried Fruit Galette

A French galette is a round, flat cake or tart filled with fruit, jam, nuts, or cheese.

PREP: 20 MIN., COOK: 25 MIN.

1 package active dry yeast
¼ cup warm water (100° to 110°)
2 cups all-purpose flour
¼ cup sugar
1 teaspoon salt
¾ cup butter, cut into pieces
1 large egg, lightly beaten
1 teaspoon vanilla extract
Fruit Filling
2 tablespoons turbinado sugar or sugar

1. Combine yeast and warm water in a 1-cup liquid measuring cup; let stand 5 minutes.
2. Combine flour, ¼ cup sugar, and salt in a large mixing bowl; cut in butter with a pastry blender until mixture is crumbly. Combine yeast mixture, egg, and vanilla; stir into flour mixture, blending well. Shape dough into a flat disc; cover and chill.
3. Roll dough into a 14-inch circle on a large greased baking sheet. Spread Fruit Filling over dough to within 3 inches of edge. Fold edges of dough over fruit, leaving center of fruit uncovered. Sprinkle dough with turbinado sugar. Bake at 400° for 25 minutes or until golden. Serve warm. **Makes** 6 servings.

Fruit Filling

PREP: 5 MIN., COOK: 10 MIN.

⅔ cup dried prunes
⅔ cup dried apricot halves
1 (8¼-ounce) can crushed pineapple
    in heavy syrup, undrained
½ cup sugar
1½ tablespoons quick-cooking tapioca

1. Cook prunes and apricots in boiling water to cover 10 minutes; drain and chop fruit. Combine prunes, apricots, pineapple, sugar, and tapioca, stirring well. **Makes** 2¼ cups.

Almond Danish

FREEZER FRIENDLY, MAKE AHEAD
Almond Danish

PREP: 30 MIN.; COOK: 30 MIN.; OTHER: 1 HR., 30 MIN.

1 cup butter, slightly softened
2 packages active dry yeast
½ cup warm water (100° to 110°)
⅓ cup sugar
¾ cup milk
2 large eggs
4¼ to 4¾ cups all-purpose flour
1 teaspoon salt
Almond Filling (opposite page), divided
1 large egg, lightly beaten
Sugar
¼ cup sliced almonds

1. Place 2 sticks butter 1 inch apart between two sheets of wax paper; roll into a 12-inch square, using a rolling pin. Place on a baking sheet, and chill.
2. Combine yeast, warm water, and ½ teaspoon sugar in a 1-cup liquid measuring cup; let stand 5 minutes.

Combine yeast mixture, remaining sugar, milk, 2 eggs, 3 cups flour, and salt in a large mixing bowl; beat at medium speed with an electric mixer 3 minutes. Gradually stir in enough remaining flour to make a soft dough. Cover and chill dough 30 minutes.
3. Place dough on a lightly floured surface; roll into an 18- x 13-inch rectangle. Peel top sheet of wax paper from chilled butter; invert butter on 1 end of dough, covering two-thirds of dough. Peel off remaining wax paper from butter. Fold uncovered third of dough over middle third; gently fold remaining third over middle third. Turn dough so that long side is toward you. Roll dough into a 24- x 12-inch rectangle. Fold ends to center; then fold dough in half. Turn dough so that the long side is toward you again. Repeat rolling and folding procedure twice; cover and chill dough 1 hour.
4. Divide dough in half. Place half of dough on a lightly floured surface; refrigerate unused portion. Roll dough into a 30- x 9-inch rectangle. Cut lengthwise into 3 strips. Gently spread ¼ cup Almond Filling

evenly down center of each strip. Fold edges of strips over filling, and seal. Place 3 ropes, side by side, on a large ungreased baking sheet; braid. Join ends of dough to make a 9-inch ring. Repeat procedure with remaining dough and filling.

5. Let dough rise in a warm place (85°), free from drafts, 30 minutes or until doubled in bulk. Brush with beaten egg; sprinkle with sugar and almonds. Bake at 350° for 25 to 30 minutes or until golden. Transfer danishes to wire racks to cool. **Makes** 2 danishes.

Almond Filling

PREP: 5 MIN.

1 (8-ounce) can almond paste, crumbled
½ cup butter, softened
½ cup sugar

1. Combine all ingredients in a bowl; beat at medium speed with an electric mixer until mixture is blended. **Makes** 1½ cups.

Note: To freeze, bake as directed; let cool. Wrap tightly in aluminum foil; freeze. To serve, let thaw, covered, in refrigerator; reheat in foil at 350° for 15 to 20 minutes.

Homemade Raisin Bread

The aroma of homemade bread baking is one of life's simple pleasures. Try this main recipe below or the Cinnamon-Raisin version, which is a bit sweeter.

PREP: 30 MIN.; COOK: 30 MIN.; OTHER: 1 HR., 45 MIN.

1 cup raisins
2 packages active dry yeast
½ cup warm water (100° to 110°)
3 tablespoons sugar
⅔ cup shortening
1⅓ cups milk
½ cup sugar
1½ teaspoons salt
6 to 6½ cups bread flour, divided
2 large eggs, lightly beaten
1 large egg, lightly beaten
2 tablespoons butter, melted

1. Place raisins in a small saucepan; add water to cover. Bring to a boil; remove from heat. Drain and cool.

2. Combine yeast and warm water in a 2-cup liquid measuring cup; stir in 3 tablespoons sugar, and let stand 5 minutes. Combine shortening, milk, ¾ cup sugar, and salt in a saucepan over medium heat until shortening melts; remove from heat. Let mixture cool to lukewarm (100° to 110°).

3. Combine yeast mixture, shortening mixture, 2 cups flour, and 2 eggs in a large mixing bowl. Beat at medium speed with an electric mixer until blended. Gradually stir in enough remaining flour to make a soft dough.

4. Turn dough out onto a floured surface; add raisins, and knead until smooth and elastic (8 to 10 minutes). Place in a well-greased bowl, turning to grease top. Cover and let rise in a warm place (85°), free from drafts, 1 hour or until doubled in bulk.

5. Punch dough down, and divide in half. Roll each half of dough into a 15- x 7-inch rectangle on a lightly floured surface; roll up, jelly-roll fashion, starting at narrow end. Pinch seams and ends to seal. Place loaves, seam side down, in 2 well-greased 9- x 5-inch loafpans. Cover and let rise 30 to 45 minutes or until doubled in bulk.

6. Brush tops of loaves with remaining beaten egg. Bake at 350° for 30 minutes or until loaves sound hollow when tapped. Brush tops of loaves with melted butter. **Makes** 2 loaves.

Cinnamon-Raisin Bread: Prepare dough as directed. Combine 3 tablespoons sugar and 1 tablespoon ground cinnamon; sift across dough before rolling up, jelly-roll fashion. Combine 1 cup sifted powdered sugar and 1½ tablespoons milk, stirring until smooth. Drizzle glaze over barely warm baked loaves.

Creamy Succotash, page 93

Southern
plate

Turnip Greens Stew

Frozen seasoning blend is a mixture of diced onion, red and green bell peppers, and celery.

PREP: 10 MIN., COOK: 35 MIN.

2 cups chopped cooked ham
1 tablespoon vegetable oil
3 cups chicken broth
2 (16-ounce) packages frozen chopped turnip greens
1 (10-ounce) package frozen seasoning blend*
1 teaspoon sugar
1 teaspoon seasoned pepper

1. Sauté ham in hot oil in a Dutch oven over medium-high heat 5 minutes or until lightly browned.
2. Add broth and remaining ingredients; bring to a boil. Cover, reduce heat to low, and simmer, stirring occasionally, 25 minutes. **Makes** 6 to 8 servings.

*1 chopped fresh onion, 1 chopped celery rib, and 1 chopped green bell pepper may be substituted for frozen seasoning blend.

Note: For testing purposes only, we used McKenzie's Seasoning Blend.

Collard Stew: Substitute 1 (16-ounce) package frozen chopped collard greens for turnip greens and 1 (16-ounce) can black-eyed peas, drained, for 2 packages turnip greens. Prepare recipe as directed, adding black-eyed peas during the last 10 minutes of cooking.

Gumbo Ya Ya

Don't skip the step of chilling Gumbo Ya Ya for eight hours. The refrigeration process not only enables you to remove solidified fat from the surface of the soup but also allows the rich flavors of the gumbo to blend and intensify.

PREP: 30 MIN., COOK: 5 HR., OTHER: 8 HR.

1 (4- to 5-pound) dressed duckling
1 (3- to 3½-pound) broiler-fryer chicken
1 gallon water
1½ teaspoons salt
½ teaspoon black pepper
1 pound smoked sausage, cut into ½-inch slices
6 ribs celery, chopped
3 large onions, chopped
2 large green bell peppers, seeded and chopped
2 garlic cloves, minced
1 tablespoon vegetable oil
1 cup bacon drippings
1 cup all-purpose flour
1 (10-ounce) can diced tomatoes and green chiles, undrained
2 teaspoons salt
1 teaspoon seasoned pepper
1 teaspoon hot sauce
1 (16-ounce) package frozen sliced okra, thawed
Hot cooked rice
Filé powder (optional)

1. Combine first 5 ingredients in a large Dutch oven or stockpot. Bring to a boil; cover, reduce heat, and simmer 1 hour or until duck and chicken are tender. Remove duck and chicken from broth, reserving broth. Let duck and chicken cool. Transfer broth to another container; set aside. Skin, bone, and coarsely chop duck and chicken; set meat aside.
2. Cook sausage and next 4 ingredients in hot oil in a Dutch oven over medium-high heat, stirring occasionally, until sausage is browned and vegetables are tender. Remove sausage and vegetables from Dutch oven; drain and set aside.
3. Combine bacon drippings and flour in Dutch oven; cook over medium heat, stirring constantly, until roux is chocolate colored (about 20 minutes). Gradually add reserved broth, stirring constantly. Stir in chopped meat, sausage mixture, tomatoes and green chiles,

2 teaspoons salt, seasoned pepper, and hot sauce.
4. Bring to a boil; cook over medium heat, uncovered, 3 hours, stirring constantly. Add okra; cook, uncovered, 30 minutes, stirring occasionally. Remove from heat; cool to almost room temperature, stirring occasionally. Cover and chill gumbo at least 8 hours.
5. Remove gumbo from refrigerator; skim as much solidified fat from top of gumbo as possible. Cook gumbo over medium heat until mixture is thoroughly heated, stirring often. Serve over rice; sprinkle with filé powder, if desired. **Makes** 12 to 15 servings.

Tortilla Soup

The slow cooker makes it easy to prepare this soup any time during the week.

PREP: 10 MIN.; COOK: 6 HR., 10 MIN.

2 (4-ounce) skinned and boned chicken breasts, cubed
2 cups frozen whole kernel corn, thawed
1 large onion, chopped
2 garlic cloves, pressed
2 (14-ounce) cans low-sodium fat-free chicken broth
1 (10¾-ounce) can tomato puree
1 (10-ounce) can diced tomatoes and green chiles
2 teaspoons ground cumin
1 teaspoon salt
1 teaspoon chili powder
⅛ teaspoon ground red pepper
⅛ teaspoon black pepper
1 bay leaf
4 (5½-inch) corn tortillas
Garnish: chopped fresh cilantro

1. Combine first 13 ingredients in a 4-quart slow cooker. Cover and cook at HIGH 6 hours. Discard bay leaf.
2. Cut tortillas into ¼-inch-wide strips; place on baking sheet.
3. Bake at 375° for 5 minutes. Stir and bake 5 more minutes or until crisp. Serve with soup. Garnish, if desired. **Makes** 6 to 8 servings.

Creole Jambalaya

Creole Jambalaya

PREP: 25 MIN., COOK: 1 HR.

2 tablespoons butter
1 large onion, chopped
1 green bell pepper, chopped
8 green onions, chopped
2 celery ribs, chopped
3 cups cubed cooked ham (1 pound)
1 pound Cajun-flavored or smoked sausage, sliced
1 (8-ounce) can tomato sauce
½ teaspoon salt
½ teaspoon ground black pepper
¼ teaspoon ground red pepper
5 cups cooked rice
Garnishes: fresh parsley sprig, chopped fresh parsley

1. Melt butter in a large skillet over medium heat. Add onion and next 3 ingredients; sauté until tender. Add ham, sausage, and next 4 ingredients. Cook, stirring occasionally, 20 minutes.
2. Stir in rice, cover, and cook, stirring occasionally, 30 minutes over low heat. Garnish, if desired. **Makes** 8 servings.

Chicken-and-Ham Jambalaya With Shrimp

PREP: 25 MIN.; COOK: 1 HR., 50 MIN.

¾ pound skinned and boned chicken thighs, cut into 1-inch cubes
¾ pound skinned and boned chicken breasts, cut into 1-inch cubes
1 teaspoon salt
⅛ teaspoon ground black pepper
⅛ teaspoon ground red pepper
2 tablespoons vegetable oil
½ pound cooked ham, cut into ½-inch cubes
2 medium-size yellow onions, chopped (about 2 cups)
1 large green bell pepper, seeded and chopped
1½ celery ribs, chopped (about 1 cup)
4 whole garlic cloves
1 (16-ounce) can diced tomatoes, undrained
3 cups chicken broth
2 pounds medium-size fresh shrimp
½ cup chopped green onion tops
2 tablespoons chopped fresh parsley
1 teaspoon hot pepper sauce
2 cups uncooked long-grain rice, rinsed and drained

1. Sprinkle chicken evenly with salt and ground peppers.
2. Cook chicken in hot oil in a Dutch oven over medium heat 8 to 10 minutes or until brown on all sides. Remove chicken with a slotted spoon to a large bowl.
3. Add ham to Dutch oven, and cook, stirring constantly, 5 minutes or until lightly browned. Add ham to chicken; set aside.

❝ As a Lowcountry native, I'm used to rice in all forms and fashions. While many folks grew up with mashed potatoes as a staple, rice was our comfort food of choice, and my mom served it with most meals.❞

DONNA FLORIO, SENIOR WRITER

4. Add onions and next 3 ingredients to Dutch oven, and cook 5 minutes, stirring to loosen any browned bits.
5. Drain tomatoes, reserving liquid: set tomatoes aside. Stir reserved liquid and chicken broth into Dutch oven. Add chicken and ham; cover and cook over low heat 45 minutes.
6. Peel shrimp; devein, if desired.
7. Mash cooked garlic against side of Dutch oven, and blend into the mixture. Add drained tomatoes, shrimp, green onions, and remaining ingredients, and bring to a boil. Cover and reduce heat to medium low; simmer, stirring occasionally, 25 minutes or until rice is tender and liquid is absorbed. **Makes** 6 to 8 servings.

MAKE AHEAD
Delta Red Beans and Rice

PREP: 15 MIN., COOK: 4 HR., OTHER: 16 HR.

1 pound dried red beans
6 cups water
1½ pounds smoked sausage, sliced
½ pound cooked ham, cubed
1 large sweet onion, chopped
2 garlic cloves, pressed
2 tablespoons olive oil
1 bunch green onions, chopped
1 cup chopped fresh parsley
1 teaspoon salt
1 teaspoon black pepper
½ teaspoon sugar
½ teaspoon dried oregano
½ teaspoon dried thyme
⅛ teaspoon ground red pepper
1 tablespoon Worcestershire sauce
¼ teaspoon hot sauce
Hot cooked rice

1. Place beans in a large Dutch oven. Cover with water 2 inches above beans; soak 8 hours. Drain.
2. Bring beans, 6 cups water, sausage, and ham to a boil in a Dutch oven. Cover, reduce heat, and simmer 3 hours.
3. Sauté onion and garlic in hot oil in a large skillet until tender. Add to bean mixture. Stir in green onions and next 9 ingredients. Cover and chill 8 hours.
4. Bring bean mixture to a simmer; cover and cook, stirring often, 1 hour. Serve over rice. **Makes** 8 to 10 servings.

MAKE AHEAD
Traditional Brisket

The rule of thumb is to smoke brisket 1 hour and
15 minutes per pound at 225° to 250° until the internal
temperature reaches 190°. The meat is safe to eat at
a lower temperature but isn't tender yet.

PREP: 40 MIN.; COOK: 6 HR., 30 MIN.; OTHER: 9 HR.

1 (5¾-pound) trimmed beef
    brisket flat
Brisket Rub
Hickory smoking chips
Basting mop*
Brisket Mopping Sauce
Brisket Red Sauce (optional)

1. Sprinkle each side of beef with ¼ cup Brisket Rub; rub thoroughly into meat. Wrap brisket in plastic wrap, and chill 8 hours.
2. Soak hickory chips in water for 8 hours. Drain.
3. Prepare smoker according to manufacturer's directions, regulating temperature with a thermometer to 225°; allow it to maintain that temperature for 1 hour before adding beef.
4. Remove beef from refrigerator, and let stand 30 minutes.
5. Place brisket on smoker rack, fat side up. Insert thermometer horizontally into thickest portion of beef. Maintain smoker temperature between 225° and 250°.
6. Add a handful (about ¼ cup) of hickory chips about every hour.
7. With basting mop, brush beef liberally with Brisket Mopping Sauce when beef starts to look dry. (Internal temperature will be about 156°.) Mop top of brisket every hour. When internal temperature reaches 170°, place brisket on a sheet of heavy-duty aluminum foil; mop liberally with Brisket Mopping Sauce. Wrap tightly, and return to smoker.
8. Remove brisket from smoker when internal temperature reaches 190° with an instant-read thermometer. Let stand 1 hour. Cut into very thin (⅛- to ¼-inch-thick) slices. Serve with Brisket Red Sauce, if desired. **Makes** 8 servings.
*Basting mops may be found in the grilling-supply section of supermarkets, restaurant-supply stores, and sporting goods stores.

Brisket Rub

PREP: 5 MIN.

¼ cup kosher salt
¼ cup sugar
¼ cup black pepper
¾ cup paprika
2 tablespoons garlic powder
2 tablespoons garlic salt
2 tablespoons onion powder
2 tablespoons chili powder
2 teaspoons ground red pepper

1. Combine all ingredients. Store in an airtight container. **Makes** 2 cups.

Brisket Mopping Sauce

PREP: 10 MIN.

1 (12-ounce) bottle beer
1 cup apple cider vinegar
1 onion, minced
4 garlic cloves, minced
½ cup water
½ cup Worcestershire sauce
¼ cup vegetable oil
2 tablespoons Brisket Rub

1. Stir together all ingredients until blended. **Makes** 4 cups.

Brisket Red Sauce

PREP: 10 MIN.

1½ cups apple cider vinegar
1 cup ketchup
¼ cup Worcestershire sauce
1 teaspoon salt
½ teaspoon ground red pepper
½ teaspoon black pepper
½ teaspoon onion powder
½ tablespoon garlic powder
½ tablespoon ground cumin
2 tablespoons unsalted butter,
    melted
½ cup firmly packed brown sugar

1. Stir together all ingredients until blended. Serve sauce heated or at room temperature. **Makes** 3½ cups.

Country-Style Pot Roast
and Gravy

FAMILY FAVORITE
Country-Style Pot Roast and Gravy

PREP: 20 MIN.; COOK: 2 HR., 45 MIN.

1 (4- to 5-pound) boneless chuck roast
1 tablespoon vegetable oil
1 (1-ounce) envelope onion soup mix
2 cups water
6 red new potatoes, quartered
2 carrots, cut into 2-inch pieces
½ (10-ounce) package red pearl onions, peeled
2 tablespoons all-purpose flour
½ cup water
¼ teaspoon salt
¼ teaspoon pepper

1. Brown roast in hot oil in a Dutch oven. Add soup mix and 2 cups water; bring to a boil. Cover, reduce heat, and simmer 2 hours.
2. Add vegetables; return to a boil. Cover, reduce heat, and simmer 30 minutes. Remove roast and vegetables to a serving platter; keep warm.
3. Remove and discard fat from pan drippings; return 1 cup drippings to Dutch oven.
4. Combine flour and ½ cup water, stirring until smooth. Add to drippings, stirring constantly. Bring to a boil over medium heat, stirring constantly, until thickened. Stir in salt and pepper. Serve with roast and vegetables. **Makes** 8 to 10 servings.

Chicken-Fried Steak

Fresh tomato slices, mashed potatoes, and black-eyed peas complete this menu. Cubing—pounding steak with a meat mallet—actually tenderizes the beef. Buy steaks already cubed at the meat counter.

PREP: 20 MIN., COOK: 18 MIN.

4 (4-ounce) cubed steaks
¼ teaspoon salt
¼ teaspoon black pepper
38 saltine crackers, crushed
     (about 1 sleeve)
1¼ cups all-purpose flour, divided
2 teaspoons salt, divided
1½ teaspoons black pepper, divided
½ teaspoon ground red pepper
½ teaspoon baking powder
4¾ cups milk, divided
2 large eggs
1 cup peanut oil

1. Sprinkle steaks evenly with ¼ teaspoon salt and ¼ teaspoon black pepper. Set aside.

2. Combine crackers, 1 cup flour, 1 teaspoon salt, ½ teaspoon black pepper, red pepper, and baking powder.

3. Whisk together ¾ cup milk and eggs. Dredge steaks in cracker mixture; dip in milk mixture, and dredge again in cracker mixture.

4. Pour oil into a 12-inch skillet; heat to 360°. (Do not use a nonstick skillet.) Fry steaks 2 to 3 minutes. Turn and fry 2 to 3 minutes or until golden. Remove steaks to a wire rack in a jelly-roll pan. Keep steaks warm in a 225° oven. Carefully drain hot oil, reserving cooked bits and 1 tablespoon drippings in skillet.

5. Whisk together remaining 4 cups milk, ¼ cup flour, 1 teaspoon salt, and 1 teaspoon black pepper. Add to reserved drippings in skillet; cook, whisking constantly, over medium-high heat, 10 to 12 minutes or until thickened. Serve over steaks and mashed potatoes. **Makes** 4 servings.

Chicken-Fried Steak

> **This recipe creates a taste that resembles a dish I grew up eating. This is an art of frying that my mother learned while living on the farm.**
>
> JOHN ALEX FLOYD, JR., FORMER EDITOR IN CHIEF

Our Best Southern
Fried Chicken

Our Best Southern Fried Chicken

PREP: 10 MIN., COOK: 30 MIN., OTHER: 8 HR.

3 quarts water
1 tablespoon salt
1 (2- to 2½-pound) broiler-fryer chicken, cut up
1 teaspoon salt
1 teaspoon pepper
1 cup all-purpose flour
2 cups vegetable oil
¼ cup bacon drippings

1. Combine 3 quarts water and 1 tablespoon salt in a large bowl; add chicken. Cover and chill 8 hours. Drain chicken; rinse with cold water, and pat dry.
2. Combine 1 teaspoon salt and pepper; sprinkle half of mixture over chicken. Combine remaining salt and pepper mixture and flour in a large, zip-top plastic freezer bag. Place 2 pieces of chicken in bag; seal. Shake to coat. Remove chicken; repeat procedure with remaining chicken, 2 pieces at a time.
3. Combine vegetable oil and bacon drippings in a 12-inch cast-iron skillet or chicken fryer; heat to 360°. Add chicken, a few pieces at a time, skin side down. Cover and cook 6 minutes; uncover and cook 9 minutes.
4. Turn chicken pieces; cover and cook 6 minutes. Uncover and cook 5 to 9 minutes, turning pieces during the last 3 minutes for even browning, if necessary. Drain chicken on paper towels; keep chicken warm.
Makes 4 servings.
Note: The oil temperature will drop when you add or turn the chicken. For best results, keep the oil temperature between 300° and 325°. You may substitute 2 cups buttermilk for the saltwater solution.

Chicken Pot Pie

This handy recipe makes four large casseroles—perfect for a crowd or for sharing with neighbors.

PREP: 10 MIN., COOK: 40 MIN., OTHER: 15 MIN.

2 recipes Pot Pie Filling, prepared 1 at a time
4 (15-ounce) packages refrigerated piecrusts

1. Divide filling evenly among 4 (15- x 12-inch) disposable aluminum roasting pans. Top each pan with 2 round piecrusts. Cut slits in piecrusts.
2. Bake at 400° for 30 to 40 minutes or until golden. Let stand 15 minutes before serving. **Makes** 100 servings (⅔ cup).

Pot Pie Filling

PREP: 1 HR., COOK: 15 MIN.

3 cups butter
2 large onions, chopped
6 celery ribs, chopped
3 cups all-purpose flour
2 (49-ounce) cans chicken broth
5 cups milk
16 cups chopped cooked chicken (about 8 roasted
    whole chickens)
3½ cups sliced carrots, cooked (about 1 pound)
3½ cups frozen green peas, thawed
1 to 2 tablespoons salt
1 tablespoon pepper
1½ teaspoons poultry seasoning
2 teaspoons hot sauce

1. Melt butter in a 4- to 6-gallon stockpot over medium heat; add onions and celery, and sauté until tender.
2. Add flour, stirring until blended; cook, stirring constantly, 2 minutes. Stir in broth and milk, stirring constantly. Bring to a boil, stirring constantly, and cook 2 minutes. Stir in chicken, sliced carrots, and remaining ingredients. **Makes** 32 cups.

To prepare this recipe to serve 8: Use ⅔ cup butter; ⅔ cup chopped onion; ⅔ cup chopped celery; ⅔ cup all-purpose flour; 3½ cups chicken broth; 1⅓ cups milk; 4 cups chopped roasted chicken breast;

1 cup sliced carrots, cooked; ½ cup frozen green peas, thawed; ¾ teaspoon salt; ¼ teaspoon pepper; ¼ teaspoon poultry seasoning; and ¼ teaspoon hot sauce in place of the Pot Pie Filling ingredients above. Follow the Chicken Pot Pie method above using a 13- x 9-inch dish and 1 (15-ounce) package refrigerated piecrusts.

King Ranch Chicken Casserole

PREP: 35 MIN., COOK: 35 MIN.

1 large onion, chopped
1 large green bell pepper, chopped
2 tablespoons vegetable oil
2 cups chopped cooked chicken
1 (10¾-ounce) can cream of chicken soup,
    undiluted
1 (10¾-ounce) can cream of mushroom soup,
    undiluted
1 (10-ounce) can diced tomatoes and green
    chiles
1 teaspoon chili powder
¼ teaspoon salt
¼ teaspoon garlic powder
¼ teaspoon pepper
12 (6-inch) corn tortillas
2 cups (8 ounces) shredded Cheddar cheese

1. Sauté onion and bell pepper in hot oil in a large skillet over medium-high heat 5 minutes or until tender. Stir in chicken and next 7 ingredients; remove from heat.
2. Tear tortillas into 1-inch pieces, and layer one-third of tortilla pieces in bottom of a lightly greased 13- x 9-inch baking dish. Top with one-third of chicken mixture and ⅔ cup cheese. Repeat layers twice.
3. Bake at 350° for 30 to 35 minutes. **Makes** 6 to 8 servings.
Note: Freeze casserole up to 1 month, if desired. Thaw in refrigerator overnight, and bake as directed.

Quick Chicken and Dumplings

Quick Chicken and Dumplings

Pick up a rotisserie chicken from your grocery deli. One whole roasted chicken yields about 3 cups chopped meat.

PREP: 10 MIN., COOK: 25 MIN.

4 cups water
3 cups chopped cooked chicken
2 (10¾-ounce) cans cream of chicken soup, undiluted
2 teaspoons chicken bouillon granules
1 teaspoon seasoned pepper
1 (6-ounce) can refrigerated buttermilk biscuits

1. Bring first 5 ingredients to a boil in a Dutch oven over medium-high heat, stirring often.
2. Separate biscuits in half, forming 2 rounds; cut each round in half. Drop biscuit pieces, 1 at a time, into boiling mixture; stir gently. Cover, reduce heat to low, and simmer, stirring occasionally, 15 to 20 minutes or until dumplings are cooked. **Makes** 4 to 6 servings.

To lighten: Use reduced-sodium, reduced-fat cream of chicken soup; reduced-fat biscuits; and chopped, cooked chicken breast halves.

Buttermilk Baked Chicken

Serve this sauce-smothered chicken with steamed asparagus, hot cooked rice, or any of your favorite sides. Sprinkle with chopped basil, parsley, or chives for a colorful garnish.

PREP: 15 MIN., COOK: 45 MIN.

¼ cup butter
4 bone-in chicken breasts, skinned
½ teaspoon salt
½ teaspoon pepper
1½ cups buttermilk, divided
¾ cup all-purpose flour
1 (10¾-ounce) can cream of mushroom soup, undiluted
Garnish: lemon wedges

1. Melt butter in a lightly greased 13- x 9-inch baking dish in a 425° oven.

2. Sprinkle chicken with salt and pepper. Dip chicken in ½ cup buttermilk, and dredge in flour. Arrange chicken, breast side down, in baking dish.

3. Bake at 425° for 25 minutes. Turn chicken, and bake 10 more minutes. Stir together remaining 1 cup buttermilk and cream of mushroom soup; pour over chicken, and bake 10 more minutes, shielding chicken with aluminum foil to prevent excessive browning, if necessary. Garnish, if desired. **Makes** 4 servings.

To lighten: Prepare recipe as directed, using light butter; nonfat buttermilk; and reduced-sodium, reduced-fat cream of mushroom soup.

Classic Fried Catfish

PREP: 10 MIN., COOK: 6 MIN.

¾ cup yellow cornmeal
¼ cup all-purpose flour
2 teaspoons salt
1 teaspoon ground red pepper
¼ teaspoon garlic powder
4 catfish fillets (about 1½ pounds)
¼ teaspoon salt
Vegetable oil

1. Combine first 5 ingredients in a large shallow dish.
2. Sprinkle catfish fillets with salt, and dredge in cornmeal mixture, coating evenly.
3. Pour vegetable oil to a depth of 3 inches into a Dutch oven; heat to 350°. Fry fillets 5 to 6 minutes or until golden; drain on paper towels. **Makes** 4 servings.

Fried Fish Tips

- Remove excess moisture from fish before dredging by patting dry with a paper towel.
- Keep one hand clean for dredging and the other hand available for frying.
- Select an oil, such as peanut oil, with a high smoke point.
- Use a large Dutch oven or deep cast-iron skillet to keep the hot oil from popping out.
- Use a deep-fat thermometer to maintain an accurate temperature.
- Don't overcrowd the skillet; fry in batches of two or three fillets at a time. Bring remaining oil back to the proper temperature before frying the next batch.
- Remove fish from skillet with a wide, slotted, curved spoon.
- To keep warm, place fried fish on a wire rack with a foil-lined pan underneath; place in a 250° oven. For a crisp texture, do not cover fillets.

Cajun-Style Grilled Catfish

Four ingredients containing pepper contribute to the Cajun flavor of this grilled fish.

PREP: 5 MIN., COOK: 10 MIN.

1 teaspoon lemon-pepper seasoning
1 teaspoon white pepper
1 teaspoon Creole seasoning
1 teaspoon blackened fish seasoning
4 catfish fillets (1½ to 2 pounds)
2 tablespoons lemon juice
Garnish: lemon wedges

1. Combine first 4 ingredients; rub seasoning on catfish. Sprinkle lemon juice on both sides of catfish.
2. Grill, covered with grill lid, over medium-hot coals (350° to 400°) 5 minutes on each side or until fish flakes easily when tested with a fork. Garnish, if desired. **Makes** 4 servings.
Note: For testing purposes only, we used Paul Prudhomme's Blackened Redfish seasoning.

Creamy Macaroni and Cheese

We like the pungent flavor of sharp and extra-sharp cheeses, but you can use whatever type you prefer.

PREP: 20 MIN., COOK: 35 MIN.

1 (8-ounce) package elbow macaroni
¼ cup butter
¼ cup all-purpose flour
¼ teaspoon salt
¼ teaspoon black pepper
⅛ teaspoon ground red pepper
⅛ teaspoon granulated garlic
1 cup half-and-half
1 cup milk
½ (10-ounce) block extra-sharp Cheddar cheese, shredded
1 (10-ounce) block sharp Cheddar cheese, shredded and divided

1. Prepare pasta according to package directions; drain and set aside.

2. Melt butter in a large skillet over medium-high heat. Gradually whisk in flour until smooth; cook, whisking constantly, 2 minutes. Stir in salt and next 3 ingredients. Gradually whisk in half-and-half and milk; cook, whisking constantly, 8 to 10 minutes or until thickened.

3. Stir in extra-sharp cheese and half of sharp cheese until smooth. Remove from heat.

4. Combine pasta and cheese mixture, and pour into 6 lightly greased (6-ounce) ramekins or 1 (8-inch square) baking dish. Sprinkle evenly with remaining sharp Cheddar cheese.

5. Bake at 375° for 20 minutes. (Bake 15 minutes longer for a crusty top.) **Makes** 6 servings.

Note: For testing purposes only, we used Kraft Cracker Barrel cheese.

Savory Green Beans

PREP: 15 MIN., COOK: 25 MIN.

1½ pounds fresh green beans
1 garlic clove, minced
2 tablespoons chopped onion
3 tablespoons olive oil or vegetable oil
½ cup boiling water
1 tablespoon fresh basil or 1 teaspoon dried basil
¾ teaspoon salt
½ teaspoon sugar
¼ teaspoon pepper

1. Wash beans; trim ends, and remove strings. Cut beans in half.
2. Sauté garlic and onion in hot oil just until tender. Add beans, boiling water, basil, salt, sugar, and pepper. Cover and cook over medium heat 20 to 25 minutes or until beans are tender. **Makes** 6 servings.

Fresh Pole Beans

Serve these beans and some of their cooking liquid with cornbread.

PREP: 15 MIN., COOK: 40 MIN.

1 pound fresh pole beans
½ pound salt pork or ham hock
2 teaspoons vegetable oil
3 cups water
½ teaspoon salt
½ teaspoon freshly ground pepper

1. Wash beans; trim ends. Cut beans into pieces, and set aside.
2. Brown salt pork on all sides in oil in a large saucepan over medium heat. Add water, salt, and pepper; bring to a boil. Cover, reduce heat, and simmer broth mixture 15 minutes.
3. Add beans. Cover and cook over medium heat 25 minutes or until beans are tender. Serve with a slotted spoon. **Makes** 4 servings.

Easy Baked Beans

Baked beans are always a welcome and favorite dish. Pair this recipe with pork chops, ham, or burgers from the grill.

PREP: 10 MIN., COOK: 50 MIN.

2 bacon slices, halved
1 small onion, diced
1 small green bell pepper, finely chopped
1 (15-ounce) can pork and beans with tomato sauce
2 teaspoons prepared mustard
1 teaspoon chili powder
¼ to ⅓ cup molasses
3 tablespoons ketchup

1. Cook bacon in a medium skillet until partially cooked; remove bacon, and set aside, reserving drippings in pan.
2. Sauté onion and green pepper in bacon drippings until tender; drain.
3. Combine sautéed onion mixture, beans, and remaining 4 ingredients, stirring well. Spoon mixture into a lightly greased 1½-quart baking dish. Top with bacon slices. Bake, uncovered, at 350° for 30 to 40 minutes or until beans are thickened and bacon is cooked. **Makes** 4 servings.

Grilled Corn With Jalapeño-Lime Butter

To make the butter a bit more kid-friendly, prepare a second batch without the jalapeño peppers.

PREP: 25 MIN., COOK: 20 MIN., OTHER: 1 HR.

¾ cup butter, softened
2 large jalapeño peppers, seeded and
    minced
2 tablespoons lime zest
1 teaspoon fresh lime juice
10 ears fresh corn, husks removed
2 tablespoons olive oil
1 tablespoon kosher salt
1 teaspoon freshly ground black pepper

1. Combine first 4 ingredients in a bowl; cover and chill until ready to serve.
2. Rub corn evenly with 2 tablespoons olive oil; sprinkle evenly with salt and black pepper.
3. Grill, covered with grill lid, over high heat (400° to 500°), turning often, 15 to 20 minutes or until corn is tender. Serve corn with flavored butter. **Makes** 10 servings.

Fried Green Tomatoes

Crispy tomatoes provide a crunchy texture that pairs well with many different types of foods.

PREP: 15 MIN., COOK: 4 MIN. PER BATCH

1 large egg, lightly beaten
½ cup buttermilk
½ cup all-purpose flour, divided
½ cup cornmeal
1 teaspoon salt
½ teaspoon pepper
3 medium-size green tomatoes, cut into
    ⅓-inch slices
Vegetable oil
Salt to taste

1. Combine egg and buttermilk; set aside.
2. Combine ¼ cup all-purpose flour, cornmeal, 1 teaspoon salt, and pepper in a shallow bowl or pan.
3. Dredge tomato slices in remaining ¼ cup flour; dip in egg mixture, and dredge in cornmeal mixture.
4. Pour oil to a depth of ¼ to ½ inch in a large cast-iron skillet; heat to 375°. Drop tomatoes, in batches, into hot oil, and cook 2 minutes on each side or until golden. Drain on paper towels or a wire rack. Sprinkle hot tomatoes with salt to taste. **Makes** 4 to 6 servings.

Fried Green Tomato Tips

- When purchasing tomatoes, make sure that they are indeed unripe tomatoes instead of a ripe green heirloom tomato.
- Select tomatoes that are firm.
- Don't slice the tomatoes too thin; otherwise they will fall apart before frying.

Fried Green Tomatoes

Tee's Corn Pudding

PREP: 15 MIN.; COOK: 1 HR., 15 MIN.; OTHER: 10 MIN.

¼ cup sugar
3 tablespoons all-purpose flour
2 teaspoons baking powder
1½ teaspoons salt
6 large eggs
2 cups whipping cream
½ cup butter, melted
6 cups fresh corn kernels (about 12 ears)*
Garnish: flat-leaf parsley sprig

1. Combine first 4 ingredients.
2. Whisk together eggs, whipping cream, and butter. Gradually add sugar mixture, whisking until smooth; stir in corn. Pour mixture into a lightly greased 2-quart baking dish.
3. Bake at 350° for 1 hour and 15 minutes or until golden brown and set. Let stand 10 minutes. Garnish, if desired. **Makes** 6 to 8 servings.
*6 cups frozen whole kernel corn or canned shoepeg corn, drained, may be substituted.
Note: This recipe may also be baked in a 13- x 9-inch baking dish at 350° for 1 hour to 1 hour and 5 minutes or until golden brown and set.

Southwestern Corn Pudding: Stir 1 (4.5-ounce) can chopped green chiles, drained, and ¼ teaspoon ground cumin into corn pudding batter. Bake as directed.

Buttermilk Fried Corn

You can serve these fried corn niblets as a side dish or sprinkle some on salads, soups, or casseroles.

PREP: 10 MIN., COOK: 3 MIN. PER BATCH, OTHER: 30 MIN.

2 cups fresh corn kernels
1½ cups buttermilk
⅔ cup all-purpose flour
⅔ cup cornmeal
1 teaspoon salt
½ teaspoon pepper
Vegetable oil

1. Combine corn kernels and buttermilk in a large bowl; let stand 30 minutes. Drain; discard buttermilk.
2. Combine flour and next 3 ingredients in a large heavy-duty, zip-top plastic freezer bag. Add corn to flour mixture, a small amount at a time, and shake bag to coat corn.
3. Pour oil to depth of 1 inch in a Dutch oven; heat to 375°. Fry corn, a small amount at a time, in hot oil 3 minutes or until corn is golden. Drain on paper towels. **Makes** 2 cups.

QUICK
Mess O' Greens With Warm Pecan Dressing

As far as greens go, this recipe is tops. A small amount of delicious dressing wilts and coats the greens perfectly. And the pecans are a nice nutty surprise. You'll need to buy 1 bunch of greens to yield 6 cups shredded.

PREP: 10 MIN., COOK: 2 MIN.

6 cups fresh mustard greens, shredded, or fresh
      turnip greens, shredded
2 tablespoons balsamic vinegar
2 teaspoons honey
1 tablespoon Dijon mustard
⅓ cup coarsely chopped pecans
1 tablespoon vegetable oil or olive oil

1. Place greens in a large bowl.
2. Stir together vinegar, honey, and mustard. Simmer vinegar mixture and pecans in hot oil in a small skillet over medium heat 2 minutes, stirring often. Remove from heat. Pour warm dressing over greens; toss. Serve immediately. **Makes** 2 servings.

FAMILY FAVORITE
Southern Black-Eyed Peas

PREP: 10 MIN., COOK: 2 HR., OTHER: 1 HR.

1 pound dried black-eyed peas
3 ham hocks
1 medium onion, chopped
2 tablespoons bacon drippings
1 bay leaf
¼ teaspoon freshly ground pepper
5 cups water
1 teaspoon salt
2 teaspoons hot sauce

1. Sort and wash peas; place in a large Dutch oven. Add water 2 inches above peas, and bring to a boil. Boil 2 minutes; cover, remove from heat, and let stand 1 hour. Drain peas.
2. Brown ham hocks and onion in bacon drippings in Dutch oven 2 minutes. Add peas, bay leaf, and pepper. Add 5 cups water. Bring to a boil; reduce heat, and simmer, partially covered, 1 to 1½ hours or until peas are tender. Discard bay leaf.
3. Remove ham hocks from saucepan. Remove meat from bones, and add meat to peas. Add salt and hot sauce to peas. Serve with a slotted spoon. **Makes** 8 cups.

Turnips Au Gratin

The mild flavor of turnips may surprise you in this well-seasoned casserole.

PREP: 10 MIN., COOK: 45 MIN.

9 medium turnips, peeled and diced (about 3 pounds)
1 teaspoon salt
1 teaspoon sugar
2 tablespoons butter
2 tablespoons all-purpose flour
1½ cups milk
¾ cup (3 ounces) shredded Cheddar cheese
1 teaspoon seasoned salt
⅛ teaspoon pepper
¼ cup fine, dry breadcrumbs

1. Combine first 3 ingredients in a Dutch oven; add water to cover. Bring to a boil; cover, reduce heat, and simmer 10 to 12 minutes or until diced turnips are tender. Drain well, and set aside.
2. Melt butter in a large heavy saucepan over low heat; add flour, stirring constantly. Gradually add milk; cook over medium heat, stirring constantly, until slightly thickened. Add cheese, seasoned salt, and pepper, stirring until cheese melts. Remove from heat; stir in diced turnips.
3. Spoon turnip mixture into a lightly greased 1½-quart casserole; sprinkle with breadcrumbs. Bake at 350° for 20 to 25 minutes or until thoroughly heated. **Makes** 6 servings.

Apple and Pecan Acorn Squash

The best flavors of fall are wrapped up in this simple stuffed acorn squash.

PREP: 10 MIN., COOK: 1 HR.

2 medium acorn squash (about 1¼ pounds each)
1 cup peeled, chopped cooking apple
¼ cup firmly packed brown sugar
¼ cup butter, melted
¼ teaspoon apple pie spice
¼ cup chopped pecans, toasted

1. Cut squash in half crosswise, and remove seeds. Cut a thin slice from bottom of each squash half to sit flat, if necessary. Place squash halves, cut sides up, in a 13- x 9-inch baking dish. Add hot water to dish to depth of 1 inch.
2. Combine apple and next 3 ingredients; spoon evenly into squash halves. Cover and bake at 350° for 1 hour or until squash is tender. Sprinkle with pecans. **Makes** 4 servings.

Bourbon Sweet Potatoes

A toasty ring of pecans crowns these mashed sweet potatoes.

PREP: 10 MIN.; COOK: 1 HR., 20 MIN.

6 medium-size sweet potatoes, unpeeled (4 pounds)
½ cup butter, melted
½ cup firmly packed brown sugar
⅓ cup orange juice
¼ cup bourbon
½ teaspoon salt
½ teaspoon pumpkin pie spice
½ cup chopped pecans

1. Cook sweet potatoes in boiling water to cover 30 to 35 minutes or until tender. Let cool to touch; peel and mash potatoes.
2. Combine sweet potato, butter, and next 5 ingredients; mash until blended. Spoon mixture into a lightly greased 1½-quart baking dish. Sprinkle chopped pecans around edge of dish. Bake at 375° for 45 minutes. **Makes** 8 servings.

Creamy Succotash

Creamy Succotash

"Succotash" is derived from an Indian word meaning "broiled corn kernels." This vegetable dish is made by cooking lima beans, corn, and sometimes bell peppers together. Bacon adds even more Southern flavor.

PREP: 15 MIN., COOK: 20 MIN.

1 (10-ounce) package frozen petite lima beans
1 (16-ounce) package frozen white shoepeg corn, thawed
2 tablespoons butter
2 tablespoons all-purpose flour
1 teaspoon sugar
½ teaspoon salt
½ teaspoon seasoned pepper
1¼ cups milk
Garnish: cooked and crumbled bacon

1. Cook lima beans according to package directions; drain and set aside.
2. Pulse corn in a food processor 8 to 10 times or until coarsely chopped. Set aside.
3. Melt butter in large skillet over medium heat; add flour, stirring until smooth. Cook, stirring constantly, 1 minute; stir in sugar, salt, and seasoned pepper. Gradually add milk, stirring until smooth.
4. Stir in chopped corn, and cook, stirring often, 12 to 15 minutes or until corn is tender and mixture is thickened. Stir in lima beans. Garnish, if desired, and serve immediately. **Makes** 6 to 8 servings.

sides **93**

Garlic-Gruyère Mashed Potatoes
PREP: 10 MIN., COOK: 15 MIN.

3 pounds Yukon Gold potatoes
¾ cup hot milk
½ cup sour cream
¼ cup butter, softened
1 teaspoon salt
⅛ teaspoon ground red pepper
1 garlic clove, minced
½ cup (2 ounces) shredded Gruyère cheese
2 green onions, thinly sliced
⅓ cup chopped baked ham (optional)
Garnish: sliced green onions

1. Peel potatoes, if desired; cut into 1-inch cubes. Cook in boiling water to cover 15 minutes or until tender. Drain and mash. Add milk and next 5 ingredients. Mash until fluffy.
2. Stir in cheese, thinly sliced green onions, and, if desired, ham. Garnish, if desired. **Makes** 8 servings.

Joy's Potato Salad
PREP: 30 MIN., COOK: 20 MIN., OTHER: 8 HR.

2 pounds small new potatoes
2 teaspoons salt, divided
1 medium-size green bell pepper, diced
12 cherry tomatoes, halved
½ small red onion, diced
3 tablespoons minced fresh basil
⅓ cup red wine vinegar
½ teaspoon pepper
2 teaspoons sugar
½ cup olive oil
Red leaf lettuce

1. Cook potatoes in boiling water to cover and 1 teaspoon salt 15 to 20 minutes or until tender; drain. Plunge into ice water to stop the cooking process; drain. Peel potatoes, and cut in half. Place potato, bell pepper, and next 3 ingredients in a large bowl.
2. Process remaining 1 teaspoon salt, vinegar, pepper, and sugar in a blender until smooth. Turn blender on high; add oil in a slow, steady stream. Pour over potato mixture; toss gently to coat.
3. Cover and chill 8 hours. Drain; serve on a lettuce-lined dish. **Makes** 6 to 8 servings.

Horseradish Potato Salad
Horseradish fans, here's a potato salad you'll love.

PREP: 15 MIN., COOK: 12 MIN.

5 large red potatoes
½ cup mayonnaise
½ cup sour cream
1 to 2 tablespoons prepared horseradish
1 tablespoon chopped fresh parsley
½ teaspoon salt
½ teaspoon freshly ground pepper
4 hard-cooked eggs, chopped
4 bacon slices, cooked and crumbled
3 green onions, sliced

1. Peel potatoes, and cut into 1-inch cubes. Cook in boiling salted water to cover 12 minutes or until tender. (Do not overcook.) Drain and cool.
2. Stir together mayonnaise and next 5 ingredients in a large bowl; add cubed potato, egg, bacon, and green onions, tossing gently. Cover and chill. **Makes** 6 servings.

Family Potato Salad

Family Potato Salad
Grate the eggs on the largest holes of a cheese grater for best results.

PREP: 20 MIN., COOK: 40 MIN.

4 pounds baking potatoes (8 large)
3 hard-cooked eggs, grated
1 cup mayonnaise
1 tablespoon spicy brown mustard
1½ teaspoons salt
¾ teaspoon pepper

1. Cook potatoes in boiling water to cover 40 minutes or until tender; drain and cool. Peel potatoes, and cut into 1-inch cubes.
2. Stir together potato cubes and eggs.
3. Stir together mayonnaise and next 3 ingredients; gently stir into potato mixture. Serve immediately, or cover and chill, if desired. **Makes** 8 to 10 servings.

Red Potato Salad: Substitute 4 pounds red potatoes (8 large red potatoes) for baking potatoes.

Potato Salad With Sweet Pickle: Add ⅓ cup sweet pickle relish to potato mixture.

Potato Salad With Onion and Celery: Add 2 celery ribs, diced, and ½ small sweet onion, diced, to potato mixture.

Light Potato Salad: Substitute 1 cup low-fat mayonnaise for regular mayonnaise.

Fried Okra Salad

Fried Okra Salad

PREP: 25 MIN., COOK: 2 MIN. PER BATCH

1½ cups self-rising yellow cornmeal
1 teaspoon salt
1 pound fresh okra
1½ cups buttermilk
Peanut oil
1 head Bibb lettuce
1 large tomato, chopped (about 1 cup)
1 medium-size sweet onion, thinly sliced
    (about ¾ cup)
1 medium-size green bell pepper, chopped
Lemon Dressing (opposite page)
3 bacon slices, cooked and crumbled

1. Combine cornmeal and salt. Dip okra in buttermilk; dredge in cornmeal mixture.
2. Pour peanut oil to a depth of 2 inches into a Dutch oven or deep cast-iron skillet; heat to 375°. Fry okra, in batches, 2 minutes or until golden, turning once. Drain on a wire rack over paper towels.
3. Arrange lettuce leaves on a serving platter; top with tomato, onion slices, and bell pepper. Add Lemon Dressing, tossing to coat. Top with fried okra, and sprinkle with crumbled bacon. Serve immediately.
Makes 6 servings.

Lemon Dressing

This also makes a tangy dipping sauce for steamed artichokes or asparagus.

PREP: 5 MIN.

¼ cup fresh lemon juice
3 tablespoons chopped fresh basil
1 teaspoon salt
1 teaspoon paprika
½ teaspoon pepper
¼ cup olive oil

1. Combine first 5 ingredients in a bowl. Add oil in a slow, steady stream, whisking until combined. **Makes** ¾ cup.

MAKE AHEAD
Ham and Blue Cheese Pasta Salad

Bow-tie pasta lends interesting shape to this salad. Other pastas, such as penne or even macaroni, will work just fine, too.

PREP: 10 MIN., COOK: 12 MIN.

3 cups bow-tie pasta, uncooked
1 cup coarsely chopped pecans, toasted
⅓ cup grated Parmesan cheese
2 tablespoons chopped fresh parsley
1 tablespoon minced fresh rosemary
½ to ¾ teaspoon freshly ground pepper
4 ounces cooked ham, cut into strips
1 (4-ounce) package blue cheese, crumbled
1 garlic clove, minced
¼ cup olive oil

1. Cook pasta according to package directions. Drain well, and place in a large serving bowl.
2. Add pecans and next 7 ingredients, tossing gently to combine. Add oil, stirring gently to coat mixture. Serve immediately, or cover and chill thoroughly, if desired. **Makes** 6 servings.

MAKE AHEAD
Basil-Marinated Tomatoes

Enjoy the sweet tang of vine-ripened tomatoes, fresh basil, and garlic in this summertime specialty.

PREP: 15 MIN., OTHER: 8 HR.

3 large tomatoes
⅓ cup olive oil
¼ cup red wine vinegar
2 to 3 tablespoons chopped fresh basil
2 tablespoons chopped onion
1 teaspoon salt
¼ teaspoon pepper
1 garlic clove, crushed

1. Cut tomatoes into ½-inch-thick slices; arrange in a thin layer in a large shallow dish.
2. Combine oil and remaining 6 ingredients in a jar; cover tightly, and shake vigorously. Pour mixture over tomato slices. Cover and marinate in refrigerator at least 8 hours before serving. **Makes** 6 servings.

MAKE AHEAD
Black Bean-and-Rice Salad

PREP: 25 MIN., OTHER: 2 HR.

½ cup canola oil
¼ cup lime juice
2 cups canned black beans, rinsed and drained*
2 cups cooked long-grain rice
½ cup chopped onion
¼ cup chopped fresh cilantro
1 (4-ounce) jar diced pimiento, drained
2 garlic cloves, pressed
½ teaspoon salt
¼ teaspoon pepper

1. Whisk together oil and lime juice in a large bowl.
2. Add remaining ingredients, and toss mixture to coat. Cover and chill salad 2 hours. **Makes** 4 to 6 servings.
*Substitute 2 cups cooked black beans for canned, if desired.

Cheese Biscuit with Chipotle Butter

Cheese Biscuits With Chipotle Butter

PREP: 10 MIN., COOK: 12 MIN.

1 (6.25-ounce) package all-purpose baking mix
1 (6-ounce) package cornbread mix
1 (8-ounce) container sour cream
1 cup (4 ounces) shredded Cheddar cheese
⅓ cup buttermilk
1 teaspoon fajita seasoning (optional)
Chipotle Butter

1. Stir together first 5 ingredients, and, if desired, fajita seasoning. Pat or roll dough out onto a lightly floured surface to ½-inch thickness. Cut dough with a 2-inch round cutter, and place rounds on a lightly greased baking sheet.

2. Bake at 400° for 10 to 12 minutes or until golden. Serve with Chipotle Butter. **Makes** 2 dozen.
Note: For testing purposes only, we used Bisquick for all-purpose baking mix.

Chipotle Butter

PREP: 5 MIN.

½ cup butter, softened
2 teaspoons chopped fresh parsley
1 canned chipotle pepper in adobo sauce, diced
2 teaspoons adobo sauce from can

1. Stir together all ingredients. **Makes** ½ cup.

Softened Butter:

Recipes often call for softened butter, but exactly how soft should it be? Butter will usually soften at room temperature in about 30 minutes, but the time can vary depending on the warmth of your kitchen. Test the butter by gently pressing the top of the stick with your index finger. If an indentation remains and the butter still holds its shape (like the stick in the center), it's perfectly softened. The butter on the left is still too firm, while the butter on the right is too soft. Avoid softening butter in the microwave as it can melt too quickly and unevenly.

Hot-Water Cornbread

PREP: 10 MIN., COOK: 6 MIN. PER BATCH

2 cups white cornmeal mix
1¼ teaspoons salt
1 teaspoon sugar
¼ teaspoon baking powder
¼ cup half-and-half
1 tablespoon vegetable oil
1¼ cups boiling water
Vegetable oil
Softened butter

1. Combine first 4 ingredients in a bowl; stir in half-and-half and 1 tablespoon oil. Gradually add 1¼ cups boiling water, stirring until batter is the consistency of grits.
2. Pour oil to a depth of ¼ inch into a large heavy skillet; place over medium-high heat. Scoop batter into a lightly greased ¼-cup measure; drop batter into hot oil in batches, and fry 3 minutes on each side or until golden. Drain well on paper towels. Serve immediately with softened butter. **Makes** 10 patties.

Country Ham Hot-Water Cornbread: Stir in 1 to 2 cups finely chopped country ham after adding boiling water.

Bacon-Cheddar Hot-Water Cornbread: Stir in 8 slices cooked and crumbled bacon, 1 cup shredded sharp Cheddar cheese, and 4 minced green onions after adding boiling water.

Southwestern Hot-Water Cornbread: Stir in 1 seeded and minced jalapeño pepper; 1 cup Mexican cheese blend; 1 cup frozen whole kernel corn, thawed; and ¼ cup minced fresh cilantro after adding boiling water.

Baked Hot-Water Cornbread: Omit skillet procedure. Pour ⅓ cup vegetable oil into a 15- x 10-inch jelly-roll pan, spreading to edges. Drop batter as directed onto pan. Bake at 475° for 12 to 15 minutes. Turn cakes, and bake 5 more minutes or until golden brown.

" I love this old-fashioned cornbread, pan-fried in small rounds; it has a crisp and buttery crust with a tender inside. "

LYDA JONES BURNETTE, TEST KITCHENS DIRECTOR

Hot-Water Cornbread

Minted Lemon
Iced Tea

Minted Lemon Iced Tea

*No Southern meal is complete without a glass of sweet tea. Adjust the amount of sugar in the tea
to suit your taste buds. Or omit the sugar, and serve unsweetened tea with Simple Syrup.*

PREP: 10 MIN.; OTHER: 2 HR., 5 MIN.

2 quarts boiling water
10 lemon zinger tea bags
1 to 1½ cups sugar
1 cup fresh mint leaves
Garnish: fresh mint sprigs, lemon slices

1. Pour 2 quarts boiling water over tea bags. Stir in
sugar and 1 cup mint leaves; steep 5 minutes. Remove
and discard tea bags and mint leaves. Chill 2 hours.
Garnish, if desired. **Makes** 2 quarts.

Simple Syrup

*Keep Simple Syrup on hand in the refrigerator to stir
into each glass. The sugar is already dissolved,
so the syrup blends in easily.*

PREP: 2 MIN., COOK: 5 MIN.

1. Bring ½ cup water and ½ cup sugar to boil over
medium-high heat in a saucepan, stirring until sugar
dissolves; boil 1 minute. Remove from heat; cool.
Cover and chill until ready to serve. Stir desired
amount into tea. **Makes** about ¾ cup.

102 Southern plate

Old-Fashioned Blackberry Cobbler

Place an aluminum foil-lined baking sheet under cobbler to catch any juices that bubble over during baking.

PREP: 10 MIN., COOK: 35 MIN.

4 cups fresh blackberries or 2 (16-ounce) packages
    frozen blackberries, thawed
¾ cup sugar
3 tablespoons all-purpose flour
1½ cups water
1 tablespoon lemon juice
Pastry
2 tablespoons butter, melted
Whipping cream
Sugar

1. Place berries in a lightly greased 2-quart baking dish. Combine ¾ cup sugar and flour; add water and lemon juice, mixing well. Pour sugar mixture over berries; bake at 350° for 15 minutes. Place Pastry over hot berries; brush with butter.
2. Bake at 425° for 20 minutes or until Pastry is golden. Serve warm with whipping cream, and sprinkle each serving with sugar. **Makes** 8 servings.

Pastry

PREP: 10 MIN.

1¾ cups all-purpose flour
2 to 3 tablespoons sugar
2 teaspoons baking powder
1 teaspoon salt
¼ cup shortening
⅓ cup whipping cream
⅓ cup buttermilk

1. Combine flour, sugar, baking powder, and salt; cut in shortening with a pastry blender until mixture is crumbly; stir in whipping cream and buttermilk. Knead dough 4 or 5 times; roll to ¼-inch thickness on a lightly floured surface. Cut dough to fit baking dish. **Makes** pastry for 1 cobbler.

Easy Peach Cobbler

PREP: 15 MIN., COOK: 45 MIN.

½ cup unsalted butter
1 cup all-purpose flour
2 cups sugar, divided
1 tablespoon baking powder
Pinch of salt
1 cup milk
4 cups fresh peach slices
1 tablespoon lemon juice
Ground cinnamon or nutmeg (optional)

1. Melt butter in a 13- x 9-inch baking dish.
2. Combine flour, 1 cup sugar, baking powder, and salt; add milk, stirring just until dry ingredients are moistened. Pour batter over butter (do not stir).
3. Bring remaining 1 cup sugar, peach slices, and lemon juice to a boil over high heat, stirring constantly; pour over batter (do not stir). Sprinkle with cinnamon, if desired.
4. Bake at 375° for 40 to 45 minutes or until golden brown. Serve cobbler warm or cool. **Makes** 10 servings.

Mrs. Floyd's Divinity

PREP: 30 MIN., COOK: 20 MIN.

2½ cups sugar
½ cup water
½ cup light corn syrup
¼ teaspoon salt
2 egg whites
1 teaspoon vanilla extract
1 cup chopped pecans, toasted
Garnish: toasted pecan halves

1. Cook first 4 ingredients in a heavy 2-quart saucepan over low heat until sugar dissolves and a candy thermometer registers 248° (about 15 minutes). Remove syrup mixture from heat.

2. Beat egg whites at high speed with an electric mixer until stiff peaks form. Pour half of hot syrup in a thin stream over egg whites, beating constantly at high speed, about 5 minutes.
3. Cook remaining half of syrup over medium heat, stirring occasionally, until a candy thermometer registers 272° (about 4 to 5 minutes). Slowly pour hot syrup and vanilla extract over egg white mixture, beating constantly at high speed until mixture holds its shape (about 6 to 8 minutes). Stir in 1 cup chopped pecans.
4. Drop mixture quickly by rounded teaspoonfuls onto lightly greased wax paper. Garnish, if desired. Cool.
Makes 4 dozen (1¾ pounds).

Mrs. Floyd's Divinity

Pralines

PREP: 20 MIN., COOK: 12 MIN., OTHER: 30 MIN.

3 cups firmly packed light brown sugar
1 cup whipping cream
2 tablespoons light corn syrup
¼ teaspoon salt
¼ cup butter
2 cups chopped pecans
1 teaspoon vanilla extract

1. Bring first 4 ingredients to a boil in a 3-quart saucepan over medium heat, stirring mixture constantly. Cook mixture, stirring occasionally, 6 to 8 minutes, or until a candy thermometer registers 236° (soft ball stage).
2. Remove mixture from heat, and add butter (do not stir). Let stand until candy thermometer reaches 150°. Stir in pecans and vanilla, using a wooden spoon; stir constantly until candy begins to thicken.
3. Drop by heaping teaspoonfuls, working rapidly, onto wax paper. Let stand until firm. **Makes** 2½ dozen.

Pecan Pie Cookies

PREP: 30 MIN.; COOK: 16 MIN. PER BATCH; OTHER: 1 HR., 35 MIN.

1 cup butter, softened
½ cup granulated sugar
½ cup dark corn syrup
2 large eggs, separated
2½ cups all-purpose flour
¼ cup butter
½ cup powdered sugar
3 tablespoons dark corn syrup
¾ cup finely chopped pecans

1. Beat 1 cup butter and granulated sugar at medium speed with an electric mixer until light and fluffy. Add ½ cup corn syrup and egg yolks, beating well. Gradually stir in flour; cover and chill 1 hour.
2. Melt ¼ cup butter in a heavy saucepan over medium heat; stir in powdered sugar and 3 tablespoons corn syrup. Cook, stirring often, until mixture boils. Remove from heat. Stir in pecans; chill 30 minutes. Shape mixture by ½ teaspoonfuls into ¼-inch balls; set aside.
3. Shape cookie dough into 1-inch balls; place 2 inches apart on lightly greased baking sheets. Beat egg whites until foamy; brush on dough balls.

4. Bake at 375° for 6 minutes. Remove from oven, and place a pecan ball in center of each cookie. Bake 8 to 10 more minutes or until lightly browned. Cool 5 minutes on baking pans; remove to wire racks to cool completely. Freeze up to 1 month, if desired. **Makes** 4½ dozen.

Rum Pecan Pie

PREP: 10 MIN., COOK: 58 MIN.

¾ cup light corn syrup
½ cup sugar
⅓ cup butter
¼ cup maple syrup
4 large eggs, lightly beaten
1 cup coarsely chopped pecans
3 tablespoons dark rum
Brandied Butter Pastry
¾ cup pecan halves

1. Cook first 4 ingredients in a medium saucepan over medium heat until butter melts and sugar dissolves; cool slightly. Gradually add eggs to syrup mixture, beating constantly with a wire whisk. Stir in chopped pecans and rum.
2. Line a 9-inch pie plate with Brandied Butter Pastry. Pour filling into pastry, and top with pecan halves. Bake at 325° for 48 minutes or until filling is set. **Makes** 1 (9-inch) pie.

Brandied Butter Pastry

PREP: 10 MIN.

1¼ cups all-purpose flour
½ teaspoon salt
¼ cup plus 2 tablespoons cold butter
3 to 4 tablespoons cold brandy

1. Combine flour and salt; cut in butter with a pastry blender until mixture is crumbly. Sprinkle with cold brandy (1 tablespoon at a time) evenly over surface; stir with a fork until dry ingredients are moistened. Shape into a ball before rolling out.
2. Roll pastry to ⅛-inch thickness on a lightly floured surface. Place in a 9-inch pie plate; trim off excess pastry along edges. Fold edges under, and crimp. **Makes** 1 (9-inch) pastry shell.

Two-Step Pound Cake

Two-Step Pound Cake

We stumbled across this procedure that broke all the rules—not adding the eggs one at a time, not alternating the milk and flour, not beating the butter and sugar together until fluffy—and found the result to be as delicious as the tradtional recipe. To make it requires a heavy-duty stand mixer with a 4-quart bowl and a paddle attachment. If you don't have the mixer, though, you can prepare the pound cake using the traditional method that follows.

PREP: 10 MIN.; COOK: 1 HR., 30 MIN.

4 cups all-purpose flour
3 cups sugar
1 pound butter, softened
¾ cup milk
6 eggs
2 teaspoons vanilla extract

1. Place flour, sugar, butter, milk, eggs, and vanilla (in that order) in a 4-quart bowl. Beat at low speed with a heavy-duty electric mixer 1 minute, stopping to scrape down sides. Beat at medium speed 2 minutes. Pour into a greased and floured 10-inch tube pan.
2. Bake at 325° for 1 hour and 30 minutes or until a long wooden pick inserted in center comes out clean.

Cool in pan on a wire rack 10 minutes. Remove cake from pan; cool cake completely on wire rack. **Makes** 1 (10-inch) cake.
Note: For testing purposes only, we used a KitchenAid Mixer.

Traditional Method:
1. Beat butter at medium speed with an electric mixer 2 minutes or until creamy. Gradually add sugar, beating until light and fluffy. Add eggs, 1 at a time, beating after each addition.
2. Add flour to butter mixture alternately with milk, beginning and ending with flour. Beat at low speed just until blended after each addition. Stir in vanilla.
3. Pour batter into a greased and floured 10-inch tube pan. Bake as directed in two-step method.

Coconut-Cream Cheese Pound Cake

*Cream cheese and coconut put this pound cake in a
rich and tender category all its own.*

PREP: 20 MIN.; COOK: 1 HR., 40 MIN.; OTHER: 15 MIN.

½ cup butter, softened
½ cup shortening
1 (8-ounce) package cream cheese, softened
3 cups sugar
6 large eggs
3 cups all-purpose flour
¼ teaspoon baking soda
¼ teaspoon salt
1 (6-ounce) package frozen flake grated coconut,
    thawed (1¾ cups)
1 teaspoon vanilla extract
1 teaspoon coconut flavoring

1. Beat butter, shortening, and cream cheese at
medium speed with an electric mixer 2 minutes or
until creamy. Gradually add sugar, beating 5 to 7 minutes. Add eggs, 1 at a time, beating after each addition
just until yellow disappears.
2. Combine flour, soda, and salt; add to butter mixture,
beating at low speed just until blended. Stir in coconut, vanilla, and coconut flavoring.
3. Pour batter into a greased and floured 10-inch tube
pan. Bake at 325° for 1 hour and 30 to 40 minutes
or until a wooden pick inserted in center comes out
clean. Cool in pan on a wire rack 10 to 15 minutes;
remove from pan, and cool completely on wire rack.
Makes 1 (10-inch) cake.
Note: We tested with Tropic Isle grated coconut.

Peach Brandy Pound Cake

PREP: 15 MIN.; COOK: 1 HR., 30 MIN.; OTHER: 15 MIN.

1 cup butter, softened
3 cups sugar
6 large eggs
3 cups all-purpose flour
¼ teaspoon baking soda
⅛ teaspoon salt
1 (8-ounce) container sour cream
½ cup peach brandy
2 teaspoons dark rum
1 teaspoon orange extract
1 teaspoon vanilla extract
½ teaspoon lemon extract
¼ teaspoon almond extract

1. Beat butter at medium speed with an electric mixer
2 minutes. Gradually add sugar, beating at medium
speed 5 minutes. Add eggs, 1 at a time, beating after
each addition just until yellow disappears.
2. Combine flour, baking soda, and salt; add to butter mixture alternately with sour cream, beginning
and ending with flour mixture. Mix at low speed just
until blended after each addition. Stir in brandy and
remaining ingredients.
3. Pour batter into a greased and floured 10-inch tube
pan. Bake at 325° for 1½ hours or until a wooden pick
inserted in center comes out clean. Cool in pan on a
wire rack 10 to 15 minutes; remove from pan, and cool
completely on wire rack. **Makes** 1 (10-inch) cake.

Pound Cake Banana Pudding

Look for pound cake in the frozen dessert case of the supermarket.

PREP: 20 MIN., COOK: 30 MIN., OTHER: 6 HR.

4 cups half-and-half
4 egg yolks
1½ cups sugar
¼ cup cornstarch
¼ teaspoon salt
3 tablespoons butter
2 teaspoons vanilla extract
1 (1-pound) pound cake, cubed
4 large ripe bananas, sliced
Meringue

1. Whisk together first 5 ingredients in a saucepan over medium-low heat; cook, whisking constantly, 13 to 15 minutes or until thickened. Remove from heat; stir in butter and vanilla until butter melts. Layer half of pound cake cubes, half of bananas, and half of pudding mixture in a 3-quart round baking dish. Repeat layers. Cover pudding, and chill 6 hours.

2. Spread Meringue over pudding.
3. Bake at 375° for 15 minutes or until golden brown.
Makes 10 to 12 servings.
Note: For testing purposes only, we used Sara Lee Family Size All Butter Pound Cake.

QUICK
Meringue

PREP: 10 MIN.

¼ cup sugar
⅛ teaspoon salt
4 egg whites
¼ teaspoon vanilla extract

1. Combine sugar and salt.
2. Beat egg whites and vanilla at high speed with an electric mixer until foamy. Add sugar mixture, 1 tablespoon at a time, and beat 2 to 3 minutes or until stiff peaks form and sugar dissolves. **Makes** about 3½ cups.

I'm not a sweets guy, but this combines two of my favorite desserts.

SCOTT JONES, EXECUTIVE EDITOR

Pound Cake
Banana Pudding

Peanut Butter Cake

Peanut butter and caramel are a luscious combination in this cake. This particular Caramel Frosting is a staff favorite—it's easy to make and tastes divine.

PREP: 15 MIN., COOK: 27 MIN., OTHER: 10 MIN.

½ cup shortening
1 cup creamy peanut butter
1 cup sugar
2 large eggs
1½ cups all-purpose flour
1 tablespoon baking powder
½ teaspoon salt
1 cup milk
½ teaspoon vanilla extract
Caramel Frosting

1. Beat shortening and peanut butter at medium speed with an electric mixer until creamy; gradually add sugar, beating well. Add eggs, 1 at a time, beating after each addition.
2. Combine flour, baking powder, and salt; add to shortening mixture alternately with milk, beginning and ending with flour mixture. Mix at low speed after each addition until blended. Stir in vanilla. Pour batter into 2 lightly greased and floured 9-inch round cake pans.
3. Bake at 350° for 25 to 27 minutes or until a wooden pick inserted in center comes out clean. Cool in pans on wire racks 10 minutes; remove from pans, and cool completely on wire racks.
4. Spread Caramel Frosting between layers and on top and sides of cake. **Makes** 1 (2-layer) cake.

Caramel Frosting

PREP: 20 MIN., COOK: 10 MIN., OTHER: 10 MIN.

2 cups sugar
1 cup butter
1 cup evaporated milk
1 teaspoon vanilla extract

1. Combine sugar, butter, and milk in a large heavy saucepan; bring to a boil over medium heat. Cover and cook 2 to 3 minutes to wash down sugar crystals from sides of pan. Uncover and cook, stirring constantly, until mixture reaches soft ball stage or candy thermometer registers 234°. Remove from heat, and add vanilla (do not stir). Cool 10 minutes. Beat at medium speed with an electric mixer 8 to 10 minutes or until frosting is spreading consistency. **Makes** 2½ cups.

MAKE AHEAD

Chocolate-Pecan Snack Cake

Chocolate morsels and pecans create a pebbled top for this cake that kids will devour.

PREP: 20 MIN., COOK: 28 MIN.

1 cup chopped dates
1 cup boiling water
1 teaspoon baking soda
½ cup shortening
1 cup sugar
2 large eggs
1 tablespoon cocoa
1 teaspoon vanilla extract
1¾ cups all-purpose flour
½ teaspoon cream of tartar
½ teaspoon salt
1 cup (6 ounces) semisweet chocolate morsels
¾ cup chopped pecans

1. Combine first 3 ingredients in a small bowl; stir well. Cool to room temperature. (Do not drain.)
2. Beat shortening at medium speed with an electric mixer 2 minutes or until creamy. Gradually add sugar, beating well. Add eggs, 1 at a time, beating just until yellow disappears. Add cocoa and vanilla; beat well.
3. Combine flour, cream of tartar, and salt; add to shortening mixture alternately with date mixture, beginning and ending with flour mixture. Mix at low speed after each addition just until blended.
4. Pour batter into a lightly greased 13- x 9-inch pan. Sprinkle chocolate morsels and pecans evenly over batter. Bake at 350° for 26 to 28 minutes. Cool in pan on a wire rack. Cut into squares to serve. Cover and store in pan. **Makes** 20 servings.

Fruit With Sour Cream
Sauce, page 131

breakfast
&
brunch

FAMILY FAVORITE
Classic Stuffed Eggs

Dress up a dozen eggs for a brunch with this classic stuffed egg recipe. Let fresh herbs from the garden be a simple garnish.

PREP: 12 MIN., COOK: 8 MIN., OTHER: 15 MIN.

12 large eggs
3 tablespoons mayonnaise
1 tablespoon sugar
1 tablespoon Dijon mustard
1 tablespoon white vinegar
1 teaspoon hot sauce
1 teaspoon Worcestershire sauce
⅛ teaspoon salt
Paprika
Garnish: fresh herb sprigs

1. Place eggs in a large saucepan or Dutch oven. Add enough water to measure at least 1 inch above eggs. Cover and quickly bring to a boil. Remove from heat. Let stand, covered, in hot water 15 minutes. Drain. Immediately run cold water over eggs or place them in ice water until cooled completely.
2. To remove shell, gently tap each egg all over, and roll between hands to loosen shell; then hold egg under cold running water as you peel the shell.
3. Slice eggs in half lengthwise, and carefully remove yolks. Mash yolks; add mayonnaise and next 6 ingredients. Stir well. Spoon egg yolk mixture into egg white halves. Sprinkle with paprika; garnish, if desired. **Makes** 2 dozen.

QUICK
Cheese-Chive Scrambled Eggs

PREP: 8 MIN., COOK: 8 MIN.

6 large eggs, lightly beaten
2 tablespoons water
¼ teaspoon seasoned salt
Dash of pepper
2 tablespoons butter
3 ounces reduced-fat cream cheese, cut into
    ¼-inch cubes and softened
1 tablespoon frozen chopped chives, thawed

1. Combine first 4 ingredients.
2. Melt butter in a large nonstick skillet over medium heat; tilt pan to coat bottom.
3. Add egg mixture to pan; top with cream cheese and chives.
4. Cook, without stirring, until mixture begins to set on bottom. Draw a spatula across bottom of pan to form large curds. Continue cooking until eggs are thickened but still moist; do not stir constantly. **Makes** 4 servings.

QUICK
Tex-Mex Egg Burritos

These breakfast burritos are a nod to the Southwest. Top them with fresh cilantro for extra kick.

PREP: 5 MIN., COOK: 15 MIN.

4 (8-inch) flour tortillas
½ pound hot ground pork sausage
6 large eggs, lightly beaten
1 (4.5-ounce) can chopped green chiles,
    undrained
Picante sauce
Shredded Cheddar cheese

1. Heat tortillas according to package directions.
2. Meanwhile, brown sausage in a large skillet, stirring until it crumbles; drain and return to skillet. Add eggs and chiles to sausage. Cook, without stirring, until mixture begins to set on bottom. Draw a spatula across bottom of pan to form large curds. Continue cooking until eggs are thickened but still moist. Do not stir constantly.
3. Spoon egg mixture evenly down centers of warm tortillas; top each with picante sauce and cheese. Fold opposite sides over filling. Serve immediately. **Makes** 4 servings.

Ham and Eggs à la Swiss

Ham and Eggs à la Swiss

Set ham, sliced cooked eggs, and cheese high atop crusty English muffins for a filling breakfast.

PREP: 8 MIN., COOK: 2 MIN.

4 English muffins, split
3 tablespoons butter, softened
½ pound thinly sliced deli ham
4 hard-cooked eggs, sliced
½ cup sour cream
½ cup mayonnaise
1 cup (4 ounces) shredded Swiss cheese
Paprika
Garnish: pickled jalapeño pepper slices

1. Spread muffins with butter. Toast muffins until lightly browned. Divide ham evenly among muffin halves. Arrange egg slices evenly over ham. Set aside.
2. Combine sour cream and mayonnaise, stirring well. Spoon mixture evenly over sandwiches; sprinkle each muffin half with shredded cheese and paprika.
3. Place sandwiches on a baking sheet. Broil 5½ inches from heat 1 to 2 minutes or until cheese melts and sandwiches are heated. Garnish, if desired. **Makes** 4 servings.

eggs & cheese **113**

Sausage Breakfast Casserole
PREP: 15 MIN.; COOK: 45 MIN.; OTHER: 8 HR., 15 MIN.

6 white bread slices
Butter
1 pound ground pork sausage
1½ cups (6 ounces) shredded longhorn cheese
6 large eggs, lightly beaten
2 cups half-and-half
½ teaspoon salt

1. Trim crusts from bread slices; reserve crusts for another use. Spread butter over 1 side of each bread slice. Place bread slices, buttered sides up, in bottom of a lightly greased 13- x 9- x 2-inch baking dish. Set aside.
2. Brown sausage in a large skillet, stirring until it crumbles; drain. Spoon sausage over bread; sprinkle with cheese. Combine eggs, half-and-half, and salt; pour over cheese. Cover and chill 8 hours or overnight.
3. Remove from refrigerator; let stand, covered, 15 minutes. Uncover and bake at 350º for 45 minutes or until golden. **Makes** 8 servings.

> **This casserole has been a staple in our house on Christmas morning since my kids were little. My oldest also requested that I bring this to school for a breakfast special treat. They all loved it and ate seconds.**

ASHLEY ARTHUR, ASSISTANT RECIPE EDITOR

Breakfast Pizza
PREP: 12 MIN., COOK: 35 MIN.

1 (8-ounce) can refrigerated crescent rolls
1 pound ground pork sausage, cooked and drained
1 cup (4 ounces) shredded sharp Cheddar cheese
1 cup (4 ounces) shredded mozzarella cheese
5 large eggs, lightly beaten
½ cup milk
¾ teaspoon dried oregano
⅛ teaspoon pepper

1. Unroll crescent rolls, separating into 8 triangles. Place triangles with elongated points toward center on a greased 12-inch pizza pan. Press perforations together to form a crust. Bake at 375º for 8 minutes on lower rack of oven. (Crust will be puffy when removed from oven.) Reduce oven temperature to 350º. Spoon sausage over crust; sprinkle with cheeses.
2. Combine eggs and remaining 3 ingredients; pour over sausage mixture. Bake at 350º on lower rack of oven for 30 to 35 minutes or until crust is golden. **Makes** 6 servings.

Brunch for a Bunch
PREP: 15 MIN., COOK: 50 MIN.

1 pound ground hot pork sausage
3 cups frozen hash brown potatoes, thawed
3 cups (12 ounces) shredded Cheddar cheese
½ cup chopped green pepper
12 large eggs, lightly beaten
2 cups milk
½ teaspoon salt
Garnishes: celery leaves, tomato wedges

1. Brown sausage in a medium skillet, stirring until it crumbles; drain. Place hash browns in a lightly greased shallow 3-quart baking dish. Layer cooked sausage, cheese, and chopped green pepper evenly over hash browns.
2. Combine eggs, milk, and salt in a large bowl, stirring with a wire whisk or fork until blended; pour egg mixture over chopped green pepper layer. Bake at 350º for 50 minutes or until golden. Garnish, if desired. **Makes** 8 servings.

Breakfast Casserole

MAKE AHEAD
Breakfast Casserole
Start the morning with a fresh balance of orange wedges, fruit juice, and this hearty standby.

PREP: 15 MIN.; COOK: 45 MIN.; OTHER: 8 HR., 35 MIN.

1 pound ground pork sausage*
10 white sandwich bread slices, cubed (6 cups)
2 cups (8 ounces) shredded sharp Cheddar cheese
6 large eggs,
2 cups milk
2 teaspoons salt
1 teaspoon dry mustard
¼ teaspoon Worcestershire sauce

1. Cook sausage in a skillet over medium heat, stirring until it crumbles and is no longer pink; drain well.

2. Place bread cubes evenly in 6 lightly greased 8-ounce individual baking dishes or ramekins; sprinkle bread cubes evenly with cheese, and top with sausage.
3. Whisk together eggs and next 4 ingredients; pour evenly over sausage mixture. Cover and chill casserole 8 hours. Let stand at room temperature 30 minutes.
4. Bake at 350° for 45 minutes or until set. Let stand 5 minutes before serving. **Makes** 6 servings.
*2 cups cubed cooked ham or light pork or turkey sausage may be substituted for sausage.
Note: You can also bake this casserole in a lightly greased 13- x 9-inch baking dish.

eggs & cheese 115

Blintz Soufflé

Blintz Soufflé

Cream cheese and cottage cheese give this casserole soufflé ultrarich taste. The blueberry sauce adorns it beautifully.

PREP: 20 MIN., COOK: 55 MIN.

1 (8-ounce) package cream cheese, softened
2 cups small-curd cottage cheese
2 egg yolks
2 tablespoons sugar
1 teaspoon vanilla extract
6 large eggs
1½ cups sour cream
½ cup orange juice
½ cup butter, softened
1 cup all-purpose flour
⅓ cup sugar
2 teaspoons baking powder
1 teaspoon orange zest
Blueberry Sauce
Garnishes: orange wedges, strawberry halves,
     mint sprigs

1. Combine first 5 ingredients in a small bowl; beat at medium speed with an electric mixer until smooth. Set mixture aside.
2. Blend eggs and next 3 ingredients in container of an electric blender until smooth. Add flour, ⅓ cup sugar, baking powder, and orange zest; blend until smooth. Pour half of batter into a lightly greased 13- x 9-inch baking dish. Spoon cream cheese mixture evenly over batter, and spread gently with a knife. Pour remaining batter over cream cheese mixture.
3. Bake at 350° for 50 to 55 minutes or until puffed and golden. Serve immediately with warm Blueberry Sauce. Garnish, if desired. **Makes** 8 servings.

Blueberry Sauce

PREP: 5 MIN., COOK: 6 MIN.

⅔ cup sugar
2 tablespoons cornstarch
Dash of ground cinnamon
Dash of ground nutmeg
Pinch of salt
1 cup water
2 cups fresh blueberries
2 tablespoons lemon juice

1. Combine first 5 ingredients in a small heavy saucepan. Gradually stir in water. Cook over medium-high heat, stirring constantly, until mixture comes to a boil; boil 1 minute. Stir in blueberries and lemon juice, and boil 1 minute, stirring constantly. Remove from heat. **Makes** 2½ cups.

Cheddar Strata

PREP: 10 MIN.; COOK: 1 HR.; OTHER: 8 HR., 30 MIN.

3 large eggs, lightly beaten
1¼ cups milk
½ cup minced onion
¼ teaspoon salt
¼ teaspoon dry mustard
¼ teaspoon black pepper
¼ teaspoon ground red pepper
⅛ teaspoon paprika
¼ teaspoon Worcestershire sauce
Butter
8 white bread slices
3 cups (12 ounces) shredded Cheddar cheese

1. Combine first 9 ingredients; set aside. Butter bread; cut off crusts, and cut each slice into small squares. Arrange a single layer of bread squares in a lightly greased 9-inch square pan; top with 1 cup cheese. Repeat layers until all bread and cheese are used. Pour egg mixture over all. Cover and chill 8 hours.
2. Remove from refrigerator; let stand at room temperature 30 minutes before baking. Bake, uncovered, at 325° for 1 hour. Serve hot. **Makes** 6 servings.

What's a Strata?

You won't find strata as a food term in most dictionaries, but you will find it in the pages of *Southern Living*. Our first strata, similar to the recipe above, debuted in 1970. It resembled a cheese soufflé but was more forgiving. You simply layered bread and cheese, covered it with a milk-and-egg mixture, and stashed it in the fridge until ready to cook, usually the next morning. The '80s brought flavor inspiration as we varied the cheese and tossed in sausage and other favorite foods. Stratas remain popular with our audience for their flavor and convenience.

Asparagus-and-Bacon Frittata

Plum tomatoes, onion, and asparagus lend garden-fresh flavor to this Italian omelet.

PREP: 20 MIN., COOK: 30 MIN.

6 large plum tomatoes
1 (12-ounce) package bacon slices
1 medium onion, chopped
2 garlic cloves, pressed
2 cups (½-inch) fresh asparagus pieces
10 large eggs, lightly beaten
½ teaspoon seasoned salt
¼ teaspoon pepper
½ cup sour cream
¼ cup fresh parsley, chopped
2 cups (8 ounces) shredded mild Cheddar
      cheese, divided

1. Cut tomatoes into thin slices. Drain tomatoes well, pressing between layers of paper towels to remove excess moisture; set aside.
2. Cook bacon in a 12-inch ovenproof skillet until crisp; remove bacon, reserving 1 tablespoon drippings in skillet. Crumble bacon, and set aside.
3. Sauté onion and garlic in reserved hot drippings 4 to 5 minutes or until tender. Add asparagus, and sauté 1 minute.
4. Beat eggs, salt, and pepper at medium-high speed with an electric mixer until foamy; stir in sour cream. Pour over vegetables in skillet. Reserve ¼ cup bacon; stir in remaining bacon, parsley, and 1 cup cheese.
5. Cook over medium-low heat 3 to 4 minutes or until eggs begin to set around edges.
6. Bake at 350° for 15 minutes. Remove from oven; top with tomato slices, reserved ¼ cup bacon, and remaining 1 cup cheese.
7. Bake 10 to 15 more minutes or until frittata appears to be set. **Makes** 8 servings.

> **The combination of cheesy goodness and Southwestern flavors makes it a crowd pleaser. The fact that it can be made ahead is just salsa on the enchilada.**
>
> DONNA FLORIO, SENIOR WRITER

(EDITOR'S CHOICE)

Breakfast Enchiladas

PREP: 20 MIN., COOK: 46 MIN.

1 (1-pound) package hot ground
    pork sausage
2 tablespoons butter
4 green onions, thinly sliced
2 tablespoons chopped fresh cilantro
14 large eggs, beaten
¾ teaspoon salt
½ teaspoon pepper
Cheese Sauce
8 (8-inch) soft taco-size flour tortillas
1 cup (4 ounces) shredded Monterey Jack cheese
    with peppers
Toppings: grape tomato halves, sliced green onions,
    chopped fresh cilantro

1. Cook sausage in a large nonstick skillet over medium-high heat, stirring frequently, 6 to 8 minutes or until sausage crumbles and is no longer pink. Remove from skillet; drain well, pressing between paper towels. Wipe skillet clean.

2. Melt butter in skillet over medium heat. Add green onions and cilantro, and sauté 1 minute. Add eggs, salt, and pepper, and cook, without stirring, 2 minutes or until eggs begin to set on bottom. Gently draw cooked edges away from sides of pan to form large pieces. Cook, stirring occasionally, 4 to 5 minutes or until eggs are thickened but still moist. (Do not over-stir.) Remove from heat, and gently fold in 1½ cups Cheese Sauce and sausage.

3. Spoon about ¾ cup egg mixture down center of each tortilla; roll up. Place, seam side down, in a lightly greased 13- x 9-inch baking dish. Pour remaining Cheese Sauce over tortillas; sprinkle with cheese.

4. Bake at 350° for 30 minutes or until sauce is bubbly. Serve with desired toppings. **Makes** 8 servings. **Note:** To make ahead, prepare the casserole as directed, without baking, and refrigerate overnight. Let it stand at room temperature for 30 minutes, and bake as directed. Make the Cheese Sauce before scrambling the eggs so the sauce will be ready to add at the proper time.

Cheese Sauce

PREP: 10 MIN., COOK: 8 MIN.

⅓ cup butter
⅓ cup all-purpose flour
3 cups milk
1 (8-oz.) block Cheddar cheese, shredded (about 2 cups)
1 (4-oz.) can chopped green chiles
¾ teaspoon salt

1. Melt butter in a heavy saucepan over medium-low heat; whisk in flour until smooth. Cook, whisking constantly, 1 minute. Gradually whisk in milk; cook over medium heat, whisking constantly, 7 minutes or until thickened. Remove from heat, and whisk in remaining ingredients until cheese is melted. **Makes** about 4 cups.

Cheese Soufflé Roll

PREP: 30 MIN., COOK: 19 MIN.

Vegetable oil
⅓ cup butter
⅓ cup all-purpose flour
1¼ cups milk
1 cup (4 ounces) shredded Cheddar cheese, divided
½ cup grated Parmesan cheese
¾ teaspoon salt
⅛ teaspoon ground red pepper
7 large eggs, separated
¼ teaspoon cream of tartar
2 tablespoons grated Parmesan cheese
Spinach-Mushroom Filling
Fresh spinach leaves

1. Lightly oil bottom and sides of a 15- x 10-inch jelly-roll pan; line with wax paper, allowing paper to extend beyond ends of pan. Lightly oil wax paper. Set aside.

2. Melt butter in a heavy saucepan over low heat; add flour, stirring until smooth. Cook 1 minute, stirring constantly. Gradually add milk; cook over medium heat, stirring constantly, until mixture is very thick. Add ½ cup Cheddar cheese, ½ cup Parmesan cheese, salt, and pepper, stirring until cheeses melt. Transfer to a large bowl.

3. Beat egg yolks at high speed with an electric mixer until thick and pale. Gradually stir about one-fourth of hot cheese mixture into egg yolks; add to remaining cheese mixture, stirring well.

4. Beat egg whites and cream of tartar at high speed until stiff peaks form. Stir a small amount of cheese mixture into beaten egg whites. Gradually fold egg white mixture into remaining cheese mixture.

5. Spread batter evenly in prepared pan. Bake at 350° for 18 minutes or until puffy and firm in center (do not overcook). Loosen edges of soufflé with a knife blade or metal spatula. Turn soufflé out onto a double layer of wax paper sprinkled with 2 tablespoons Parmesan cheese. Carefully peel wax paper off top of soufflé. Spread soufflé evenly with Spinach-Mushroom Filling. Starting with long side, and using wax paper for support, carefully roll up soufflé, jelly-roll fashion.

6. Carefully slide roll, seam side down, onto a large baking sheet; sprinkle with remaining ½ cup Cheddar cheese. Broil 5½ inches from heat 1 minute or until cheese melts. Carefully transfer roll to a spinach leaf-lined serving platter. **Makes** 8 servings.

Spinach-Mushroom Filling

PREP: 10 MIN., COOK: 8 MIN.

1 (10-ounce) package frozen chopped spinach
3 cups chopped fresh mushrooms
¼ cup finely chopped green onions
2 tablespoons butter, melted
½ cup sour cream
½ teaspoon garlic salt

1. Cook spinach according to package directions; drain well, pressing between layers of paper towels to remove excess moisture. Set aside.

2. Cook mushrooms and green onions in butter in a large skillet over medium-high heat, stirring constantly, until tender; stir in spinach, sour cream, and garlic salt. Cook 3 minutes or until mixture is thoroughly heated. Remove from heat, and keep warm. **Makes** 2½ cups.

Chiles Rellenos
With Red Sauce

Chiles Rellenos With Red Sauce

PREP: 15 MIN., COOK: 30 MIN.

8 canned whole mild green chiles (about four
    4-ounce cans) or 8 fresh poblano or
    Anaheim chiles
1 (8-ounce) package Monterey Jack cheese
    with peppers
½ cup all-purpose flour
¼ teaspoon salt
⅛ teaspoon pepper
4 large eggs, separated
¼ cup all-purpose flour
Vegetable oil
Red Sauce (opposite page)
Tomatillo salsa (store-bought; optional)
Garnish: fresh cilantro

1. If using canned chiles, rinse chiles, and remove seeds; pat dry. If using fresh chiles, place on a baking sheet. Broil 5½ inches from heat 5 to 10 minutes on each side or until chiles look blistered. Place chiles in a zip-top plastic bag; seal and let stand 10 minutes. Peel off skins; remove seeds.

2. Cut block of cheese into 8 crosswise strips; place a strip of cheese inside each chile. (If chiles tear, overlap torn sides; batter will hold chiles together.)

3. Combine ½ cup flour, salt, and pepper in a shallow bowl; set aside. Beat egg yolks until thick and pale. Beat egg whites in a large bowl at high speed with an electric mixer until stiff peaks form. Gently fold yolks and ¼ cup flour into beaten egg whites.

4. Pour oil to depth of 2 inches into a Dutch oven; heat to 375°. Dredge each stuffed chile in dry flour mixture; dip in egg batter.

5. Fry chiles, a few at a time, in hot oil until golden, turning once; drain on paper towels. Serve warm with Red Sauce, and if desired, tomatillo salsa. Garnish, if desired. **Makes** 4 servings.

Red Sauce

PREP: 5 MIN., COOK: 10 MIN.

4 garlic cloves, crushed
¼ cup butter, melted
¼ cup all-purpose flour
1 cup beef broth
1 (8-ounce) can tomato sauce
1 tablespoon chili powder
1 teaspoon rubbed sage
1 teaspoon ground cumin

1. Cook garlic in butter in a medium saucepan over medium heat 3 minutes, stirring constantly; add flour, stirring until smooth. Cook 1 minute, stirring constantly. Gradually add beef broth and tomato sauce, stirring constantly. Add chili powder, sage, and cumin; cook, stirring constantly, until mixture is thickened and bubbly. **Makes** 2 cups.

Swiss Alpine Quiche

PREP: 12 MIN., COOK: 48 MIN., OTHER: 10 MIN.

½ (15-ounce) package refrigerated piecrusts
1 (10-ounce) package frozen chopped broccoli
2 cups chopped cooked ham
2 cups (8 ounces) shredded Swiss cheese
3 tablespoons minced onion
3 large eggs, lightly beaten
1½ cups milk
⅛ teaspoon salt
⅛ teaspoon pepper

1. Fit piecrust into a 9-inch pie plate according to package directions; fold edges under and crimp. Prick bottom and sides of pastry with a fork. Bake at 400° for 3 minutes; remove from oven, and gently prick with a fork. Bake 5 more minutes. Set aside.
2. Cook broccoli according to package directions, omitting salt; drain well. Layer half each of broccoli, ham, and cheese in pastry shell; repeat layers. Sprinkle onion evenly over top.
3. Combine eggs and remaining 3 ingredients; stir with a wire whisk until blended. Pour over layers in pastry shell. Bake at 450° for 10 minutes. Reduce oven temperature to 325°, and bake 30 minutes or until set and golden. Let stand 10 minutes. **Makes** 8 servings.

Greek Spinach Quiche

Feta and oregano give this quiche Grecian flair.

PREP: 10 MIN., COOK: 43 MIN., OTHER: 10 MIN.

½ (15-ounce) package refrigerated piecrusts
3 large eggs, lightly beaten
1 cup milk
¼ cup butter, melted
2 tablespoons all-purpose flour
2 tablespoons grated Parmesan cheese
¼ teaspoon salt
¼ teaspoon dried oregano
Dash of ground nutmeg
1 (10-ounce) package frozen chopped spinach, thawed and well drained
1 cup crumbled feta cheese

1. Fit piecrust into a 9-inch pie plate according to package directions; fold edges under and crimp. Prick bottom and sides of pastry with a fork. Bake at 400° for 3 minutes; remove from oven, and gently prick with a fork. Bake 5 more minutes. Set aside.
2. Combine eggs and next 7 ingredients; stir with a wire whisk until blended. Stir in spinach and feta cheese; pour into pastry shell. Bake at 350° for 35 minutes or until quiche is set and golden. Let stand 10 minutes. **Makes** 8 servings.

Canadian Bacon-and-Brie Quiche

PREP: 15 MIN., COOK: 35 MIN., OTHER: 5 MIN.

16 Canadian bacon slices
1 (8-ounce) Brie round
8 large eggs, lightly beaten
½ cup mayonnaise
½ teaspoon white pepper
½ teaspoon grated Parmesan cheese
½ teaspoon Italian seasoning

1. Arrange bacon slices on bottom and up sides of a lightly greased 9-inch pie plate, slightly overlapping slices.
2. Remove rind from Brie, and cut cheese into cubes.
3. Stir together eggs, cubed Brie, mayonnaise, and next 3 ingredients in a bowl. Pour mixture into prepared pie plate.
4. Bake at 375° for 30 to 35 minutes or until a knife inserted in center comes out clean. Let quiche stand 5 minutes before serving. **Makes** 8 servings.

Pizza Quiche
PREP: 12 MIN., COOK: 50 MIN., OTHER: 10 MIN.

½ (15-ounce) package refrigerated piecrusts
¾ cup (3 ounces) shredded Swiss cheese
¾ cup (3 ounces) shredded mozzarella cheese
½ cup chopped pepperoni
1 green onion, chopped
3 large eggs, lightly beaten
1 cup half-and-half
½ teaspoon salt
¾ teaspoon dried oregano

1. Fit piecrust into a 9-inch pieplate according to package directions; fold edges under and crimp. Prick bottom and sides of pastry with a fork. Bake at 325° for 5 minutes. Cool.

2. Combine cheeses, pepperoni, and onion; sprinkle into pastry shell. Combine eggs, half-and-half, salt, and oregano; mix well, and pour over cheese mixture in pastry shell. Bake at 325° for 45 minutes. Let stand 10 minutes before serving. **Makes** 8 servings.

Ham-and-Grits Crustless Quiche
PREP: 10 MIN., COOK: 35 MIN., OTHER: 15 MIN.

½ cup water
¼ teaspoon salt
⅓ cup quick-cooking yellow grits, uncooked
1 (12-ounce) can evaporated milk
1½ cups chopped cooked ham
1 cup (4 ounces) shredded sharp
    Cheddar cheese
1 tablespoon chopped fresh parsley
1 teaspoon dry mustard
1 to 2 teaspoons hot sauce
3 large eggs, lightly beaten

1. Bring water and salt to a boil in a large saucepan; stir in grits. Remove from heat; cover and let stand 5 minutes (mixture will be thick). Stir in milk and remaining ingredients. Pour into a greased 9½-inch quiche dish or deep-dish pieplate. Bake at 350° for 30 to 35 minutes. Let stand 10 minutes before serving. **Makes** 8 servings.

Chile Cheese Quiche
PREP: 12 MIN., COOK: 58 MIN., OTHER: 10 MIN.

½ (15-ounce) refrigerated piecrusts
1 cup (4 ounces) shredded Cheddar cheese
1½ cups (6 ounces) shredded Monterey Jack cheese, divided
1 (4.5-ounce) can chopped green chiles, drained
3 large eggs, lightly beaten
1 cup half-and-half
⅛ teaspoon salt
⅛ teaspoon pepper

1. Fit piecrust into a 9-inch pie plate according to package directions; fold edges under and crimp. Prick bottom and sides of pastry with a fork. Bake at 400° for 3 minutes; remove from oven, and gently prick with a fork. Bake 5 more minutes. Set aside.

2. Layer Cheddar cheese, ¾ cup Monterey Jack cheese, green chiles, and remaining ¾ cup Monterey Jack cheese in pastry shell. Combine eggs and remaining ingredients; pour into pastry shell. Bake at 350° for 50 minutes or until set. Let stand 10 minutes before serving. **Makes** 8 servings.

Three-Cheese and Chile Casserole
Green chiles come in handy for a multitude of dishes. Here they add a Western accent to a favorite cheesy egg casserole.

PREP: 8 MIN., COOK: 35 MIN.

8 large eggs, lightly beaten
½ cup all-purpose flour
1 teaspoon baking powder
1 (16-ounce) carton small-curd cottage cheese
2 cups (8 ounces) shredded Monterey Jack cheese
2 cups (8 ounces) shredded Cheddar cheese
2 (4.5-ounce) cans chopped green chiles
¼ cup butter, melted
½ teaspoon garlic powder
½ teaspoon chili powder

1. Combine eggs, flour, and baking powder, stirring well. Stir in cheeses and remaining ingredients. Pour mixture into a lightly greased 13- x 9-inch baking dish.

2. Bake, uncovered, at 325° for 35 minutes. **Makes** 8 servings.

Cheese Grits Casserole
PREP: 20 MIN., COOK: 1 HR., OTHER: 5 MIN.

4 cups water
1 teaspoon salt
1 cup quick-cooking grits, uncooked
2 cups (8 ounces) shredded sharp Cheddar
      cheese
⅔ cup milk
⅓ cup butter
1 teaspoon Worcestershire sauce
¼ teaspoon ground red pepper
4 large eggs, lightly beaten
Paprika

1. Bring water and salt to a boil in a large saucepan;
stir in grits. Return to a boil. Cover, reduce heat, and
simmer 5 minutes, stirring occasionally.
2. Remove from heat. Add cheese and next 4 ingredients, stirring until cheese and butter melt. Add eggs;
stir well.
3. Spoon mixture into a lightly greased 2-quart baking
dish; sprinkle with paprika.
4. Bake, uncovered, at 350° for 1 hour or until thoroughly heated and lightly browned. Let casserole stand
5 minutes before serving. **Makes** 8 servings.

Stovetop Garlic-Cheese Grits
PREP: 5 MIN., COOK: 10 MIN.

4 cups water
1 cup quick-cooking grits, uncooked
½ teaspoon salt
1 (6-ounce) tube pasteurized processed cheese
      food with garlic
⅛ teaspoon ground red pepper

1. Bring water to a boil in a large saucepan or Dutch
oven; stir in grits and salt.
2. Return to a boil; cover, reduce heat, and simmer
5 minutes, stirring occasionally. Remove from heat;
add cheese and pepper, stirring until cheese melts.
Serve hot. **Makes** 6 servings.

Hominy-and-Cheese Grits
*You can't go wrong with this recipe! It's easy to make
and is a fine dish with any course.*

PREP: 20 MIN., COOK: 45 MIN.

5 cups water
1 teaspoon salt
1⅓ cups quick-cooking white grits, uncooked
1 (15-ounce) can yellow hominy, drained
½ cup butter
2 cups (8 ounces) shredded sharp Cheddar
      cheese
½ cup grated Parmesan cheese

1. Bring water and salt to a boil in a heavy Dutch oven;
gradually stir in grits. Return to a boil; reduce heat,
and cook 4 to 5 minutes, stirring occasionally.
2. Stir in hominy, butter, and Cheddar cheese; spoon
into a lightly greased 13- x 9-inch baking dish.
Sprinkle with Parmesan cheese.
3. Bake at 350° for 45 minutes or until set. **Makes**
12 servings.

Hot Tomato Grits

PREP: 10 MIN., COOK: 30 MIN., OTHER: 5 MIN.

2 bacon slices, chopped
2 (14½-ounce) cans chicken broth
½ teaspoon salt
1 cup quick-cooking grits, uncooked
2 large ripe tomatoes, peeled and chopped
2 tablespoons canned chopped green chiles
1 cup (4 ounces) shredded Cheddar cheese
Garnish: cooked and crumbled bacon

1. Cook bacon in a heavy saucepan over medium-high heat until crisp. (Do not drain.) Gradually add broth and salt; bring to a boil. Stir in grits, tomatoes, and chiles; return to a boil, stirring often. Reduce heat, and simmer, stirring often, 15 to 20 minutes. Stir in cheese; cover and let stand 5 minutes or until cheese melts. Garnish, if desired. **Makes** 6 servings.
Note: To reduce fat and calories, drain bacon on paper towels, and wipe skillet clean. Substitute 2% reduced-fat sharp Cheddar cheese for regular.

Ham-Stuffed Biscuits
With Mustard Butter

Ham-Stuffed Biscuits With Mustard Butter

PREP: 1 HR.; COOK: 12 MIN. PER BATCH; OTHER: 1 HR., 5 MIN.

1 (¼-ounce) envelope active dry yeast
½ cup warm water (100° to 110°)
2 cups buttermilk
5½ cups all-purpose flour
¼ cup sugar
1½ tablespoons baking powder
1½ teaspoons salt
½ teaspoon baking soda
¾ cup shortening
Mustard Butter
2 pounds thinly sliced cooked ham

1. Combine yeast and ½ cup warm water in a 4-cup liquid measuring cup, and let mixture stand 5 minutes. Stir in buttermilk.
2. Combine flour and next 4 ingredients in a large bowl; cut in shortening with a pastry blender or fork until mixture resembles coarse meal. Add buttermilk mixture, stirring with a fork just until dry ingredients are moistened.
3. Turn dough out onto a well-floured surface, and knead 4 to 5 times.
4. Roll dough to ½-inch thickness; cut with a 2-inch round cutter, and place on lightly greased baking sheets. Cover and let rise in a warm place (85°), free from drafts, 1 hour.
5. Bake at 425° for 10 to 12 minutes or until golden. Split each biscuit, and spread evenly with Mustard Butter. Place ham slices between biscuit halves. **Makes** 5 dozen.

Mustard Butter

PREP: 5 MIN.

1 cup butter, softened
2 tablespoons minced sweet onion
2 tablespoons spicy brown mustard

1. Stir together all ingredients until blended. **Makes** about 1 cup.

Classic Cream Scones

PREP: 15 MIN., COOK: 15 MIN.

2 cups all-purpose flour
¼ cup sugar
2 teaspoons baking powder
⅛ teaspoon salt
⅓ cup butter, cubed
½ cup whipping cream
1 large egg
1½ teaspoons vanilla extract
1 egg white
1 teaspoon water
Sugar

1. Combine first 4 ingredients. Cut in butter with a pastry blender or two forks until mixture resembles coarse meal.
2. Whisk together cream, egg, and vanilla; add to flour mixture, stirring just until dry ingredients are moistened.
3. Turn dough out onto a lightly floured surface. Pat dough to ½-inch thickness; cut with a 2½-inch round cutter, and place on baking sheets.
4. Whisk together egg white and 1 teaspoon water; brush mixture over tops of scones. Sprinkle scones with additional sugar.
5. Bake at 425° for 13 to 15 minutes or until lightly browned. **Makes** 1 dozen.

Classic Cream Scones

Parmesan Cheese Muffins

You probably have most of these ingredients in your pantry and refrigerator.
Mix up your menu with some of our muffin variations.

PREP: 10 MIN., COOK: 18 MIN.

2 cups self-rising flour
¾ cup shredded Parmesan cheese
2 tablespoons sugar
1 cup milk
¼ cup vegetable oil
2 large eggs

1. Combine first 3 ingredients in a large bowl; make a well in center of mixture.
2. Whisk together milk, oil, and eggs until well blended. Add to flour mixture, and stir just until dry ingredients are moistened.
3. Spoon mixture into lightly greased muffin pans, filling two-thirds full.

4. Bake at 400° for 15 to 18 minutes or until golden brown. **Makes** 1 dozen.

Breakfast Muffins: Add 1 cup cooked and crumbled ground pork sausage to flour mixture. Proceed with recipe as directed.

Blueberry Muffins: Omit Parmesan cheese. Increase sugar to ½ cup; proceed with recipe as directed, folding 1 cup fresh or frozen blueberries into prepared batter.

Cranberry-Orange Muffins: Omit Parmesan cheese, and add ¾ cup sweetened dried cranberries and 1 tablespoon grated orange rind to flour mixture. Increase sugar to ½ cup, and proceed as directed.

Sausage-Cheddar Muffins

*Serve these savory muffins for breakfast
or with soup and salad.*

PREP: 10 MIN., COOK: 30 MIN.

½ pound ground pork sausage
2 cups all-purpose flour
2 tablespoons sugar
1 tablespoon baking powder
¼ teaspoon salt
1 cup milk
1 large egg, lightly beaten
¼ cup butter, melted
½ cup (2 ounces) shredded sharp
    Cheddar cheese
Vegetable cooking spray

1. Brown sausage in a large skillet, stirring until it
crumbles; drain. Set sausage aside.
2. Combine flour and next 3 ingredients; make a well
in center of mixture.
3. Combine milk, egg, and butter; add to dry mixture, stirring just until moistened. Stir in sausage and
cheese.
4. Place paper baking cups in muffin pans, and coat
lightly with cooking spray. Spoon batter into cups,
filling two-thirds full.
5. Bake at 375° for 20 minutes or until golden. Remove
from pans immediately. **Makes** 1 dozen.

FAMILY FAVORITE, QUICK
Cinnamon Toast Rollups

PREP: 10 MIN., COOK: 12 MIN.

½ cup granulated sugar
¼ cup firmly packed light
    brown sugar
½ teaspoon ground cinnamon
1 (8-ounce) can refrigerated
    crescent rolls
¼ cup butter, melted

1. Stir together first 3 ingredients.
2. Unroll crescent dough; brush with melted butter,
and sprinkle evenly with sugar mixture.

3. Separate dough into triangles. Roll up each triangle,
starting with shortest side; place on a lightly greased
baking sheet.
4. Bake at 350° for 10 to 12 minutes or until golden
brown; remove to a wire rack to cool. **Makes** 8 rollups.

FAMILY FAVORITE, QUICK
Pecan Crescent Twists

PREP: 15 MIN., COOK: 12 MIN.

2 (8-ounce) cans refrigerated
    crescent rolls
3 tablespoons butter, melted and divided
½ cup chopped pecans
¼ cup powdered sugar
1 teaspoon ground cinnamon
⅛ teaspoon ground nutmeg
½ cup powdered sugar
2½ teaspoons maple syrup or milk

1. Unroll crescent rolls, and separate each can into
2 rectangles, pressing perforations to seal. Brush
evenly with 2 tablespoons melted butter.
2. Stir together chopped pecans and next 3 ingredients; sprinkle 3 tablespoons pecan mixture onto each
rectangle, pressing in gently.
3. Roll up, starting at 1 long side, and twist. Cut 6 shallow ½-inch-long diagonal slits in each roll.
4. Shape rolls into rings, pressing ends together; place
on a lightly greased baking sheet. Brush rings evenly
with remaining 1 tablespoon butter.
5. Bake at 375° for 12 minutes or until rings are
golden.
6. Stir together ½ cup powdered sugar and maple
syrup until glaze is smooth; drizzle over warm rings.
Cut rings in half, and serve. **Makes** 8 servings.

Mixed-Fruit Granola

Mixed-Fruit Granola

PREP: 10 MIN., COOK: 35 MIN.

3 cups uncooked regular oats
½ cup wheat germ
½ cup sunflower kernels
½ cup chopped pecans
½ cup honey
¼ cup sesame seeds
2 tablespoons vegetable oil
½ tablespoon ground cinnamon
1½ teaspoons vanilla extract
1½ cups chopped mixed dried fruit
Yogurt (optional)

1. Combine first 9 ingredients in a bowl; spread evenly on 2 lightly greased jelly-roll pans.
2. Bake at 350° for 25 to 30 minutes, stirring every 7 minutes. Cool. Stir in dried fruit. Serve with yogurt, if desired. **Makes** 7½ cups.
Note: Store in an airtight container up to 2 weeks.

Fruit With Sour Cream Sauce

PREP: 15 MIN., COOK: 5 MIN., OTHER: 1 HR.

⅓ cup sugar
1 cup water
6 fresh mint leaves
1 (8-ounce) can pineapple chunks in juice, drained
1 banana, sliced
1 Granny Smith apple, chopped
1 cup seedless green grapes
1 cup sliced strawberries
Sour Cream Sauce
Garnish: fresh mint sprigs

1. Bring first 3 ingredients to a boil in a saucepan, and cook, stirring constantly, 4 to 5 minutes or until sugar mixture reaches a syrup consistency. Discard mint leaves, and cool sugar syrup completely.
2. Combine pineapple, banana, apple, grapes, and strawberries in a large bowl. Pour syrup over fruit mixture; toss gently. Cover and chill at least 1 hour. Serve with Sour Cream Sauce, and garnish, if desired. **Makes** 4 servings.

Sour Cream Sauce

PREP: 10 MIN.

⅓ cup butter, softened
1 cup powdered sugar
½ cup sour cream
½ teaspoon lemon juice
¼ teaspoon vanilla extract

1. Beat butter and powdered sugar at medium speed with an electric mixer until smooth. Add sour cream, lemon juice, and vanilla, beating until mixture is creamy. Cover and chill until ready to serve or up to 8 hours. **Makes** about 1¾ cups.

Fruit With Sour
Cream Sauce

Maple Coffee

*This recipe easily doubles for a larger crowd. To make
sweetened whipped cream, use 1 to 2 tablespoons
sugar to 1 cup whipping cream.*

PREP: 5 MIN., COOK: 5 MIN.

2 cups half-and-half
½ cup maple syrup
2 cups hot brewed coffee
Sweetened whipped cream

1. Cook half-and-half and maple syrup in a saucepan
over medium heat, stirring constantly, until thoroughly heated. (Do not boil.) Stir in coffee, and serve
with sweetened whipped cream. **Makes** 4½ cups.

Orange-Scented Mocha

Nothing is more comforting on a chilly winter day than sitting by the fireplace with your hands wrapped around a toasty warm mug.

PREP: 10 MIN., COOK: 9 MIN.

3 cups milk
1 cup semisweet chocolate morsels
4 (2-inch) orange rind strips
½ teaspoon instant espresso or ¾ teaspoon instant coffee granules
⅛ teaspoon ground nutmeg
Sweetened whipped cream
Garnishes: orange rind strips and curls, ground nutmeg

1. Combine first 5 ingredients in heavy medium saucepan. Cook over medium heat, whisking often, 3 to 4 minutes or until chocolate is melted. Increase heat to medium-high, and cook, whisking often, 4 to 5 minutes or just until mixture begins to boil. Remove from heat; discard orange rind strips. Serve immediately with sweetened whipped cream. Garnish, if desired. **Makes** about 3½ cups (about 4 servings).
Note: This recipe can be prepared up to 2 hours ahead. Let stand at room temperature. Before serving, bring to a light boil, whisking occasionally; remove from heat, and serve immediately.

Minted Hot Chocolate Mix

PREP: 10 MIN.

3 (4½-inch) soft peppermint candy sticks
1 cup sugar
¾ cup instant nonfat dry milk
¾ cup powdered nondairy coffee creamer
½ cup unsweetened cocoa

1. Place peppermint sticks in a zip-top plastic freezer bag; seal bag, and crush candy with a mallet.
2. Combine crushed candy and remaining ingredients in an airtight container, and store at room temperature up to 1 month. **Makes** 3 cups dry mix (about 16 servings).
Note: For testing purposes only, we used King Leo Peppermint Sticks.

Kane's Peppery Bloody Mary

PREP: 10 MIN.

1 teaspoon chopped fresh basil
1 teaspoon chopped fresh cilantro
1 teaspoon chopped fresh chives
1⅓ cups tomato juice
½ cup pepper vodka
6 tablespoons fresh lemon juice
1½ to 3 teaspoons green hot sauce
1 teaspoon Worcestershire sauce
Large pinch of celery salt
Pinch of sea salt
Freshly ground pepper to taste
Garnishes: pickled okra, lemon wedges

1. Combine first 3 ingredients in a cocktail shaker. Press leaves against bottom of cup using a wooden spoon to release flavors; stir in tomato juice and next 7 ingredients. Transfer half of mixture to a 2-cup glass measuring cup.
2. Place ice in cocktail shaker, filling halfway full. Cover with lid, and shake vigorously until thoroughly chilled. Strain into a glass over ice. Repeat procedure with remaining tomato mixture. Garnish, if desired. **Makes** 2 servings.
Note: For testing purposes only, we used Absolut Peppar Vodka and Tabasco Green Pepper Sauce.

> **This is my husband Kane's specialty drink that he makes for our annual laid-back Christmas Eve Brunch. He says that lots of fresh lemon juice is the key to a great Bloody Mary.**

LYDA JONES BURNETTE, TEST KITCHENS DIRECTOR

Italian Club Sandwich, page 144

weeknight favorites

Linguine With Fresh Tomato Sauce

Linguine With Fresh Tomato Sauce

This makes a great meatless main dish or a flavorful side. You'll love the quick, no-cook sauce. (also pictured on back cover)

PREP: 10 MIN., COOK: 10 MIN.

1 (12-ounce) package uncooked linguine
4 large tomatoes, finely chopped
3 tablespoons shredded fresh basil
1 tablespoon olive oil
½ teaspoon salt
¼ teaspoon freshly ground pepper
1 (2¼-ounce) can sliced ripe olives, drained
¾ cup crumbled feta cheese

1. Cook linguine according to package directions; drain and place in a large serving bowl.
2. Combine tomato and next 4 ingredients; toss gently.
3. Top linguine with tomato mixture, and sprinkle with olives and feta cheese. **Makes** 6 servings.

(EDITOR'S CHOICE)
Beefy Slow-cooker Spaghetti Sauce

This makes enough sauce for several meals, so serve some today and freeze the rest. You can also cook this on top of the stove over very low heat, stirring often, for several hours or until the meat is tender.

PREP: 20 MIN., COOK: 6 HR.

1 (3- to 3½-pound) boneless chuck roast, trimmed
2 teaspoons salt, divided
2 tablespoons olive oil
2 garlic cloves, minced
1 large onion, chopped
4 (14.5-ounce) cans Italian-style diced tomatoes, undrained
1 (15-ounce) can tomato sauce
1 (12-ounce) can tomato paste
1 tablespoon sugar
2 teaspoons dried basil
2 teaspoons dried oregano
1 teaspoon dried crushed red pepper
Hot cooked spaghetti (optional)

1. Sprinkle roast evenly with 1 teaspoon salt. Cook roast in hot oil in a large skillet over medium-high heat 3 minutes on each side or until browned.
2. Combine minced garlic, remaining 1 teaspoon salt, and next 8 ingredients in a 6-quart slow cooker; gently add roast.
3. Cook, covered, on HIGH 6 hours or until roast is very tender. Remove roast from slow cooker, and shred using 2 forks. Skim off any fat from tomato sauce, if desired, and return shredded meat to sauce. Serve over hot cooked spaghetti, if desired. **Makes** about 3 quarts.
Note: Freeze spaghetti sauce in airtight containers for up to 6 weeks, if desired.

Three-Cheese Tortellini With Tomatoes

Here's a simple pasta dish for any night of the week. Make it a meatless entrée for two or an easy side for six. Look for cheese-filled tortellini in the refrigerated section of the supermarket.

PREP: 10 MIN., COOK: 16 MIN.

1 (9-ounce) package refrigerated cheese-filled tortellini, uncooked
2 garlic cloves, minced
1 jalapeño pepper, seeded and chopped
½ medium-size green pepper, chopped
2 tablespoons chopped onion
2 tablespoons olive oil
2 large tomatoes, chopped
1 teaspoon salt
½ teaspoon dried oregano
½ teaspoon dried basil
½ cup freshly grated Parmesan cheese
Freshly ground pepper

1. Cook tortellini according to package directions; drain. Keep warm.
2. Sauté garlic and next 3 ingredients in oil 3 minutes or until crisp-tender. Add tomato, salt, oregano, and basil. Cook 3 minutes, stirring constantly. Spoon mixture over tortellini, and toss gently. Sprinkle with Parmesan cheese and freshly ground pepper. Serve hot. **Makes** 6 servings.

> **This recipe is inspired by my mother's spaghetti, which uses a chuck roast rather than ground beef for its rich meat flavor. It's a huge favorite in my family—my nieces and their children are thrilled when Grandma makes spaghetti for them.**

DONNA FLORIO, SENIOR WRITER

Pepperoni Spaghetti

PREP: 12 MIN., COOK: 35 MIN.

1 medium onion, chopped
1 green pepper, chopped
1 pound ground chuck
1 (3.5-ounce) package sliced pepperoni, chopped
1 (26-ounce) jar pasta sauce with mushrooms
½ (16-ounce) package spaghetti, cooked
1 cup (4 ounces) shredded mozzarella cheese
1 tablespoon grated Parmesan cheese

1. Combine onion, green pepper, and ground chuck in a large skillet. Cook over medium heat until meat browns, stirring until it crumbles. Remove from heat; drain. Return meat mixture to skillet. Add pepperoni and pasta sauce; bring to a boil. Cover, reduce heat, and simmer 20 minutes, stirring occasionally.
2. Arrange spaghetti in a greased 13- x 9-inch baking dish; top with meat sauce. Sprinkle mozzarella cheese over sauce; bake, uncovered, at 400° for 5 minutes. Remove from oven; top with Parmesan cheese. Serve hot. **Makes** 8 servings.

Chicken Fettuccine Supreme

PREP: 12 MIN., COOK: 30 MIN.

¼ cup butter
1¼ pounds skinned and boned chicken breasts, cut into bite-size pieces
3 cups sliced fresh mushrooms
1 cup chopped green onions
1 small sweet red pepper, cut into thin strips
1 garlic clove, crushed
½ teaspoon salt
½ teaspoon pepper
10 ounces fettuccine, cooked
¾ cup half-and-half
½ cup butter, melted
¼ cup chopped fresh parsley
¼ teaspoon salt
¼ teaspoon pepper
½ cup grated Parmesan cheese
1 cup chopped pecans, toasted

1. Melt ¼ cup butter in a large skillet over medium heat; add chicken, and cook, stirring constantly, until browned. Remove chicken from skillet, reserving pan drippings in skillet; set chicken aside.
2. Add mushrooms and next 5 ingredients to pan drippings in skillet, and sauté until vegetables are tender.
3. Add chicken; reduce heat, and cook 15 minutes or until chicken is tender. Set aside, and keep warm.
4. Place fettuccine in a large bowl. Add half-and-half and next 4 ingredients to fettuccine; toss gently to combine.
5. Add chicken mixture and Parmesan cheese to fettuccine; toss gently to combine. Sprinkle with pecans, and serve immediately. **Makes** 4 servings.

Easy Measuring, Easy Freezing

- 1 to 1¼ pounds uncooked lean ground beef, turkey, or sausage = about 2½ to 3 cups cooked and crumbled
- 1¼ to 1½ pounds uncooked chicken breasts = about 3 cups cooked and cubed
- Preshredded cheeses are convenient and freeze great but can be costly. Consider shredding your own cheese (2 [8-ounce] blocks of cheese, shredded = about 4 cups). Partially freezing the block, especially softer cheeses such as Swiss and Monterey Jack, makes shredding a breeze.
- Chopped onions show up as an ingredient in lots of recipes. You can freeze them after chopping, but freeze them raw.
- Pint- to gallon-size, zip-top plastic freezer bags are excellent choices for storing food items. (A pint-size zip-top plastic freezer bag is perfect for 1 cup cubed cooked chicken breasts.) Also check out the great plastic freezer container choices that go from freezer to microwave to dishwasher. They come in several sizes. Whichever you choose, make sure you purchase good-quality bags and containers that are designed for the freezer.
- Label your items for freezing, including the amount and date. If properly stored, shredded cheeses and cooked meats can be frozen up to 3 months.

FREEZEABLE, MAKE AHEAD
Chicken 'n' Spinach Pasta Bake

You'll find this dish perfect for company but also speedy enough for weeknight meals.

PREP: 15 MIN., COOK: 1 HR.

8 ounces uncooked rigatoni
1 tablespoon olive oil
1 cup finely chopped onion (about 1 medium)
1 (10-ounce) package frozen chopped spinach,
    thawed
3 cups cubed cooked chicken breasts
1 (14.5-ounce) can Italian-style diced tomatoes
1 (8-ounce) container chive-and-onion cream cheese
½ teaspoon salt
½ teaspoon pepper
1½ cups (6 ounces) shredded mozzarella cheese

1. Prepare rigatoni according to package directions.
2. Meanwhile, spread oil on bottom of an 11- x 7-inch baking dish; add onion in a single layer.

3. Bake at 375° for 15 minutes or just until tender. Transfer onion to a large bowl, and set aside.
4. Drain chopped spinach well, pressing between layers of paper towels.
5. Stir rigatoni, spinach, chicken, and next 4 ingredients into onion in bowl. Spoon mixture into baking dish, and sprinkle evenly with shredded mozzarella cheese.
6. Bake, covered, at 375° for 30 minutes; uncover and bake 15 more minutes or until bubbly. **Makes** 4 to 6 servings.

Sausage 'n' Spinach Pasta Bake: Substitute 3 cups cooked, crumbled hot Italian sausage for 3 cups cubed cooked chicken breasts. Reduce salt to ¼ teaspoon, and omit ½ teaspoon pepper. Proceed with recipe as directed.

Saucy Manicotti

FAMILY FAVORITE
Saucy Manicotti

PREP: 30 MIN., COOK: 1 HR.

1 (8-ounce) package uncooked manicotti shells

1 (16-ounce) package Italian sausage, casings removed

1 large onion, chopped

9 garlic cloves, pressed and divided

1 (26-ounce) jar seven-herb tomato pasta sauce

1 (8-ounce) container chive-and-onion cream cheese, softened

6 cups (24 ounces) shredded mozzarella cheese, divided

¾ cup freshly grated Parmesan cheese

1 (15-ounce) container ricotta cheese

¾ teaspoon freshly ground pepper

1. Cook manicotti shells according to package directions, and drain.

2. Cook sausage, onion, and 5 garlic cloves in a large Dutch oven over medium-high heat 6 minutes, stirring until sausage crumbles and is no longer pink. Stir in pasta sauce; bring to a boil. Remove from heat.

3. Combine cream cheese, 4 cups mozzarella cheese, next 3 ingredients, and remaining 4 garlic cloves in a large bowl, stirring until blended. Cut a slit down length of each cooked manicotti shell.

4. Spoon 1 cup sauce mixture into a lightly greased 13- x 9-inch baking dish. Spoon cheese mixture evenly into manicotti shells. Arrange stuffed shells over sauce in dish, seam sides down. Spoon remaining sauce over stuffed shells. Sprinkle evenly with remaining 2 cups cheese.

5. Bake, covered, at 350° for 50 minutes or until bubbly. **Makes** 7 servings.

Note: For testing purposes only, we used Ragú 7-Herb Tomato Pasta Sauce.

140 weeknight favorites

Lasagna Maria

Sausage and pepperoni add chunks of flavor to this favorite multilayered casserole.

PREP: 12 MIN., COOK: 28 MIN.

1 pound ground pork sausage
1 (26-ounce) jar spaghetti sauce
½ cup water
1 large egg, lightly beaten
1 (15-ounce) carton ricotta cheese
¼ cup grated Parmesan cheese
1 tablespoon dried parsley flakes
½ teaspoon dried oregano
¼ teaspoon pepper
1 (8-ounce) package lasagna noodles,
    cooked
2 cups (8 ounces) shredded mozzarella
    cheese, divided
1 (7-ounce) jar sliced mushrooms, drained
1 (3.5-ounce) package sliced pepperoni

1. Brown sausage in a skillet over medium heat, stirring until it crumbles; drain. Stir in spaghetti sauce and water; set aside. Combine egg and next 5 ingredients, stirring well.

2. Spread about ½ cup meat sauce in a lightly greased 13- x 9-inch pan. Layer 3 lasagna noodles, half of the ricotta cheese mixture, one-third of mozzarella cheese, and one-third of remaining meat sauce; repeat layers. Top with remaining noodles. Arrange mushrooms and pepperoni slices on top. Spoon remaining meat sauce on top.

3. Bake, uncovered, at 375° for 20 minutes. Sprinkle with remaining mozzarella cheese, and bake 5 more minutes. **Makes** 6 servings.

Note: If desired, sauté 2 cups sliced fresh mushrooms in 1 tablespoon olive oil 3 minutes over medium-high heat instead of using mushrooms in a jar.

Lasagna Maria

Stuffed Focaccia With Roasted Pepper Vinaigrette

PREP: 20 MIN., COOK: 8 MIN.

1 (9-inch) round loaf focaccia
1 (3-ounce) goat cheese log, crumbled
1 whole deli-roasted chicken
½ cup Roasted Pepper Vinaigrette
3 cups mixed salad greens
½ pint grape or cherry tomatoes, halved

1. Cut focaccia in half horizontally, using a serrated knife; place, cut sides up, on a baking sheet.
2. Bake at 400° for 6 to 8 minutes or until lightly browned. Spread cut sides evenly with goat cheese.
3. Remove meat from chicken, and coarsely chop. Place chicken in a medium bowl, and toss with Roasted Pepper Vinaigrette. Top bottom half of focaccia with chicken mixture, and layer with salad greens and tomatoes; cover with top of bread, cut side down. Cut into 6 wedges. **Makes** 6 servings.

Roasted Pepper Vinaigrette

PREP: 5 MIN.

1 cup bottled oil-and-vinegar dressing
½ (12-ounce) jar roasted red bell peppers, drained

1. Process dressing and roasted peppers in a blender or food processor until smooth, stopping to scrape down sides. Store in refrigerator up to 2 weeks. **Makes** 1½ cups.

Spinach-Walnut Pitas

You won't miss meat in these pitas filled with toasty nuts, artichoke hearts, avocado, and zucchini.

PREP: 10 MIN.

2 (6-ounce) jars marinated artichoke hearts
4 cups torn spinach, lightly packed
1 cup chopped iceberg lettuce
1 small zucchini, thinly sliced
2 green onions, sliced
2 avocados, seeded and coarsely chopped
½ cup toasted chopped walnuts
2 tablespoons toasted sesame seeds
Piquant French Dressing
6 (6-inch) pita bread rounds, cut in half

1. Drain artichoke hearts, reserving ⅓ cup liquid for dressing.
2. Combine artichokes, spinach and next 6 ingredients in a large bowl. Toss with Piquant French Dressing. Spoon mixture into pita bread halves. Serve immediately. **Makes** 6 servings.

Piquant French Dressing
PREP: 10 MIN., OTHER: 1 HR.

3 tablespoons sugar
3 tablespoons lemon juice
¾ teaspoon salt
¾ teaspoon paprika
¾ teaspoon dry mustard
¼ teaspoon pepper
¾ teaspoon celery seeds
¾ teaspoon grated onion
2 garlic cloves, halved
⅓ cup reserved artichoke liquid

1. Process first 9 ingredients in an electric blender until blended, stopping once to scrape down sides. With blender on high, gradually add artichoke liquid in a slow, steady stream; blend until dressing is thickened. Cover and chill at least 1 hour. Stir dressing before serving. **Makes** ¾ cup.

BLT Croissant Sandwiches

Goat cheese and tangy sun-dried tomatoes send this sandwich upscale. Red leaf lettuce provides a pretty ruffly edge.

PREP: 12 MIN., COOK: 7 MIN., OTHER: 8 HR.

1 (3-ounce) package cream cheese, softened
1 (3-ounce) package goat cheese, softened
¼ cup chopped oil-packed sun-dried tomatoes
1 tablespoon chopped fresh basil or 1 teaspoon
    dried basil
6 large croissants, split horizontally
12 bacon slices, cooked
3 plum tomatoes, sliced
6 red leaf lettuce leaves

1. Combine cream cheese and goat cheese, stirring until smooth; stir in chopped tomato and basil. Cover and chill 8 hours, if desired, to develop stronger flavor. Let mixture stand at room temperature to soften slightly before spreading on bread.
2. Spread cheese mixture evenly over cut surfaces of croissant halves. Place croissant halves, cheese sides up, on an ungreased baking sheet.
3. Bake, uncovered, at 325° for 5 to 7 minutes or until cheese mixture is thoroughly heated. Place 2 bacon slices on bottom half of each croissant; top evenly with tomato slices, lettuce leaves, and croissant tops. Serve immediately. **Makes** 6 servings.

Italian Club Sandwich

QUICK
Italian Club Sandwiches

PREP: 25 MIN., COOK: 6 MIN.

½ (16-ounce) Italian bread loaf
¼ cup Italian dressing
⅓ cup shredded Parmesan cheese
½ cup mayonnaise
½ cup mustard
½ pound thinly sliced Genoa salami
½ pound thinly sliced mortadella or bologna
4 (1-ounce) provolone cheese slices
Romaine lettuce leaves
3 plum tomatoes, sliced
8 bacon slices, cooked and cut in half
Wooden picks
Garnish: pimiento-stuffed green olives

1. Cut bread diagonally into 12 (¼-inch-thick) slices; arrange on a baking sheet. Brush slices evenly with Italian dressing, and sprinkle with Parmesan cheese.
2. Bake at 375° for 5 to 6 minutes or until lightly toasted.
3. Spread untoasted sides of bread slices evenly with mayonnaise and mustard. Layer 4 bread slices, mayonnaise sides up, with salami, mortadella, and provolone. Top with 4 bread slices, mayonnaise sides up; layer with lettuce, tomato, and bacon. Top with remaining 4 bread slices, mayonnaise side down. Cut in half, and secure with wooden picks. Garnish, if desired. **Makes** 4 servings.

Taco Burgers

Pile this "burger" high with your choice of taco toppings.

PREP: 10 MIN., COOK: 22 MIN.

1½ pounds ground chuck
1 small onion, chopped
1 (8-ounce) can tomato sauce
1 (1¼-ounce) package taco seasoning mix
6 hamburger buns
1 small onion, sliced and separated into rings
1½ cups shredded lettuce
3 medium tomatoes, chopped
1 cup (4 ounces) finely shredded Cheddar cheese
½ cup sliced pimiento-stuffed olives

1. Brown ground chuck and chopped onion in a large skillet, stirring until meat crumbles; drain well. Add tomato sauce and taco seasoning to meat mixture; stir well. Bring to a boil; reduce heat, and simmer, uncovered, 5 minutes.

2. Split and toast hamburger buns. Place onion rings on bottom half of each bun; top with meat mixture. Top each sandwich with lettuce, tomato, cheese, and olives. Replace bun tops. **Makes** 6 servings.

Taco Burgers

Hickory Burgers

Barbecue sauce ties beef and ham together in this juicy burger.
Ham gives the burgers a smoky pink appearance.

PREP: 10 MIN., COOK: 10 MIN.

1 pound ground chuck
1 pound ground cooked ham
1 (8-ounce) container sour cream
¼ cup finely chopped onion
¾ teaspoon salt
¼ teaspoon pepper
Hickory-flavored barbecue sauce
8 slices American cheese
8 hamburger buns, split and toasted
Tomato slices
Sweet pickle slices
Lettuce
Onion slices

1. Combine first 6 ingredients in a large bowl; shape into 8 patties. (Mixture will be sticky.) Grill patties, uncovered, over medium-hot coals (350° to 400°) 4 to 5 minutes on each side or until beef is no longer pink, basting often with barbecue sauce. Top patties with cheese during last 2 to 3 minutes of grilling time.
2. Serve on buns. Top with tomato slices, pickles, lettuce, and onion. **Makes** 8 servings.
Note: For testing purposes only, we used KC Master-piece Hickory-Flavored Barbecue Sauce.

Grilled Reubens

PREP: 12 MIN., COOK: 10 MIN.

1 (16-ounce) bottle Thousand Island dressing
18 rye bread slices
12 Swiss cheese slices
2 cups canned sauerkraut, drained
2 pounds corned beef, thinly sliced
Softened butter
Pimiento-stuffed olives (optional)
Wooden picks

1. Spread 1⅓ cups salad dressing evenly on 1 side of 12 bread slices. Layer 1 cheese slice, 2 heaping

tablespoons sauerkraut, and about 4 slices corned beef over each prepared bread slice. Stack bread to make 6 (2-layer) sandwiches. Spread 1 side of each of remaining 6 slices with remaining dressing, and place, dressing sides down, on sandwiches.
2. Spread butter over top of each sandwich. Place sandwiches, buttered sides down, on a moderately hot griddle or skillet; cook until bread is golden.
3. Spread butter on ungrilled sides of sandwiches; turn carefully, and cook until bread is golden. Skewer olives on wooden picks, if desired, and secure sandwiches with wooden picks. Serve immediately. **Makes** 6 servings.

Grilled Pesto-Pepperoni Sandwiches

Make this speedy sandwich on a griddle. It takes only six
ingredients, but it tastes like much more.

PREP: 8 MIN., COOK: 8 MIN.

1 (6-ounce) package sliced mozzarella cheese,
    cut into thirds
8 (1-inch-thick) Italian bread slices
¼ cup pizza sauce
¼ cup pesto sauce
20 pepperoni slices
2 tablespoons butter, softened

1. Arrange 1 cheese slice on each of 4 slices of bread; spread evenly with pizza sauce. Top each with another cheese slice, and spread evenly with pesto sauce. Arrange pepperoni slices over pesto sauce; top with remaining cheese slices and remaining bread slices.
2. Spread half of butter on tops of sandwiches. Invert sandwiches onto a hot nonstick skillet or griddle; cook over medium heat until browned. Spread remaining butter on ungrilled sides of sandwiches; turn and cook until browned. Serve immediately. **Makes** 4 servings.

Chorizo, Black Bean, and Corn Quesadillas

PREP: 25 MIN., COOK: 15 MIN.

4 (4-inch) chorizo sausage links, chopped
1 (15-ounce) can black beans, drained and
    rinsed
½ cup frozen whole kernel corn, thawed
½ teaspoon ground cumin
⅓ cup Cilantro Pesto
4 (8-inch) flour tortillas
1 (8-ounce) package shredded Mexican
    cheese blend*

1. Cook sausage in a large skillet over medium heat 5 minutes or until browned. Add black beans, corn, and cumin, and cook, stirring occasionally, 3 to 4 minutes or until thoroughly heated.
2. Spread Cilantro Pesto evenly on each tortilla. Spoon chorizo mixture on half of each tortilla; sprinkle with cheese. Wipe skillet clean.
3. Cook, tortilla sides down, in lightly greased skillet over medium-high heat 1 minute or until lightly browned. Fold tortillas over filling. Serve immediately with remaining pesto. **Makes** 6 servings.
*1 (8-ounce) package shredded Monterey Jack cheese may be substituted.

MAKE AHEAD
Cilantro Pesto

PREP: 10 MIN.

3 bunches fresh cilantro, stems removed
1½ tablespoons fresh lime juice
2 tablespoons olive oil
1 garlic clove
½ teaspoon salt
2 tablespoons water

1. Process all ingredients in a food processor until smooth, stopping to scrape down sides. Store in refrigerator up to 1 week. **Makes** about ½ cup.

Black Bean Soup

PREP: 20 MIN.; COOK: 5 HR., 15 MIN.; OTHER: 8 HR.

1 (16-ounce) package dried black beans
3 quarts water
2 chicken bouillon cubes
½ small onion
¼ small green bell pepper
6 garlic cloves, minced
2 tablespoons olive oil
1½ teaspoons sugar
1 teaspoon dried oregano
1 teaspoon ground cumin
1 teaspoon salt
½ teaspoon pepper
Garnish: minced red onion

1. Rinse and sort beans according to package directions.
2. Soak beans in water to cover in a 6-quart stockpot 8 hours. Rinse and drain beans.
3. Bring beans, 3 quarts water, and bouillon to a boil. Cover, reduce heat to low, and simmer 3 hours. Do not drain.
4. Process ½ small onion and bell pepper in a blender or food processor until smooth, stopping to scrape down sides.
5. Sauté garlic in hot oil in a large skillet over medium-high heat 1 minute. Add onion mixture; cook, stirring constantly, 4 minutes.
6. Stir onion-and-garlic mixture into beans. Add sugar and next 4 ingredients. Simmer, uncovered, 1½ to 2 hours or until beans are tender and soup is thick. Garnish, if desired. **Makes** 8 servings.

Garden Vegetable Soup

PREP: 20 MIN., COOK: 50 MIN.

2 tablespoons butter
1 cup thinly sliced carrot
1 cup sliced celery with leaves
1 cup chopped onion
1 garlic clove, crushed
9 medium tomatoes, peeled and chopped
2 teaspoons salt
½ teaspoon pepper
1 (14½-ounce) can beef or vegetable
    broth
½ pound fresh green beans, cut into
    1-inch pieces
1 medium zucchini, halved lengthwise and
    sliced
¼ cup chopped fresh parsley
1 tablespoon chopped fresh oregano or
    1 teaspoon dried oregano
1 tablespoon chopped fresh basil or
    1 teaspoon dried basil
Freshly grated Parmesan cheese (optional)

1. Heat butter in a large Dutch oven over medium-high heat. Add carrot and next 3 ingredients; sauté 5 minutes or until onion is tender. Add tomato, salt, and pepper; bring to a boil. Reduce heat, and simmer 15 minutes, stirring occasionally.
2. Add broth and green beans; simmer 20 minutes. Add zucchini and next 3 ingredients; simmer 10 minutes. Spoon into soup bowls; sprinkle with cheese, if desired. **Makes** about 11 cups.

Baked Potato Soup

To bake potatoes in the microwave, prick each several times with a fork. Microwave 1 inch apart on paper towels at HIGH 14 minutes or until done, turning and rearranging after 5 minutes. Let cool.

PREP: 30 MIN., COOK: 30 MIN.

5 large baking potatoes, baked
¼ cup butter
1 medium onion, chopped
⅓ cup all-purpose flour
1 quart half-and-half
3 cups milk
1 teaspoon salt
⅛ teaspoon ground white pepper
2 cups (8 ounces) shredded Cheddar
    cheese
8 bacon slices, cooked and crumbled

1. Peel potatoes, and coarsely mash with a fork.
2. Melt butter in a Dutch oven over medium heat; add onion, and sauté until tender. Add flour, stirring until smooth.
3. Stir in potatoes, half-and-half, and next 3 ingredients; cook over low heat until thoroughly heated. Top each serving with cheese and bacon. **Makes** about 12 cups.

Easy Brunswick Stew

Easy Brunswick Stew

Make preparation a breeze by stopping at your supermarket deli or favorite barbecue restaurant for shredded pork.

PREP: 15 MIN., COOK: 50 MIN.

3 pounds shredded cooked pork
4 cups water
4 cups frozen cubed hash brown potatoes
3 (14½-ounce) cans diced tomatoes with garlic and onion
1 (14½-ounce) can whole kernel corn, drained
1 (14½-ounce) can cream-style corn
½ cup barbecue sauce
1 tablespoon hot sauce
1½ teaspoons salt
1 teaspoon pepper
2 cups frozen lima beans (optional)

1. Stir together shredded pork, 4 cups water, next 8 ingredients, and, if desired, lima beans in a 6-quart stockpot. Bring mixture to a boil; cover, reduce heat, and simmer, stirring often, 45 minutes. **Makes** 5 quarts.

Mexican Chili

PREP: 10 MIN., COOK: 30 MIN.

2 pounds ground chuck
1 cup chopped onion
¾ cup chopped green pepper
1 garlic clove, minced
1 (16-ounce) can kidney beans, drained
1 (14½-ounce) can diced tomatoes
2 (8-ounce) cans tomato sauce
1 tablespoon plus 1 teaspoon chili powder
2 teaspoons ground cumin
½ teaspoon salt
½ teaspoon dried basil
¼ teaspoon pepper
¼ teaspoon hot sauce
1 fresh or canned green chile, seeded and chopped
Shredded Cheddar cheese (optional)
Corn chips (optional)

1. Combine first 4 ingredients in a Dutch oven; cook over medium heat until meat is browned, stirring until it crumbles. Drain. Add beans and next 9 ingredients; cover, reduce heat, and simmer 20 minutes, stirring occasionally. If desired, top with cheese, and serve with corn chips. **Makes** 9 cups.

Chicken-Corn Chowder

This soup can be made ahead and thinned with milk when reheating.

PREP: 10 MIN., COOK: 20 MIN.

1 tablespoon butter
1 (8-ounce) package sliced fresh mushrooms
1 medium onion, chopped
2 (14-ounce) cans chicken broth
1 (16-ounce) package frozen white shoepeg corn
2 cups cubed cooked chicken breast
1 (10¾-ounce) can condensed cream of chicken soup
½ cup uncooked orzo
1 tablespoon sugar
½ teaspoon dried basil
½ teaspoon dried rosemary or thyme
½ teaspoon salt
½ teaspoon pepper
1 cup milk
2 tablespoons all-purpose flour

1. Melt butter in a large Dutch oven over medium-high heat; add mushrooms and onion, and sauté 5 minutes or until tender.
2. Add chicken broth and next 9 ingredients; simmer 10 minutes or until orzo is tender.
3. Stir together milk and flour in a small bowl; gradually stir into chowder, and simmer 5 minutes. **Makes** 6 servings.

Easy Cream of Corn Soup

Simple soups are the solution when you're in a hurry. Try this yummy corn soup which starts with cans of cream-style corn.

PREP: 10 MIN., COOK: 10 MIN.

2 tablespoons minced onion
2 tablespoons butter
2 tablespoons all-purpose flour
1 teaspoon salt
¼ teaspoon pepper
1 (14¾-ounce) can cream-style corn
1 (8¾-ounce) can cream-style corn
3 cups milk or half-and-half
Salt and pepper to taste

1. Sauté onion in butter in a saucepan over medium heat until tender. Stir in flour, salt, and pepper. Cook over low heat, stirring constantly, until smooth. Stir in corn; bring to a boil, and boil 1 minute.
2. Stir in milk. Heat thoroughly (do not boil). Remove from heat; cool slightly. Process in container of an electric blender until smooth, if desired. Add additional salt and pepper to taste. **Makes** 5 cups.

Marinated Baked Ham

Bake this ham one night and you can enjoy leftovers in sandwiches or diced in casseroles for up to a week.

PREP: 10 MIN.; COOK: 2 HR.; OTHER: 8 HR., 10 MIN.

1 (7- to 8-pound) fully cooked ham half
2 cups orange juice
2 cups ginger ale
⅓ cup firmly packed brown sugar
¼ cup orange marmalade
1 teaspoon dry mustard

1. Place first 3 ingredients in a large plastic zip-top freezer bag. Seal bag; marinate in refrigerator 8 hours, turning bag occasionally.
2. Remove ham from marinade, reserving marinade. Place ham, fat side up, in a shallow roasting pan lined with heavy-duty aluminum foil. Bake, uncovered, at 325° for 1½ hours, basting often with marinade.
3. Remove ham from oven; reduce oven temperature to 300°. Slice skin from ham; score fat in a diamond design. Combine brown sugar, marmalade, and mustard; spread over scored fat. Bake ham, uncovered, 30 more minutes. Let stand 10 minutes before carving. **Makes** 16 servings.

Ham Fried Rice

For fast rice, cook 2 (3.5-ounce) bags quick-cooking long-grain rice.

PREP: 15 MIN., COOK: 20 MIN.

3 bacon slices
1½ cups chopped cooked ham
1 red or green bell pepper, chopped
½ cup sliced fresh mushrooms
3 green onions, chopped
1 celery rib, chopped
1 large garlic clove, minced
½ teaspoon dried crushed red pepper
3½ cups cooked rice
2 large eggs, lightly beaten
¼ cup soy sauce

1. Cook bacon slices in a large skillet or wok over medium-high heat until crisp. Remove bacon slices, and drain on paper towels, reserving drippings in skillet. Crumble bacon, and set aside.

2. Add chopped ham to hot drippings in skillet, and stir-fry 3 minutes or until ham is lightly browned. Add bell pepper and next 5 ingredients, and stir-fry 5 minutes. Add rice, and stir-fry 3 minutes or until thoroughly heated.

3. Push rice mixture to sides of skillet, forming a well in center. Pour eggs into well, and cook, stirring occasionally, until eggs are set. Stir rice mixture into eggs; stir in soy sauce and crumbled bacon. Spoon rice mixture into serving bowls. **Makes** 4 to 6 servings.

Stir-fry Pork and Cashews

Stir-fry Pork and Cashews

PREP: 10 MIN., COOK: 6 MIN.

½ pound boneless pork loin, cut into ½-inch pieces
3 tablespoons stir-fry sauce
1 tablespoon frozen orange juice concentrate, thawed
1½ teaspoons cornstarch
1 tablespoon vegetable oil
½ cup dry-roasted or unsalted cashews
Hot cooked rice
Garnish: green onions

1. Stir together first 4 ingredients.
2. Stir-fry pork mixture in hot oil in a large nonstick skillet 4 to 6 minutes; stir in cashews. Serve immediately with rice. Garnish, if desired. **Makes** 2 servings.
Note: To serve 4, use ⅓ cup stir-fry sauce, ¼ cup vegetable oil, and double all other ingredients. Proceed as directed.

FAMILY FAVORITE
Sweet-and-Sour Pork

PREP: 20 MIN., COOK: 15 MIN.

½ cup all-purpose flour
¼ cup cornstarch
½ teaspoon salt
½ cup water
1 large egg, lightly beaten
1½ pounds boneless pork, cut into ¾-inch pieces
Vegetable oil
1 (20-ounce) can pineapple chunks, undrained
½ cup firmly packed brown sugar
½ cup white vinegar
1 tablespoon soy sauce
2 tablespoons cornstarch
2 tablespoons water
2 tablespoons vegetable oil
2 large carrots, thinly sliced
1 green pepper, seeded and cut into ¾-inch pieces
1 small onion, cut into thin wedges
1 garlic clove, minced
Hot cooked rice

1. Combine first 5 ingredients in a bowl; stir with a wire whisk until well blended. Add pork, stirring mixture well.
2. Pour oil to depth of 2 inches into a large heavy saucepan; heat to 375°. Carefully drop pork into hot oil, and fry 5 minutes or until golden. Drain on paper towels. Arrange pork in a single layer on a baking sheet; place in a 200° oven to keep warm while frying remaining pork.
3. Drain pineapple, reserving juice. Set pineapple aside. Add enough water to juice to make 1 cup. Combine juice, brown sugar, vinegar, and soy sauce; stir until sugar dissolves. Set aside. Combine 2 tablespoons cornstarch and 2 tablespoons water, stirring until smooth; set aside.
4. Pour 2 tablespoons oil around top of a preheated wok (or in a large skillet), coating sides; heat at medium-high (375°) for 2 minutes. Add carrot and next 3 ingredients; stir-fry 3 to 5 minutes or until crisp-tender. Stir in juice mixture. Bring to a boil, and boil 1 minute. Stir in cornstarch mixture; cook, stirring constantly, until thickened. Add pork and pineapple; stir-fry until thoroughly heated. Serve over rice. **Makes** 6 servings.

Herb-Crusted Pork With New Potatoes

PREP: 15 MIN., COOK: 45 MIN.

2 pounds new potatoes
¼ cup butter, melted
2 tablespoons prepared horseradish
½ teaspoon salt
½ teaspoon freshly ground pepper
½ cup fine, dry breadcrumbs
⅓ cup chopped fresh basil
3 tablespoons chopped fresh thyme
1 tablespoon freshly ground pepper
3 tablespoons olive oil
1 teaspoon kosher salt
1½ pounds pork tenderloins
2 tablespoons chopped fresh parsley

1. Peel a 1-inch strip around center of each potato. Place potatoes in a large bowl. Add butter and next 3 ingredients, tossing gently. Place potatoes on a lightly greased rack in a broiler pan.
2. Bake at 425° for 20 minutes; remove from oven.
3. Stir together breadcrumbs and next 5 ingredients. Moisten pork tenderloins with water; press crumb mixture over tenderloins, and place on rack with potatoes.
4. Bake at 425° for 25 more minutes or until potatoes are tender and a meat thermometer inserted in thickest part of tenderloins registers 160°.
5. Sprinkle potatoes with parsley, and slice tenderloins. **Makes** 4 servings.

"Serve this pork-and-bean mixture spooned over cornbread or rolled up burrito style in flour tortillas. You can make hearty nachos, quesadillas, or tacos with it too."

MARIAN COOPER CAIRNS, TEST KITCHENS PROFESSIONAL

Chalupa Dinner Bowl

(EDITOR'S CHOICE)
Chalupa Dinner Bowl
PREP: 30 MIN.; COOK: 11 HR., 5 MIN.

1 pound dried pinto beans
1 (3½-pound) bone-in pork loin roast
2 (4-ounce) cans chopped green chiles
2 garlic cloves, chopped
1 tablespoon chili powder
2 teaspoons salt
1 teaspoon dried oregano
1 teaspoon ground cumin
1 (32-ounce) container chicken broth
1 (10-ounce) can diced tomatoes and green chiles
    with lime juice and cilantro
8 taco salad shells
1 small head iceberg lettuce, shredded
Toppings: shredded Monterey Jack cheese, pickled
    jalapeño slices, halved grape tomatoes, sour
    cream, chopped avocado

1. Rinse and sort beans according to package
directions.
2. Place pinto beans in a 6-quart slow cooker; add
roast and next 6 ingredients. Pour chicken broth
evenly over top of roast.
3. Cover and cook on HIGH 1 hour; reduce to LOW,
and cook 9 hours. Or, cover and cook on HIGH
6 hours. Remove bones and fat from roast; pull roast
into large pieces with two forks. Stir in diced tomatoes
and green chiles. Cook, uncovered, on HIGH 1 more
hour or until liquid is slightly thickened.
4. Heat taco salad shells according to package directions; place shredded lettuce evenly into shells. Spoon
about 1 cup pork-and-bean mixture into each shell
using a slotted spoon. Serve with desired toppings.
Makes 8 servings.
Note: For testing purposes only, we used RO-TEL
Mexican Festival tomatoes and a Rival Recipe
Smart-Pot slow cooker. Times may vary depending
on the slow cooker used.

Peppercorn Pork Roast
PREP: 20 MIN.; COOK: 1 HR., 45 MIN.

2 tablespoons olive oil
1 (4½-pound) rolled boneless pork loin roast
1 tablespoon mustard seeds
3 tablespoons cracked black peppercorns or
    multicolored peppercorns
2 tablespoons all-purpose flour
1 tablespoon dry mustard
2 teaspoons dried thyme
1 teaspoon brown sugar
¼ cup butter, softened
2 tablespoons Dijon mustard
1 tablespoon all-purpose flour
1½ cups apple cider, divided
1 tablespoon cider vinegar
1 teaspoon Dijon mustard
3 tablespoons apple brandy
½ teaspoon salt
¼ teaspoon ground black pepper

1. Heat oil in a heavy skillet over medium-high heat.
Add roast; brown on all sides. Place roast in a roasting
pan, and cool slightly.
2. Combine mustard seeds and peppercorns in a
heavy-duty, zip-top plastic freezer bag; seal. Crush
spices with a meat mallet or rolling pin.
3. Combine crushed spices, 2 tablespoons flour, and
next 3 ingredients; stir in ¼ cup butter and 2 tablespoons Dijon mustard. Spread mixture on top and
sides of roast.
4. Bake at 475° for 20 minutes; reduce heat to 325°.
Loosely cover with aluminum foil; bake 1 hour and
10 minutes or until a meat thermometer inserted
into thickest portion registers 160°. Remove roast
from pan, reserving 2 tablespoons drippings; keep
roast warm.
5. Combine reserved drippings, 1 tablespoon flour,
2 tablespoons apple cider, cider vinegar, and 1 teaspoon Dijon mustard; set aside.
6. Bring remaining apple cider to a boil in a saucepan over medium-high heat; boil 8 minutes or until
reduced to ¾ cup. Stir in brandy; boil 1 minute.
7. Whisk in flour mixture, salt, and pepper; cook over
medium-high heat until thickened. Serve with roast.
Makes 10 servings.

Margarita Pork Kabobs

PREP: 10 MIN., COOK: 10 MIN., OTHER: 30 MIN.

1 cup frozen margarita mix concentrate, thawed
1 teaspoon ground coriander
3 garlic cloves, minced
2 teaspoons lime zest
2 pounds pork tenderloin, cut into 1-inch cubes
3 ears fresh corn
1 tablespoon water
1 large onion, quartered
1 large green pepper, cut into 1-inch pieces
1 large sweet red pepper, cut into 1-inch pieces
Vegetable Cooking Spray

1. Combine first 4 ingredients in a shallow dish; add pork. Cover and marinate in refrigerator 30 minutes, turning occasionally.
2. Cut each ear of corn into 4 pieces. Place corn and 1 tablespoon water in an 8-inch square microwave-safe dish. Cover with heavy-duty plastic wrap, folding back one corner to allow steam to escape. Microwave at HIGH 4 minutes, giving dish a half turn after 2 minutes.
3. Remove pork from marinade, discarding marinade. Thread pork, corn, onion, and peppers onto skewers.
4. Coat grill rack with cooking spray; place on grill over medium-hot coals (350° to 400°). Place kabobs on rack; grill, covered with grill lid, 5 minutes on each side or until pork is done. **Makes** 4 servings.

Pork Medallions in Mustard Sauce

PREP: 10 MIN.; COOK: 25 MIN.; OTHER: 8 HR., 10 MIN.

3 tablespoons vegetable oil
1 tablespoon coarse-grained mustard
½ teaspoon salt
½ teaspoon pepper
2 (¾-pound) pork tenderloins
¼ cup dry white wine, divided
Mustard Sauce

1. Combine first 4 ingredients; rub over tenderloins. Place tenderloins in a large heavy-duty, zip-top plastic freezer bag. Seal bag; marinate in refrigerator 8 hours, turning bag occasionally.
2. Place tenderloins on a lightly greased rack in a shallow roasting pan; brush with half of wine. Insert meat thermometer into thickest part of 1 tenderloin. Bake at 400° for 25 minutes or until thermometer registers 160°, brushing with remaining half of wine after 10 minutes. Let stand 10 minutes before slicing. Cut tenderloins into ¼-inch slices; arrange slices evenly on four dinner plates. Spoon Mustard Sauce evenly around slices. **Makes** 4 servings.

Mustard Sauce

PREP: 5 MIN., COOK: 15 MIN.

1¾ cups whipping cream
¼ cup coarse-grained mustard
¼ teaspoon salt
⅛ teaspoon ground white pepper

1. Cook whipping cream in a medium saucepan over medium heat until reduced to 1¼ cups (about 15 minutes), stirring often. Add mustard, salt, and pepper; cook just until mixture is heated, stirring constantly. **Makes** 1⅓ cups.

Pan-Fried Pork Chops

Pan-Fried Pork Chops

PREP: 10 MIN., COOK: 2 MIN. PER BATCH

½ cup all-purpose flour
1 teaspoon salt
1 teaspoon seasoned pepper
1½ pounds wafer-thin boneless pork chops
¼ cup vegetable oil

1. Combine first 3 ingredients in a shallow dish, and dredge pork chops in flour mixture.
2. Fry pork chops, in 3 batches, in hot oil in a large skillet over medium-high heat 1 minute on each side or until browned. Drain on paper towels. **Makes** 6 to 8 servings.

Spicy-Sweet Ribs and Beans

PREP: 30 MIN.; COOK: 10 HR., 25 MIN.

2 (16-ounce) cans pinto beans, drained
4 pounds country-style pork ribs, trimmed
1 teaspoon garlic powder
½ teaspoon salt
½ teaspoon pepper
1 medium onion, chopped
1 (10.5-ounce) jar red jalapeño jelly
1 (18-ounce) bottle hickory-flavored barbecue sauce
1 teaspoon green hot sauce

1. Place beans in a 5-quart electric slow cooker; set aside.
2. Cut ribs apart; sprinkle with garlic powder, salt, and pepper. Place ribs on a broiling pan.
3. Broil 5½ inches from heat 18 to 20 minutes or until browned, turning once. Add ribs to slow cooker, and sprinkle with onion.
4. Combine jelly, barbecue sauce, and hot sauce in a saucepan; cook over low heat, stirring occasionally, until jelly melts. Pour over ribs; stir gently.
5. Cover and cook on HIGH 5 to 6 hours or on LOW 9 to 10 hours. Remove ribs. Drain bean mixture, reserving sauce. Skim fat from sauce. Arrange ribs over bean mixture; serve with sauce. **Makes** 8 servings.
Note: For testing purposes only, we used Kraft Thick 'n Spicy Hickory Smoke Barbecue Sauce and Tabasco Green Pepper Sauce.

Oven-Barbecued Pork Ribs

Country-style ribs are long and chunky, providing ample meat for hearty eaters. They make great picnic food, and you don't even need a grill.

PREP: 25 MIN.; COOK: 2 HR., 30 MIN.

2 tablespoons vegetable oil, divided
4 pounds country-style pork ribs
½ cup dry sherry
½ cup water
½ cup firmly packed brown sugar
1 teaspoon salt
1 teaspoon celery seeds
1 teaspoon chili powder
⅛ teaspoon pepper
2 cups water
¼ cup white vinegar
¼ cup Worcestershire sauce
1 (12-ounce) bottle chili sauce
1 medium onion, chopped

1. Add 1 tablespoon oil to a large nonstick skillet; place over medium-high heat until hot. Brown half of ribs in skillet; set aside. Brown remaining ribs in remaining 1 tablespoon oil. Return ribs to skillet; add sherry and ½ cup water. Bring to a boil. Cover, reduce heat, and simmer 1½ hours.
2. Meanwhile, combine brown sugar and remaining 9 ingredients in a 2-quart saucepan. Bring to a boil; simmer, uncovered, over medium heat 1 hour.
3. Transfer ribs to a 13- x 9-inch pan; pour sauce over ribs. Bake, uncovered, at 300° for 1 hour, basting occasionally. **Makes** 4 servings.

Sweet-and-Tangy Ribs

These delectable ribs cook in two stages. First you apply a seasoning rub and bake them; then finish them on the grill the next day, basting with a tangy-sweet sauce.

PREP: 20 MIN.; COOK: 1 HR., 30 MIN.; OTHER: 8 HR.

4 pounds country-style ribs
1 (12-ounce) can beer
1 teaspoon black pepper
½ teaspoon seasoned salt
½ teaspoon garlic powder
¼ teaspoon dried crushed red pepper
2 green onions, chopped
1 tablespoon vegetable oil
1 cup barbecue sauce
½ cup peach preserves
2 tablespoons white wine vinegar

1. Place ribs on two layers of heavy-duty aluminum foil. Pour beer over ribs. Combine black pepper and next 3 ingredients; sprinkle over ribs. Seal foil packet tightly. Bake at 350° for 1 hour. Cool. Cover and chill ribs overnight.
2. Sauté green onions in oil in a large skillet over medium-high heat until tender. Add barbecue sauce, preserves, and vinegar; stir well. Simmer 1 minute; remove from heat.
3. Grill ribs, uncovered, over medium-hot coals (350° to 400°) 20 to 30 minutes, basting heavily with barbecue sauce mixture the last 5 minutes. Serve ribs with remaining barbecue sauce mixture. **Makes** 4 servings.

Planet Barbecue

Southern barbecue varies as much as our accents. Agreement ends there. North Carolinians brush pork with a peppery-vinegary sauce. Georgians like their BBQ sauce sweeter and red on pork ribs or on chicken. In South Carolina, mustard-based sauces are mopped on pork or chicken. Alabamians prefer a thin, tangy tomato-based sauce on pork. Tennessee BBQers guard their top secret recipes for spices rubbed over pork. Texans claim there's no point to BBQ if beef isn't the base. And don't even let us start on the side dishes!

Smothered Swiss Steak

SLOW COOKER
Smothered Swiss Steak

A cola soft drink is the secret ingredient for these slow-cooked steaks with a juicy tomato-based sauce.
Start table talk by asking everyone to guess the surprise flavoring.

PREP: 15 MIN.; COOK: 1 HR., 35 MIN.

½ teaspoon salt
6 (4-ounce) cube steaks
½ cup all-purpose flour
1 teaspoon seasoned pepper
4½ tablespoons vegetable oil
1 medium onion, diced
1 medium-size green pepper, diced
1 (14.5-ounce) can petite diced tomatoes
1 (12-ounce) cola soft drink
1 tablespoon beef bouillon granules
2 tablespoons tomato paste

1. Sprinkle salt evenly on both sides of cube steaks. Combine flour and pepper in a shallow dish. Dredge steaks in flour mixture.

2. Brown 2 steaks in 1½ tablespoons hot oil in a large nonstick skillet over medium-high heat 3 minutes on each side; drain on paper towels. Repeat procedure with remaining steaks and oil. Drain drippings from skillet, reserving 1 tablespoon in skillet.

3. Sauté onion and green pepper in hot drippings 7 minutes or until tender. Add diced tomatoes and next 3 ingredients to skillet. Bring to a boil, and cook, stirring often, 5 minutes or until slightly thickened. Return steaks to skillet; cover and cook over low heat 55 to 60 minutes or until tender. **Makes** 6 servings.
Note: To prepare this recipe in the slow cooker, place seared cubed steaks in a 5-quart slow cooker. After cola mixture has cooked 5 minutes, spoon it over seared cube steaks. Cover and cook on LOW 5 hours.

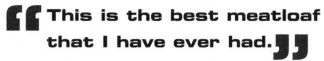

" This is the best meatloaf that I have ever had. "

MARIAN COOPER CAIRNS, TEST KITCHENS PROFESSIONAL

(**EDITOR'S CHOICE**)
Simple Meatloaf

Ground chuck offers lots of flavor and is less expensive, but we chose lean ground beef because it has less fat.

PREP: 10 MIN., COOK: 1 HR., OTHER: 5 MIN.

1½ pounds 85% lean ground beef
¾ cup quick-cooking oats
¾ cup milk
¼ cup chopped onion
1 large egg, lightly beaten
1½ teaspoons salt
¼ teaspoon pepper
⅓ cup ketchup
2 tablespoons brown sugar
1 tablespoon yellow mustard

1. Combine first 7 ingredients in a large bowl just until blended; place in a lightly greased 9- x 5-inch loaf pan.
2. Stir together ketchup, brown sugar, and yellow mustard; pour evenly over meatloaf.
3. Bake at 350° for 1 hour. Remove from oven; let stand 5 minutes, and remove from pan before slicing. **Makes** 6 servings.
Note: Wrap meatloaf in plastic wrap and aluminum foil, and freeze up to 1 month. Thaw in refrigerator overnight.

Leftover Tips

Leftover meatloaf is a wonderful thing. While it's warm and comforting when snuggled up to mashed potatoes, meatloaf is downright luscious layered on bread with mayonnaise or tomato sauce. Use your favorite recipe for the basic loaf, or try the one offered here. And because you can't just conjure up meatloaf out of the air when the urge for a sandwich strikes, double the recipe and freeze one to keep on hand. One of these midnights, you'll be really glad you did.

QUICK
Italian Meatloaf Sandwich

This great flavor combo also works with leftover roast beef or pot roast.

PREP: 15 MIN., BAKE: 15 MIN.

1 (14-ounce) French bread loaf
8 (1-inch-thick) cold meatloaf slices
1 cup marinara or spaghetti sauce
1 (8-ounce) package shredded Italian cheese blend
¼ teaspoon dried Italian seasoning

1. Cut bread into fourths; cut quarters in half horizontally. Place bread quarters, cut sides up, on a baking sheet. Top each bread bottom with 2 meatloaf slices, 2 tablespoons marinara sauce, and ¼ cup cheese. Top each bread top with 2 tablespoons marinara sauce and ¼ cup cheese; sprinkle with Italian seasoning.
2. Bake at 375° for 10 to 15 minutes or until cheese melts and meat is thoroughly heated. Top bread bottoms with bread tops; serve sandwiches immediately. **Makes** 4 servings.

Basil-Tomato Meatloaf Sandwich

You'll love the flavor boost when you stir fresh basil into mayonnaise.

PREP: 10 MIN.

½ cup mayonnaise
1 tablespoon chopped fresh basil
8 hearty white bread slices
8 (½-inch-thick) cold meatloaf slices
1 cup shredded iceberg lettuce
2 plum tomatoes, sliced
Salt and pepper to taste

1. Stir together ½ cup mayonnaise and 1 tablespoon chopped fresh basil. Spread 1 tablespoon mayonnaise mixture on 1 side of each bread slice. Top 4 bread slices, mayonnaise sides up, evenly with meatloaf slices, shredded lettuce, and tomato slices; sprinkle with salt and pepper to taste. Top with remaining bread slices, mayonnaise sides down. **Makes** 4 servings.
Note: For testing purposes only, we used Sara Lee Honey White Bakery Bread.

Southwestern Beef Tips and Noodles

The wonderful earthy essence of cumin spices this old-fashioned entrée with Southwestern flavor. Using Mexican-style tomatoes kicks up the heat.

PREP: 20 MIN., COOK: 1 HR.

¼ cup all-purpose flour
2 pounds boneless top sirloin roast, cut into
    ½-inch cubes
¼ cup vegetable oil
1 (14½-ounce) can diced tomatoes or
    Mexican-style diced tomatoes, undrained
1 medium onion, chopped
¼ cup chopped green pepper
1 garlic clove, minced
1 teaspoon ground cumin
¼ teaspoon salt
¼ teaspoon pepper
Hot cooked egg noodles

1. Place flour in a heavy-duty, zip-top plastic freezer bag. Add beef cubes; seal bag, and shake until meat is coated with flour.
2. Brown beef in hot oil in a Dutch oven, stirring often. Add tomatoes and next 6 ingredients; bring to a boil. Cover, reduce heat, and simmer 30 minutes. Uncover and simmer 30 more minutes or until beef tips are tender, stirring occasionally. Serve over egg noodles. **Makes** 6 servings.

(EDITOR'S CHOICE)
Beef-and-Green Onion Stir-fry

You can substitute presliced steak for the sirloin. Look for it in the meat department of your grocery store. Serve the stir-fry over hot cooked rice, if desired.

PREP: 15 MIN., COOK: 10 MIN.

1½ bunches green onions
1 pound top round steak*
3 tablespoons cornstarch, divided
3 tablespoons lite soy sauce
1 medium-size red bell pepper, thinly sliced
2 tablespoons vegetable oil
1 teaspoon sesame oil (optional)
1 cup beef broth
2 tablespoons rice wine vinegar
¼ to ½ teaspoon dried crushed red pepper
Peanuts (optional)

1. Thoroughly wash green onions. Remove root ends and tips of onions; cut into 2-inch pieces. Place pieces in a large bowl.
2. Cut steak across the grain into thin slices, and add to green onions in bowl. Sprinkle with 2 tablespoons cornstarch and soy sauce, tossing to coat.
3. Sauté beef mixture and red bell pepper, in 2 batches, in hot vegetable oil and, if desired, sesame oil in a large nonstick skillet over medium-high heat 3 minutes or until beef is done and bell pepper is crisp-tender. Whisk together beef broth, vinegar, red pepper flakes, and remaining 1 tablespoon cornstarch. Add to beef mixture in skillet, and bring to a boil. Cook 1 minute or until thickened. Top with peanuts, if desired. **Makes** 4 servings.
*1 pound skinned and boned chicken breasts may be substituted.

❝This is one of my family's most requested meals. It's perfect for weeknights. I serve it over jasmine rice, which I let cook while I prep and cook the other ingredients. That way everything finishes at the same time.❞

ASHLEY LEATH, ASSISTANT RECIPE EDITOR

Easy Chicken Cassoulet

PREP: 25 MIN.; COOK: 1 HR., 15 MIN.; OTHER: 10 MIN.

8 skinned and boned chicken thighs (about
    2 pounds)
½ teaspoon salt
¾ teaspoon pepper, divided
3 tablespoons olive oil
1 (8-ounce) package sliced fresh mushrooms
2 to 3 teaspoons minced fresh or dried rosemary
½ cup dry white wine
2 (15-ounce) cans navy beans, rinsed, drained,
    and divided
1 cup grated Parmesan cheese
¾ cup fine, dry breadcrumbs*
1 (14.5-ounce) can chicken broth
2 tablespoons butter, cut up

1. Sprinkle chicken evenly with salt and ½ teaspoon
pepper. Brown chicken, in batches, on both sides
in hot oil in a large skillet over medium-high heat.
Remove chicken; chop and set aside.

2. Add mushrooms and rosemary to skillet, and sauté
3 minutes.

3. Stir in white wine, and cook 5 minutes. Remove
from heat, and add 1 can navy beans.

4. Spoon bean mixture evenly into 4 (2-cup) crocks or
baking dishes. Top evenly with chopped chicken.

5. Sprinkle evenly with ½ cup Parmesan cheese, ½ cup
breadcrumbs, and remaining ¼ teaspoon pepper. Top
evenly with remaining can navy beans. Drizzle with
chicken broth. Sprinkle evenly with remaining ½ cup
Parmesan cheese and remaining ¼ cup breadcrumbs;
dot with butter.

6. Bake, covered loosely with aluminum foil, at 350°
for 40 minutes. Remove foil, and bake 20 more
minutes or until golden brown. Let stand 10 minutes.
Makes 4 servings.

*Soft breadcrumbs may be substituted for fine, dry
breadcrumbs.

Plum Good Chicken Fajitas

We love the flavor of this homemade plum sauce. Make it ahead, and keep it in your refrigerator up to 2 weeks.

PREP: 15 MIN., COOK: 17 MIN.

Plum Sauce (opposite page)
1 red bell pepper, cut into strips
1 green bell pepper, cut into strips
1 large red onion, sliced
2 tablespoons olive oil
2 pounds skinned and boned chicken breasts
8 (8-inch) flour tortillas, warmed
Lime wedges
Toppings: guacamole, pico de gallo

1. Prepare Plum Sauce as directed. Remove and reserve 1 cup for basting. Keep remaining sauce warm.
2. Sauté bell peppers and onion in hot oil in a large skillet over medium-high heat 3 minutes or until crisp-tender. Keep warm.

3. Grill chicken over medium-high heat (350° to 400°) 7 minutes on each side or until done, basting often with 1 cup reserved Plum Sauce. Cut chicken into thin strips. Serve with sautéed vegetables, remaining Plum Sauce, warm tortillas, lime wedges, and desired toppings. **Makes** 8 servings.

Skillet Fajitas: Prepare Plum Sauce, and sauté vegetables as directed. Cut chicken into thin strips. Cook, in batches, in 1 tablespoon olive oil in a large skillet over medium-high heat, stirring often, 10 minutes or until done. Cook chicken and ¼ cup Plum Sauce until thoroughly heated.

Plum Sauce

PREP: 15 MIN., COOK: 20 MIN.

1 tablespoon butter
1 small onion, chopped
1 (7.6-ounce) jar Asian plum sauce
½ (6-ounce) can frozen lemonade concentrate
½ cup chili sauce
¼ cup soy sauce
1 tablespoon dry mustard
1 teaspoon ground ginger
1 teaspoon Worcestershire sauce
¼ teaspoon hot sauce

1. Melt butter in a medium saucepan over medium-high heat; add chopped onion, and sauté until tender. Stir in plum sauce and remaining ingredients. Bring sauce to a boil; reduce heat, and simmer 15 minutes. **Makes** about 2 cups.

FAMILY FAVORITE
Easy Chicken Enchiladas

PREP: 15 MIN., COOK: 25 MIN.

2 cups chopped cooked chicken
2 cups sour cream
1 (10¾-ounce) can cream of chicken soup
1½ cups (6 ounces) shredded Monterey Jack cheese
1½ cups (6 ounces) shredded Colby Jack cheese
1 (4.5-ounce) can chopped green chiles, drained
2 tablespoons chopped onion
¼ teaspoon pepper
⅛ teaspoon salt
10 (10-inch) corn tortillas
Vegetable oil
1 cup (4 ounces) shredded Colby Jack cheese
Salsa

1. Combine first 9 ingredients; stir well. Fry tortillas, 1 at a time, in 2 tablespoons oil in a skillet 5 seconds on each side or until softened; add additional oil, if necessary. Drain.
2. Place heaping ½ cup chicken mixture on each tortilla; roll up each tortilla, and place, seam side down, in a 13- x 9-inch baking dish.
3. Cover and bake at 350° for 20 minutes. Sprinkle with 1 cup cheese, and bake, uncovered, 5 more minutes. Serve with salsa. **Makes** 5 servings.

FAMILY FAVORITE
Chicken Divan

Chicken Divan nestles broccoli spears next to chicken in a subtle curried cream sauce.

PREP: 15 MIN., COOK: 56 MIN.

4 bone-in chicken breasts, skinned
½ teaspoon salt
¼ teaspoon pepper
2 tablespoons butter
¼ cup all-purpose flour
1 cup milk
1 egg yolk, beaten
1 cup sour cream
½ cup mayonnaise
½ teaspoon lemon zest
2 tablespoons lemon juice
½ teaspoon salt
¼ to ½ teaspoon curry powder
2 (10-ounce) packages frozen broccoli spears, thawed and drained
⅓ cup grated Parmesan cheese
Paprika

1. Place first 3 ingredients in a large saucepan; add water to cover. Bring to a boil. Cover, reduce heat, and simmer 15 to 20 minutes or until chicken is tender. Drain, reserving ½ cup broth. Let chicken cool slightly. Bone and chop chicken; set aside.
2. Melt butter in a small heavy saucepan over low heat; add flour, stirring until smooth. Cook 1 minute, stirring constantly. Gradually add milk and reserved broth; cook over medium heat, stirring constantly, until thickened and bubbly.
3. Stir one-fourth of hot mixture into egg yolk; add to remaining hot mixture and cook 1 minute, stirring constantly. Remove from heat; stir in sour cream and next 5 ingredients.
4. Layer half each of broccoli, chicken, and sauce in a greased 2-quart baking dish. Repeat layers. Sprinkle with Parmesan cheese.
5. Bake, uncovered, at 350° for 30 to 35 minutes. Sprinkle with paprika. **Makes** 4 servings.

Slow-Roasted Chicken

This easy entrée first bakes covered and then uncovered for even browning. The broth in the pan helps keep the meat moist.

PREP: 10 MIN.; COOK: 1 HR., 30 MIN.

1 (4- to 4½-pound) whole chicken
1 onion, cut into 1-inch pieces
6 garlic cloves
½ teaspoon salt
¼ teaspoon pepper
2 tablespoons olive oil
1 cup chicken broth

1. Remove giblets from chicken. Place giblets, onion, and garlic in a shallow roasting pan.
2. Tuck wings under; tie legs together with string, if desired. Place chicken, breast side up, over giblets and vegetables; sprinkle with salt and pepper. Drizzle chicken and giblet mixture with oil. Add broth to roasting pan.
3. Cover and bake at 350° for 1 hour. Uncover and bake 30 more minutes or until a meat thermometer inserted in chicken thigh registers 170°. **Makes** 4 to 6 servings.

MAKE AHEAD
Greek Baked Chicken

PREP: 10 MIN., COOK: 35 MIN., OTHER: 8 HR.

⅓ cup olive oil
¼ cup lemon juice
1 teaspoon salt
½ teaspoon dried oregano
¼ teaspoon pepper
1 (2½- to 3-pound) broiler-fryer

1. Stir together first 5 ingredients.
2. Place chicken in a shallow dish or large heavy-duty, zip-top plastic freezer bag; pour oil mixture over chicken. Cover or seal; marinate in refrigerator 8 hours.
3. Remove chicken from marinade, discarding marinade. Tuck wings under, and tie legs together with string, if desired. Place chicken, breast side up, on a rack in a shallow roasting pan.
4. Bake at 450° for 35 minutes or until a meat thermometer inserted in chicken thigh registers 170°.
Makes 3 servings.

FAMILY FAVORITE, QUICK
Parmesan Baked Chicken

Here's an easy oven-fried recipe.

PREP: 5 MIN., COOK: 30 MIN.

½ cup fine, dry breadcrumbs
¼ cup grated Parmesan cheese
½ teaspoon dried basil
½ teaspoon dried thyme
¼ teaspoon salt
4 skinned and boned chicken breasts
¼ cup butter, melted

1. Combine first 5 ingredients in a heavy-duty, zip-top plastic freezer bag; seal bag, and shake well.
2. Dip chicken in butter. Add 1 piece of chicken at a time to breadcrumb mixture; seal bag, and shake until well coated. Place chicken on a greased baking sheet. Bake at 400° for 25 to 30 minutes or until done. **Makes** 4 servings.

How to Flatten Chicken

A zip-top plastic freezer bag keeps the chicken in place and prevents contamination as you flatten it with a meat mallet.

Chicken Breasts Lombardy

*This easy chicken bake is elegant enough for entertaining too. Serve it over pasta
with a side of steamed green beans.*

PREP: 20 MIN., COOK: 59 MIN.

1 (8-ounce) package sliced fresh mushrooms
2 tablespoons butter, melted
6 skinned and boned chicken breasts
½ cup all-purpose flour
⅓ cup butter
¾ cup Marsala*
½ cup chicken broth
½ teaspoon salt
⅛ teaspoon pepper
½ cup (2 ounces) shredded mozzarella cheese
½ cup grated Parmesan cheese
2 green onions, chopped

1. Cook mushrooms in 2 tablespoons butter in a large nonstick skillet over medium heat, stirring constantly, 3 to 5 minutes or just until tender. Remove from heat; set aside.

2. Cut each chicken breast in half lengthwise. Place chicken between 2 sheets of heavy-duty plastic wrap; flatten to ⅛-inch thickness, using a meat mallet or rolling pin.

3. Dredge chicken pieces in flour. Cook chicken, in batches, in 1 to 2 tablespoons butter in a large nonstick skillet over medium heat 3 to 4 minutes on each side or until golden. Place chicken in a lightly greased 13- x 9-inch baking dish, overlapping edges. Repeat procedure with remaining chicken and butter. Reserve pan drippings in skillet. Sprinkle mushrooms evenly over chicken.

4. Add wine and broth to skillet. Bring to a boil; reduce heat, and simmer, uncovered, 10 minutes, stirring occasionally. Stir in salt and pepper. Pour sauce over chicken. Combine cheeses and green onions; sprinkle over chicken.

5. Bake, uncovered, at 450° for 12 to 14 minutes or until cheese melts. **Makes** 6 servings.

*⅔ cup dry white wine plus 2 tablespoons brandy may be substituted for Marsala.

Praline Chicken

Praline Chicken

Speak of pralines, and most people think of the sugar-pecan candy icon of New Orleans. In this recipe,
the traditional candy ingredients are drizzled over chicken for a delectable entrée.

PREP: 14 MIN., COOK: 28 MIN.

6 skinned and boned chicken breasts
2 teaspoons Creole seasoning
¼ cup butter, melted
1 tablespoon vegetable oil
⅓ cup maple syrup
2 tablespoons brown sugar
1 cup chopped pecans, toasted

1. Sprinkle both sides of chicken with Creole seasoning. Cook chicken in butter and oil in a large skillet over medium-high heat 4 to 5 minutes on each side or until done. Remove chicken, reserving drippings in skillet. Place chicken on a serving platter; set aside, and keep warm.

2. Add maple syrup and sugar to drippings in skillet; bring to a boil. Stir in pecans, and cook 1 minute or until thoroughly heated. Spoon pecan mixture over chicken. **Makes** 6 servings.

Turkey Piccata

Add colorful pasta to brighten up this tangy dish.

PREP: 15 MIN., COOK: 5 MIN.

2 tablespoons lemon juice, divided
½ pound turkey breast cutlets
1½ tablespoons all-purpose flour
½ teaspoon paprika
¼ teaspoon ground white pepper
2 tablespoons olive oil
¼ cup dry white wine
1 tablespoon drained capers
1½ teaspoons chopped fresh parsley

1. Drizzle 1 tablespoon lemon juice over cutlets. Combine 1½ tablespoons flour, paprika, and white pepper; dredge cutlets in flour mixture.

2. Cook turkey cutlets in 2 tablespoons hot oil in a medium nonstick skillet over medium-high heat 2 minutes on each side or until browned. Transfer cutlets to a serving platter; keep warm.

3. Combine wine and remaining 1 tablespoon lemon juice in skillet; bring to a boil over medium heat, stirring constantly. Add capers, and cook 1 minute. Pour caper mixture over cutlets, and sprinkle with parsley. **Makes** 2 servings.

Turkey Piccata

Parmesan Corn Muffins

PREP: 10 MIN., COOK: 15 MIN.

2 cups white cornmeal mix
¾ cup all-purpose flour
½ cup grated Parmesan cheese
¼ teaspoon ground red pepper
2½ cups fat-free buttermilk
½ cup egg substitute
2 tablespoons vegetable oil
Vegetable cooking spray

1. Combine first 4 ingredients in a large mixing bowl, and make a well in center of mixture.
2. Stir together buttermilk, egg substitute, and oil; add to dry ingredients, stirring just until moistened. Spoon into muffin pans coated with cooking spray, filling two-thirds full.
3. Bake at 425° for 15 minutes or until golden. Remove from pans immediately, and cool on wire racks. **Makes** 17 muffins.

Per muffin: Calories 118; Fat 3.7g (sat 1g, mono 1.5g, poly 0.9g); Protein 5g; Carb 16g; Fiber 1g; Chol 5mg; Iron 1.2mg; Sodium 284mg; Calc 138mg

Berry-and-Spice Whole-Wheat Muffins

PREP: 15 MIN., COOK: 21 MIN., OTHER: 5 MIN.

¼ cup firmly packed light brown sugar
1 tablespoon all-purpose flour
3 tablespoons chopped pecans
1 tablespoon butter, melted
1 cup all-purpose flour
1 cup whole-wheat flour
¼ cup sugar
¾ teaspoon baking powder
¾ teaspoon baking soda
½ teaspoon ground cinnamon
¼ teaspoon ground allspice
1 egg
1¼ cups buttermilk
1½ tablespoons vegetable oil
1 cup fresh or frozen blueberries

1. Combine brown sugar, 1 tablespoon all-purpose flour, and pecans in a small bowl. Stir in melted butter; set aside.

2. Combine 1 cup all-purpose flour, whole-wheat flour, and next 5 ingredients in a large bowl; make a well in center of mixture.
3. Stir together egg, buttermilk, and oil; add to dry ingredients, stirring just until moistened. Fold in blueberries.
4. Spoon about ⅓ cup batter into each of 12 lightly greased muffin cups. Sprinkle batter evenly with reserved pecan mixture.
5. Bake at 375° for 19 to 21 minutes or until lightly browned. Cool in pans on wire rack 5 minutes. Remove from pans, and cool slightly on wire rack. Serve warm. **Makes** 1 dozen.

Per muffin: Calories 168; Fat 5g; (sat 1.2g, mono 2, poly 1.4g); Protein 4.2g; Carb 28g; Fiber 2g; Chol 21mg; Iron 1.2mg; Sodium 151mg; Calc 61mg

Fruit-and-Bran Muffins

PREP: 15 MIN., COOK: 20 MIN., OTHER: 5 MIN.

1 cup fat-free milk
2 cups O-shaped sweetened oat-and-wheat bran cereal
1 large Granny Smith apple, peeled and diced
1¼ cups uncooked oat bran hot cereal
⅓ cup golden raisins
¼ cup firmly packed dark brown sugar
¼ cup egg substitute
1 tablespoon baking powder
½ teaspoon ground cinnamon
¼ teaspoon ground nutmeg
3 tablespoons applesauce
Vegetable cooking spray

1. Bring milk to a boil in a large saucepan; remove from heat, and stir in O-shaped cereal. Let stand 5 minutes or until cereal is softened.
2. Stir in apple and next 8 ingredients until blended.
3. Place paper baking cups in muffin pans, and lightly coat with cooking spray. Spoon batter evenly into cups.
4. Bake at 375° for 18 to 20 minutes or until a wooden pick inserted in center comes out clean. **Makes** 1 dozen.
Note: For testing purposes only, we used Cracklin' Oat Bran Cereal for sweetened cereal and Hodgson Mill Oat Bran Hot Cereal for uncooked cereal.

Per muffin: Calories 150; Fat 2.9g (sat 0.6g, mono 1.1g, poly 0.4g); Protein 5.2g; Carb 27.3g; Fiber 4.1g; Chol 0.5mg; Iron 1.9mg; Sodium 158mg; Calc 118mg

Blueberry-Cinnamon Muffins

Blueberry-Cinnamon Muffins

To prevent the berries from bleeding, toss them in flour, and then gently fold them into the batter.

PREP: 25 MIN., COOK: 20 MIN., OTHER: 5 MIN.

¼ cup uncooked regular oats
2 tablespoons brown sugar
1 teaspoon ground cinnamon, divided
¼ cup butter, softened
1 cup granulated sugar
½ cup egg substitute
1 teaspoon vanilla extract
2 cups all-purpose flour
1 teaspoon baking soda
½ teaspoon baking powder
½ teaspoon salt
1¼ cups fat-free buttermilk
1 cup fresh blueberries
Vegetable cooking spray

1. Stir together oats, brown sugar, and ½ teaspoon cinnamon; set aside.

2. Beat butter and granulated sugar at medium speed with an electric mixer until fluffy. Add egg substitute, beating until blended. Stir in vanilla.

3. Combine all-purpose flour, baking soda, baking powder, salt, and remaining ½ teaspoon cinnamon; add to butter mixture alternately with buttermilk, ending with flour mixture.

4. Gently stir in blueberries. Spoon batter evenly into muffin pans coated with cooking spray, filling two-thirds full. Sprinkle evenly with oat mixture.

5. Bake at 350° for 15 to 20 minutes or until tops are golden. Cool muffins in pans 5 minutes; remove from pans, and cool on wire racks. **Makes** 15 muffins.

Per muffin: Calories 174; Fat 4g (sat 2g, mono 1.1g, poly 0.4g); Protein 3.7g; Carb 31g; Fiber 0.9g; Chol 9mg; Iron 1.1mg; Sodium 249mg; Calc 39mg

Grilled Burgers With Tahini Sauce

PREP: 20 MIN., COOK: 12 MIN.

1 pound extra-lean ground beef
1 teaspoon Greek seasoning
4 pita rounds
4 lettuce leaves
8 large tomato slices
4 thin red onion slices
Tahini Sauce
¼ cup feta cheese (optional)

1. Combine beef and Greek seasoning. Shape into 4 patties.
2. Grill, covered with grill lid, over medium-high heat (350° to 400°) 5 to 6 minutes on each side or until beef is no longer pink.
3. Cut off and discard 2 inches of bread from 1 side of each pita round, forming a pocket. Line each with 1 lettuce leaf, 2 tomato slices, and 1 red onion slice.

Add burger. Drizzle each with 2 tablespoons Tahini Sauce; sprinkle with 1 tablespoon cheese, if desired. **Makes** 4 servings.

Tahini Sauce:
Look for tahini paste in the ethnic food aisle of major supermarkets. You can make this sauce a few days ahead.

PREP: 10 MIN.

¼ cup tahini paste
¼ cup water
2 tablespoons fresh lemon juice
⅛ teaspoon garlic powder
¼ teaspoon salt

1. Whisk together all ingredients.

Per serving (including sauce): Calories 377; Fat 13g (sat 2.8g, mono 4.7g, poly 4.3g); Protein 26.4g; Carb 41g; Fiber 3g; Chol 48mg; Iron 4mg; Sodium 551mg; Calc 81mg

Grilled Flank Steak With
Molasses Barbecue Glaze

Grilled Flank Steak With Molasses Barbecue Glaze

*Serve this flavorful steak with wild rice and a tossed salad. Or host a fiesta,
and offer it with flour tortillas and your favorite Tex-Mex toppings.*

PREP: 10 MIN., COOK: 12 MIN., OTHER: 2 HR.

½ cup molasses
¼ cup coarse-grained mustard
1 tablespoon olive oil
1 (1½-pound) flank steak

1. Whisk together first 3 ingredients.
2. Place steak in a shallow dish or large zip-top
plastic freezer bag. Pour molasses mixture over steak,
reserving ¼ cup for basting. Cover or seal, and chill,
turning occasionally, 2 hours. Remove meat from
marinade, discarding marinade.
3. Grill, covered with grill lid, over medium-high
heat (350° to 400°) 6 minutes on each side or to
desired degree of doneness, brushing often with
reserved ¼ cup marinade. Cut steak diagonally across
the grain into very thin strips. **Makes** 6 servings.

Per serving: Calories 256; Fat 9g (sat 3.1g, mono 4.3g, poly 0.5g); Protein 22.5g; Carb 20.3g;
Fiber 0g; Chol 45mg; Iron 2.8mg; Sodium 186mg; Calc 68mg

Creamy Lamb Curry

Serve this aromatic, full-flavored dish over basmati rice, a nutty-tasting long-grain variety. Look for garam masala, a fragrant spice mixture, in Indian markets or in the spice or ethnic sections of supermarkets. It's available in the McCormick Gourmet Collection, or find it online at www.ethnicgrocer.com. The flavor makes it worth the search.

PREP: 20 MIN.; COOK: 1 HR., 15 MIN.

2 pounds lean boneless lamb, cut into 2-inch pieces
½ teaspoon salt
Vegetable cooking spray
1 medium onion, chopped (1 cup)
1 (1-inch) piece fresh ginger, peeled and minced
2 garlic cloves, minced
2 teaspoons ground coriander
1 teaspoon ground cumin
⅛ teaspoon ground cloves
2 bay leaves
1 (1-inch) cinnamon stick
2 cups fat-free reduced-sodium chicken broth
1 (14.5-ounce) can diced tomatoes, undrained
½ cup plain nonfat yogurt
1 tablespoon garam masala
8 fresh mint leaves, chopped

1. Sprinkle lamb pieces with salt.
2. Cook lamb, in batches, in a Dutch oven coated with cooking spray over medium-high heat, stirring often, 5 minutes or until lamb is lightly browned. Remove and set aside.
3. Sauté onion and ginger in a Dutch oven coated with cooking spray over medium-high heat 1 to 2 minutes.
4. Add garlic; cook 1 minute. Stir in coriander and next 4 ingredients. Add cooked lamb, broth, and tomatoes; bring to a boil. Cover, reduce heat, and simmer 1 hour or until lamb is tender. Remove bay leaves and cinnamon stick. Remove from heat; add yogurt and garam masala, stirring until blended. Sprinkle with mint. **Makes** 6 servings.

Per serving: Calories 257; Fat 11g (sat 4.5g, mono 4g, poly 0.5g); Protein 29.6g; Carb 9.2g; Fiber 1.3g; Chol 101mg; Iron 2.4mg; Sodium 512mg; Calc 109mg

FAMILY FAVORITE
Apple-a-Day Pork Chops

PREP: 20 MIN., COOK: 30 MIN.

6 (4-ounce) boneless pork loin chops
Vegetable cooking spray
1½ teaspoons dried crushed rosemary
½ to ¾ teaspoon salt
½ to ¾ teaspoon freshly ground pepper
1 medium-size Red Delicious apple, peeled and chopped
½ cup golden raisins
½ cup currants
2 teaspoons olive oil
¾ cup Marsala or apple cider
Garnishes: rosemary sprigs, apple slices

1. Coat both sides of pork chops evenly with cooking spray.
2. Combine rosemary, salt, and pepper. Rub mixture evenly on both sides of pork, and set aside.
3. Cook apple, raisins, and currants in hot oil in a large skillet over medium-high heat, stirring often, 5 minutes. Add ¼ cup Marsala, stirring constantly, until most of the liquid is evaporated. Add remaining ½ cup Marsala, and cook 15 minutes or until mixture is thickened. Keep warm.
4. Cook pork chops in a large skillet coated with cooking spray over medium-high heat 5 minutes on each side or until done. Top with apple mixture. Garnish, if desired. **Makes** 6 servings.

Per serving: Calories 286; Fat 10.9g (sat 3.3g, mono 5g, poly 1.1g); Protein 24.5g; Carb 23g; Fiber 1.4g; Chol 68mg; Iron 1.9mg; Sodium 276mg; Calc 38mg

FAMILY FAVORITE, QUICK
Fried Pork Chops With Cream Gravy

PREP: 5 MIN., COOK: 25 MIN.

1 cup all-purpose flour
1 teaspoon Cajun seasoning
¼ teaspoon garlic powder
¼ teaspoon pepper
8 (4-ounce) boneless center-cut pork chops
1 cup nonfat buttermilk
Vegetable cooking spray
3 tablespoons vegetable oil
1 cup fat-free milk
¼ teaspoon salt
Garnish: coarsely ground pepper

1. Reserve 2 tablespoons flour, and set aside. Place remaining flour in a shallow dish.
2. Combine Cajun seasoning, garlic powder, and ¼ teaspoon pepper. Rub pork chops evenly on both sides with seasoning mixture.
3. Dip pork in buttermilk; dredge in flour. Lightly coat both sides of pork with cooking spray.
4. Cook pork, in batches, in hot oil in a large heavy skillet over medium-high heat 5 minutes on each side or until golden brown. Drain on paper towels.
5. Add reserved 2 tablespoons flour to pan drippings in skillet; stir in milk and salt, and cook, stirring constantly, until thickened and bubbly. Serve immediately with pork. Garnish, if desired. **Makes** 8 servings.

Per serving: Calories 267; Fat 12.3g (sat 3.7g, mono 4.9g, poly 2.6g); Protein 26.2g; Carb 11.2g; Fiber 0.3g; Chol 69mg; Iron 1.5mg; Sodium 250mg; Calc 63mg

Grilled Pork Tenderloin With Orange Marmalade

Add some vitamin-packed green veggies, such as sautéed Brussels sprouts, to your plate. You can also sauté bell pepper and onion, and stir it into the marmalade.

PREP: 20 MIN., COOK: 35 MIN., OTHER: 1 HR.

1 cup pineapple juice
¼ cup apple cider vinegar
¼ cup lite soy sauce
1 (1½-pound) package pork tenderloins
1 (12-ounce) jar orange marmalade*

1. Combine first 3 ingredients in a shallow dish or large zip-top plastic freezer bag; add pork tenderloins. Cover or seal, and chill 1 hour.

2. Cook orange marmalade in a small saucepan over medium heat until melted. Remove and reserve ¼ cup for basting; keep remaining marmalade warm.

3. Remove pork from marinade, discarding marinade.

4. Grill pork, covered with grill lid, over medium-high heat (350° to 400°) 25 minutes or until a meat thermometer inserted into thickest portion registers 160°, basting with reserved ¼ cup marmalade the last 5 minutes. Serve with remaining warm marmalade. **Makes** 6 servings.

*1 (10.5-ounce) jar red pepper jelly or 1 (10.5-ounce) jar jalapeño pepper jelly may be substituted for orange marmalade.

Per serving: Calories 317; Fat 5.1g (sat 1.8g, mono 2g, poly 0.5g); Protein 25g; Carb 43g; Fiber 1.2g; Chol 75mg; Iron 1.4mg; Sodium 141mg; Calc 18mg

Make-Ahead Pork Dumplings

This recipe makes a bunch, so ask a friend to help you assemble the dumplings; then freeze some for later.

PREP: 2 HR., COOK: 25 MIN.

1½ pounds lean boneless pork loin chops, cut into chunks
1 (12-ounce) package 50%-less-fat ground pork sausage
1½ teaspoons salt
15 water chestnuts, finely chopped
1 to 2 tablespoons minced fresh ginger
½ cup cornstarch
2 teaspoons lite soy sauce
½ cup fat-free low-sodium chicken broth
¼ cup sugar
1 teaspoon teriyaki sauce
1 teaspoon sesame oil
¼ cup chopped fresh parsley
4 green onions, diced
2 (16-ounce) packages won ton wrappers
Oyster sauce (optional)
Thai chili sauce (optional)

1. Process pork loin in a food processor until finely chopped.
2. Combine pork loin, pork sausage, and next 11 ingredients.
3. Cut corners from won ton wrappers to form circles. Drop 1 teaspoon mixture onto middle of each skin. Gather up won ton sides, letting dough pleat naturally. Lightly squeeze the middle while tapping the bottom on a flat surface so it will stand upright.
4. Arrange dumplings in a bamboo steam basket over boiling water. Cover and steam 20 to 25 minutes. Serve with sauces, if desired. **Makes** 116 dumplings.
Note: To freeze, arrange dumplings on a baking sheet; freeze for 2 hours. Place in zip-top plastic freezer bags; label and freeze for up to 3 months. To cook dumplings from frozen state, steam for 22 to 25 minutes.

Per dumpling: Calories 40; Fat 0.8g (sat 0.2g, mono 0.3g, poly 0.2g); Protein 2.5g; Carb 6g; Fiber 0.2g; Chol 6mg; Iron 0.4mg; Sodium 101mg; Calc 7mg

Marinated Chicken Strips and Vegetables

PREP: 25 MIN., COOK: 15 MIN., OTHER: 2 HR.

¾ cup lite soy sauce
⅔ cup honey
⅓ cup dry sherry*
½ teaspoon garlic powder
¼ teaspoon ground ginger
1½ pounds fresh asparagus spears
6 (6-ounce) skinned and boned chicken breasts, cut into ¼-inch strips
¼ cup stone-ground mustard
2 tablespoons sesame seeds, toasted
3 medium tomatoes, cut into wedges
8 cups mixed salad greens
Honey-mustard dressing

1. Stir together first 5 ingredients; set ½ cup mixture aside.
2. Pour remaining soy sauce mixture evenly into 2 zip-top plastic freezer bags. Snap off tough ends of asparagus, and place asparagus spears in 1 bag. Add chicken to remaining bag. Seal and chill at least 2 hours.
3. Drain chicken and asparagus, discarding marinade. Place chicken on a lightly greased roasting pan. Place asparagus in a lightly greased 13- x 9-inch pan.
4. Stir together reserved ½ cup soy sauce mixture, mustard, and sesame seeds. Pour ½ cup mixture over chicken and remaining ¼ cup over asparagus.
5. Bake chicken at 425° for 5 minutes. Place asparagus in oven, and bake chicken and asparagus 10 minutes or until chicken is done. Cool, if desired. Place separately in zip-top freezer bags, and chill 8 hours, if desired.
6. Arrange chicken, asparagus, and tomato over salad greens, and drizzle with honey-mustard dressing.
Makes 6 servings.
*Substitute ⅓ cup pineapple juice for sherry, if desired.

Per serving: Calories 324; Fat 6.2g (sat 1.8g, mono 0.9g, poly 1.1g); Protein 30.6g; Carb 37g; Fiber 3.8g; Chol 72mg; Iron 3.8mg; Sodium 834mg; Calc 109mg

> I love this easy, no-mess recipe because no pots and pans are required. Simply use a glass measuring cup to heat the broth in the microwave, place dry couscous in the serving bowl, and then add the broth. Once the remaining ingredients are stirred in, the dish is ready to serve.

MARIAN COOPER CAIRNS, TEST KITCHENS PROFESSIONAL

Mediterranean Chicken
Couscous

(EDITOR'S CHOICE)

Mediterranean Chicken Couscous

PREP: 15 MIN., COOK: 5 MIN., OTHER: 5 MIN.

1¼ cups low-sodium fat-free chicken broth
1 (5.6-ounce) package toasted pine nut couscous mix
3 cups chopped cooked chicken
¼ cup chopped fresh basil
1 (4-ounce) package crumbled feta cheese
1 pint grape tomatoes, halved
1 teaspoon grated lemon rind
1½ tablespoons fresh lemon juice
¼ teaspoon pepper
Garnish: fresh basil leaves

1. Heat broth and seasoning packet from couscous in the microwave on HIGH for 3 to 5 minutes or until broth begins to boil. Place couscous in a large bowl, and stir in broth mixture. Cover and let stand 5 minutes.
2. Fluff couscous with a fork; stir in chicken and next 6 ingredients. Serve warm or cold. Garnish, if desired. **Makes** 8 servings.
Note: You'll need to buy a ⅔-ounce package of fresh basil and 1 rotisserie chicken to get the right amount of basil and chicken for this recipe. Substitute 4 teaspoons of dried basil if you can't find fresh.

Per serving: Calories 212; Fat 6.8g (sat 3.1g; mono 1.9g; poly 1.1g); Protein 21.3g; Carb 16.9; Fiber 1.4g; Chol 58mg; Iron 1.2mg; Sodium 455mg; Calc 89mg

Oven-Baked Barbecue Chicken

Use any delicious leftovers in tacos or wraps
with Cheddar cheese and bacon.

PREP: 10 MIN.; COOK: 1 HR., 40 MIN.

3 cups spicy tomato juice
½ cup cider vinegar
3 tablespoons vegetable oil
2 to 3 garlic cloves, minced
1 bay leaf
2 teaspoons salt
1 teaspoon sugar
½ teaspoon black pepper
¼ teaspoon ground red pepper (optional)
4½ teaspoons Worcestershire sauce
2 cups all-purpose flour
10 chicken thighs, skinned
10 chicken legs, skinned

1. Stir together first 10 ingredients in a saucepan over medium-high heat; bring to a boil. Reduce heat, and simmer 10 minutes.
2. Place flour in a shallow dish; dredge chicken pieces on both sides. Arrange thighs, bone side up, and legs in a lightly greased roasting pan. Pour tomato juice mixture evenly over chicken.
3. Bake, uncovered, at 350° for 1½ hours or until done, basting occasionally. Discard bay leaf. **Makes** 10 servings.

Per serving: Calories 341; Fat 11.1g (sat 2.5g, mono 3.1g, poly 4g); Protein 41.9g; Carb 16g; Fiber 0.7g; Chol 161mg; Iron 3.2mg; Sodium 687mg; Calc 33mg

Maple-Balsamic Chicken

PREP: 10 MIN., COOK: 25 MIN.

8 skinned and boned chicken thighs
¾ teaspoon salt
¾ teaspoon paprika
¾ teaspoon dried thyme
1 tablespoon olive oil
1 (14-ounce) can chicken broth
⅓ cup maple syrup
⅓ cup balsamic vinegar
½ teaspoon freshly ground black pepper
¼ teaspoon ground red pepper
3 tablespoons chunky peanut butter

1. Sprinkle chicken evenly with salt, paprika, and thyme.
2. Cook chicken in hot oil in a large nonstick skillet over medium-high heat 2 minutes on each side or until golden. Stir in chicken broth and next 4 ingredients, and bring to a boil. Cover, reduce heat to low, and simmer 15 minutes. Remove chicken to a serving platter, and keep warm. Reserve liquid in skillet.
3. Whisk peanut butter into reserved liquid, and boil over medium-high heat, uncovered, 5 minutes or until sauce is thickened; spoon sauce evenly over chicken. **Makes** 4 servings.

Per serving: Calories 369; Fat 15.8g (sat 2.8g, mono 7.5g, poly 3.7g); Protein 31g; Carb 24.7g; Fiber 1.4g; Chol 119mg; Iron 2.4mg; Sodium 1,296mg; Calc 43mg

FAMILY FAVORITE
Breaded Chicken Drumsticks

A colorful blend of spices coats these
drumsticks that bake in the oven to crispy perfection.
Dark meats, such as drumsticks, are juicier due to their
higher fat content. But don't dismay—most of the fat's
in the skin, which you remove before baking.

PREP: 10 MIN., COOK: 1 HR.

½ cup fine, dry breadcrumbs
2 teaspoons onion powder
2 teaspoons curry powder
½ teaspoon dry mustard
¼ teaspoon salt
¼ teaspoon garlic powder
¼ teaspoon paprika
¼ to ½ teaspoon ground red pepper
12 chicken drumsticks, skinned (3 pounds)
¼ cup milk
Vegetable cooking spray

1. Combine first 8 ingredients in a shallow dish. Dip chicken in milk; coat with crumb mixture, and place in a lightly greased 13- x 9-inch baking dish. Coat chicken with cooking spray. Bake, uncovered, at 375° for 1 hour or until done. **Makes** 6 servings.

Per serving: Calories 208; Fat 6.4g (sat 1.6g, mono 1.7g, poly 1.5g); Protein 27.8g; Carb 8.2g; Fiber 0.8g; Chol 104mg; Iron 2mg; Sodium 279mg; Calc 49mg

Spicy Oven-Fried Catfish
With Lemon Cream

Spicy Oven-Fried Catfish With Lemon Cream

PREP: 15 MIN., COOK: 30 MIN.

6 (6-ounce) catfish fillets
1 teaspoon salt, divided
¼ teaspoon black pepper
1½ cups Japanese breadcrumbs (panko)*
¼ teaspoon garlic powder
¼ teaspoon ground red pepper
4 egg whites
Vegetable cooking spray
Lemon Cream
Garnishes: lemon wedges, parsley sprigs

1. Sprinkle fillets evenly with ¾ teaspoon salt and
¼ teaspoon black pepper. Set aside.
2. Combine breadcrumbs, remaining ¼ teaspoon
salt, garlic powder, and ground red pepper in a
shallow bowl.
3. Whisk egg whites in a shallow bowl until frothy. Dip
fillets in egg whites, and dredge in breadcrumb mixture.
4. Coat fillets evenly on both sides with cooking spray.
Arrange fillets on a wire rack coated with cooking

spray in an aluminum foil-lined 15- x 10-inch
jelly-roll pan. (Do not overlap fillets.)
5. Bake at 375° for 25 to 30 minutes or until fish is
golden brown. Serve with Lemon Cream. Garnish, if
desired. **Makes** 6 servings.
*1 cup plain, dry breadcrumbs may be substituted.
Note: Look for panko breadcrumbs in Asian markets
or on the ethnic food aisle of your grocery store.

Lemon Cream

PREP: 10 MIN.

1 (8-ounce) container light sour cream
1 tablespoon chopped fresh parsley
½ teaspoon lemon zest
2 tablespoons fresh lemon juice
¼ teaspoon salt

1. Stir together all ingredients until blended. Cover
and chill until ready to serve. **Makes** about 1 cup.

Per serving (including sauce): Calories 337; Fat 10.1g (sat 4.1g, mono 1.4g, poly 1.5g);
Protein 35g; Carb 24.6g; Fiber 1g; Chol 118mg; Iron 0.6mg; Sodium 480mg; Calc 93mg

Baked Salmon With Caribbean Fruit Salsa

A whole salmon fillet makes a dramatic presentation. Ask the butcher at your grocery store to remove salmon skin.

PREP: 5 MIN., COOK: 25 MIN., OTHER: 2 HR.

1 (3-pound) whole skinless salmon fillet
1 tablespoon Caribbean jerk seasoning*
1½ tablespoons olive oil
Caribbean Fruit Salsa
Garnish: lime wedges

1. Place salmon fillet in a roasting pan; sprinkle evenly on 1 side with jerk seasoning. Drizzle with oil. Cover and chill 2 hours.
2. Bake salmon at 350° for 20 to 25 minutes or until fish flakes with a fork. Serve with Caribbean Fruit Salsa. Garnish, if desired **Makes** 8 servings.
*Substitute Jamaican jerk seasoning, if desired. Caribbean jerk seasoning has a hint of sweetness.

Per serving: Calories 346; Fat 16.4g (sat 2.5g, mono 7g, poly 5.4g); Protein 39.1g; Carb 9.2g; Fiber 1.4g; Chol 108mg; Iron 1.8mg; Sodium 192mg; Calc 35mg

Caribbean Fruit Salsa

This salsa's also great as an appetizer served with tortilla chips.

PREP: 20 MIN., OTHER: 2 HR.

1 mango (about ½ pound), peeled and diced*
1 papaya (about ½ pound), peeled and diced*
1 medium-size red bell pepper, diced
1 medium-size green bell pepper, diced
1 cup diced fresh pineapple
1 small red onion, diced
3 tablespoons chopped fresh cilantro
2 tablespoons fresh lime juice
1 tablespoon olive oil

1. Stir together all ingredients. Cover and chill at least 2 hours. **Makes** 5 cups.
*Substitute 1 cup each diced, refrigerated jarred mango and papaya, if desired.

Per ¼ cup: Calories 24; Fat 0.8g (sat 0.1g, mono 0.5g, poly 0.1g); Protein 0.3g; Carb 4.6g; Fiber 0.7g; Chol 0mg; Iron 0.1mg; Sodium 1mg; Calc 6mg

Moroccan Broiled Fish

PREP: 13 MIN., COOK: 10 MIN., OTHER: 30 MIN.

2 garlic cloves, halved
1 (2-inch) piece fresh ginger, chopped (about 2 tablespoons chopped)
½ cup chopped fresh cilantro
1 small jalapeño pepper, seeded and quartered
1 teaspoon salt
½ teaspoon ground hot paprika
½ teaspoon ground turmeric
½ teaspoon ground coriander
2 teaspoons vegetable oil
2 pounds catfish, grouper, or flounder fillets (about 6 fillets)
Fresh lime wedges (optional)

1. Process first 9 ingredients in a food processor until finely chopped.
2. Spread spice mixture evenly over both sides of each fillet. Cover and chill 30 minutes.
3. Place fillets on a lightly greased rack in a broiler pan. Broil fish 5½ inches from heat 10 minutes or until fish flakes with a fork. Serve with fresh lime wedges, if desired. **Makes** 6 servings.
Note: For a different serving idea, prepare recipe as directed, let cooked fish stand 15 minutes, and then flake with a fork. Serve on warm flour tortillas with a squeeze of lime and a dollop of sour cream.

Per serving: Calories 198; Fat 11.1g (sat 2.3g, mono 5.6g, poly 2.3g); Protein 22.3g; Carb 1.1g; Fiber 0.3g; Chol 75mg; Iron 1.2mg; Sodium 483mg; Calc 15mg

Crab Burgers

Tomato wedges are a colorful accompaniment to these seafood burgers.

PREP: 25 MIN., COOK: 10 MIN., OTHER: 1 HR.

1 pound fresh crabmeat
2 cups soft breadcrumbs
1 small onion, chopped
½ green bell pepper, chopped
⅓ cup light mayonnaise
1 large egg
¼ teaspoon salt
¼ teaspoon pepper
Vegetable cooking spray
6 lettuce leaves
3 English muffins, split
Roasted Red Pepper Sauce
Garnish: flat-leaf parsley sprigs

1. Drain and flake crabmeat, removing any bits of shell.
2. Stir together crabmeat and next 7 ingredients. Shape into 6 (3½-inch) patties. Chill 1 hour.

3. Cook patties in a nonstick skillet coated with cooking spray over medium-high heat 5 minutes on each side or until lightly browned. Place lettuce on muffin halves. Top with crab burgers; spoon Roasted Red Pepper Sauce over burgers. Garnish, if desired. **Makes** 6 servings.

Roasted Red Pepper Sauce

PREP: 5 MIN.

1 (7-ounce) jar roasted red bell peppers, drained
3 tablespoons light mayonnaise
1 garlic clove
⅛ teaspoon dried crushed red pepper

1. Process all ingredients in a food processor until smooth. **Makes** ⅔ cup.

Per serving (including sauce): Calories 272; Fat 9.6g (sat 1.5g, mono 0.6g, poly 0.6g); Protein 21g; Carb 25.4g; Fiber 0.9g; Chol 96mg; Iron 2.1mg; Sodium 826mg; Calc 127mg

Shrimp Tacos With Spicy Cream Sauce

PREP: 20 MIN., COOK: 8 MIN., OTHER: 15 MIN.

1 (16-ounce) container fat-free sour cream
2 teaspoons chili powder, divided
1 teaspoon ground cumin, divided
¾ teaspoon ground red pepper, divided
¾ teaspoon salt, divided
¼ teaspoon ground cinnamon
¾ cup water
1 pound unpeeled, medium-size raw shrimp
3 tablespoons orange juice
2 garlic cloves, minced
2 teaspoons olive oil
1 avocado, chopped
8 (6-inch) corn tortillas, warmed

1. Whisk together sour cream, 1 teaspoon chili powder, ½ teaspoon cumin, ½ teaspoon red pepper, ¼ teaspoon salt, and cinnamon. Add ¾ cup water, stirring until smooth. Cover and chill until ready to serve.

2. Peel shrimp, and devein, if desired; chop. Combine remaining 1 teaspoon chili powder, ½ teaspoon cumin, ¼ teaspoon red pepper, and ½ teaspoon salt in a shallow dish or zip-top plastic freezer bag; add orange juice and shrimp, turning to coat. Cover or seal, and chill 15 minutes. Remove shrimp from marinade, discarding marinade.

3. Sauté garlic in hot oil in a large skillet over medium-high heat 2 to 3 minutes. Add shrimp, and cook 5 minutes or just until shrimp turn pink. Serve with sour cream mixture and avocado in warm tortillas. **Makes** 8 servings.

Per serving: Calories 212; Fat 6.2g (sat 1g, mono 3.6g, poly 1.1g); Protein 13g; Carb 26g; Fiber 3g; Chol 72mg; Iron 2mg; Sodium 391mg; Calc 140mg

Pecan Shrimp With Orange Dipping Sauce

PREP: 25 MIN., COOK: 15 MIN.

1½ pounds unpeeled, large raw shrimp
1 teaspoon seasoned salt
3 egg whites
1½ cups Japanese breadcrumbs (panko)*
⅔ cup ground pecans
2 tablespoons all-purpose flour
Vegetable cooking spray
Orange Dipping Sauce (opposite page)

1. Peel shrimp, leaving tails on, and devein, if desired. Sprinkle shrimp evenly with seasoned salt. Set aside.
2. Whisk egg whites in a small bowl until frothy. Set aside.

3. Combine breadcrumbs, pecans, and flour in a shallow bowl. Set aside.
4. Place a wire rack coated with cooking spray in an aluminum foil-lined 15- x 10-inch jelly-roll pan.
5. Dip shrimp, 1 at a time, in egg whites, and dredge in breadcrumb mixture. Arrange shrimp on rack. Coat shrimp evenly with cooking spray.
6. Bake at 425° for 10 to 15 minutes or just until shrimp turn pink, turning after 5 to 7 minutes. Serve with Orange Dipping Sauce. **Makes** 6 servings.
*1½ cups plain, dry breadcrumbs may be substituted.
Note: Look for panko breadcrumbs in Asian markets or on the ethnic food aisle of your grocery store.

Orange Dipping Sauce:

PREP: 5 MIN.

¾ cup orange marmalade
¼ cup orange juice
2 tablespoons lemon juice
1 teaspoon stone-ground mustard
½ teaspoon dried crushed red pepper

1. Microwave marmalade in a small glass bowl at HIGH 20 seconds or until melted.
2. Stir in remaining ingredients. Serve immediately. **Makes** about 1 cup.

Per serving (including sauce): Calories 336; Fat 9g (sat 0.9g, mono 4.5g, poly 2.7g); Protein 23g; Carb 41.7g; Fiber 1.9g; Chol 168mg; Iron 3.2mg; Sodium 530mg; Calc 59mg

MAKE AHEAD
Marinated Shrimp
A cool and easy dish for a summer cookout.

PREP: 30 MIN., COOK: 2 MIN., OTHER: 1 HR.

2 pounds unpeeled, large raw shrimp
6 cups water
2 teaspoons salt
½ cup sugar
1½ cups white vinegar
1 cup vegetable oil
¼ cup capers, undrained
1½ teaspoons celery salt
1 teaspoon salt
1 medium-size red onion, sliced and separated
    into rings

1. Peel shrimp, and devein, if desired. Bring water and 2 teaspoons salt to a boil; add shrimp, and cook 2 minutes or just until shrimp turn pink. Drain; rinse with cold water. Chill.
2. Whisk together sugar and next 5 ingredients in a large shallow dish; add shrimp alternately with onion. Cover and chill 1 to 6 hours, turning often. Drain and discard marinade before serving. **Makes** 10 appetizer servings.

Per serving: Calories 80; Fat 1.4g (sat 0.3g, mono 0.4g, poly 0.6g); Protein 14.5g; Carb 1.4g; Fiber 0.2g; Chol 134mg; Iron 2.2mg; Sodium 198mg; Calc 29mg

New Orleans Barbecue Shrimp
Spicy, buttery, and decidedly hands-on, this dish is a New Orleans classic. Serve with a green salad and corn on the cob for a complete meal.

PREP: 5 MIN., COOK: 20 MIN., OTHER: 2 HR.

4 pounds unpeeled, large raw shrimp or 6 pounds
    shrimp with heads on
½ cup butter
½ cup olive oil
¼ cup chili sauce
¼ cup Worcestershire sauce
2 lemons, sliced
4 garlic cloves, chopped
2 tablespoons Creole seasoning
1 tablespoon chopped fresh parsley
2 tablespoons lemon juice
1 teaspoon paprika
1 teaspoon dried oregano
1 teaspoon ground red pepper
½ teaspoon hot sauce

1. Spread shrimp in a shallow, aluminum foil-lined broiler pan.
2. Combine butter and remaining ingredients in a medium saucepan over low heat, stirring until butter melts; pour over shrimp. Cover and chill 2 hours, turning shrimp every 30 minutes.
3. Bake, uncovered, at 400° for 20 minutes, turning shrimp once. Serve with French bread. **Makes** 8 servings.

Per serving: Calories 396; Fat 24.7g (sat 14.9g, mono 6.2g, poly 1.6g); Protein 36.5g; Carb 6.3g; Fiber 0.3g; Chol 396mg; Iron 6mg; Sodium 2,254mg; Calc 91mg

Barbecue Shrimp Notes

• Offer plenty of napkins, paper towels, or, if you have them, bibs. (If you don't like getting your hands dirty when you eat, this isn't the dish for you.)
• Leftover shrimp keep well in the refrigerator for a day or two. Be careful not to overcook them when reheating.

White Spaghetti and Meatballs

White Spaghetti and Meatballs

Lean chicken, garlic, and warm spices combine in these hand-shaped meatballs with a creamy white wine sauce.

PREP: 30 MIN., COOK: 58 MIN., OTHER: 20 MIN.

1½ pounds skinned and boned chicken breasts,
    cut into chunks
1 large garlic clove
1 large egg
10 saltine crackers, finely crushed
1 teaspoon Italian seasoning
Vegetable cooking spray
1 (8-ounce) package spaghetti, uncooked
1 (8-ounce) package sliced fresh mushrooms
⅛ teaspoon ground nutmeg
1 teaspoon olive oil
1 large garlic clove, minced
2 tablespoons all-purpose flour
½ cup dry white wine
3 cups low-sodium, fat-free chicken broth
1 (8-ounce) package ⅓-less-fat cream cheese
¼ teaspoon ground red pepper
¼ cup chopped fresh flat-leaf parsley
Garnish: flat-leaf parsley sprig

1. Process chicken and garlic clove in a food processor until ground.

2. Stir together chicken mixture, egg, and next 2 ingredients in a large bowl. Cover and chill 20 minutes.
3. Shape mixture into 1-inch balls. Place a rack coated with cooking spray in an aluminum foil-lined broiling pan. Arrange meatballs on rack; lightly spray meatballs with cooking spray.
4. Bake at 375° for 13 minutes or until golden and thoroughly cooked.
5. Cook pasta according to package directions, omitting salt and oil; drain.
6. Sauté mushrooms and nutmeg in hot oil in a Dutch oven over medium-high heat 8 to 10 minutes or until mushrooms are tender.
7. Add minced garlic; sauté 1 minute. Sprinkle with flour; cook, stirring constantly, 1 minute. Add wine, stirring to loosen browned particles from bottom of pan. Whisk in broth. Bring to a boil; reduce heat, and simmer, stirring occasionally, 15 minutes. Add cream cheese, whisking until smooth and sauce is thickened.
8. Add meatballs, red pepper, and parsley to sauce; simmer 10 minutes. Serve sauce with meatballs over pasta. Garnish, if desired. **Makes** 6 servings.

Per serving: Calories 431; Fat 11.2g (sat 5.2g, mono 3.5g, poly 1.1g); Protein 40g; Carb 39g; Fiber 1.7g; Chol 122mg; Iron 3.8mg; Sodium 629mg; Calc 78mg

Won Ton Spinach Lasagna

Won ton wrappers replace noodles in this clever dish. Find them in the produce section of the supermarket.

PREP: 25 MIN., COOK: 45 MIN., OTHER: 10 MIN.

2 cups (8 ounces) shredded part-skim mozzarella
    cheese, divided
1½ teaspoons dried basil, divided
¾ teaspoon ground red pepper, divided
1 (15-ounce) container fat-free ricotta cheese
1 (10-ounce) package frozen chopped spinach,
    thawed and well drained
1 cup shredded carrots
½ cup shredded Parmesan cheese
¼ cup egg substitute
½ teaspoon garlic powder
1 (26-ounce) jar tomato pasta sauce
Vegetable cooking spray
½ (16-ounce) package won ton wrappers

1. Stir together 1 cup mozzarella cheese, 1 teaspoon basil, ¼ teaspoon red pepper, ricotta, and next 5 ingredients in a large bowl. Set aside.

2. Stir together pasta sauce and remaining ½ teaspoon each of basil and ground red pepper. Spread ½ cup sauce mixture in bottom of a 13- x 9-inch baking dish coated with cooking spray.

3. Arrange 1 layer of won ton wrappers over sauce, slightly overlapping. Top with one-third cheese mixture. Spoon one-third remaining sauce mixture over cheese mixture. Repeat layers twice, ending with sauce mixture. Sprinkle evenly with remaining 1 cup mozzarella cheese.

4. Bake at 350° for 45 minutes or until bubbly and cheese melts. Let stand 10 minutes before serving.
Makes 8 servings.

Per serving: Calories 272; Fat 7.1g (sat 3.9g, mono 1.9g, poly 0.5g); Protein 21g; Carb 31g; Fiber 3.6g; Chol 27mg; Iron 2.9mg; Sodium 757mg; Calc 535mg

Won Ton Spinach Lasagna

Easy Mexican Lasagna

This simple and delicious one-dish supper calls for almost no preparation (especially if you buy precooked cut-up chicken).

PREP: 15 MIN., COOK: 1 HR.

3 cups chopped cooked chicken breast
1 (15-ounce) can black beans, rinsed and drained
⅔ cup canned diced tomatoes and green chiles
1 teaspoon garlic powder
1 teaspoon ground cumin
½ teaspoon pepper
1 (10¾-ounce) can fat-free cream of chicken soup
1 (10¾-ounce) can fat-free cream of mushroom soup
1 (10-ounce) can enchilada sauce
Vegetable cooking spray
9 (6-inch) corn tortillas
1 cup (4 ounces) shredded reduced-fat Cheddar cheese
1 cup (4 ounces) shredded Monterey Jack cheese
Toppings: shredded lettuce, fat-free sour cream, mild chunky salsa

1. Cook first 6 ingredients in a saucepan over medium heat 10 minutes or until thoroughly heated.
2. Stir together chicken and mushroom soups and enchilada sauce in a saucepan; cook, stirring often, 10 minutes or until thoroughly heated.
3. Spoon one-third of sauce into a 13- x 9-inch baking dish coated with cooking spray; top with 3 tortillas. Spoon half of chicken mixture and one-third of sauce over tortillas; sprinkle with half of Cheddar cheese. Top with 3 tortillas; repeat layers once with remaining chicken, sauce, Cheddar cheese, and tortillas, ending with tortillas. Sprinkle with Monterey Jack cheese.
4. Bake at 350° for 30 to 40 minutes or until lasagna is bubbly. Serve with desired toppings. **Makes** 8 servings.
*To lower sodium, substitute reduced-sodium soups, canned tomato products, and cheeses.

Per serving: Calories 303; Fat 13.6g (sat 7g, mono 2.7g, poly 0.8g); Protein 25g; Carb 24g; Fiber 3.7g; Chol 65mg; Iron 1.2mg; Sodium 896mg; Calc 250mg

Pasta With Spring Vegetables

Great as a vegetarian dish, or add some chopped grilled chicken.

PREP: 25 MIN., COOK: 20 MIN.

12 ounces uncooked whole grain spaghetti or fettuccine
1 pound fresh asparagus
1 pound broccoli florets
½ cup rice vinegar
¼ cup peanut oil
3 tablespoons sesame oil
1 medium cucumber
3 large carrots, thinly sliced
1 (8-ounce) can sliced water chestnuts, drained
5 large radishes, thinly sliced (optional)
¾ teaspoon salt
¼ teaspoon pepper

1. Cook pasta according to package directions; remove pasta with tongs, reserving boiling water. Drain pasta, and set aside.
2. Snap off tough ends of asparagus; cut asparagus into ½-inch pieces. Add asparagus and broccoli to boiling water, and cook 3 minutes; drain. Plunge asparagus and broccoli into ice water to stop the cooking process; drain and set aside.
3. Whisk together vinegar and oils. Pour over pasta, and toss.
4. Cut cucumber in half lengthwise; remove seeds, and thinly slice cucumber. Add cucumber, asparagus, broccoli, carrot, chestnuts, radishes, if desired, and salt and pepper to pasta mixture; toss well. **Makes** 6 main-dish servings.
Note: For testing purposes only, we used Barilla Plus Whole Grain Spaghetti.

Per serving: Calories 404; Fat 17.2g (sat 2.8g, mono 7.3g, poly 6.4g); Protein 12.5g; Carb 56.4g; Fiber 13.1g; Chol 0mg; Iron 3.3mg; Sodium 638mg; Calc 93mg

Noodles With Peanut-Basil Sauce

Stir in grilled chicken, shrimp, or pork for a fresh spin on a one-dish meal.

PREP: 20 MIN., COOK: 10 MIN.

1 cup fresh snow peas
½ (16-ounce) package uncooked fettuccine
½ cup lite coconut milk
¾ cup vegetable broth
½ cup crunchy peanut butter
3 tablespoons lite soy sauce
2 tablespoons lime juice
1 garlic clove, minced
2 teaspoons sugar
¾ teaspoon ground coriander
1 cup firmly packed basil leaves,
    shredded and divided
Toppings: chopped dry-roasted peanuts, bean
    sprouts, dried crushed red pepper

1. Trim snow peas, and cut in half diagonally.
2. Bring water to a boil in a large heavy saucepan; add snow peas, and cook 45 seconds. Drain. Plunge into ice water to stop the cooking process; drain and set aside.
3. Cook pasta according package directions; drain.
4. Whisk together coconut milk and next 7 ingredients in a large saucepan. Cook over medium-low heat, whisking occasionally, 5 minutes or until mixture is thoroughly heated. Add snow peas, hot cooked pasta, and ¾ cup basil; toss and place on a serving platter.
5. Sprinkle with remaining ¼ cup basil. Serve with desired toppings. **Makes** 6 side-dish servings.

Per serving (not including toppings): Calories 293; Fat 12.7g (sat 2.8g, mono 5.4g, poly 3.8g); Protein 11.2g; Carb 37.2g; Fiber 4g; Chol 0mg; Iron 2.3mg; Sodium 633mg; Calc 43.6mg

Eggplant Parmesan With Feta

This Italian dish is great served over pasta with a fresh green salad. If you want a simple baked eggplant, just complete the first 3 steps with the first 7 ingredients.

PREP: 35 MIN.; COOK: 1 HR., 11 MIN.

½ small eggplant
1 teaspoon salt, divided
1 teaspoon pepper, divided
1 cup Italian breadcrumbs
½ cup grated Parmesan cheese, divided
½ cup egg substitute
Vegetable cooking spray
1 medium onion, chopped
2 garlic cloves, minced
1 (28-ounce) can crushed tomatoes
1 teaspoon sugar
1 teaspoon dried basil
½ teaspoon dried oregano
1 (16-ounce) container 1% low-fat cottage cheese*
½ cup crumbled feta cheese

1. Cut eggplant crosswise into ⅛-inch-thick slices. Sprinkle evenly with ¾ teaspoon salt and ½ teaspoon pepper.
2. Combine breadcrumbs and 3 tablespoons Parmesan cheese. Dip eggplant into egg substitute. Dredge in breadcrumb mixture. Coat eggplant evenly on both sides with cooking spray. Arrange slices on a rack coated with cooking spray; place rack inside a roasting pan.
3. Bake at 375° for 16 minutes, turning after 8 minutes.
4. Sauté onion and garlic in a large saucepan coated with cooking spray over medium-high heat 5 minutes or until onion is tender. Add tomatoes, remaining ¼ teaspoon salt, remaining ½ teaspoon pepper, sugar, basil, and oregano; bring to a boil. Reduce heat, and simmer, stirring often, 10 minutes or until thickened.
5. Spoon 1 cup tomato mixture into an 8-inch-square baking dish coated with cooking spray, and arrange one-third of eggplant slices in a single layer over tomato mixture.
6. Stir together cottage cheese and feta cheese; spoon ⅓ cup cheese mixture over eggplant. Spoon 1 cup tomato mixture over cheese mixture. Repeat layers twice, ending with tomato mixture. Sprinkle with remaining Parmesan cheese.
7. Bake at 350° for 35 to 40 minutes or until bubbly and golden brown. **Makes** 6 servings.
*Part-skim ricotta cheese may be substituted for cottage cheese, if desired.

Per serving: Calories 279; Fat 7.6g (sat 3.8g, mono 1.6g, poly 0.7g); Protein 22.2g; Carb 32g; Fiber 5g; Chol 20mg; Iron 3.7g; Sodium 1,215mg; Calc 299mg

Overnight Slaw

PREP: 15 MIN., COOK: 4 MIN., OTHER: 8 HR.

6 cups shredded cabbage (about 1¾ pounds)*
1 cup shredded red cabbage*
½ cup shredded carrot
½ cup chopped red bell pepper
2 green onions, diagonally sliced
1½ tablespoons sugar
3 tablespoons white wine vinegar
3 tablespoons vegetable oil
½ teaspoon celery seed
1 teaspoon coarse-grained Dijon mustard
¼ teaspoon salt
⅛ teaspoon pepper
½ (4-ounce) package crumbled feta cheese

1. Combine first 5 ingredients in a large bowl. Stir together sugar and next 6 ingredients in a small saucepan; bring to a boil.
2. Boil 1 minute. Remove from heat; cool completely. Pour dressing over cabbage mixture; toss well. Cover and chill 8 hours. Toss with feta cheese just before serving. **Makes** 8 servings.
*Substitute 1 (16-ounce) package slaw mix, if desired.

Per (1-cup) serving: Calories 98; Fat 7g (sat 1.5g, mono 3.5g, poly 1.7g); Protein 2.2g; Carb 7.7g; Fiber 0.7g; Chol 6mg; Iron 0.6mg; Sodium 188mg; Calc 70mg

> **Because I travel so much, I love the make-ahead aspect of this dish. It's much healthier to reach for this crunchy slaw than a bag of chips.**
>
> ELEANOR GRIFFIN, EDITOR-IN-CHIEF

MAKE AHEAD
Baked Cheese Grits

Yummy cheese grits are as at home on the dinner plate as they are at the breakfast table. Serve them alongside grilled pork or chicken.

PREP: 15 MIN., COOK: 40 MIN.

2⅔ cups water
⅔ cup quick-cooking grits
2 tablespoons light butter
2 large eggs, lightly beaten
½ (8-ounce) loaf light pasteurized prepared cheese product, cut into ½-inch pieces
¼ teaspoon salt
¼ teaspoon ground red pepper
Vegetable cooking spray

1. Bring 2⅔ cups water to a boil; add grits, and cook, stirring often, 5 minutes or until thickened. Remove from heat. Add butter and next 4 ingredients, stirring until blended. Spoon mixture into a 2-quart baking dish coated with cooking spray.
2. Bake at 350° for 40 minutes or until lightly browned. **Makes** 3½ cups.
Note: Casserole may be chilled up to 8 hours. Let stand at room temperature 30 minutes; bake as directed.

Per (½-cup) serving: Calories 131; Fat 5g (sat 1.9g, mono 1.3g, poly 1g); Protein 6.3g; Carb 14g; Fiber 0.3g; Chol 67mg; Iron 0.3mg; Sodium 389mg; Calc 101mg

MAKE AHEAD

Confetti Twice-Baked Potatoes

PREP: 15 MIN.; COOK: 1 HR., 10 MIN.; OTHER: 10 MIN.

4 medium baking potatoes
½ cup fat-free sour cream
¼ cup fat-free milk
2 tablespoons butter
¼ cup chopped fresh basil
¼ cup chopped fresh parsley
2 green onions, chopped
2 garlic cloves, minced
Butter-flavored vegetable cooking spray
2 plum tomatoes, chopped
½ cup (2 ounces) shredded reduced-fat sharp
    Cheddar cheese

1. Bake potatoes at 375° for 1 hour or until tender; cool 10 minutes. Reduce oven temperature to 350°.
2. Cut potatoes in half lengthwise; carefully scoop out pulp into a large bowl, leaving shells intact. Stir together pulp, sour cream, milk, and butter; stir in basil and next 3 ingredients.
3. Coat insides of potato shells with cooking spray. Spoon potato mixture evenly into shells; sprinkle evenly with tomato and cheese.
4. Bake potatoes at 350° for 10 minutes or until thoroughly heated and cheese is melted. **Makes** 8 servings.
Note: To make ahead, place unbaked stuffed potato halves, covered, in the refrigerator. Bring potato halves to room temperature before baking at 350°.

Per serving (1 potato half): Calories 129; Fat 3.7g (sat 2.3g, mono 1g, poly 0.2g); Protein 4.6g; Carb 20g; Fiber 1.9g; Chol 11mg; Iron 1.2mg; Sodium 96mg; Calc 80mg

Creamy Hash Brown Casserole

PREP: 10 MIN., COOK: 1 HR., OTHER: 10 MIN.

1 (32-ounce) package frozen hash brown potatoes
1 (10¾-ounce) can fat-free cream of chicken soup
1 (8-ounce) container light sour cream
1 small onion, chopped
1 (5-ounce) can low-fat evaporated milk
¼ cup light butter, melted
½ teaspoon salt
¼ teaspoon pepper
1 teaspoon dried rosemary (optional)
Vegetable cooking spray
1 cup (4 ounces) shredded reduced-fat
    Cheddar cheese

1. Stir together first 8 ingredients and, if desired, rosemary in a large bowl.
2. Spoon mixture into an 11- x 7-inch baking dish coated with cooking spray. Sprinkle cheese evenly over top.
3. Bake at 350° for 1 hour or until bubbly and golden. Remove from oven, and let stand 10 minutes. **Makes** 6 servings.

Per serving: Calories 308; Fat 13g (sat 7.4g, mono 0.4g, poly 0.5g); Protein 13g; Carb 37g; Fiber 2.6g; Chol 44mg; Iron 1.7mg; Sodium 811mg; Calc 230mg

MAKE AHEAD
Layered Potato Salad

PREP: 15 MIN., COOK: 30 MIN., OTHER: 1 HR.

4 pounds red potatoes, unpeeled
1 (8-ounce) container fat-free sour cream
¾ cup light mayonnaise
2 tablespoons Creole mustard
½ teaspoon pepper
¼ teaspoon salt
1 bunch green onions, chopped (about 1 cup)
¾ cup chopped Italian parsley
3 reduced-fat, reduced-sodium bacon slices, cooked
    and crumbled

1. Bring potatoes and water to cover to a boil in a large Dutch oven over medium-high heat. Boil 25 minutes or until tender. Drain and let cool.
2. Cut potatoes into thin slices.

3. Stir together sour cream and next 4 ingredients.
4. Layer one-third each of potatoes, sour cream mixture, green onions, and parsley in a large glass bowl. Repeat layers twice, ending with parsley. Cover and chill 1 hour. Sprinkle with bacon just before serving. **Makes** 12 servings.
Note: Salad may be prepared a day in advance and chilled.

Per serving: Calories 192; Fat 5.8g (sat 1g, mono 0g, poly .01g); Protein 4.8g; Carb 30g; Fiber 3.4g; Chol 8mg; Iron 1.5mg; Sodium 270mg; Calc 51mg

QUICK
Tangy Spinach Salad

Turkey bacon helps keep this salad on the light side.

PREP: 15 MIN., COOK: 7 MIN.

6 turkey bacon slices
3 tablespoons lemon juice
2 tablespoons brown sugar
2 tablespoons Dijon mustard
1 (10-ounce) package fresh spinach, torn
1 (8-ounce) package sliced fresh
    mushrooms

1. Cook bacon in a large skillet over medium-high heat until crisp; remove bacon, reserving drippings in skillet. Crumble bacon, and set aside.
2. Add lemon juice, brown sugar, and mustard to skillet; cook over low heat, stirring constantly, 1 minute.
3. Toss together spinach, mushrooms, and lemon juice mixture. Sprinkle with bacon. **Makes** 4 servings.

Per serving: Calories 104; Fat 4g (sat 0.8g, mono 1.5g, poly 1g); Protein 6.2g; Carb 11.3g; Fiber 3.6g; Chol 15mg; Iron 3.1mg; Sodium 583mg; Calc 87mg

Thai Pork Salad

Thai Pork Salad

Don't let the long ingredient list stop you. All you really have to do is sauté the ground pork and then stir in the flavor. The slaw can be made ahead of time.

PREP: 20 MIN., COOK: 10 MIN.

1 pound ground pork
Vegetable cooking spray
½ cup chopped fresh cilantro
½ cup fresh lime juice
¼ cup chopped fresh mint leaves
1 tablespoon light brown sugar
1 tablespoon fish sauce
3 green onions, finely chopped
1 teaspoon minced fresh ginger
1 teaspoon sesame oil
½ teaspoon ground red pepper
Asian Slaw
Garnishes: fresh cilantro sprigs,
    cucumber curls, chopped jicama

1. Sauté pork in a large skillet coated with cooking spray over medium-high heat 8 to 10 minutes or until meat crumbles and is no longer pink. Drain and cool.

2. Stir together pork, chopped cilantro, and next 8 ingredients. Serve with Asian Slaw. Garnish, if desired. **Makes** 6 servings.
Note: Fish sauce may be found in Asian markets and large supermarkets.

Asian Slaw

PREP: 10 MIN.

2 tablespoons rice vinegar
2 tablespoons lite soy sauce
2 teaspoons light brown sugar
2 tablespoons olive oil
1 (16-ounce) package broccoli slaw mix

1. Stir together first 4 ingredients. Drizzle over slaw mix, tossing to coat. **Makes** 6 servings.

Per serving (including slaw): Calories 218; Fat 11.8g (sat 3.3g, mono 5.8g, poly 1.6g); Protein 20g; Carb 9g; Fiber 2.6g; Chol 57mg; Iron 1.8mg; Sodium 220mg; Calc 62mg

Chicken-Blueberry Salad

PREP: 20 MIN., COOK: 12 MIN., OTHER: 1 HR.

3 tablespoons olive oil
½ cup rice wine vinegar
2 teaspoons minced fresh ginger
1 garlic clove, minced
¼ teaspoon salt
½ teaspoon pepper
3 skinned and boned chicken breasts
1 celery rib, chopped
½ cup diced sweet onion
½ cup chopped red bell pepper
1 cup shredded carrot
4 cups torn mixed salad greens
1 cup fresh blueberries

1. Whisk together first 6 ingredients. Reserve half of vinegar mixture, and chill.
2. Place chicken in a shallow dish or heavy-duty zip-top plastic freezer bag; pour remaining vinegar mixture over chicken. Cover or seal, and chill at least 1 hour.
3. Remove chicken from marinade; discard marinade. Grill over medium-high heat (350° to 400°) 6 minutes on each side or until done. Cut into thin slices.
4. Combine celery and next 3 ingredients; add reserved vinegar mixture, tossing to coat.
5. Place chicken over salad greens. Top with celery mixture; sprinkle with berries. **Makes** 4 servings.

Per serving: Calories 183; Fat 4.8g (sat 0.8g, mono 2.8g, poly 0.7g); Protein 21g; Carb 14g; Fiber 3.3g; Chol 49mg; Iron 1.2mg; Sodium 127mg; Calc 48mg

Chicken-Blueberry Salad

Banana Pudding

PREP: 20 MIN., COOK: 33 MIN., OTHER: 30 MIN.

⅓ cup all-purpose flour
Dash of salt
2½ cups 1% low-fat milk
1 (14-ounce) can fat-free sweetened condensed milk
2 egg yolks, lightly beaten
2 teaspoons vanilla extract
2¼ to 3 cups sliced ripe bananas
45 to 50 reduced-fat vanilla wafers (depending on baking dishes)
4 egg whites
¼ cup sugar

> **As a dietitian, I hear angels sing whenever I taste a lightened recipe that's just as rich and sumptuous as its traditional version.**
>
> SHANNON SLITER SATTERWHITE, FOOD EDITOR

1. Combine flour and salt in a medium saucepan. Gradually stir in 1% milk, sweetened condensed milk, and yolks, and cook over medium heat, stirring constantly, 8 minutes or until thickened. Remove from heat; stir in vanilla.

2. Layer 3 banana slices, 3½ tablespoons pudding mixture, and 3 vanilla wafers in each of 8 (1-cup) ramekins or individual baking dishes. Top each with 6 banana slices, 3½ tablespoons pudding, and 3 vanilla wafers.

3. Beat egg whites at high speed with an electric mixer until foamy. Add sugar, 1 tablespoon at a time, beating until stiff peaks form and sugar dissolves (2 to 4 minutes). Spread about ½ cup meringue over each pudding.

4. Bake at 325° for 25 minutes or until golden. Let cool at least 30 minutes. **Makes** 8 servings.

Note: A 2-quart baking dish may be used instead of ramekins. Layer about one-third each of banana slices, pudding mixture, and vanilla wafers. Repeat layers; top with remaining bananas and pudding mixture. Arrange remaining wafers around inside edge of dish. Gently push wafers into pudding. Spread meringue evenly over pudding; bake as directed.

Per serving: Calories 359; Fat 3.6g (sat 1g, mono 0.7g, poly 0.3g); Protein 11g; Carb 70.7g; Fiber 1.3g; Chol 58mg; Iron 1.1mg; Sodium 234mg; Calc 242mg

Light Tiramisù

*This creamy, coffee-inspired concoction has less
than half the fat of the traditional version.*

PREP: 15 MIN., COOK: 30 MIN., OTHER: 2 HR.

½ cup granulated sugar
1 cup whipping cream, divided
2 cups fat-free milk
½ cup egg substitute
2 egg yolks
1 tablespoon all-purpose flour
½ vanilla bean, split
1 (8-ounce) package fat-free cream cheese,
    softened
1 (8-ounce) package ⅓-less-fat cream
    cheese, softened
½ cup brewed espresso or dark-roast coffee
3 tablespoons Marsala
3 (3-ounce) packages ladyfingers
3 tablespoons powdered sugar
1 tablespoon unsweetened cocoa

1. Stir together granulated sugar, ½ cup cream, milk,
and next 4 ingredients in a heavy saucepan. Cook over
medium heat, stirring constantly, 30 minutes or until
thickened. Cool completely. Discard vanilla bean.
Whisk in cream cheeses.
2. Stir together espresso and Marsala. Layer one-fourth
of ladyfingers in a trifle bowl; brush with espresso
mixture. Top with one-fourth of cream cheese mixture. Repeat 3 times with remaining ladyfingers, coffee
mixture, and cream cheese mixture.
3. Beat remaining ½ cup whipping cream at high speed
with an electric mixer until foamy; gradually add powdered sugar, beating until soft peaks form. Spoon over
cream cheese mixture, and sprinkle with cocoa. Cover
and chill 2 hours. **Makes** 10 servings.
Note: This can also be prepared in a 13- x 9-inch
baking dish, layering ladyfingers and cream cheese
mixture. Spread with whipped cream mixture.

Per serving: Calories 345; Fat 16.6g (sat 9.5g, mono 4.3g, poly 1.1g); Protein 12.3g;
Carb 35g; Fiber 0.4g; Chol 182mg; Iron 1.4mg; Sodium 325mg; Calc 166mg

Black-Eyed Susans

*Get out your cookie gun for this recipe. Let the kids
help add chocolate morsels.*

PREP: 20 MIN., COOK: 8 MIN. PER BATCH

½ cup butter, softened
½ cup granulated sugar
½ cup firmly packed light brown sugar
1 cup creamy peanut butter
1 large egg
1½ tablespoons warm water
1 teaspoon vanilla extract
1½ cups all-purpose flour
½ teaspoon salt
½ teaspoon baking soda
½ cup semisweet chocolate morsels

1. Beat butter and sugars at medium speed with an
electric mixer until light and fluffy. Add peanut butter
and next 3 ingredients, beating well.
2. Combine flour, salt, and baking soda. Add to butter
mixture, beating until blended.
3. Use a cookie gun fitted with a flower-shaped disc to
make cookies, following manufacturer's instructions.
Place cookies on lightly greased baking sheets. Place a
chocolate morsel in center of each cookie.
4. Bake at 350° for 8 minutes or until lightly browned.
Remove to wire racks to cool. Freeze up to 1 month, if
desired. **Makes** 8 dozen.

Per cookie: Calories 45; Fat 2.6g (sat 1.1g, mono 1g, poly 0.4g); Protein 1g; Carb 4.7g;
Fiber 0.3g; Chol 5mg; Iron 0.2mg; Sodium 39mg; Calc 3mg

Battered Catfish and
Chips, page 253

mouthwatering
entrées

Grilled Steaks Balsamico

Grilled Steaks Balsamico
PREP: 15 MIN., COOK: 18 MIN., OTHER: 2 HR.

⅔ cup balsamic vinaigrette
¼ cup fig preserves
4 (6- to 8-ounce) boneless beef chuck-eye steaks
1 teaspoon salt
1 teaspoon freshly ground pepper
1 (6.5-ounce) container buttery garlic-and-herb
    spreadable cheese

1. Process vinaigrette and preserves in a blender until smooth. Place steaks and vinaigrette mixture in a shallow dish or a large zip-top plastic freezer bag. Cover or seal, and chill at least 2 hours. Remove steaks from marinade, discarding marinade.
2. Grill, covered with grill lid, over medium-high heat (350° to 400°) 5 to 7 minutes on each side or to desired degree of doneness. Remove to a serving platter, and sprinkle evenly with salt and pepper; keep warm.
3. Heat cheese in a small saucepan over low heat, stirring often, 2 to 4 minutes or until melted. Serve cheese sauce with steaks. **Makes** 4 servings.
Note: For testing purposes only, we used Alouette Garlic & Herbs Spreadable Cheese.

GRILL FAVORITE, FAMILY FAVORITE
Italian Sirloin Steaks
PREP: 15 MIN., COOK: 14 MIN., OTHER: 2 HR.

4 garlic cloves, pressed
¼ cup olive oil
2 teaspoons dried basil
2 teaspoons dried oregano
2 teaspoons dried parsley
1 teaspoon dried rosemary
2 (¾-inch-thick) top-sirloin steaks (about 2 pounds)
1¼ teaspoons salt, divided
1 teaspoon pepper

1. Stir together first 6 ingredients in a small bowl. Sprinkle steaks evenly with 1 teaspoon salt and pepper; rub with garlic mixture. Cover and chill steaks at least 2 hours. Sprinkle steaks evenly with remaining ¼ teaspoon salt.

2. Grill steaks, covered with grill lid, over medium-high heat (350° to 400°) 7 minutes on each side or to desired degree of doneness. Cut steaks in half. **Makes** 4 servings.

GRILL FAVORITE, FAMILY FAVORITE
Marinated London Broil
London broil, an extra-thick cut of boneless top round steak, serves six to eight people relatively inexpensively. Keep a close watch for buy-one-get-one-free sales.

PREP: 5 MIN.; COOK: 30 MIN.; OTHER: 24 HR., 10 MIN.

1 (12-ounce) can cola soft drink
1 (10-ounce) bottle teriyaki sauce
1 (2½- to 3-pound) London broil

1. Combine cola and teriyaki sauce in a shallow dish or large zip-top plastic freezer bag; add London broil. Cover or seal, and chill 24 hours, turning occasionally. Remove London broil from marinade, discarding marinade.
2. Grill, covered with grill lid, over medium heat (300° to 350°) 12 to 15 minutes on each side or to desired degree of doneness. Let stand 10 minutes; cut diagonally into thin slices across the grain. **Makes** 6 to 8 servings.

Beef Tips on Rice
PREP: 10 MIN.; COOK: 2 HR., 15 MIN.

3 tablespoons all-purpose flour
1 teaspoon salt
½ teaspoon pepper
½ teaspoon paprika
2 pounds boneless top sirloin roast,
    cut into 1-inch cubes
2 tablespoons vegetable oil
2 large onions, chopped
1 beef bouillon cube
¾ cup boiling water
Hot cooked rice

1. Combine first 4 ingredients in a zip-top plastic freezer bag; shake to mix. Add beef cubes; seal bag, and shake until meat is coated. Brown beef in hot oil in a Dutch oven, stirring often. Add onion, and cook until tender.
2. Dissolve bouillon cube in boiling water; add to beef mixture.
3. Cover, reduce heat, and simmer 2 hours, stirring occasionally. Serve over rice. **Makes** 6 servings.
Note: Sometimes you can find meat labeled "beef tips" in the grocery; if so, the work of cutting into cubes has already been done for you.

"This is a true family pleaser. My kids love the mild recipe—and they always eat the rice."

ASHLEY ARTHUR, ASSISTANT RECIPE EDITOR

Pepper Steak
PREP: 17 MIN.; COOK: 1 HR., 12 MIN.

1½ pounds boneless top round steak
2 tablespoons vegetable oil
2 medium tomatoes, peeled and coarsely
    chopped
2 medium-sized green peppers, seeded
    and cut into strips
1 small onion, sliced
1 cup water
¼ cup soy sauce
½ teaspoon beef bouillon granules
½ teaspoon pepper
¼ teaspoon salt
¼ teaspoon garlic powder
¼ teaspoon ground ginger
2 tablespoons cornstarch
2 tablespoons water
Hot cooked rice

1. Flatten steak to ¼-inch thickness with a meat mallet or rolling pin; slice steak across the grain into thin strips. Brown steak on both sides in hot oil in a Dutch oven; drain. Add chopped tomato and next 9 ingredients; cover and simmer 1 hour.
2. Combine cornstarch and 2 tablespoons water; add to steak mixture. Cook 2 minutes or until thickened, stirring constantly. Serve over rice. **Makes** 4 servings.

Strip Steak With Rosemary Butter

PREP: 15 MIN., COOK: 8 MIN., OTHER: 1 HR.

½ cup butter, softened
1 tablespoon fresh rosemary
2 teaspoons lemon zest, divided
Salt and pepper to taste
1 tablespoon dried Italian seasoning
1½ tablespoons olive oil
2 garlic cloves, minced
1 teaspoon pepper
½ teaspoon salt
4 (6-ounce) beef strip steaks (½ inch thick)

1. Stir together butter, rosemary, 1 teaspoon lemon zest, and salt and pepper to taste. Cover and chill until ready to serve.

2. Combine Italian seasoning and next 4 ingredients in a small bowl. Stir in remaining 1 teaspoon lemon zest. Rub mixture over steaks. Cover and chill 1 hour.

3. Grill steaks, covered with grill lid, over medium-high heat (350° to 400°) 3 to 4 minutes on each side or to desired degree of doneness. Serve with rosemary butter. **Makes** 2 servings.

Strip Steak With Rosemary Butter

Cilantro-Garlic Sirloin With
Zesty Corn Salsa

GRILL FAVORITE
Cilantro-Garlic Sirloin With Zesty Corn Salsa

Chopping up the sirloin and tossing it into a salad with the salsa as a dressing is also very good.

PREP: 15 MIN.; COOK: 24 MIN.; OTHER: 2 HR., 10 MIN.

1 cup (1 bunch) fresh cilantro, packed
2 garlic cloves
3 tablespoons fresh lime juice
1 tablespoon lime zest
½ teaspoon salt
½ teaspoon ground cumin
¼ to ½ teaspoon ground red pepper
2 pounds top sirloin steak (1¼ inches thick)
Zesty Corn Salsa (opposite page)
Garnish: fresh cilantro sprig

1. Process first 7 ingredients in a food processor or blender until blended, and rub cilantro mixture over sirloin steak. Chill 2 hours.
2. Grill, covered with grill lid, over medium-high heat (350° to 400°) 10 to 12 minutes on each side or to desired degree of doneness. Let stand 10 minutes.
3. Cut steak diagonally across the grain into thin slices. Serve with Zesty Corn Salsa. Garnish, if desired.
Makes 8 servings.

Zesty Corn Salsa

PREP: 15 MIN., COOK: 20 MIN.

6 ears fresh corn, husks removed
¼ cup fresh lime juice
2 teaspoons olive oil
½ teaspoon lime zest
1 small jalapeño pepper, minced
¼ teaspoon salt
¼ teaspoon ground cumin

1. Grill corn, covered with grill lid, over medium-high heat (350° to 400°) 10 minutes on each side or until browned on all sides. Remove from grill; cool.
2. Cut corn from cob into a bowl; stir in juice and remaining ingredients. **Makes** 2 cups (about 8 servings).

GRILL FAVORITE
Grilled Flank Steak

Leftovers make great fajitas or a low-carb green salad topper.

PREP: 10 MIN.; COOK: 14 MIN.; OTHER: 8 HR., 5 MIN.

2 tablespoons dry red wine
1 tablespoon red wine vinegar
1 tablespoon prepared horseradish
1 tablespoon ketchup
1 teaspoon dried thyme
1 teaspoon minced garlic
½ teaspoon pepper
2 pounds flank steak

1. Combine first 7 ingredients in a shallow dish or zip-top plastic freezer bag; add steak. Cover or seal, and chill 8 hours, turning occasionally.
2. Remove steak from marinade, discarding marinade.
3. Grill, covered with grill lid, over high heat (400° to 500°) about 7 minutes on each side or to desired degree of doneness. Let stand 5 minutes. Cut diagonally across the grain into thin slices. **Makes** 6 servings.

GRILL FAVORITE, FAMILY FAVORITE
Fajitas With Pico de Gallo

PREP: 20 MIN., COOK: 8 MIN., OTHER: 4 HR.

1 garlic bulb
1 large yellow bell pepper, cut into strips
1 large red bell pepper, cut into strips
1 large green bell pepper, cut into strips
2 large onions, sliced
1 cup lime juice
1 tablespoon pepper
2 (1½-pound) flank steaks
Vegetable cooking spray
16 (8-inch) flour tortillas
Pico de Gallo
Sour cream

1. Separate garlic bulb into cloves; peel and crush cloves.
2. Combine garlic and next 6 ingredients in a shallow dish or large zip-top plastic freezer bag; add steak. Cover or seal, and chill 4 hours, turning occasionally.
3. Remove steak and vegetables from marinade; discard marinade.
4. Coat vegetables with vegetable cooking spray. Place in a grill basket. Grill steak and vegetables, covered with grill lid, over high heat (400° to 500°) about 4 minutes on each side or until steak reaches desired degree of doneness and vegetables are tender.
5. Cut steak diagonally across the grain into very thin slices. Serve steak, peppers, and onion with tortillas, Pico de Gallo, and sour cream. **Makes** 8 servings.

Pico de Gallo

PREP: 10 MIN.

6 medium tomatoes, diced
1 medium onion, diced
¼ cup chopped fresh cilantro
1 to 2 serrano chile peppers, seeded and minced
1 tablespoon olive oil
1 teaspoon salt

1. Stir together all ingredients; chill. **Makes** 7 cups.

Marinated Beef Tenderloin

PREP: 10 MIN.; COOK: 18 MIN.; OTHER: 8 HR., 15 MIN.

1 (5- to 6-pound) beef tenderloin, trimmed
2 (16-ounce) bottles zesty Italian salad dressing
⅓ cup Allegro meat and vegetable marinade
    or soy sauce
⅓ cup Burgundy or other dry red wine
1 teaspoon soy sauce
1 clove garlic, minced
½ teaspoon lemon-pepper marinade or
    lemon-pepper seasoning
Lettuce leaves
Horseradish Sauce

1. Place meat in a large shallow dish or zip-top plastic freezer bag. Combine salad dressing and next 5 ingredients, and pour over meat. Cover or seal, and refrigerate 8 hours, turning occasionally.
2. Drain, discarding marinade. Cook, covered with grill lid over high heat 3 minutes; turn and cook 3 minutes. Reduce heat to low, and cook, covered, 12 minutes or until a meat thermometer inserted in thickest portion registers 140°. Let stand 15 minutes before slicing.
3. Place tenderloin on a lettuce-lined tray. Serve tenderloin with Horseradish Sauce and sliced French bread. **Makes** 20 to 24 appetizer servings.

Horseradish Sauce

PREP: 5 MIN.

1 cup mayonnaise
1½ tablespoons prepared horseradish

1. Combine mayonnaise and horseradish in a small bowl. **Makes** 1 cup.

> **This is one of my favorite recipes to prepare when I take dinner to friends.**
>
> ELEANOR GRIFFIN, EDITOR-IN-CHIEF

Aunt Mary's Pot Roast

To reduce the fat in this recipe, substitute an eye-of-round roast for the chuck roast. Both cuts of meat become fall-apart tender when cooked with slow, moist heat.

PREP: 10 MIN.; COOK: 3 HR, 10 MIN.

1 (3- to 4-pound) chuck roast
1 (12-ounce) can beer
1 (0.7-ounce) envelope Italian dressing mix
Roasted Vegetables (optional)

1. Brown roast on all sides in a lightly oiled 5-quart cast-iron Dutch oven over high heat. Remove from heat, and add beer and dressing mix.
2. Bake, covered, at 300° for 3 hours or until tender, turning once. Serve with Roasted Vegetables, if desired. **Makes** 6 servings.

Roasted Vegetables

Slow roasting in a cast-iron skillet accentuates the natural sweetness of these root vegetables. If desired, you may omit the olive oil and add vegetables to the Dutch oven with the pot roast during the last hour of baking.

PREP: 10 MIN., COOK: 45 MIN.

1½ pounds new potatoes, cut in half
1 (1-pound) package baby carrots
2 medium onions, quartered
1 tablespoon olive oil
Salt and pepper to taste

1. Toss potatoes, baby carrots, and onions with olive oil, and season to taste with salt and pepper.
2. Bake at 300° in a large cast-iron skillet for 45 minutes, stirring once. **Makes** 6 servings.

MAKE AHEAD
Italian Pot Roast

To make ahead, chill baked roast overnight. Cut into thin slices, and place in a 13- x 9-inch baking dish.
Top with gravy. Bake at 350° for 30 minutes or until thoroughly heated. Serve with roasted potatoes.

PREP: 35 MIN.; COOK: 3 HR., 30 MIN.

1 (4½-pound) rib-eye roast, trimmed*
2 tablespoons vegetable oil
1 (15-ounce) can tomato sauce
½ cup red wine
2 large tomatoes, chopped
1 medium onion, minced
4 garlic cloves, minced
1 tablespoon salt
1 tablespoon pepper
2 teaspoons chopped fresh or 1 teaspoon dried basil
2 teaspoons chopped fresh or 1 teaspoon dried oregano
1 (16-ounce) package red potatoes, cut into wedges
½ teaspoon salt
¼ teaspoon pepper
3 tablespoons all-purpose flour
1 cup beef broth or water
Garnish: chopped fresh parsley

1. Cook roast in hot oil in a large Dutch oven over medium-high heat 5 to 6 minutes or until browned on all sides.
2. Combine tomato sauce and next 8 ingredients; pour sauce mixture over roast in Dutch oven.
3. Bake, covered, at 325° for 3 hours or until roast is tender. Remove roast from Dutch oven, and keep warm; reserve drippings in Dutch oven.
4. Place potato wedges in a lightly greased 15- x 10-inch jelly-roll pan. Bake at 450° for 30 minutes. Sprinkle with ½ teaspoon salt and ¼ teaspoon pepper.
5. Skim fat from drippings in Dutch oven. Whisk together flour and beef broth until smooth; add to drippings. Cook mixture, stirring constantly, over low heat 8 minutes or until thickened.
6. Cut roast into thin slices. Arrange roast and potatoes on a serving platter. Garnish, if desired. Serve with tomato gravy. **Makes** 6 to 8 servings.
*1 (4½-pound) boneless beef rump roast, trimmed, may be substituted. Bake, covered, at 325° for 2 hours and 20 minutes or until tender.

Pot Roast Jardinière

This tender roast simmers several hours with no attention needed. Just remember to add the vegetables the last hour of cooking. They make it a complete one-dish meal.

PREP: 20 MIN.; COOK: 3 HR., 30 MIN.

1 (3- to 4-pound) boneless chuck roast
1 teaspoon salt
¼ teaspoon pepper
1 tablespoon vegetable oil or olive oil
1 (10½-ounce) can beef broth, undiluted
4 carrots, scraped, cut in half crosswise, and
    sliced lengthwise
2 medium turnips, peeled and quartered
8 boiling onions or 2 small onions, quartered
1 teaspoon fresh or dried rosemary
¼ cup all-purpose flour
¼ cup water
Garnish: fresh herbs

1. Rub roast with salt and pepper. Brown roast in hot oil over medium heat in a Dutch oven. Add broth; bring mixture to a boil. Cover, reduce heat, and simmer 2½ hours.
2. Add vegetables and rosemary to Dutch oven. Cover and cook 1 more hour or until meat and vegetables are tender. Remove roast and vegetables with a slotted spoon to a serving platter, reserving liquid in pan.
3. Whisk together flour and water until smooth. Whisk into reserved liquid in Dutch oven; cook over medium heat until thickened, stirring constantly. Serve gravy with roast and vegetables. Garnish, if desired. **Makes** 6 servings.

Baked Spicy Beef Chimichangas

PREP: 15 MIN., COOK: 23 MIN.

1 pound ground round
1 medium onion, chopped
2 garlic cloves, pressed
2 cups (8 ounces) Mexican blend shredded
    cheese, divided
1 (16-ounce) can refried beans
1 (4.5-ounce) can chopped green chiles,
    drained
½ cup picante sauce
12 (8-inch) flour tortillas
Toppings: salsa, sour cream, shredded lettuce

1. Cook first 3 ingredients in a large skillet over medium-high heat 8 to 10 minutes or until beef is no longer pink, stirring until beef crumbles. Remove from heat, and drain.
2. Stir in 1½ cups cheese and next 3 ingredients. Place ¼ cup beef mixture just below center of each tortilla. Fold opposite sides of tortillas over filling, forming rectangles. Secure with wooden picks.
3. Place on a baking sheet; coat with vegetable cooking spray.
4. Bake at 425° for 8 minutes; turn chimichangas, and bake 5 more minutes. Remove picks, and serve immediately with remaining ½ cup cheese and desired toppings. **Makes** 12 servings.
Note: For testing purposes only we used Sargento 4 Cheese Mexican Recipe Blend Shredded Cheese.

Traditional Spicy Beef Chimichangas: Pour vegetable oil to depth of 2 inches into a Dutch oven; heat to 375°. Fry chimichangas, a few at a time, 1½ minutes on each side or until golden. Drain and serve hot.

Baked Linguine With Meat Sauce

FAMILY FAVORITE
Baked Linguine With Meat Sauce

PREP: 40 MIN., COOK: 30 MIN., OTHER: 5 MIN.

2 pounds lean ground beef
2 garlic cloves, minced
1 (28-ounce) can crushed tomatoes
1 (8-ounce) can tomato sauce
1 (6-ounce) can tomato paste
1 teaspoon salt
2 teaspoons sugar
8 ounces uncooked linguine
1 (16-ounce) container sour cream
1 (8-ounce) package cream cheese,
    softened
1 bunch green onions, chopped
2 cups (8 ounces) shredded sharp
    Cheddar cheese

1. Cook beef and garlic in a Dutch oven, stirring until beef crumbles and is no longer pink. Stir in tomatoes and next 4 ingredients; simmer 30 minutes. Set mixture aside.

2. Cook pasta according to package directions; drain. Place pasta in a lightly greased 13- x 9-inch baking dish.

3. Stir together sour cream, cream cheese, and green onions. Spread over pasta. Top with meat sauce.

4. Bake at 350° for 20 to 25 minutes or until thoroughly heated. Sprinkle with Cheddar cheese, and bake 5 more minutes or until cheese melts. Let stand 5 minutes. Serve with a salad and bread, if desired. **Makes** 8 servings.

Note: To lighten dish, use no-salt-added tomato products, light sour cream, light cream cheese, and reduced-fat Cheddar cheese.

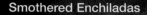

Smothered Enchiladas

PREP: 10 MIN., COOK: 25 MIN.

2 pounds ground beef
1 (1.25-ounce) package mild taco seasoning mix
1 (4.5-ounce) can chopped green chiles, divided
2 (10¾-ounce) cans cream of chicken soup
1 (16-ounce) container sour cream
8 (8-inch) flour tortillas
2 cups (8 ounces) shredded Cheddar cheese
Garnishes: salsa, sour cream, green onion curls, chopped fresh cilantro

1. Cook ground beef in a large skillet, stirring until it crumbles and is no longer pink; drain. Stir in taco seasoning mix and half of chopped green chiles; set aside.
2. Stir together remaining green chiles, soup, and sour cream. Pour half of soup mixture into a lightly greased 13- x 9-inch baking dish. Spoon beef mixture evenly down centers of tortillas; roll up. Place, seam sides down, over soup mixture in baking dish; top evenly with remaining soup mixture and cheese.
3. Bake, uncovered, at 350° for 25 minutes or until thoroughly heated. Garnish, if desired. **Makes** 8 servings.

(EDITOR'S CHOICE)
Italian Meatballs

PREP: 20 MIN., COOK: 35 MIN.

½ pound mild Italian sausage,
    casings removed
¾ pound ground turkey
1 cup fine, dry breadcrumbs
¾ cup minced onion
4 large eggs, lightly beaten
¾ cup grated Parmesan cheese
1 tablespoon minced garlic
½ teaspoon salt
½ teaspoon pepper
2 teaspoons dried Italian seasoning
Marinara Sauce
Hot cooked spaghetti
Freshly grated Parmesan cheese (optional)

1. Combine sausage, ground turkey, and next 8 ingredients in a large bowl until well blended.
2. Gently shape meat mixture into 30 (1½-inch) balls.
3. Bring Marinara Sauce to a boil in a Dutch oven over medium heat, stirring occasionally; reduce heat, and simmer. Add 10 meatballs, and cook 6 to 8 minutes or until meatballs are done. Remove meatballs from sauce, and keep warm; repeat procedure with remaining meatballs.
4. Return all cooked meatballs to sauce, reduce heat to low, and cook 10 more minutes. Serve over hot cooked spaghetti, and, if desired, sprinkle with Parmesan cheese. **Makes** 30 meatballs (6 to 8 servings).

❝❝ We adapted and scaled down this recipe from *Barbara Jean's Cookbook* by Barbara Jean Barta, owner of the Barbara Jean's restaurant chain. Make a large batch of these, and freeze them in meal-size portions to cook during the week. ❞❞

REBECCA KRACKE GORDON, ASSISTANT TEST KITCHENS DIRECTOR

Marinara Sauce

PREP: 5 MIN., COOK: 10 MIN.

1 cup beef broth
½ cup dry red wine
½ cup water
1 (26-ounce) jar marinara sauce
1 (8-ounce) can tomato sauce with basil,
    garlic, and oregano

1. Stir together all ingredients. Cook over medium heat, stirring occasionally, 10 minutes or until thoroughly heated. **Makes** about 6 cups.

FAMILY FAVORITE
Hamburger-Rice Skillet

PREP: 18 MIN., COOK: 30 MIN.

1 pound ground chuck
1 small onion, chopped
1 small green bell pepper, chopped
1 (10-ounce) can mild diced tomatoes and
    green chiles
1½ cups water
1 cup uncooked long-grain rice
1 (1.25-ounce) package mild taco seasoning mix
½ teaspoon salt
2 cups chopped lettuce
3 green onions, chopped
1 tomato, chopped
1 avocado, sliced
1 (2¼-ounce) can sliced olives, drained
1 cup (4 ounces) shredded Mexican
    four-cheese blend
Tortilla chips
Salsa

1. Cook first 3 ingredients in a large skillet over medium-high heat, stirring until beef crumbles and is no longer pink; drain.
2. Stir in tomatoes and green chiles and next 4 ingredients. Cook, covered, over medium heat 15 minutes, stirring occasionally. Uncover and cook 15 more minutes; remove from heat.
3. Sprinkle lettuce and next 5 ingredients over hamburger mixture. Stand tortilla chips around edge of skillet; serve with chips and salsa. **Makes** 6 servings.

Pork-Stuffed Poblanos With Walnut Cream Sauce

PREP: 25 MIN., COOK: 55 MIN., OTHER: 10 MIN.

8 large poblano chile peppers
1 pound ground pork
1 tablespoon olive oil
1 medium onion, chopped
1 large garlic clove, minced
1 teaspoon ground cumin
¾ teaspoon ground cinnamon
¼ teaspoon ground red pepper
2 large tomatoes, chopped
1 small apple, chopped
⅓ cup raisins
⅓ cup diced almonds, toasted
1 tablespoon cider vinegar
1 teaspoon salt
1 cup tomato sauce
1 teaspoon sugar
¼ teaspoon salt
¼ teaspoon dried crushed red pepper
Walnut Cream Sauce
Garnish: cinnamon sticks

1. Broil chile peppers on an aluminum foil-lined baking sheet 5 inches from heat about 5 minutes on each side or until peppers look blistered.
2. Place chile peppers in a zip-top plastic freezer bag; seal and let stand 10 minutes to loosen skins. Peel peppers. Split chile peppers open lengthwise, keeping stems intact; remove and discard seeds. Set aside.
3. Cook pork in hot oil in a large skillet over medium-high heat, stirring until it crumbles and is no longer pink; drain. Add chopped onion and next 4 ingredients; cook, stirring often, 7 minutes or until onion is tender.
4. Stir in tomato and next 4 ingredients. Cover, reduce heat, and simmer 5 minutes. Stir in 1 teaspoon salt.
5. Stir together tomato sauce and next 3 ingredients in a small saucepan over low heat 5 minutes. Spoon about ½ cup pork mixture into each pepper, and place in a lightly greased 13- x 9-inch baking dish. Pour tomato sauce mixture over peppers.
6. Bake, covered, at 350° for 30 minutes. Top with Walnut Cream Sauce. Garnish, if desired. **Makes** 8 servings.

Note: Small green bell peppers may be substituted for poblanos chile peppers. (Do not broil.) Proceed as directed. Bake 45 minutes or until peppers are tender.

Walnut Cream Sauce

PREP: 10 MIN.

1 (3-ounce) package cream cheese, softened
½ cup walnuts, toasted
½ cup sour cream
¼ cup milk
1 teaspoon ground cinnamon
½ teaspoon ground red pepper
½ teaspoon sugar
¼ teaspoon salt

1. Process all ingredients in a food processor or blender until smooth, stopping to scrape down sides. **Makes** 1½ cups.

GRILL FAVORITE
Maple Spareribs

PREP: 15 MIN., COOK: 2 HR.

3 to 4 pounds pork spareribs
1 cup maple syrup
⅓ cup soy sauce
1 tablespoon garlic powder
3 tablespoons sweet cooking rice wine
2 teaspoons salt
½ teaspoon sugar

1. Bring ribs and water to cover to a boil in a large Dutch oven; reduce heat, and simmer 30 minutes. Drain. Place ribs in a lightly greased 13- x 9-inch pan.
2. Stir together maple syrup and remaining ingredients; pour over ribs in dish.
3. Prepare hot fire by piling charcoal on 1 side of grill, leaving other side empty. (For gas grills, light only 1 side.) Arrange ribs over unlit side, reserving sauce in dish.
4. Grill spareribs, covered with grill lid, 1 hour and 30 minutes, basting occasionally with reserved sauce. **Makes** 4 servings.
Note: For testing purposes only, we used Kikkoman Aji-Mirin Sweet Cooking Rice Wine.

Maple Spareribs

Pork 'n' Avocado Enchiladas

PREP: 10 MIN., COOK: 50 MIN.

2 bacon slices
1 medium onion, chopped
1 garlic clove, minced
2 (10-ounce) cans diced tomatoes and
    green chiles
1 pound breakfast pork chops
1 (16-ounce) container sour cream
2 cups (8 ounces) shredded Mexican
    four-cheese blend, divided
1 (3-ounce) package cream cheese,
    softened
2 medium avocados, chopped
¼ cup chopped fresh cilantro
1 teaspoon ground cumin
½ teaspoon salt
10 (8-inch) flour tortillas

1. Cook bacon in a large skillet until crisp; remove and drain on paper towels, reserving 1 tablespoon drippings in skillet. Crumble bacon, and set aside.
2. Sauté onion and garlic in hot drippings 2 to 3 minutes or until onion is tender; add tomatoes and green chiles and pork chops to skillet. Cover, reduce heat, and cook 8 to 10 minutes. Remove pork, and cut into thin strips. Cook tomato mixture, uncovered, 5 to 7 minutes or until liquid evaporates. Set tomato mixture aside.
3. Stir together pork, bacon, sour cream, 1 cup shredded cheese, and next 5 ingredients.
4. Spoon pork mixture down center of each tortilla; roll up tortillas, and place, seam sides down, in a lightly greased 13- x 9-inch baking dish.
5. Bake enchiladas at 350° for 15 minutes. Sprinkle with remaining 1 cup shredded cheese; top with tomato mixture, and bake 10 minutes. **Makes** 4 to 6 servings.

Pork 'n' Avocado Enchiladas

Grillades and Grits

PREP: 15 MIN., COOK: 35 MIN.

3 tablespoons all-purpose flour
1 teaspoon Creole seasoning, divided
1 pound lean breakfast pork cutlets,
    trimmed
2 teaspoons olive oil
1 cup finely diced onion
1 cup finely diced celery
½ cup finely diced green bell pepper
1 (14.5-ounce) can no-salt-added diced
    tomatoes
1 (14-ounce) can low-sodium fat-free
    chicken broth
Creamy Grits

1. Combine flour and ½ teaspoon Creole seasoning in a shallow dish. Dredge pork in flour mixture.
2. Cook pork, in 2 batches, in ½ teaspoon hot oil per batch in a large skillet over medium-high heat 2 minutes on each side or until done. Remove from skillet, and keep warm.
3. Add remaining 1 teaspoon oil to skillet. Sauté diced onion, celery, and bell pepper in hot oil 3 to 5 minutes or until vegetables are tender. Stir in remaining ½ teaspoon Creole seasoning. Stir in diced tomatoes and chicken broth, and cook 2 minutes, stirring to loosen particles from bottom of skillet. Simmer 15 to 18 minutes or until liquid reduces to about 2 tablespoons. Serve tomato mixture over Creamy Grits and pork. **Makes** 4 servings.

Creamy Grits

PREP: 5 MIN., COOK: 20 MIN.

1 (14-ounce) can low-sodium, fat-free chicken broth
1 cup fat-free milk
½ cup quick-cooking grits

1. Bring broth and milk to a boil in a medium saucepan over medium-high heat; reduce heat to low, and whisk in ½ cup grits. Cook, whisking occasionally, 15 to 20 minutes or until creamy and thickened. **Makes** 2 cups.

Cornflake-Coated Pork Chops

PREP: 10 MIN., COOK: 35 MIN.

2 large eggs, lightly beaten
2 tablespoons milk
5 cups cornflake cereal, crushed (about 2 cups
    crushed)
6 boneless pork chops (about ¾-inch thick)
2 teaspoons lemon pepper
1 teaspoon salt
1 teaspoon garlic powder
1 large lemon, halved
Garnish: halved lemon slices

1. Stir together eggs and milk in a shallow dish. Place cornflake crumbs in a separate shallow dish. Sprinkle pork evenly with lemon pepper, salt, and garlic powder. Dip pork chops in egg mixture, and dredge in cornflake crumbs. Place chops on a lightly greased rack on a baking sheet.
2. Bake at 350° for 30 to 35 minutes or until done. Squeeze lemon juice evenly over chops, and garnish, if desired. **Makes** 6 servings.

Stuffed Pork Chops

Stuffed with fontina cheese, chopped Granny Smith apples, and herbs, these pork chops become something spectacular without losing their homey appeal.

PREP: 30 MIN., COOK: 50 MIN.

6 bacon slices
2 Granny Smith apples, peeled and diced
2 shallots, finely chopped
1 tablespoon chopped fresh ginger
1 tablespoon chopped fresh sage
1 cup fontina cheese, cubed
6 (1½-inch-thick) center-cut pork loin chops
1⅛ teaspoons salt
1¼ teaspoons pepper
2 tablespoons olive oil

1. Cook bacon in a large skillet until crisp; remove bacon, and drain on paper towels, reserving 2 table-spoons drippings in skillet. Crumble bacon, and set aside.
2. Sauté apples, shallots, and ginger in hot drippings 5 minutes or until tender. Remove from heat; stir in sage.
3. Stir together apple mixture, bacon, and cheese in a bowl. Cut a horizontal slit through thickest portion of each pork chop, cutting to, but not through, other side to form a pocket. Sprinkle both sides and pocket of each pork chop with salt and pepper. Spoon apple mixture evenly into pockets, and secure with wooden picks.
4. Cook pork chops, in 2 batches, in hot olive oil in a large skillet over medium-high heat 1 to 2 minutes on each side or until golden. Place pork chops in a lightly greased roasting pan or large shallow baking dish. Bake at 425° for 25 to 30 minutes or until done.
Makes 6 servings.

Saucy Pork Chops With Orange Slices

Sweet orange marmalade is slightly less bitter than traditional orange marmalade. Either works fine in this recipe. If your chops are thinner than ours, reduce the grilling time.
(also pictured on back cover)

PREP: 10 MIN., COOK: 22 MIN., OTHER: 35 MIN.

4 (1¼-inch-thick) bone-in pork rib chops
      or loin chops*
½ cup orange juice
2 teaspoons soy sauce
¼ teaspoon dried crushed red pepper
1 teaspoon salt
¾ teaspoon black pepper
¼ cup sweet orange marmalade
½ cup bottled barbecue sauce
4 (¼-inch-thick) orange slices

1. Pierce pork chops with a fork several times on each side. Combine pork chops and next 3 ingredients in a large shallow dish or large zip-top plastic freezer bag. Cover or seal, and chill for 30 minutes.
2. Remove chops from marinade, discarding marinade. Sprinkle chops evenly with salt and black pepper.
3. Stir together marmalade and barbecue sauce in a small bowl. Brush one side of pork chops evenly with half of marmalade mixture.
4. Grill chops, marmalade mixture side up and covered with grill lid, over medium-high heat (350° to 400°) 10 minutes. Turn pork chops, and brush evenly with remaining half of marmalade mixture. Grill 10 minutes or until done. Remove chops from grill, and let stand 5 minutes.
5. Grill orange slices, covered with grill lid, over medium-high heat 1 minute on each side. Serve with pork chops. **Makes** 4 servings.
*4 (1¼-inch-thick) boneless pork loin chops may be substituted. Reduce grilling time to 8 minutes on each side or until done.
Note: For testing purposes only, we used Jack Daniel's Original No. 7 Barbecue Recipe Grilling Sauce.

Saucy Pork Chop With
Orange Slices

Grilled Maple Chipotle Pork Chops on Smoked Gouda Grits

PREP: 10 MIN., COOK: 20 MIN.

½ cup barbecue sauce

½ cup maple syrup

2 chipotle peppers in adobo sauce, seeded
    and minced

1 teaspoon adobo sauce from can

6 (1¼-inch-thick) bone-in pork loin chops

1 teaspoon salt

1 teaspoon pepper

Smoked Gouda Grits (opposite page)

1. Whisk together first 4 ingredients, and set aside.

2. Sprinkle pork chops evenly with salt and pepper.

3. Grill, covered with grill lid, over medium-high heat (350° to 400°) 20 minutes or until a meat thermometer inserted into thickest portion registers 155°, turning once. Baste with half of barbecue sauce mixture the last 5 minutes of cooking or when meat thermometer registers 145°. Let pork stand until thermometer registers 160°.

4. Spoon Smoked Gouda Grits evenly onto 6 serving plates; top each with a pork chop, and drizzle evenly with remaining barbecue sauce mixture. **Makes** 6 servings.

Smoked Gouda Grits

PREP: 5 MIN., COOK: 10 MIN.

6 cups low-sodium chicken broth or water
2 cups milk
1 teaspoon salt
½ teaspoon ground white pepper
2 cups uncooked quick-cooking grits
1⅔ cups shredded smoked Gouda cheese
3 tablespoons unsalted butter

1. Bring first 4 ingredients to a boil in a medium saucepan; gradually whisk in grits. Cover, reduce heat, and simmer, stirring occasionally, 5 minutes or until thickened. Add cheese and butter, stirring until melted. **Makes** 6 to 8 servings.

Pork Chops and Gravy

PREP: 8 MIN.; COOK: 2 HR., 30 MIN.

½ cup all-purpose flour
1½ teaspoons dry mustard
½ teaspoon salt
½ teaspoon garlic powder
6 (1-inch-thick) lean pork chops
1 (10¾-ounce) can condensed chicken
     broth, undiluted
2 tablespoons vegetable oil

1. Combine first 4 ingredients in a shallow dish; dredge chops in flour mixture, and set aside. Combine remaining flour mixture and chicken broth in a 3½-quart slow cooker.
2. Pour oil into a large skillet; place over medium-high heat until hot. Cook chops in hot oil just until browned on both sides; place in slow cooker.
3. Cook, covered, on HIGH 2 to 2½ hours or until tender. Serve with hot rice or mashed potatoes. **Makes** 6 servings.

QUICK
Garlic-Parmesan Pork Chops

PREP: 5 MIN., COOK: 37 MIN.

6 (½-inch-thick) boneless pork loin chops
½ teaspoon salt
½ teaspoon pepper
¼ cup milk
2 tablespoons Dijon mustard
1 cup Italian-seasoned breadcrumbs
¼ cup butter, divided
1½ teaspoons jarred minced garlic
¾ cup whipping cream
⅓ cup white wine or chicken broth
½ cup grated Parmesan cheese

1. Sprinkle pork chops evenly with salt and pepper.
2. Stir together milk and mustard. Dip pork chops in milk mixture; dredge in breadcrumbs. Place pork chops on a rack in a broiler pan.
3. Bake pork chops at 375° for 30 minutes or until done.
4. Melt 1 tablespoon butter in a saucepan over medium-high heat; add garlic, and sauté 2 to 3 minutes. Stir in cream, wine, and cheese; reduce heat, and simmer 3 to 4 minutes (do not boil). Whisk in remaining 3 tablespoons butter until melted. Serve with chops. **Makes** 4 to 6 servings.

Slow-Roasted Pork

Serve shredded pork over Caribbean Rice and Peas (page 284).

PREP: 15 MIN., COOK: 7 HR., OTHER: 4 HR.

1 medium onion, finely chopped
4 garlic cloves, crushed
½ cup fresh orange juice
½ cup fresh grapefruit juice
⅓ cup fresh lemon juice
2 tablespoons brown sugar
3 bay leaves, crumbled
2 teaspoons salt
2 teaspoons chili powder
1 teaspoon ground allspice
1 teaspoon ground black pepper
1 (5- to 6-pound) Boston butt pork roast
    or pork shoulder
1 tablespoon vegetable oil
Garnishes: lemon slices, lemon zest,
    fresh parsley sprigs

1. Combine first 11 ingredients in a large bowl. Add pork roast, turning to coat with marinade. Cover and refrigerate roast at least 4 hours or overnight.
2. Remove roast from marinade, reserving marinade. Brown all sides of roast in hot oil in a Dutch oven. Add reserved marinade.
3. Bake, covered, at 275° for 6 to 7 hours or until meat can be shredded. Garnish, if desired. **Makes** 8 servings.

Honey-Garlic Pork Tenderloin

PREP: 5 MIN., COOK: 26 MIN., OTHER: 1 HR.

6 tablespoons lemon juice
6 tablespoons honey
2½ tablespoons soy sauce
1½ tablespoons dry sherry or chicken broth
3 garlic cloves, pressed
¾ pound pork tenderloin

1. Stir together first 5 ingredients in a shallow dish or zip-top plastic freezer bag; remove ½ cup mixture, and set aside. Prick pork several times with a fork, and place in remaining mixture. Cover or seal, and chill 1 hour.
2. Remove pork, discarding marinade.
3. Grill, covered with grill lid, over medium heat (300° to 350°) 11 to 13 minutes on each side or until a meat thermometer inserted into thickest portion registers 160°, basting with reserved ½ cup mixture. **Makes** 2 servings.

Asian Pork Tenderloin

PREP: 20 MIN.; COOK: 25 MIN.; OTHER: 8 HR., 5 MIN.

⅓ cup lite soy sauce
¼ cup sesame oil
⅓ cup packed light brown sugar
2 tablespoons Worcestershire sauce
2 tablespoons lemon juice
4 garlic cloves, crushed
1 tablespoon dry mustard
1½ teaspoons pepper
1½ to 2 pounds pork tenderloin

1. Whisk together first 8 ingredients. Place pork in a shallow dish; add marinade, turning pork to coat. Cover and chill 8 hours. Remove pork from marinade, discarding marinade. Place in a foil-lined roasting pan.
2. Bake at 450° for 25 minutes or until a meat thermometer registers 160°. Let pork stand 5 minutes. **Makes** 6 servings.

Festive Pork Roast

A blend of Asian spices, red wine, and sugar create a delectable taste bud sensation.

PREP: 30 MIN.; COOK: 2 HR., 30 MIN.; OTHER: 8 HR., 10 MIN.

1½ cups dry red wine
⅔ cup firmly packed brown sugar
½ cup ketchup
½ cup water
¼ cup vegetable oil
4 garlic cloves, minced
3 tablespoons soy sauce
2 teaspoons curry powder
1 teaspoon ground ginger
½ teaspoon pepper
1 (5-pound) boneless rolled pork roast
4 teaspoons cornstarch

1. Combine first 10 ingredients in a large shallow dish or zip-top plastic freezer bag; add pork. Cover or seal, and chill 8 hours, turning occasionally.
2. Remove pork from marinade, reserving 2½ cups marinade. Bring reserved marinade to a boil in a small saucepan; whisk in cornstarch, and cook, stirring constantly, 2 to 3 minutes or until thickened. Cool.
3. Pat pork dry, and place on a rack in a shallow roasting pan.
4. Bake pork at 325° for 2½ hours or until meat thermometer inserted into thickest portion registers 170°, basting with ¼ cup reserved sauce during the last 15 minutes. Allow roast to stand 10 minutes before slicing. Serve with reserved sauce. **Makes** 8 to 10 servings.

Orange-Cranberry Glazed Pork Tenderloins

Prepare cranberry basting sauce up to 8 hours ahead; chill until ready to use.

PREP: 35 MIN., COOK: 40 MIN.

1 (16-ounce) can whole-berry cranberry sauce
1 teaspoon orange zest
⅔ cup fresh orange juice
2 teaspoons balsamic vinegar
⅛ teaspoon salt
½ teaspoon pepper
¼ teaspoon ground allspice
⅛ teaspoon ground cinnamon
⅛ teaspoon ground cloves
1½ pounds pork tenderloin, trimmed
Garnishes: fresh rosemary sprigs, whole cranberries

1. Bring first 9 ingredients to a boil in a large saucepan. Reduce heat, and simmer mixture, stirring occasionally, 20 minutes.
2. Place pork in a lightly greased, shallow roasting pan.
3. Bake at 425° for 40 minutes or until a meat thermometer inserted into thickest portion registers 160°, basting occasionally with half of cranberry mixture. Slice pork, and serve with remaining cranberry mixture. Garnish, if desired. **Makes** 6 servings.

Grilled Pork Tenderloin With Gingered Jezebel Sauce

PREP: 5 MIN., COOK: 25 MIN., OTHER: 30 MIN.

½ cup lite soy sauce
2 tablespoons dark brown sugar
2 green onions, chopped
2 tablespoons sherry (optional)
3 pounds pork tenderloin
Gingered Jezebel Sauce
Garnish: fresh rosemary

1. Combine first 3 ingredients and, if desired, sherry in a shallow dish or large zip-top plastic freezer bag; add pork. Cover or seal, and chill 20 minutes.
2. Remove pork from marinade, discarding marinade. Grill pork, covered with grill lid, over medium-high heat (350° to 400°) 25 minutes or until meat thermometer inserted into thickest portion registers 155°, turning once and basting with ½ cup Gingered Jezebel Sauce the last 5 to 10 minutes. Let stand 10 minutes or until thermometer registers 160°. Slice and serve with remaining ¾ cup Gingered Jezebel Sauce. Garnish, if desired. **Makes** 6 servings.

Gingered Jezebel Sauce
Ginger replaces dry mustard in this version of Jezebel sauce.

PREP: 5 MIN., COOK: 2 MIN.

⅔ cup pineapple preserves
⅓ cup apple jelly
2 tablespoons prepared horseradish
1 tablespoon grated fresh ginger

1. Microwave pineapple preserves and apple jelly in a glass bowl at HIGH 2 minutes or until melted. Stir in remaining ingredients. **Makes** 1¼ cups.

Grilled Pork Tenderloin With
Gingered Jezebel Sauce

QUICK
Sausage and Peppers With Parmesan Cheese Grits

PREP: 15 MIN., COOK: 15 MIN.

1 (19-ounce) package sweet Italian sausage
3 red, yellow, or green bell peppers, cut into strips
1 large sweet onion, cut in half and thinly sliced
2 garlic cloves, minced
1 to 2 teaspoons dried Italian seasoning
½ teaspoon garlic powder
1 teaspoon salt
½ teaspoon pepper
Parmesan Cheese Grits
Garnish: shredded Parmesan cheese

1. Remove sausage casings, and discard. Cook sausage and next 7 ingredients in a large skillet over medium-high heat, stirring until sausage crumbles and is no longer pink and vegetables are tender. Serve over Parmesan Cheese Grits; garnish, if desired. **Makes** 4 servings.

Parmesan Cheese Grits

PREP: 3 MIN., COOK: 5 MIN.

1 cup grits
4 cups water
¾ teaspoon salt
1 tablespoon butter
1 (5-ounce) package shredded
    Parmesan cheese

1. Cook grits according to package directions, using 4 cups water. Stir in salt, butter, and Parmesan cheese. **Makes** 4 servings.

230 mouthwatering entrées

Ham-and-Greens Pot Pie With Cornbread Crust

PREP: 10 MIN., COOK: 50 MIN.

4 cups chopped cooked ham
2 tablespoons vegetable oil
3 tablespoons all-purpose flour
3 cups chicken broth
1 (16-ounce) package frozen seasoning blend
1 (16-ounce) package frozen chopped
    collard greens
1 (16-ounce) can black-eyed peas, rinsed
    and drained
½ teaspoon dried crushed red pepper
Cornbread Crust Batter

1. Sauté ham in hot oil in a Dutch oven over medium-high heat 5 minutes or until lightly browned. Add flour, and cook, stirring constantly, 1 minute. Gradually add chicken broth, and cook, stirring constantly, 3 minutes or until broth begins to thicken.
2. Bring mixture to a boil, and add seasoning blend and collard greens; return to a boil, and cook, stirring often, 15 minutes. Stir in black-eyed peas and crushed red pepper; spoon hot mixture into a lightly greased 13- x 9-inch baking dish. Pour Cornbread Crust Batter evenly over hot filling mixture.
3. Bake at 425° for 20 to 25 minutes or until cornbread is golden brown and set. **Makes** 8 to 10 servings.
Note: For testing purposes only, we used McKenzie's Seasoning Blend.

Cornbread Crust Batter

PREP: 5 MIN.

1½ cups white cornmeal mix
½ cup all-purpose flour
1 teaspoon sugar
2 large eggs, lightly beaten
1½ cups buttermilk

1. Combine first 3 ingredients; make a well in the center of mixture. Add eggs and buttermilk to corn-meal mixture, stirring just until moistened. **Makes** 1 (13- x 9-inch) crust.

Ham-Broccoli Pot Pie

Convenience items make this one-dish meal
very easy to prepare.

PREP: 20 MIN., COOK: 35 MIN.

1 (10-ounce) package frozen chopped broccoli,
    thawed
1 (11-ounce) can sweet whole kernel corn,
    drained
1 (10¾-ounce) can cream of mushroom soup,
    undiluted
2 cups diced cooked ham
2 cups (8 ounces) shredded Colby-Jack
    cheese blend
1 (8-ounce) container sour cream
½ teaspoon pepper
½ teaspoon dried mustard
½ (15-ounce) package refrigerated piecrusts

1. Arrange chopped broccoli in a lightly greased 11- x 7-inch baking dish.
2. Stir together corn and next 6 ingredients. Spoon over broccoli.
3. Unfold piecrust; pat or roll into an 11- x 7-inch rectangle, and place over ham mixture. Crimp edges, and cut 4 slits for steam to escape.
4. Bake at 400° for 30 to 35 minutes or until golden. **Makes** 6 servings.

Cola-Can Chicken

The cola can serves as a poultry rack to hold the chicken upright, and the cola left in the can moistens the chicken from the inside out as it grills.

PREP: 20 MIN., COOK: 1 HR., OTHER: 5 MIN.

2 tablespoons Barbecue Rub, divided
1 (3½- to 4-pound) whole chicken
3 tablespoons vegetable oil
1 (12-ounce) can cola soft drink
Cola Barbecue Sauce

1. Sprinkle 1 teaspoon Barbecue Rub inside body cavity and ½ teaspoon inside neck cavity of chicken.
2. Rub oil over skin. Sprinkle with 1 tablespoon Barbecue Rub, and rub over skin.
3. Pour out half of cola (about ¾ cup), and reserve for Cola Barbecue Sauce, leaving remaining cola in can. Make 2 additional holes in top of can. Spoon remaining 1½ teaspoons rub into cola can. Cola will start to foam.
4. Place chicken upright onto the cola can, fitting can into cavity. Pull legs forward to form a tripod, allowing chicken to stand upright.
5. Prepare a fire by piling charcoal on 1 side of grill, leaving other side empty. (For gas grills, light only 1 side.) Place a drip pan on unlit side, and place food rack on grill. Place chicken upright over drip pan. Grill, covered with grill lid, 1 hour or until golden and a meat thermometer registers 170°.
6. Remove chicken from grill, and let stand 5 minutes; carefully remove can. Serve with Cola Barbecue Sauce. **Makes** 2 to 4 servings.

Barbecue Rub

Leftover sauce can be stored in the refrigerator for a later use as long as it hasn't come into contact with raw meat.

PREP: 5 MIN.

1 tablespoon mild chili powder
2 teaspoons salt
2 teaspoons light brown sugar
1 teaspoon black pepper
1 teaspoon ground cumin
½ teaspoon garlic powder
¼ teaspoon ground red pepper

1. Combine all ingredients. **Makes** 3 tablespoons.

Cola Barbecue Sauce

PREP: 15 MIN., COOK: 8 MIN.

1 tablespoon butter
½ small onion, minced
1 tablespoon minced fresh ginger
1 garlic clove, minced
¾ cup reserved cola
¾ cup ketchup
½ teaspoon lemon zest
2 tablespoons fresh lemon juice
2 tablespoons Worcestershire sauce
2 tablespoons steak sauce
½ teaspoon pepper
½ teaspoon liquid smoke
Salt to taste

1. Melt butter in a heavy saucepan over medium heat. Add onion, ginger, and garlic; sauté 3 minutes or until tender.
2. Stir in reserved cola; bring mixture to a boil. Stir in ketchup and remaining ingredients; bring to a boil. Reduce heat, and simmer 5 minutes. **Makes** about 1½ cups.
Note: For testing purposes only, we used A.I. Steak Sauce.

Lexington-Style
Grilled Chicken

Lexington-Style Grilled Chicken

PREP: 15 MIN., COOK: 40 MIN., OTHER: 2 HR.

2 cups cider vinegar
¼ cup firmly packed dark brown sugar
¼ cup vegetable oil
3 tablespoons dried crushed red pepper
4 teaspoons salt
2 teaspoons pepper
2 (2½- to 3-pound) cut-up whole chickens*

1. Stir together first 6 ingredients until blended.
2. Place half each of vinegar mixture and chicken in a large zip-top plastic freezer bag; seal. Repeat procedure with remaining vinegar mixture and chicken, placing in a separate zip-top plastic freezer bag. Chill chicken at least 2 hours or up to 8 hours, turning occasionally.
3. Remove chicken from marinade, discarding marinade.
4. Grill chicken, covered with grill lid, over medium-high heat (350° to 400°) 35 to 40 minutes or until done, turning occasionally. **Makes** 8 to 10 servings.
*8 skinned and boned chicken breast halves and 8 skinned and boned chicken thighs may be substituted for whole chickens. Chill in marinade at least 1 to 2 hours, turning occasionally. Grill chicken, covered with grill lid, over medium-high heat (350° to 400°) 4 to 5 minutes on each side or until done.

Chicken Marbella

Chicken Marbella

Choose a mixture of everyone's favorite cuts of chicken—such as one package each of bone-in breasts, legs, thighs, and wings—or purchase pick-of-the-chick packages or chicken quarters to equal 8 pounds.

PREP: 10 MIN., COOK: 1 HR., OTHER: 8 HR.

1 (12-ounce) package pitted, bite-size dried plums
1 (3.5-ounce) jar capers
1 (0.5-ounce) bottle dried oregano
6 bay leaves
1 garlic bulb, minced (about 1 tablespoon)
1 cup pimiento-stuffed olives
½ cup red wine vinegar
½ cup olive oil
1 tablespoon coarse sea salt
2 teaspoons pepper
8 pounds mixed chicken pieces
1 cup brown sugar
1 cup dry white wine
¼ cup fresh parsley, chopped

1. Combine first 10 ingredients in a large zip-top plastic freezer bag or a large bowl. Add chicken pieces, turning to coat well; seal or cover and chill for at least 8 hours (overnight is best), turning chicken occasionally.

2. Arrange chicken in a single layer in pan. Pour marinade evenly over chicken, and sprinkle evenly with brown sugar; pour wine around pieces.

3. Bake at 350° for 50 minutes to 1 hour, basting frequently.

4. Remove chicken, dried plums, olives, and capers to serving platter. Drizzle with ¾ cup pan juices; sprinkle parsley evenly over top. Serve with remaining pan juices. **Makes** 8 to 10 servings.

Tandoori Chicken

This spicy chicken dish calls for quite a few ingredients, but it's well worth it. High-heat roasting makes for a short cooking time.

PREP: 20 MIN., COOK: 35 MIN., OTHER: 8 HR.

6 tablespoons fresh lime juice (about 3 limes)
3 tablespoons plain yogurt
1 to 2 small jalapeño or serrano chile peppers, seeded and minced
1½ teaspoons salt
1 teaspoon ground turmeric
1 teaspoon ground coriander
1 teaspoon ground cumin
½ teaspoon ground ginger
½ teaspoon garlic powder
½ teaspoon ground red pepper
¼ teaspoon ground cinnamon
¼ teaspoon ground cloves
2 tablespoons vegetable oil, divided
3 pounds chicken pieces
Garnishes: lime wedges, jalapeño or serrano chile peppers

1. Stir together first 12 ingredients and 1 tablespoon vegetable oil in a large bowl until blended.
2. Skin chicken breasts. Remove breast bones by inserting a sharp knife tip between bone and meat, cutting gently to remove as much meat as possible. Cut breast halves into thirds. Cut deep slits, 1 inch apart, into remaining chicken pieces. (Do not skin pieces.) Place chicken in a large bowl with spice mixture. Thoroughly rub spice mixture into slits. Cover and chill 8 hours.
3. Drizzle remaining 1 tablespoon oil in a large aluminum foil-lined roasting pan. Arrange chicken in a single layer in pan.
4. Bake chicken at 450° for 35 minutes or until done.
5. Arrange chicken on a serving platter. Garnish, if desired. **Makes** 8 servings.
Note: For testing purposes only, we used Butterball Best of the Fryer, a cut-up mix of chicken breasts, thighs, legs, and wings.

Chicken Mediterranean

PREP: 8 MIN.; COOK: 15 MIN.; OTHER: 2 HR., 5 MIN.

½ pound skinned and boned chicken breasts, cut into cubes
4 garlic cloves, minced
2 tablespoons olive oil
1 (14½-ounce) can diced tomatoes, undrained
¼ cup kalamata olives, pitted and chopped
½ teaspoon dried parsley flakes
½ teaspoon dried basil
½ teaspoon dried oregano
⅓ cup crumbled feta cheese
4 ounces penne pasta, cooked

1. Combine first 3 ingredients in a zip-top plastic freezer bag. Seal and chill 2 hours.
2. Cook chicken mixture in a large skillet over medium-high heat 8 minutes or until chicken is done; remove from skillet. Add tomatoes and next 4 ingredients to skillet. Reduce heat, and simmer, stirring often, 7 minutes.
3. Return chicken to skillet. Sprinkle with feta cheese, and remove from heat. Cover and let stand 5 minutes. Serve immediately over hot cooked pasta. **Makes** 2 servings.
Note: To serve 4, use 1 (14½-ounce) can diced tomatoes, and double all other ingredients. Cook chicken mixture 8 to 10 minutes or until done; remove from skillet. Add tomatoes and next 4 ingredients to skillet. Reduce heat, and simmer, stirring often, 7 to 8 minutes. Proceed as directed.

Chicken in Lemon Marinade
PREP: 15 MIN., COOK: 24 MIN., OTHER: 2 HR.

⅔ cup vegetable oil
½ cup lemon juice
1 tablespoon Worcestershire sauce
⅛ teaspoon hot sauce
1 small onion, grated
1 teaspoon salt
1 teaspoon pepper
1 teaspoon celery salt
6 skinned and boned chicken breasts

1. Process first 8 ingredients in a blender until smooth, stopping to scrape down sides. Reserve ¼ cup lemon juice mixture, and chill.
2. Place chicken in a shallow dish or zip-top plastic freezer bag; pour remaining lemon juice mixture over chicken. Cover or seal, and chill 2 hours, turning chicken occasionally.
3. Remove chicken from marinade, discarding marinade; place chicken on a lightly greased rack in a broiler pan.
4. Broil 7 inches from heat (with electric oven door partially open) 11 to 12 minutes on each side or until tender, basting chicken frequently with reserved ¼ cup lemon juice mixture. **Makes** 6 servings.

Chicken-Artichoke Pasta With Rosemary
PREP: 25 MIN., COOK: 25 MIN.

4 skinned and boned chicken breasts, cut into
    1-inch pieces
½ teaspoon salt
1 teaspoon freshly ground pepper
½ cup butter, divided
1 small sweet onion, halved and sliced
2 garlic cloves, pressed
6 plum tomatoes, seeded and chopped
1 (8-ounce) package sliced fresh mushrooms
1 (12-ounce) jar marinated artichoke heart
    quarters, drained
1 to 2 tablespoons chopped fresh rosemary
⅓ cup dry white wine
2 cups whipping cream
1 (9-ounce) package refrigerated
    fettuccine, cooked
¾ cup freshly grated Parmesan cheese

1. Sprinkle chicken evenly with salt and pepper.
2. Melt ¼ cup butter in a Dutch oven over medium-high heat; add chicken, and cook 5 minutes or until lightly browned. Remove chicken with a slotted spoon, and set aside.
3. Add onion and next 5 ingredients to Dutch oven; sauté 10 minutes or until vegetables are tender. Drain and remove from Dutch oven.
4. Add remaining ¼ cup butter, wine, and whipping cream to Dutch oven. Cook over medium heat, stirring constantly, 10 minutes or until thickened. Add chicken, vegetables, cooked fettuccine, and Parmesan cheese, tossing gently. Serve immediately. **Makes** 4 servings.

Chicken With Polenta

Chicken With Polenta

To prepare this recipe ahead of time, grill the chicken, cut into strips, and chill.
Make the polenta just before serving, and reheat the chicken in the microwave.

PREP: 30 MIN.; COOK: 1 HR., 15 MIN.

5 cups chicken broth, divided
1⅓ cups yellow cornmeal*
¾ cup half-and-half
1 cup grated Parmesan cheese
8 to 10 skinned and boned chicken breasts
1 teaspoon salt, divided
¼ teaspoon ground black pepper
2 red bell peppers, diced
1 large Vidalia onion, diced
1 tablespoon olive oil
3 cups fresh corn kernels (about 4 ears)
¾ cup dry white wine
½ cup orange juice
⅛ to ¼ teaspoon ground red pepper
Garnish: chopped fresh chives

1. Bring 4½ cups chicken broth to a boil in a 3-quart saucepan over medium heat. Gradually whisk in cornmeal. Reduce heat to low, and simmer, stirring often, 30 minutes. Remove from heat; stir in half-and-half and cheese.

2. Sprinkle chicken with ½ teaspoon salt and ¼ black pepper.

3. Grill chicken over medium-high heat (350° to 400°) 7 minutes on each side or until done. Cool to touch, and cut into thin strips; set aside.

4. Sauté bell pepper and onion in hot oil in a large nonstick skillet over medium heat 7 minutes or until tender. Add corn; sauté 4 minutes. Stir in wine; simmer 5 minutes. Stir in juice, remaining ½ cup broth, remaining ½ teaspoon salt, and ground red pepper; simmer 10 minutes or until slightly thickened. Serve over polenta and chicken strips. Garnish, if desired. **Makes** 10 servings.

*1 cup regular grits may be substituted for cornmeal. Bring 4 cups chicken broth to a boil, and stir in grits. Cover, reduce heat, and simmer 5 minutes. Remove from heat; stir in half-and-half and cheese.

Chicken Parmesan

PREP: 10 MIN., COOK: 26 MIN.

1 cup Italian-seasoned breadcrumbs
2 tablespoons all-purpose flour
½ teaspoon ground red pepper
2 skinned and boned chicken breasts
2 egg whites, lightly beaten
1 tablespoon olive oil
Tomato Sauce (opposite page)
1 cup shredded mozzarella cheese
¼ cup freshly grated Parmesan cheese

1. Combine breadcrumbs, flour, and ground red pepper in a small bowl, and set aside.

2. Place chicken breasts between 2 sheets of heavy-duty plastic wrap, and flatten to ¼-inch thickness using a meat mallet or rolling pin.

3. Dip 1 chicken breast in egg whites, and coat with breadcrumb mixture. Dip again in egg mixture, and coat again in breadcrumb mixture.

4. Repeat procedure with remaining chicken breast.

5. Cook chicken in hot oil over medium heat 2 to 3 minutes on each side or until done.

6. Place chicken breasts in a single layer in a lightly greased 8-inch square baking dish. Top evenly with Tomato Sauce and cheeses.

7. Bake at 350° for 20 minutes or until cheeses melt. **Makes** 2 servings.

Chicken Parmesan

Tomato Sauce

PREP: 5 MIN., COOK: 27 MIN.

½ small onion, chopped
2 garlic cloves, minced
1 tablespoon olive oil
1 (14½-ounce) can diced tomatoes with basil,
    garlic, and oregano
¼ cup red wine
½ teaspoon ground red pepper
½ teaspoon salt
¼ cup chopped fresh basil

1. Sauté onion and garlic in hot oil over medium heat
5 to 7 minutes or until tender. Add tomatoes, wine, and
red pepper; simmer 20 minutes or until thoroughly
heated. Add salt and basil. **Makes** 1½ cups.

Apple-Bacon Stuffed Chicken Breasts

PREP: 30 MIN., COOK: 25 MIN.

2 bacon slices, diced
½ cup peeled, chopped Granny Smith apple
½ cup dried cranberries, divided
1 tablespoon fine, dry breadcrumbs
½ teaspoon poultry seasoning
½ teaspoon ground cinnamon
4 skinned and boned chicken breasts
2 tablespoons butter
1 cup apple juice
2 tablespoons apple brandy or apple juice
¼ teaspoon salt
2 teaspoons cornstarch
1 tablespoon water
¼ cup coarsely chopped pecans
2 tablespoons chopped fresh parsley

1. Cook bacon in a large skillet over medium heat until
crisp; remove bacon, reserving 1 tablespoon drippings
in skillet.
2. Sauté chopped apple in reserved drippings over
medium-high heat 4 minutes. Remove from heat; stir
in bacon, ¼ cup cranberries, and next 3 ingredients.
3. Cut a 3½-inch-long horizontal slit through the
thickest portion of each chicken breast, cutting to, but
not through, other side, forming a pocket. Stuff apple
mixture evenly into each pocket. Wipe skillet clean.

4. Melt butter in skillet over medium heat. Add
chicken, and cook 8 to 10 minutes on each side or
until done. Remove chicken, and keep warm.
5. Add remaining ¼ cup cranberries, apple juice, apple
brandy, and salt to skillet. Stir together cornstarch
and 1 tablespoon water until smooth; stir into juice
mixture, and cook, stirring constantly, 1 minute or
until thickened. Spoon over chicken, and sprinkle with
pecans and parsley. **Makes** 4 servings.

QUICK
Toasted Almond Chicken

*A mixture of cream, mustard, and orange
marmalade becomes a tasty sauce for this
chicken sprinkled with almonds.*

PREP: 8 MIN., COOK: 16 MIN.

6 skinned and boned chicken breasts
⅛ teaspoon salt
⅛ teaspoon black pepper
3 tablespoons butter, divided
1½ cups whipping cream
2 tablespoons orange marmalade
1 tablespoon Dijon mustard
⅛ teaspoon ground red pepper
1 (2.25-ounce) package sliced almonds, toasted

1. Place each chicken breast between 2 sheets of heavy-
duty plastic wrap, and flatten to ¼-inch thickness
using a meat mallet or rolling pin. Sprinkle with salt
and black pepper.
2. Melt 1½ tablespoons butter in a large skillet over
medium-high heat. Add half of chicken, and cook
2 minutes on each side or until golden. Remove
chicken from skillet. Repeat procedure with remaining
butter and chicken.
3. Reduce heat to medium; add whipping cream and
next 3 ingredients to skillet, stirring well. Add chicken;
sprinkle with almonds, and cook 8 minutes or until
sauce thickens. **Makes** 6 servings.

King Ranch Chicken

PREP: 30 MIN.; COOK: 1 HR., 5 MIN.; OTHER: 5 MIN.

4 skinned and boned chicken breasts
¼ teaspoon salt
¼ teaspoon pepper
2 tablespoons butter
1 green bell pepper, chopped
1 medium onion, chopped
2 (10-ounce) cans diced tomatoes and green chiles
1 (10¾-ounce) can cream of mushroom soup, undiluted
1 (10¾-ounce) can cream of chicken soup, undiluted
12 (6-inch) corn tortillas, cut into quarters
2 cups (8 ounces) shredded Cheddar cheese, divided
Garnish: flat-leaf parsley sprigs

1. Sprinkle chicken breasts with salt and pepper; place in a lightly greased 13- x 9-inch baking dish.
2. Bake at 325° for 20 minutes or until done; cool. Coarsely chop chicken.
3. Melt butter in a large skillet over medium heat; add bell pepper and onion, and sauté until crisp-tender. Remove from heat, and stir in chicken, tomatoes and green chiles, and soups.
4. Place one-third of tortilla quarters in bottom of a lightly greased 13- x 9-inch baking dish; top with one-third chicken mixture, and sprinkle evenly with ⅔ cup cheese. Repeat layers twice, reserving last ⅔ cup cheese.
5. Bake at 325° for 35 minutes; sprinkle with reserved Cheddar cheese, and bake 5 more minutes. Let stand 5 minutes before serving. Garnish, if desired. **Makes** 6 to 8 servings.

Chicken Curry

Multiple toppings make this curried dish intriguing.

PREP: 20 MIN., COOK: 1 HR.

6 bone-in chicken breasts, skinned
2 garlic cloves, halved
2 bay leaves
4 whole peppercorns
1 teaspoon salt
3 tablespoons butter
1 large carrot, scraped and sliced
½ cup chopped celery
1 onion, chopped
1 Golden Delicious apple, peeled,
    and chopped
1½ tablespoons curry powder
½ teaspoon hot chili powder
3 tablespoons all-purpose flour
¾ teaspoon salt
¼ teaspoon ground mace
¼ teaspoon ground allspice
¼ teaspoon nutmeg
¼ teaspoon ground cinnamon
¼ teaspoon ground cloves
Hot cooked rice
Assorted condiments
Garnish: fresh cilantro

1. Place first 5 ingredients in a Dutch oven; add water to cover. Bring to a boil; cover, reduce heat, and simmer over medium heat 30 minutes or until chicken is tender. Drain, reserving broth. Bone chicken; cut into bite-size pieces.
2. Melt butter in Dutch oven over medium heat. Add carrot, celery, onion, and apple; cook 10 to 15 minutes or until tender, stirring often. Add curry and chili powders; cook 5 minutes, stirring occasionally. Stir in 1 cup reserved broth. Remove from heat; cool slightly.
3. Process mixture in an electric blender until smooth. Add flour; process until blended. Return mixture to Dutch oven; cook over medium heat 5 minutes. Gradually whisk in 2 cups reserved broth; bring to a simmer, and cook 5 minutes. Add ¾ teaspoon salt and next 5 ingredients. Stir in chicken. Serve over rice with the following condiments: flaked coconut, peanuts, chopped green onions, chutney, and currants. Garnish, if desired. **Makes** 6 servings.

Hearty Tex-Mex Squash-Chicken Casserole

PREP: 45 MIN., COOK: 35 MIN.

1 (10-ounce) package frozen chopped spinach,
    thawed
3 medium-size yellow squash, thinly sliced
1 large red bell pepper, cut into ½-inch pieces
1 yellow onion, thinly sliced
2 tablespoons peanut oil
3 cups shredded cooked chicken or turkey
12 (6-inch) corn tortillas, cut into 1-inch pieces
1 (10¾-ounce) can cream of celery soup, undiluted*
1 (8-ounce) container sour cream*
1 (8-ounce) jar picante sauce
1 (4.5-ounce) can chopped green chiles, undrained
1 (1.4-ounce) envelope fajita seasoning
2 cups (8 ounces) shredded sharp Cheddar
    cheese, divided*

1. Drain chopped spinach well, pressing between paper towels to remove excess moisture.
2. Sauté squash, bell pepper, and onion in hot oil in a large skillet over medium-high heat 6 minutes or until tender. Remove from heat. Stir in spinach, chicken, next 6 ingredients, and 1½ cups cheese. Spoon into a lightly greased 13- x 9-inch baking dish.
3. Bake at 350° for 30 minutes. Sprinkle evenly with remaining ½ cup cheese, and bake 5 more minutes. **Makes** 6 to 8 servings.
*Reduced-sodium, reduced-fat cream of celery soup; light sour cream; and reduced-fat sharp Cheddar cheese may be substituted.

Maw-Maw's Chicken Pie
PREP: 15 MIN., COOK: 40 MIN.

4 cups chopped cooked chicken
1 (10¾-ounce) can cream of chicken soup,
    undiluted
1½ cups chicken broth
2 tablespoons cornstarch
1½ cups self-rising flour
1 cup buttermilk
½ cup butter, melted

1. Place chopped chicken in a lightly greased
12- x 8-inch baking dish. Whisk together soup, broth,
and cornstarch; pour mixture evenly over chicken.
2. Whisk together flour, buttermilk, and butter; spoon
batter evenly over chicken mixture.
3. Bake at 400° for 40 minutes or until crust is golden
brown. **Makes** 8 servings.

> **This simple recipe gives rise to a golden, cakelike crust that won rave reviews at the tasting table. Try replacing a portion of the chicken with an equal amount of frozen, thawed vegetables, or stir a cup of shredded cheese into the soup mixture. We especially enjoyed the pie with broccoli and Cheddar cheese.**
>
> ASHLEY LEATH, ASSISTANT RECIPE EDITOR

Chicken-and-Wild Rice Casserole
PREP: 2 MIN., COOK: 42 MIN., OTHER: 10 MIN.

1 (6.2-ounce) package fast-cooking long-grain and
    wild rice mix
2 (10½-ounce) cans low-sodium chicken broth
1 (8-ounce) package fresh mushroom slices
3 cups chopped cooked chicken
⅔ cup Italian dressing
1 (8-ounce) container sour cream

1. Cook rice in a large saucepan according to package
directions, using 2 cans chicken broth instead of water.
Add mushrooms before the last 5 minutes.
2. Stir in chicken, dressing, and sour cream; spoon into
a lightly greased 2-quart baking dish.
3. Bake at 325° for 30 minutes or until thoroughly
heated. Let stand 10 minutes. **Makes** 6 servings.

Chicken Enchiladas
PREP: 15 MIN., COOK: 40 MIN.

3 cups chopped cooked chicken
2 cups (8 ounces) shredded Monterey Jack cheese
    with peppers
½ cup sour cream
1 (4.5-ounce) can chopped green chiles, drained
⅓ cup chopped fresh cilantro
8 (8-inch) flour tortillas
Vegetable cooking spray
1 (8-ounce) container sour cream
1 (8-ounce) jar tomatillo salsa
Toppings: diced tomatoes, chopped avocado,
    chopped green onions, sliced ripe olives,
    chopped fresh cilantro

1. Stir together first 5 ingredients. Spoon chicken mixture evenly down center of each tortilla, and roll up.
Arrange, seam side down, in a lightly greased
13- x 9-inch baking dish. Coat tortillas with vegetable
cooking spray.
2. Bake at 350° for 35 to 40 minutes or until golden
brown.
3. Stir together 8-ounce container sour cream and
salsa. Spoon over hot enchiladas; sprinkle with desired
toppings. **Makes** 4 servings.

Chicken Enchiladas

Chicken Cannelloni With Roasted
Red Bell Pepper Sauce

Chicken Cannelloni With Roasted Red Bell Pepper Sauce

For quick weeknight solutions, prepare and stuff cannelloni shells. Wrap tightly with wax paper; freeze until ready to serve. Let thaw in the refrigerator. Unwrap and place in a baking dish; top with your favorite supermarket pasta sauce, and bake as directed.

PREP: 30 MIN., COOK: 30 MIN.

1 (8-ounce) package cannelloni or manicotti shells
4 cups finely chopped cooked chicken
2 (8-ounce) containers chive-and-onion cream cheese
1 (10-ounce) package frozen chopped spinach, thawed and well drained
1 cup (8 ounces) shredded mozzarella cheese
½ cup Italian-seasoned breadcrumbs
¾ teaspoon garlic salt
1 teaspoon seasoned pepper
Roasted Red Bell Pepper Sauce
Garnish: chopped fresh basil or parsley

1. Cook pasta according to package directions; drain.
2. Stir together chicken and next 6 ingredients.
3. Cut pasta shells lengthwise through the other side. Spoon about ½ cup chicken mixture into each shell, gently pressing cut sides together. Place, cut sides down, in 2 lightly greased 11- x 7-inch baking dishes. Pour Roasted Red Bell Pepper Sauce evenly over shells.
4. Bake, covered, at 350° for 25 to 30 minutes or until thoroughly heated. Garnish, if desired. **Makes** 6 to 8 servings.

Roasted Red Bell Pepper Sauce
This sauce is also great over your favorite noodles.

PREP: 5 MIN.

2 (7-ounce) jars roasted red bell peppers, drained
1 (16-ounce) jar creamy Alfredo sauce
1 (3-ounce) package shredded Parmesan cheese

1. Process all ingredients in a blender until smooth, stopping to scrape down sides. **Makes** 3½ cups.
Note: For testing purposes only, we used Bertolli Creamy Alfredo Sauce.

Heavenly Chicken Lasagna

PREP: 30 MIN., COOK: 50 MIN., OTHER: 10 MIN.

1 tablespoon butter
½ large onion
1 (10¾-ounce) can reduced-fat cream of chicken soup, undiluted
1 (10-ounce) container refrigerated reduced-fat Alfredo sauce
1 (7-ounce) jar diced pimiento, undrained
1 (6-ounce) jar sliced mushrooms, drained
⅓ cup dry white wine
½ teaspoon dried basil
1 (10-ounce) package frozen chopped spinach, thawed
1 cup cottage cheese
1 cup ricotta cheese
½ cup grated Parmesan cheese
1 large egg, lightly beaten
9 lasagna noodles, cooked
2½ cups chopped cooked chicken
3 cups (12 ounces) shredded sharp Cheddar cheese, divided

1. Melt butter in a skillet over medium-high heat. Add onion, and sauté 5 minutes or until tender. Stir in soup and next 5 ingredients. Reserve 1 cup sauce.
2. Drain spinach well, pressing between layers of paper towels.
3. Stir together spinach, cottage cheese, and next 3 ingredients.
4. Place 3 lasagna noodles in a lightly greased 13- x 9-inch baking dish. Layer with half each of sauce, spinach mixture, and chicken. Sprinkle with 1 cup Cheddar cheese. Repeat procedure. Top with remaining 3 noodles and reserved 1 cup sauce. Cover and chill up to 1 day ahead.
5. Bake at 350° for 45 minutes. Sprinkle with remaining 1 cup Cheddar cheese, and bake 5 more minutes or until cheese is melted. Let stand 10 minutes before serving. **Makes** 8 to 10 servings.
Note: For testing purposes only, we used Cantadina Light Alfredo Sauce, found in the dairy section of the supermarket.

Smoked Turkey Breast

You won't need a smoker or gas grill for this smoked turkey recipe. Three hours on your charcoal grill give this bird its unbeatable smoky flavor.

PREP: 10 MIN., COOK: 3 HR., OTHER: 45 MIN.

1 (5- to 6-pound) bone-in turkey breast
1 teaspoon seasoned salt
1 teaspoon dried crushed red pepper
1 tablespoon seasoned salt
1½ teaspoons dried basil
1 teaspoon paprika
Vegetable cooking spray
Hickory chips

1. Split turkey breastbone so it will lie flat on grill. Combine 1 teaspoon seasoned salt and crushed red pepper; sprinkle mixture over underside of turkey breast. Combine 1 tablespoon seasoned salt, basil, and paprika; sprinkle mixture over top of turkey breast. Coat both sides of turkey breast with cooking spray.
2. Prepare charcoal fire in 1 end of grill; let burn 15 to 20 minutes. Soak hickory chips in water at least 15 minutes; place chips on coals. Place turkey breast on end of grill opposite hot coals; close grill lid. Cook 2½ to 3 hours or until a meat thermometer inserted in thickest part of breast registers 170°. Let stand 10 minutes before carving. **Makes** 12 servings.

Sesame-Crusted Turkey Mignons

PREP: 20 MIN., COOK: 24 MIN.

½ cup sesame seeds, toasted
¼ cup olive oil
1 garlic clove, minced
1 tablespoon chopped fresh chives
1 tablespoon soy sauce
2 teaspoons lemon juice
1 teaspoon grated fresh ginger
½ teaspoon sesame oil
2 (11-ounce) packages turkey mignons*
Creamy Wine Sauce
Hot cooked noodles
Garnishes: lemon slices and fresh parsley sprigs

1. Stir together first 8 ingredients; dredge turkey in sesame seed mixture. Place on a lightly greased rack in a broiler pan.
2. Broil 5½ inches from heat 12 minutes on each side or until done. Serve with Creamy Wine Sauce over hot cooked noodles. Garnish, if desired. **Makes** 4 servings.
*2 turkey tenderloins, cut in half, may be substituted for turkey mignons.

Creamy Wine Sauce

PREP: 5 MIN., COOK: 15 MIN.

1 cup fruity white wine*
2 teaspoons lemon juice
¼ cup whipping cream
2 tablespoons soy sauce
⅓ cup butter

1. Bring wine and lemon juice to a boil in a saucepan over medium-high heat. Boil 6 to 8 minutes or until mixture is reduced by half. Whisk in whipping cream. Cook 3 to 4 minutes, whisking constantly, until thickened.
2. Reduce heat to simmer, and whisk in soy sauce and butter until butter is melted. **Makes** about ¾ cup.
*Substitute white grape juice for wine, if desired.

Sesame-Crusted Turkey Mignons

Catfish Pecan With
Lemon-Thyme-Pecan Butter

Catfish Pecan With Lemon-Thyme-Pecan Butter

This is one of our favorite catfish dishes ever. Keep the cooked fish warm in a low oven for up to 30 minutes.

PREP: 25 MIN., COOK: 28 MIN.

1½ cups pecan halves, divided
¾ cup all-purpose flour
1½ teaspoons Creole seasoning, divided
1 large egg
1 cup milk
8 (6-ounce) catfish, flounder, redfish, or bass fillets
1 cup butter, divided
2 large lemons, halved
1 tablespoon Worcestershire sauce
6 large fresh thyme sprigs
Kosher salt and pepper to taste
Garnishes: fresh thyme, lemon slices

1. Process ¾ cup pecans, flour, and 1 teaspoon Creole seasoning in a food processor until finely ground; place pecan mixture in a large shallow bowl, and set aside.
2. Whisk together egg and milk in a large bowl, and set aside.
3. Sprinkle both sides of fillets evenly with remaining ½ teaspoon Creole seasoning.

4. Dip catfish fillets in egg mixture, draining off excess; dredge fillets in pecan mixture, coating both sides, and shake off excess.
5. Melt 2 tablespoons butter in a large nonstick skillet over medium heat until butter starts to bubble. Place 2 fillets in skillet, and cook 2 to 3 minutes on each side or until golden. Drain on a wire rack in a jelly-roll pan, and keep warm in a 200° oven. Wipe skillet clean, and repeat procedure with remaining fillets.
6. Wipe skillet clean. Melt remaining ½ cup butter in skillet over high heat; add remaining ¾ cup pecans, and cook, stirring occasionally, 2 to 3 minutes or until toasted. Squeeze juice from lemon halves into skillet; place halves, cut sides down, in skillet. Stir in Worcestershire sauce, thyme, salt, and pepper, and cook 30 seconds or until thyme wilts and becomes very aromatic. Remove and discard lemon halves and wilted thyme.
7. Place fish on a serving platter; spoon pecan mixture over fish. Garnish, if desired. **Makes** 8 servings.

Spicy Catfish With Vegetables and Basil Cream

This recipe, developed by our Test Kitchens, shows the versatility and creativity of sautéing.

PREP: 25 MIN., COOK: 25 MIN.

3 tablespoons butter, divided
1 (16-ounce) package frozen whole
    kernel corn, thawed
1 medium onion, chopped
1 medium-size green bell pepper, chopped
1 medium-size red bell pepper, chopped
¾ teaspoon salt
¾ teaspoon pepper
½ cup all-purpose flour
¼ cup yellow cornmeal
1 tablespoon Creole seasoning
4 (6- to 8-ounce) catfish fillets
⅓ cup buttermilk
1 tablespoon vegetable oil
½ cup whipping cream
2 tablespoons chopped fresh basil
Garnish: fresh basil sprigs

1. Melt 2 tablespoons butter in a large skillet over medium-high heat. Add corn, onion, and peppers; sauté 6 to 8 minutes or until tender. Stir in salt and pepper; spoon onto serving dish, and keep warm.
2. Combine flour, cornmeal, and Creole seasoning in a large shallow dish. Dip fillets in buttermilk, and dredge in flour mixture.
3. Melt remaining 1 tablespoon butter with oil in skillet over medium-high heat. Cook fillets, in batches, 2 to 3 minutes on each side or until golden. Remove and arrange over vegetables.
4. Add cream to skillet, stirring to loosen particles from bottom of skillet. Add chopped basil, and cook, stirring often, 1 to 2 minutes or until thickened. Serve sauce with fillets and vegetables. Garnish, if desired. **Makes** 4 servings.

Barbecue Baked Catfish

PREP: 20 MIN., COOK: 12 MIN.

¾ cup ketchup
¼ cup butter
1 tablespoon balsamic vinegar
1 tablespoon Worcestershire sauce
1 teaspoon Dijon mustard
½ teaspoon Jamaican jerk seasoning
1 garlic clove, minced
10 (3- to 4-ounce) catfish fillets
⅛ teaspoon pepper
Garnish: chopped fresh parsley

1. Stir together ketchup and next 6 ingredients in a small saucepan over medium-low heat; cook ketchup mixture 10 minutes, stirring occasionally.
2. Sprinkle catfish with pepper; arrange in an even layer in a lightly greased aluminum foil-lined broiler pan. Pour sauce over catfish.
3. Bake catfish at 400° for 10 to 12 minutes or until fish flakes with a fork. Garnish, if desired. **Makes** 5 servings.

Red Snapper Louisiane

Red Snapper Louisiane

A buttery artichoke and almond topping smothers this skillet-fried snapper. It's a rich dish and great for company. Just add crisp salad greens to the meal.

PREP: 12 MIN., COOK: 18 MIN.

4 red snapper fillets (2 to 2½ pounds)
¼ teaspoon salt
¼ teaspoon pepper
1 large egg, lightly beaten
1 cup milk
½ cup all-purpose flour
Vegetable oil
1 (14-ounce) can quartered artichoke hearts, drained
1 cup sliced fresh mushrooms
¼ cup butter, melted
⅓ cup sliced almonds, toasted
1 teaspoon Worcestershire sauce
1 teaspoon lemon juice
1 teaspoon white wine vinegar or tarragon vinegar

1. Sprinkle fillets with salt and pepper. Combine egg and milk in a shallow bowl, mixing well. Dip fillets in milk mixture, and dredge in flour.
2. Pour oil to depth of 2 inches into a Dutch oven or large deep skillet; heat to 350°.
3. Fry fillets in 2 batches in hot oil 5 minutes or until golden, turning to brown both sides. Drain on paper towels. Remove to a serving platter, and keep warm.
4. Cook artichoke hearts and mushrooms in butter in a large skillet over medium-high heat, stirring gently, until mushrooms are tender. Add almonds and remaining 3 ingredients; cook 1 minute. Spoon over fish, serve immediately. **Makes** 4 servings.
Note: You can substitute other white fillets such as grouper, flounder, Mingo snapper, or other types of snapper, if desired.

Peppered Snapper

A medley of peppers and onions tops these fillets and keeps them moist as they bake.

PREP: 10 MIN., COOK: 31 MIN.

2 medium onions, cut into ½-inch slices
1 red bell pepper, cut into ½-inch slices
1 or 2 jalapeno peppers, seeded and cut
    into thin strips
2 tablespoons olive oil
½ teaspoon salt, divided
¼ cup rice vinegar
1½ teaspoons chopped fresh oregano or
    ½ teaspoon dried oregano
6 red snapper fillets (2½ to 3 pounds)
½ teaspoon pepper
Garnish: lemon wedges

1. Cook onion, sliced red pepper, and jalapeño pepper strips in oil in a skillet over medium-high heat 10 minutes or until tender, stirring often. Add ¼ teaspoon salt, vinegar, and oregano. Cook 1 minute; set aside.
2. Sprinkle fish fillets with remaining salt and pepper; place fillets in a lightly greased 13- x 9-inch baking dish. Top with vegetable mixture. Bake, uncovered, at 350° for 20 minutes or until fish flakes easily when tested with a fork. Garnish, if desired.
Makes 6 servings.

GRILL FAVORITE
Grilled Marinated Grouper

If you can't find grouper, you can substitute another mild fish such as orange roughy or tilapia in this recipe.

PREP: 12 MIN., COOK: 16 MIN., OTHER: 1 HR.

1 (1-pound) grouper fillet, cut into 4 pieces
½ teaspoon lemon zest
3 tablespoons fresh lemon juice
1 teaspoon prepared horseradish
¼ teaspoon dried oregano
¼ teaspoon dried basil
¼ teaspoon salt
⅛ teaspoon pepper
1 small garlic clove, halved
2 tablespoons olive oil

1. Arrange fish in a shallow dish. Combine lemon zest and next 7 ingredients in container of an electric blender. Cover and process 20 seconds. With blender running, add oil in a slow stream. Pour mixture over fish, and turn to coat. Cover and marinate in refrigerator 8 hours, turning fish occasionally.
2. Remove fish from marinade. Place marinade in a saucepan; bring to a boil. Remove from heat. Coat grill rack with cooking spray; place on grill over medium-hot coals (350° to 400°). Arrange fish in a grill basket coated with cooking spray. Grill, covered, 7 to 8 minutes on each side or until fish flakes easily when tested with a fork. Baste with marinade.
Makes 4 servings.

Baked Fish With Parmesan-Sour Cream Sauce

Tilapia, flounder, or any other white fish works in place of orange roughy.

PREP: 10 MIN., COOK: 25 MIN.

1½ pounds orange roughy fillets
1 (8-ounce) container sour cream
¼ cup shredded Parmesan cheese
½ teaspoon paprika
½ teaspoon salt
¼ teaspoon pepper
2 tablespoons Italian-seasoned
   breadcrumbs
2 tablespoons butter, melted

1. Place fillets in a single layer in a lightly greased 13- x 9-inch baking dish. Stir together sour cream and next 4 ingredients; spread mixture evenly over fillets. Sprinkle with breadcrumbs, and drizzle with butter.
2. Bake at 350° for 20 to 25 minutes or until fish flakes easily with a fork. **Makes** 4 to 6 servings.

Coconut Fried Shrimp

PREP: 25 MIN., COOK: 2 MIN. PER BATCH

1 pound unpeeled, medium-size raw shrimp
¾ cup biscuit mix
1 tablespoon sugar
¾ cup beer
¾ cup all-purpose flour
2½ cups flaked coconut
Vegetable oil
Orange-Lime Dip

1. Peel shrimp, leaving the tails intact; devein, if desired, and set shrimp aside.
2. Combine biscuit mix, sugar, and beer, stirring until smooth; set mixture aside.
3. Coat shrimp with flour; dip into beer mixture, allowing excess to drain. Gently roll coated shrimp in flaked coconut.
4. Pour vegetable oil to a depth of 3 inches into a large saucepan; heat to 350°. Cook shrimp, a few at a time, 1 to 2 minutes or until golden; drain on paper towels, and serve immediately with Orange-Lime Dip. **Makes** about 3 dozen.

Orange Lime Dip

PREP: 3 MIN., COOK: 5 MIN.

1 (10-ounce) jar orange marmalade
3 tablespoons spicy brown mustard
1 tablespoon fresh lime juice

1. Combine all ingredients in a small saucepan; cook over medium heat, stirring constantly, until marmalade melts. Remove from heat; cool. Dip may be stored in refrigerator up to 1 week. **Makes** about 1¼ cups.

Garlic Shrimp

FAMILY FAVORITE
Garlic Shrimp

A crusty Parmesan-breadcrumb topping is dusted over these big garlicky shrimp before serving.
Grill or toast some French bread for sopping up the aromatic juices.

PREP: 15 MIN., COOK: 25 MIN.

2 dozen large unpeeled raw shrimp
¼ cup olive oil
¼ cup chopped fresh parsley
3 garlic cloves, minced
½ teaspoon dried crushed red pepper
¼ teaspoon pepper
¼ cup butter, melted
½ cup French breadcrumbs (homemade), toasted
½ cup freshly grated Parmesan cheese

1. Peel shrimp, leaving tails on, if desired; devein, if desired. Arrange shrimp in an 11- x 7-inch baking dish; pour oil over shrimp. Combine parsley and next 3 ingredients; sprinkle over shrimp. Cover and bake at 300° for 15 minutes.

2. Turn shrimp over; drizzle with butter, and sprinkle with breadcrumbs and cheese. Bake, uncovered, 5 to 10 more minutes. **Makes** 2 servings.

MAKE AHEAD
Shellfish Crêpes in Wine-Cheese Sauce

PREP: 30 MIN.; COOK: 20 MIN.; OTHER: 3 HR., 30 MIN.

½ cup butter, divided
2 cups chopped cooked shrimp (about 1 pound)
½ pound fresh crabmeat
2 green onions, minced
¼ cup dry vermouth*
⅛ teaspoon salt
¼ teaspoon pepper
½ tablespoon butter, melted
Wine-Cheese Sauce (opposite page)
Crêpes (opposite page)
2 cups (8 ounces) shredded Swiss cheese
Garnish: sliced green onions

1. Melt ¼ cup butter in a large skillet over medium-high heat. Add shrimp, crabmeat, and green onions, and sauté for 1 minute. Stir in vermouth*, salt, and pepper. Bring mixture to a boil, and cook 7 minutes or until most of liquid is absorbed. Remove mixture from heat, and set aside.
2. Drizzle ½ tablespoon melted butter into a 13- x 9-inch baking dish.
3. Stir 2 cups Wine-Cheese Sauce into shrimp mixture. Spoon about 3 tablespoons shrimp mixture down center of each Crêpe.
4. Roll up, and place, seam side down, in prepared dish. Spoon remaining 2 cups Wine-Cheese Sauce over Crêpes. Sprinkle with Swiss cheese, and dot with remaining ¼ cup butter. Cover and chill for 3 hours. Let stand at room temperature 30 minutes.
5. Bake at 450° for 20 minutes or until thoroughly heated. Garnish, if desired. **Makes** 12 servings.
*Clam juice may be substituted for vermouth.

Wine-Cheese Sauce

PREP: 10 MIN., COOK: 10 MIN.

¼ cup cornstarch
¼ cup milk
⅓ cup dry vermouth*
3 cups whipping cream
¼ teaspoon salt
¼ teaspoon pepper
2 cups (8 ounces) shredded Swiss cheese

1. Whisk together cornstarch and milk in a small bowl.
2. Bring vermouth* to a boil in a large skillet, and cook until vermouth is reduced to 1 tablespoon. Remove from heat, and whisk in cornstarch mixture. Add whipping cream, salt, and pepper; cook over medium-high heat, whisking constantly, 2 minutes or until mixture comes to a boil. Boil 1 minute or until mixture is thickened. Add Swiss cheese; reduce heat, and simmer, whisking constantly, 1 minute or until sauce is smooth. **Makes** 4 cups.
*Clam juice may be substituted for vermouth.

Crêpes

PREP: 8 MIN., COOK: 36 MIN., OTHER: 1 HR.

4 large eggs
2 cups all-purpose flour
1 cup cold water
1 cup cold milk
¼ cup butter, melted
½ teaspoon salt

1. Process all ingredients in a blender or food processor until smooth, stopping to scrape down sides. Cover and chill 1 hour.
2. Place a lightly greased 8-inch nonstick skillet over medium heat until skillet is hot.
3. Pour 3 tablespoons batter into skillet; quickly tilt in all directions so batter covers bottom of skillet.
4. Cook 1 minute or until crêpe can be shaken loose from skillet. Turn crêpe, and cook about 30 seconds. Repeat procedure with remaining batter. Stack crêpes between sheets of wax paper. **Makes** 2 dozen.
Note: To make ahead, prepare Crêpes as directed, and freeze up to 1 month. Casserole may be prepared 1 day ahead; cover and chill. Let stand at room temperature 30 minutes before baking; proceed as directed.

Crabmeat-Parmesan Quiche

Decked with lump crabmeat, this dish will have guests gobbling it up for brunch, lunch, or dinner.

PREP: 15 MIN., COOK: 52 MIN., OTHER: 15 MIN.

½ (15-ounce) package refrigerated piecrusts
3 to 4 green onions, chopped
2 teaspoons olive oil
2 (6-ounce) cans lump crabmeat, rinsed and drained
1 teaspoon lemon zest
½ teaspoon Old Bay seasoning
⅛ teaspoon ground red pepper
1 cup half-and-half
3 large eggs
¼ teaspoon salt
¼ teaspoon black pepper
1 (5-ounce) package shredded Parmesan cheese

1. Unfold piecrust, and place on a lightly floured surface. Roll to ⅛-inch thickness. Carefully place piecrust in a 9-inch pieplate; fold edges under, and crimp.
2. Bake on lowest oven rack at 400° for 8 minutes. Remove from oven; cool.
3. Sauté chopped green onions in hot oil in a large skillet over medium-high heat 2 minutes. Stir in crabmeat and next 3 ingredients; sauté 2 minutes.
4. Whisk together half-and-half and next 3 ingredients in a large bowl; stir in cheese and crabmeat mixture. Pour into prepared crust.
5. Bake quiche on lowest oven rack at 400° for 35 to 40 minutes or until set. Let stand 15 minutes. **Makes** 6 servings.

Triple Seafood Casserole

Loaded with scallops, shrimp, and crab, this casserole feeds the whole family.

PREP: 15 MIN., COOK: 55 MIN., OTHER: 10 MIN.

1 pound unpeeled, medium-size raw shrimp
1 cup dry white wine
1 tablespoon chopped fresh parsley
1 tablespoon butter
1 teaspoon salt
1 medium onion, thinly sliced
1 pound fresh bay scallops
3 tablespoons butter
3 tablespoons all-purpose flour
1 cup half-and-half
½ cup (2 ounces) shredded Swiss cheese
2 teaspoons lemon juice
⅛ teaspoon pepper
½ pound fresh crabmeat
1 (4½-ounce) can sliced mushrooms, drained
1 cup soft breadcrumbs (homemade)
¼ cup grated Parmesan cheese

1. Peel and devein shrimp. Combine wine and next 4 ingredients in a large Dutch oven; bring to a boil. Add shrimp and scallops. Cook 3 to 5 minutes or until shrimp turn pink, stirring often. Drain, reserving ⅔ cup cooking liquid.
2. Melt 3 tablespoons butter in Dutch oven over low heat; add flour, stirring until smooth. Cook 1 minute, stirring constantly. Gradually add half-and-half; cook over medium heat, stirring constantly, until thickened and bubbly. Stir in Swiss cheese. Gradually stir in reserved cooking liquid, lemon juice, and pepper. Stir in shrimp mixture, crabmeat, and mushrooms.
3. Spoon mixture into a lightly greased 11- x 7-inch baking dish. Cover and bake at 350° for 40 minutes or until bubbly. Combine breadcrumbs and Parmesan cheese; sprinkle over casserole. Bake, uncovered, 5 more minutes. Let stand 10 minutes before serving. **Makes** 6 servings.

Fried Soft-Shell Crabs

You don't have to do much to enhance the naturally sweet flavor of soft-shell crabs. This particular coating is a bit peppery—and we like it that way. Serve the crabs hot alongside French rolls and slaw.

PREP: 25 MIN., COOK: 2 MIN. PER BATCH

8 fresh or frozen soft-shell crabs, thawed
1 cup all-purpose flour
3 tablespoons Old Bay seasoning
2 teaspoons black pepper
1 teaspoon ground red pepper
1 teaspoon garlic powder
1 large egg, lightly beaten
½ cup milk
Vegetable oil

1. To clean crabs, remove spongy substance (gills) that lie under the tapering points on either side of back shell. Place crabs on their backs, and remove the small piece at the lower part of shell that terminates in a point (the apron). Wash crabs thoroughly; drain well.
2. Combine flour and next 4 ingredients; set aside. Combine egg and milk; stir well.
3. Pour oil to depth of 1 inch into a large Dutch oven; heat oil to 350°. Dip crabs into egg mixture; dredge in flour mixture. Fry crabs 1 to 2 minutes or until golden; drain on paper towels. Serve hot. **Makes** 4 servings.

Chesapeake Bay
Crab Cakes

Chesapeake Bay Crab Cakes

*The secret to great crab cakes is buying very fresh lumps of crabmeat
and not overstirring the crab mixture before shaping it.*

PREP: 25 MIN., COOK: 6 MIN. PER BATCH

¼ cup minced onion
2 tablespoons minced green bell pepper
¼ cup butter, melted
1 pound fresh lump crabmeat, drained
1¼ cups soft breadcrumbs (homemade),
    toasted and divided
1 tablespoon chopped fresh parsley
1 tablespoon mayonnaise
1 tablespoon lemon juice
1 teaspoon Old Bay seasoning
1 teaspoon dry mustard
1 teaspoon Worcestershire sauce
Dash of ground red pepper
1 large egg, lightly beaten
Vegetable oil
Garnishes: fresh parsley, lemon wedges

1. Cook onion and bell pepper in butter in a large skillet over medium-high heat, stirring constantly, until tender. Remove from heat; stir in crabmeat, ¾ cup breadcrumbs, parsley, and next 7 ingredients. Shape mixture into 8 patties; dredge patties in remaining breadcrumbs.
2. Pour oil to depth of ¼ inch into a large heavy skillet. Fry patties in hot oil over medium-high heat 3 minutes on each side or until golden. Drain on paper towels. Garnish, if desired. Serve hot with cocktail sauce and tartar sauce. **Makes** 4 servings.

Three-Cheese Pasta
Bake, page 275

pasta, rice, and grain favorites

Herbed Seafood Pasta

Herbed Seafood Pasta

PREP: 15 MIN., COOK: 7 MIN.

1 (16-ounce) package fettuccine
½ pound unpeeled medium-size raw shrimp
2 tablespoons olive oil
5½ tablespoons Herb-Pesto Butter, divided
½ pound large sea scallops
6 green onions, cut into 2-inch strips
1 cup freshly grated Parmesan cheese, divided

1. Prepare pasta according to package directions; drain and set aside. Keep warm.
2. Peel shrimp, and devein, if desired.
3. Heat olive oil and 2 tablespoons Herb-Pesto Butter in a large skillet over medium-high heat. Add shrimp, scallops, and green onions; cook, stirring often, 3 to 5 minutes or just until shrimp turn pink. Stir in 2 more tablespoons Herb-Pesto Butter. Remove seafood mixture from skillet, and keep warm.
4. Melt remaining 1½ tablespoons Herb-Pesto Butter in skillet; remove from heat. Add warm pasta and ½ cup Parmesan cheese, tossing to coat. Divide pasta mixture evenly among 4 pasta bowls; top evenly with seafood mixture and remaining ½ cup cheese. Serve immediately. **Makes** 4 servings.

Herb-Pesto Butter
Serve remaining Herb-Pesto Butter on bread, warm pasta, grilled vegetables, steak, or chicken breasts.

PREP: 10 MIN.

1½ cups fresh basil leaves
½ cup chopped fresh parsley
¼ cup pine nuts
3 tablespoons Marsala or white wine
2 tablespoons chopped fresh oregano leaves
8 garlic cloves, chopped
1 cup butter, softened
1 to 2 tablespoons olive oil

1. Process first 6 ingredients in a food processor until smooth, stopping to scrape down sides. Add butter and 1 tablespoon olive oil, and process until combined; add remaining 1 tablespoon oil, if necessary, to achieve desired consistency. **Makes** 2 cups.

Meaty Manicotti

This manicotti earned high marks in our Test Kitchens. The slow-simmered tomato sauce produces delicious results for a great company dish. Just add a salad and garlic bread.

PREP: 25 MIN.; COOK: 2 HR., 5 MIN.; OTHER: 5 MIN.

½ pound Italian link sausage
1 pound ground chuck
2 medium onions, chopped
5 garlic cloves, minced
2 (15-ounce) cans tomato sauce
1 (14½-ounce) can plum tomatoes, undrained
  and chopped
1 (12-ounce) can tomato paste
1½ teaspoons dried oregano
1¼ teaspoons dried basil
1 teaspoon sugar
½ teaspoon salt
½ teaspoon pepper
½ teaspoon dried thyme
½ teaspoon dried rosemary
¼ teaspoon dried marjoram
⅛ teaspoon ground red pepper
1 (15-ounce) carton ricotta cheese
1 (8-ounce) package cream cheese, softened
½ (8-ounce) container cream cheese
  with chives, softened
½ cup grated Parmesan cheese
4 garlic cloves, crushed
½ teaspoon pepper
½ teaspoon dried thyme
½ teaspoon dried oregano
4 cups (16 ounces) shredded mozzarella
  cheese, divided
1 (8-ounce) package manicotti shells, cooked

1. Remove sausage from casings. Cook sausage, beef, onion, and garlic in a large Dutch oven until beef is browned, stirring until meats crumble; drain well. Return meats to Dutch oven.
2. Add tomato sauce and next 11 ingredients; bring to a boil. Cover, reduce heat, and simmer 1½ hours, stirring occasionally.
3. Combine ricotta cheese and next 7 ingredients in a large bowl; stir in 3 cups mozzarella. Stuff mixture evenly into manicotti shells.

4. Spoon half of meat sauce into a lightly greased lasagna pan or 2 lightly greased 2½-quart shallow baking dishes. Arrange stuffed shells over sauce. Spoon remaining sauce over shells.
5. Cover and bake at 350° for 35 minutes or until thoroughly heated. Sprinkle with remaining 1 cup mozzarella cheese. Let stand 5 minutes before serving. **Makes** 7 servings.

Chicken-Tomato Fettuccine

PREP: 12 MIN.; COOK: 10 MIN.

6 ounces fettuccine, uncooked
1 (8-ounce) jar dried tomatoes in oil,
  undrained
1 small onion, chopped
2 garlic cloves, minced
4 skinned and boned chicken breasts,
  cut into strips
3 tablespoons chopped fresh or 1 tablespoon
  dried basil
1 cup half-and-half
½ teaspoon salt
¼ teaspoon pepper

1. Cook fettuccine according to package directions.
2. Drain tomatoes, reserving ¼ cup oil; coarsely chop tomatoes.
3. Sauté onion and garlic in 2 tablespoons reserved oil over medium-high heat until tender. Add chicken; cook 6 minutes or until done, stirring occasionally. Add tomato and basil; cook 2 minutes, stirring occasionally. Stir in remaining oil, half-and-half, salt, and pepper. Toss with fettuccine. **Makes** 4 servings.

Pasta Mexicana

PREP: 10 MIN., COOK: 10 MIN.

2 (9-ounce) packages refrigerated angel hair pasta
¾ cup Mojo de Ajo (opposite page)
Toppings: freshly grated Parmesan cheese, sliced
    fresh chives

1. Cook angel hair pasta according to package directions in a Dutch oven; drain. Return pasta to Dutch oven, and toss with ¾ cup Mojo de Ajo. Serve pasta immediately with desired toppings. **Makes** 8 servings.

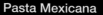

Pasta Mexicana

Mojo de Ajo

Guajillo [gwah-HEE-yoh] chiles are dried peppers with a bright tangy taste and kick of heat. Find them at grocery stores and supercenters alongside other Hispanic ingredients. Cook the chiles in hot oil for just seconds to mellow out the flavor and for easy crumbling. Don't let the ¾ cup minced garlic scare you away. The flavor smoothes out as it cooks.

PREP: 10 MIN., COOK: 5 MIN., OTHER: 10 MIN.

¾ cup olive oil
3 whole guajillo chiles*
¾ cup jarred minced garlic
5 tablespoons fresh lime juice
1½ teaspoons salt

1. Heat oil in a 2-quart saucepan over medium heat to 350°. Using tongs, submerge 1 chile into oil, and cook 5 seconds; remove and drain on paper towels. Let cool 5 minutes or until completely cool. Repeat with remaining 2 chiles. Remove and discard stems. Process remaining portion of chiles in food processor 30 seconds to 1 minute or until crumbled into small flakes.
2. Cook garlic in hot oil in same saucepan over medium heat, stirring occasionally, 3 to 4 minutes or until golden. Let stand 5 minutes.
3. Stir in chile flakes, lime juice, and salt. Store in an airtight container in refrigerator up to 5 days. Allow mixture to come to room temperature before using. **Makes** about 1½ cups.
*2 tablespoons sweet paprika may be substituted. Omit Step 1; proceed with recipe as directed, stirring in paprika with lime juice and salt in Step 3.

QUICK
Garlic-Herb Pasta
PREP: 10 MIN., COOK: 18 MIN.

8 ounces uncooked thin spaghetti
5 garlic cloves, minced
2 tablespoons olive oil
2 pounds plum tomatoes, cut into eighths
3 tablespoons minced fresh parsley
3 tablespoons thinly sliced or chopped fresh basil
1 teaspoon salt
¼ teaspoon freshly ground pepper
Freshly grated Parmesan cheese

1. Cook pasta according to package directions; drain. Place pasta in a serving bowl, and keep warm.
2. Sauté garlic in hot oil in a large skillet over medium heat 1 minute. Stir in tomatoes and next 4 ingredients. Cook, stirring occasionally, 5 minutes or until thoroughly heated and tomatoes release juices. Pour over pasta; toss to combine. Sprinkle with Parmesan cheese. **Makes** 4 servings.

Fettuccine With Wilted Greens
PREP: 20 MIN., COOK: 40 MIN.

1 (16-ounce) package fettuccine
8 chicken cutlets (about 2½ pounds)
1 teaspoon salt
½ teaspoon pepper
1 cup all-purpose flour
½ cup extra-virgin olive oil
2 sweet onions, thinly sliced
2 (8-ounce) packages sliced fresh mushrooms
2 teaspoons minced garlic
½ cup chicken broth
1 cup white wine
1 teaspoon salt
1 teaspoon pepper
2 (9-ounce) packages fresh spinach, thoroughly washed
Freshly grated Parmesan cheese

1. Cook pasta in a Dutch oven according to package directions. Drain, return to Dutch oven, and keep warm.
2. Sprinkle chicken with 1 teaspoon salt and ½ teaspoon pepper. Dredge in flour.
3. Sauté chicken, in batches, in hot oil in a large skillet over medium-high heat 3 to 5 minutes on each side or until chicken is browned. Remove and keep warm.
4. Add onions, mushrooms, and garlic to skillet; sauté 5 to 7 minutes or until mushrooms are lightly browned. Stir in chicken broth and next 3 ingredients, and cook 3 to 5 minutes or until liquid is reduced by half, stirring to loosen particles from bottom of skillet.
5. Add mushroom mixture and spinach to pasta in Dutch oven, tossing to coat. Cook, covered, over medium-low heat 4 to 6 minutes or until greens are wilted. Spoon into a serving dish, and top evenly with chicken and Parmesan cheese. **Makes** 8 servings.

Linguine Carbonara

Linguine Carbonara

Strips of prosciutto ham and crisp bacon toss meaty flavor into this creamy, rich pasta.

PREP: 10 MIN., COOK: 10 MIN.

½ pound bacon, cut into 1-inch pieces
¼ cup olive oil
1 medium onion, chopped
1 cup chopped fresh parsley (about 1 bunch)
4 ounces fontina cheese, cubed
3 ounces prosciutto, cut into strips
1 (1-pound) package linguine or spaghetti
4 egg yolks, lightly beaten
¾ cup half-and-half, heated
1 teaspoon salt
Freshly ground pepper to taste
1 cup freshly grated Parmesan cheese, divided
Garnish: fresh parsley sprigs

1. Cook bacon in a large skillet over medium heat until crisp. Drain on paper towels. Pour off drippings; add oil and onion to skillet; sauté until onion is tender. Set aside.
2. Combine parsley, fontina cheese, and prosciutto in a small bowl.
3. Cook linguine in a Dutch oven according to package directions; drain. Return hot linguine to Dutch oven; immediately stir in egg yolks. Add bacon, onion, parsley mixture, heated half-and-half, salt, pepper, and ½ cup Parmesan cheese. Cook over low heat until thoroughly heated, stirring constantly; transfer to serving dish. Sprinkle with remaining ½ cup Parmesan cheese. Garnish, if desired. Serve immediately. **Makes** 8 servings.

Pesto Pasta

Fresh herbs give pesto its classic color, and olive oil helps it cling to hot cooked pasta. Stir in grilled chicken strips to make this a main dish.

PREP: 10 MIN.

½ cup tightly packed fresh basil leaves
¼ cup minced fresh parsley
¼ cup grated Parmesan cheese
2 tablespoons pine nuts or chopped walnuts
¼ cup olive oil
¼ teaspoon salt
¼ teaspoon pepper
1 garlic clove, halved
6 ounces linguine, cooked

1. Process all ingredients except linguine in blender until smooth, stopping once to scrape down sides.
2. Combine pesto mixture and linguine; toss gently. Serve immediately. **Makes** 4 servings.

Fresh Tomato Sauce
With Linguine

Fresh Tomato Sauce With Linguine

PREP: 20 MIN., COOK: 10 MIN.

1 (16-ounce) package linguine
3 garlic cloves, thinly sliced
½ teaspoon dried crushed red pepper
3 tablespoons olive oil
4 cups cherry or grape tomatoes, halved
½ cup fresh basil leaves, coarsely chopped
2 tablespoons chopped fresh parsley
2 tablespoons red wine vinegar
½ to 1 teaspoon salt
Garnishes: shaved Parmesan cheese,
    fresh basil sprig

1. Cook linguine according to package directions; drain.
2. Sauté garlic and crushed red pepper in hot oil in a large skillet over low heat. Add tomatoes and next 4 ingredients; cook 3 to 5 minutes.
3. Toss together pasta and tomato mixture; garnish, if desired. **Makes** 6 servings.

" This tasty, easy-to-prepare sauce has just the right touch of spice. "
VANESS MCNEIL ROCCHIO, TEST KITCHEN SPECIALIST/FOOD STYLING

Pasta Antipasto

Serve this colorful antipasto as a chilled summer salad, entrée, or appetizer.

PREP: 10 MIN., OTHER: 8 HR.

2 (6-ounce) jars marinated artichoke hearts,
    undrained
¾ cup Italian dressing
¼ teaspoon freshly ground pepper
1 pint cherry tomatoes, halved
½ cup pimiento-stuffed olives
½ cup ripe olives or kalamata olives, pitted
½ pound fresh mushrooms
1 medium-size green bell pepper, seeded and
    cut into strips
8 ounces rotini (corkscrew pasta), cooked
3 to 4 ounces sliced pepperoni
3 to 4 ounces sliced salami
Freshly grated Parmesan cheese

1. Drain artichoke hearts, reserving ½ cup artichoke liquid. Add Italian dressing and pepper to artichoke liquid; stir well.
2. Combine artichoke hearts, tomatoes, olives, mushrooms, and bell pepper in a bowl. Add three-fourths of marinade to vegetable mixture, tossing gently. Cover and marinate in refrigerator 8 hours. Add remaining marinade to cooked pasta, tossing gently. Cover and marinate in refrigerator 8 hours.
3. Arrange pepperoni and salami slices around outer edges of a serving platter. Spoon pasta in a ring within meat, using a slotted spoon. Spoon vegetable mixture in center of platter, using a slotted spoon. Top with cheese. **Makes** 8 servings.

Pasta With Beans and Greens

Besides being a delicious and colorful main dish, this recipe boasts generous amounts of protein, fiber, complex carbohydrates, iron, and calcium.

PREP: 20 MIN., COOK: 21 MIN.

8 ounces uncooked bow-tie pasta
1 large onion, chopped
1 (6-ounce) package portobello mushroom caps,
    halved and sliced*
2 teaspoons olive oil
4 cups chopped fresh kale or spinach
    (about 6 ounces)
1 cup reduced-sodium chicken broth
2 garlic cloves, minced
½ teaspoon salt
½ teaspoon pepper
1 (15-ounce) can great Northern beans,
    rinsed and drained
¼ cup shredded Parmesan cheese

1. Cook pasta according to package directions; drain. Place pasta in a large bowl; set aside.
2. Sauté onion and mushrooms in hot oil in a large skillet over medium heat 5 minutes. Add kale and next 4 ingredients; cook, stirring often, 15 minutes or until kale is tender. Add beans, and cook 1 minute.
3. Add bean mixture to pasta; toss gently. Sprinkle with cheese. **Makes** 6 servings.
*1 (8-ounce) package sliced fresh mushrooms may be substituted.

Spicy Vegetables With Penne

PREP: 30 MIN., COOK: 15 MIN., OTHER: 30 MIN.

½ cup dried tomatoes
½ cup boiling water
12 ounces uncooked penne pasta
2 medium-size sweet onions, chopped
2 small zucchini, chopped
1 medium-size green bell pepper, chopped
1 medium-size red bell pepper, chopped
1 cup sliced fresh mushrooms
2 garlic cloves, minced
2 tablespoons olive oil
1 (24-ounce) jar hot-and-spicy pasta sauce
½ cup chopped fresh basil
½ teaspoon salt

1. Stir together dried tomatoes and ½ cup boiling water in a bowl; let stand 30 minutes. Drain, chop, and set aside.
2. Cook pasta according to package directions.
3. Sauté onion and next 5 ingredients in hot oil in a large skillet over medium-high heat 6 to 8 minutes or until vegetables are tender. Stir in chopped tomatoes.
4. Stir in pasta sauce; bring to a boil. Reduce heat to medium; stir in basil and salt, and simmer, stirring occasionally, 5 minutes. Serve over pasta. **Makes** 6 servings.
Note: For testing purposes only, we used Newman's Own Fra Diavolo Hot-and-Spicy Pasta Sauce.

QUICK
Pasta Provençale

This ridged pasta dish highlights some of the finest ingredients used daily in Mediterranean cuisine.

PREP: 10 MIN., COOK: 10 MIN.

2 medium zucchini, halved lengthwise and sliced,
    or 3 large yellow squash, sliced, or 1 of each
1 (8-ounce) package sliced fresh mushrooms
3 garlic cloves, minced
1 green bell pepper, chopped
¼ cup chopped onion
2 tablespoons olive oil
1 (14½-ounce) can diced tomatoes, undrained
1 tablespoon chopped fresh or ¼ teaspoon
    dried basil
1 tablespoon fresh oregano leaves or
    ⅛ teaspoon dried oregano
¼ teaspoon salt
¼ teaspoon pepper
5 ounces penne pasta, cooked
¼ cup freshly grated Parmesan cheese
Garnish: fresh herbs

1. Sauté first 5 ingredients in olive oil in a large skillet or Dutch oven over medium-high heat 3 minutes. Add tomatoes, basil, oregano, salt, and pepper; stir well. Bring mixture to a boil; reduce heat, and simmer 1 minute. Remove from heat; transfer to a serving bowl. Add pasta and Parmesan cheese; toss gently. Garnish, if desired. Serve hot. **Makes** 6 servings.

Pasta Provençale

" Mac-and-cheese happens to be one of my favorite foods. Loaded with three types of cheese, this one is a sure winner. "

SHANNON SLITER SATTERWHITE, FOOD EDITOR

Three-Cheese Pasta Bake

(EDITOR'S CHOICE)
Three-Cheese Pasta Bake
(also pictured on cover)

PREP: 20 MIN., COOK: 22 MIN.

1 (8-ounce) package penne pasta
2 tablespoons butter
2 tablespoons all-purpose flour
1½ cups milk
½ cup half-and-half
1 cup (4 ounces) shredded white Cheddar
    cheese
¼ cup grated Parmesan cheese
2 cups (8 ounces) shredded Gruyère
    cheese, divided*
1 teaspoon salt
¼ teaspoon pepper
Pinch of ground nutmeg

1. Prepare pasta according to package directions.
2. Meanwhile, melt butter in a medium saucepan over medium heat. Whisk in flour until smooth; cook, whisking constantly, 1 minute. Gradually whisk in milk and half-and-half; cook, whisking constantly, 3 to 5 minutes or until thickened. Stir in Cheddar cheese, Parmesan cheese, 1 cup Gruyère cheese, and next 3 ingredients until smooth.
3. Stir together pasta and cheese mixture, and pour into 4 lightly greased 8-ounce baking dishes or 1 lightly greased 11- x 7-inch baking dish. (If using 8-ounce baking dishes, place them in a jelly-roll pan for easy baking, and proceed as directed.) Top with remaining 1 cup Gruyère cheese.
4. Bake at 350° for 15 minutes or until golden and bubbly. **Makes** 4 servings.
*Swiss cheese may be substituted.
Note: To make ahead, proceed with recipe through Step 3. (Do not top with remaining Gruyère cheese.) Cover and chill up to 8 hours. Let stand at room temperature 30 minutes. Bake at 350° for 20 to 25 minutes or until bubbly. Increase oven temperature to 400°. Top pasta mixture with remaining Gruyère cheese, and bake 10 more minutes or until golden.

QUICK
Penne Pasta With Bacon and Cream
This rich penne dish is hearty enough to be an entrée.

PREP: 5 MIN., COOK: 25 MIN.

15 bacon slices
1 (8-ounce) package sliced fresh mushrooms
2 garlic cloves, minced
16 ounces penne pasta, cooked
1 cup freshly grated Parmesan cheese
2 cups whipping cream
½ teaspoon pepper
4 green onions, sliced

1. Cook bacon in a large skillet over medium heat until crisp; remove bacon, reserving 2 tablespoons drippings in skillet. Coarsely crumble bacon.
2. Sauté sliced mushrooms and garlic in reserved drippings 3 minutes or until tender. Stir in pasta, Parmesan cheese, whipping cream, and pepper; simmer over medium-low heat, stirring often, until sauce thickens (about 5 minutes). Stir in bacon and green onions. Serve hot. **Makes** 6 servings.

FAMILY FAVORITE, QUICK
Tuscan Pasta With Tomato-Basil Cream
This dish features chopped tomatoes and basil that freshen up jarred sauce in 15 minutes.

PREP: 10 MIN., COOK: 5 MIN.

1 (20-ounce) package refrigerated
     four-cheese ravioli*
1 (16-ounce) jar sun-dried tomato Alfredo sauce
2 tablespoons white wine
2 medium-size fresh tomatoes, chopped**
½ cup chopped fresh basil
⅓ cup grated Parmesan cheese
Garnish: fresh basil strips

1. Prepare pasta according to package directions.
2. Meanwhile, pour Alfredo sauce into a medium saucepan. Pour wine into sauce jar; cover tightly, and shake well. Stir wine mixture into saucepan. Stir in chopped tomato and ½ cup chopped basil, and cook over medium-low heat 5 minutes or until thoroughly heated. Toss with pasta, and top evenly with ⅓ cup grated Parmesan cheese. Garnish, if desired. **Makes** 4 to 6 servings.
*1 (13-ounce) package three-cheese tortellini may be substituted.
**1 (14.5-ounce) can petite diced tomatoes, fully drained, may be substituted.
Note: For testing purposes only, we used Buitoni Four Cheese Ravioli and Classico Sun-dried Tomato Alfredo Pasta Sauce.

Pasta Shells Stuffed With Five Cheeses

PREP: 15 MIN., COOK: 55 MIN.

1 (14½-ounce) can stewed tomatoes, undrained
1 (8-ounce) can mushroom stems and
    pieces, drained
1 (8-ounce) can tomato sauce
1 (6-ounce) can tomato paste
½ cup dry white wine
1 teaspoon dried oregano
1 teaspoon dried thyme
1 garlic clove, minced
1 (8-ounce) package cream cheese, softened
1 large egg, lightly beaten
1 cup (4 ounces) shredded mozzarella cheese
1 cup low-fat cottage cheese
¼ cup grated Parmesan and Romano
    cheese blend
2 teaspoons dried basil
½ teaspoon dried oregano
½ teaspoon dried thyme
⅛ teaspoon lemon zest
Pinch of ground nutmeg
16 jumbo dried pasta shells, cooked

1. Process tomatoes in container of a blender or food processor until smooth. Pour puréed tomatoes into a Dutch oven; stir in mushroom stems and pieces and next 6 ingredients. Bring to a boil; reduce heat, and simmer, uncovered, 20 minutes or until thickened. Spoon mushroom mixture into a lightly greased 11- x 7-inch baking dish.
2. Combine cream cheese and next 9 ingredients. Stuff shells evenly with cheese mixture; arrange over mushroom mixture in baking dish. Cover and bake at 350° for 25 to 30 minutes or until thoroughly heated.
Makes 4 servings.

QUICK
Green Bean Alfredo With Cheese Ravioli

PREP: 20 MIN., COOK: 23 MIN.

1 (1-pound) package frozen cheese-filled
    ravioli
3 tablespoons butter
1 pound fresh green beans, trimmed
2 garlic cloves, pressed
½ teaspoon chopped fresh rosemary
1½ cups whipping cream
¾ cup dry white wine or chicken broth
¾ teaspoon freshly ground pepper
¼ cup grated Parmesan cheese, divided
Garnish: fresh rosemary sprigs

1. Cook pasta according to package directions; keep warm.
2. Melt butter in a large nonstick skillet over medium-high heat; add green beans, garlic, and rosemary, and sauté 6 minutes or until beans are crisp-tender. Remove mixture, and set aside.
3. Add whipping cream to skillet, and bring to a boil, stirring constantly. Cook, stirring constantly, 10 minutes.
4. Return green bean mixture to skillet; add wine and pepper, and cook 5 minutes. Stir in 2 tablespoons cheese. Serve over ravioli, and sprinkle evenly with remaining 2 tablespoons cheese. Garnish, if desired.
Makes 6 servings.

Spinach-Stuffed Manicotti

PREP: 20 MIN., COOK: 35 MIN.

1 (10-ounce) package frozen chopped
    spinach, thawed
½ (8-ounce) package cream cheese,
    softened
1 cup ricotta cheese
1 cup (4 ounces) shredded mozzarella cheese
½ cup freshly grated Parmesan cheese
1 teaspoon dried Italian seasoning
¼ teaspoon salt
8 manicotti shells, cooked
2 cups pasta sauce, divided
½ cup freshly grated Parmesan cheese

1. Press spinach between layers of paper towels to remove excess moisture. Combine spinach, cream cheese, and next 5 ingredients, stirring well. Stuff mixture evenly into manicotti shells.
2. Pour ½ cup pasta sauce into a lightly greased 11- x 7-inch baking dish; arrange stuffed shells over sauce. Spoon remaining 1½ cups pasta sauce over shells.
3. Cover and bake at 350° for 30 minutes or until thoroughly heated. Sprinkle with ½ cup Parmesan cheese; bake, uncovered, 5 more minutes or until cheese melts. **Makes** 4 servings.

Mozzarella-and-Olive Orzo

Orzo is a pearl-colored, rice-shaped pasta that cooks quicker than most rice. This Greek-inspired side dish will serve a crowd.

PREP: 20 MIN., COOK: 58 MIN.

1 (12-ounce) block mozzarella cheese
16 ounces orzo, uncooked
2 tablespoons butter
2 tablespoons olive oil
1½ cups chopped onion
2 cups chopped celery
2 tablespoons all-purpose flour
1 cup chicken broth
1 (28-ounce) can plum tomatoes, drained
1 tablespoon fresh or 1 teaspoon dried basil
½ teaspoon dried crushed red pepper
2 (2¼-ounce) cans sliced ripe olives, drained
¼ teaspoon salt

1. Cut 4 ounces mozzarella into thin strips; cut remaining cheese into cubes. Set aside.
2. Cook orzo in a large saucepan according to package directions; drain and transfer to a large bowl.
3. Heat butter and oil in saucepan over medium heat until butter melts; add onion, and sauté until tender. Add celery. Sauté 5 minutes.
4. Stir in flour, and sauté 3 minutes. Stir in broth and next 3 ingredients. Cook 5 minutes, stirring constantly.
5. Stir broth mixture, cheese cubes, olives, and salt into orzo; spoon into a lightly greased shallow 3-quart baking dish. Arrange cheese strips on top.
6. Bake, uncovered, at 350° for 45 minutes or until slightly crisp on top. **Makes** 10 servings.

Hands-off Risotto With Zucchini

PREP: 15 MIN., COOK: 40 MIN., OTHER: 12 MIN.

1 pound zucchini
5¼ cups chicken broth
2 tablespoons butter
1 small onion, chopped (about ½ cup)
1¼ cups long-grain rice
3 carrots, shredded
¼ cup freshly grated Parmesan cheese
2 tablespoons finely chopped fresh oregano
1 teaspoon lemon zest
2 tablespoons lemon juice
Garnishes: oregano sprig, lemon zest

1. Cut zucchini in half lengthwise; cut each half into ¼-inch slices.

2. Microwave broth in a 2-quart. microwave-safe bowl at HIGH 6 to 7 minutes or until very hot.

3. Melt butter in a large Dutch oven over medium heat; add onion, and sauté 4 to 5 minutes or until tender. Stir in rice, and cook, stirring constantly, 2 minutes. Stir in hot broth, and bring to a boil over medium-high heat. Cover, reduce heat to low, and simmer 10 minutes.

4. Stir in zucchini and carrot. Cover and cook 10 to 12 more minutes or until rice is tender. Stir in cheese and next 3 ingredients, stirring until cheese is melted. Remove from heat; cover and let stand 10 to 12 minutes or until liquid is absorbed. Garnish, if desired. **Makes** 8 (1-cup) servings.

Note: For testing purposes only, we used Mahatma Extra Long-Grain Enriched White Rice.

Hands-off Risotto
With Zucchini

Pistachio Risotto With Saffron

Using Arborio rice makes the best risotto; find it in large supermarkets, specialty food stores, or online.

PREP: 15 MIN., COOK: 45 MIN.

¼ cup unsalted butter
1 medium-size yellow onion, chopped
1 teaspoon saffron threads
1¾ cups uncooked Arborio rice
1 cup dry white vermouth*
5 cups chicken broth
1 cup freshly grated Parmesan
    cheese
3 tablespoons coarsely chopped
    pistachios

1. Melt butter in a large skillet over medium-high heat; add onion, and sauté 5 minutes. Add saffron, and sauté 1 minute.
2. Add rice, and cook, stirring constantly, 2 minutes. Reduce heat to medium; add vermouth and 2 cups broth. Cook, stirring constantly, until liquid is absorbed.
3. Repeat procedure with remaining broth, ½ cup at a time. (Cooking time is 30 to 45 minutes.)
4. Remove from heat, stir in cheese and pistachios. **Makes** 8 cups.
*1 cup chicken broth may be substituted for vermouth.

QUICK
Spinach-Parmesan Couscous

Couscous cooks in mere minutes. It's simple and healthy food, combined here with some of the best flavors of the Mediterranean—garlic, olive oil, lemon, and Parmesan.

PREP: 10 MIN., COOK: 8 MIN., OTHER: 5 MIN.

1 medium onion, chopped
1 garlic clove, crushed
2 tablespoons olive oil
1 (14½-ounce) can chicken broth
1 (10-ounce) package frozen
    chopped spinach
1 (10-ounce) package couscous
¾ cup freshly grated Parmesan
    cheese
½ cup chopped pecans, toasted
2 tablespoons lemon juice
½ teaspoon salt
½ teaspoon freshly ground pepper

1. Sauté onion and garlic in hot oil in a large saucepan until tender. Add broth and spinach; cook until spinach thaws, stirring occasionally. Bring to a boil, stirring occasionally.
2. Stir in couscous; cover, remove from heat, and let stand 5 minutes or until liquid is absorbed.
3. Stir in cheese and remaining ingredients. Serve immediately. **Makes** 8 servings.

Orphan's Rice

PREP: 10 MIN., COOK: 30 MIN., OTHER: 10 MIN.

1 tablespoon butter
¾ cup pecan halves
½ cup slivered almonds
⅓ cup pine nuts
½ small onion, minced
1 garlic clove, minced
2 tablespoons vegetable oil
1 (10-ounce) package yellow rice
3 cups low-sodium chicken broth
2 bacon slices, cooked and crumbled
¼ cup finely chopped ham
1 tablespoon minced fresh parsley

1. Melt butter in a skillet over medium heat. Add pecan halves, almonds, and pine nuts, and sauté, stirring often, 3 minutes or until almonds are light golden brown.

2. Sauté onion and garlic in hot oil in a saucepan over medium-high heat 5 minutes or until tender. Add rice, and sauté, stirring constantly, 1 minute. Add broth, and cook rice 18 minutes. Remove from heat.

3. Stir in nuts, bacon, ham, and parsley. Cover and let stand 10 minutes. **Makes** 6 to 8 servings.

Note: We like to use three different nuts for this recipe; however, feel free to use all of the same variety.

Southern Sausage-Rice Dressing
PREP: 1 HR., COOK: 45 MIN.

2 garlic bulbs
2 teaspoons olive oil
2 cups cooked rice
1 recipe Basic Cornbread, crumbled
1 (16-ounce) package ground pork sausage
3 tablespoons butter
1 medium onion, diced
1 medium-size red or green bell pepper, diced
1 large carrot, diced
½ cup chopped fresh parsley
1 tablespoon poultry seasoning
1½ tablespoons chopped fresh or 1 to 2 teaspoons
     rubbed sage
½ teaspoon salt
½ teaspoon pepper
4 cups chicken broth

1. Cut off pointed ends of garlic bulbs; place garlic on a piece of aluminum foil, and drizzle with olive oil. Fold foil to seal.
2. Bake at 350° for 45 minutes; cool. Squeeze pulp from garlic cloves into a large bowl. Add rice and cornbread.
3. Cook sausage in a large skillet over medium heat, stirring until it crumbles and is no longer pink; drain sausage on paper towels, and wipe skillet clean.
4. Melt butter in a skillet over medium-high heat. Add onion, bell pepper, and carrot, and sauté 3 minutes or until tender.
5. Stir sausage, vegetables, parsley, and next 4 ingredients into rice mixture. Add broth; stir to moisten. Spoon into a lightly greased 13- x 9-inch baking dish. Cover and chill 8 hours, if desired; remove from refrigerator, and let stand at room temperature 30 minutes.
6. Bake, covered, at 350° for 45 minutes or until thoroughly heated. **Makes** 12 servings.

Basic Cornbread
PREP: 10 MIN., COOK: 25 MIN.

2 cups buttermilk self-rising white cornmeal mix
½ cup all-purpose flour
¼ cup butter, melted
1 large egg, lightly beaten
2 cups buttermilk

1. Heat a well-greased ovenproof skillet at 450° for 5 minutes.
2. Stir together all ingredients in a bowl. Pour batter into hot skillet.
3. Bake at 450° for 20 minutes or until golden brown.
Makes 1 (9-inch) cornbread (about 5 cups crumbled).

QUICK
Lemon Rice Pilaf
Long-grain rice has long, slender kernels that cook up separate, light, and fluffy.

PREP: 15 MIN., COOK: 12 MIN.

2 tablespoons butter
4 celery ribs, sliced
6 green onions, chopped
3 cups hot cooked rice
2 tablespoons lemon zest
½ teaspoon salt
¼ teaspoon pepper

1. Melt butter in a large skillet over medium-high heat; add celery and green onions, and sauté until celery is tender. Stir in rice and remaining ingredients; cook over low heat 2 minutes or until thoroughly heated.
Makes 6 servings.

Hoppin' John

Hoppin' John

This New Year's Day recipe of good-luck peas and rice is a universal favorite.

PREP: 15 MIN., COOK: 55 MIN.

1 cup sliced celery
⅔ cup chopped onion
1 garlic clove, minced
1 tablespoon vegetable oil
1 (16-ounce) package frozen black-eyed peas
¾ pound cubed cooked ham
2½ cups chicken broth
¼ teaspoon dried crushed red pepper
1 bay leaf
1 cup uncooked long-grain rice
Freshly ground pepper
Garnish: celery leaves

1. Cook first 3 ingredients in hot oil in a Dutch oven over medium-high heat, stirring constantly, until tender. Stir in peas and next 4 ingredients. Bring to a boil; cover, reduce heat, and simmer 30 minutes. Stir in rice; cover and cook 20 to 25 minutes or until liquid is absorbed and rice is tender. Discard bay leaf before serving. Sprinkle with freshly ground pepper. Garnish, if desired. **Makes** 4 servings.

Caribbean Rice and Peas

Pigeon peas, nicknamed no-eye peas, are of African origin. They're yellow-gray in color and are about the size of green peas. (pictured on page 226)

PREP: 10 MIN., COOK: 30 MIN.

1 small onion, finely chopped
2 garlic cloves, pressed
1 tablespoon olive oil
2 cups basmati rice
2½ cups water
1 (10¾-ounce) can condensed
    chicken broth
½ cup unsweetened coconut milk
1 (15-ounce) can pigeon peas, rinsed
    and drained*
1 tablespoon chopped fresh parsley
2 teaspoons lemon zest
1 teaspoon salt
Garnish: fresh parsley sprigs

1. Sauté onion and garlic in hot oil in a Dutch oven over medium-high heat 1 to 2 minutes or until translucent. Add rice and next 3 ingredients; bring to a boil. Cover, reduce heat, and simmer 25 minutes or until liquid is absorbed and rice is tender.
2. Stir in peas, parsley, lemon zest, and salt. Garnish, if desired. **Makes** 8 to 10 servings.
*Substitute 1 (15-ounce) can field peas for pigeon peas, if desired.

Serrano Chile Polenta

Serve this polenta just as you would mashed potatoes.

PREP: 10 MIN., COOK: 5 MIN.

3 cups water
1 cup white cornmeal
½ cup butter, cut into pieces
1 cup grated Parmesan cheese
2 serrano chiles, seeded and chopped,
    or 2 jalapeño peppers
1 tablespoon chopped fresh cilantro
¼ teaspoon salt
¼ teaspoon pepper

1. Bring 3 cups water to a boil in a large heavy saucepan; gradually add cornmeal, whisking until smooth. Cook 3 to 5 minutes or until thickened. Remove from heat.
2. Whisk in butter and remaining ingredients. Serve warm, or spread polenta into a lightly greased 9-inch square pan. Cool slightly. Cut into desired shapes. **Makes** 4 servings.

Tomato Gravy

You'll love the flavor of this gravy over hot cooked grits. We tried it with canned tomatoes but prefer the flavor and texture of fresh.

PREP: 10 MIN., COOK: 30 MIN.

2 garlic cloves, minced
1 medium onion, finely chopped
2 tablespoons olive oil
4 large tomatoes, chopped
½ cup whipping cream
½ teaspoon salt
½ teaspoon ground red pepper
½ teaspoon dried thyme
Hot cooked grits

1. Sauté garlic and onion in hot oil in a medium skillet over medium heat 5 minutes or until tender. Stir in tomatoes; reduce heat to low, and simmer, stirring occasionally, 20 minutes.

2. Stir in whipping cream and remaining ingredients; simmer, stirring occasionally, 4 to 5 minutes or until slightly thickened. Serve over hot cooked grits. **Makes** 2½ cups.

Tomato-and-Watermelon
Salad, page 301

sensational
salads

Pear Salad With
Raspberry Cream

Pear Salad With Raspberry Cream

This salad makes a beautiful presentation and a delicious combination of flavors.

PREP: 20 MIN.

¾ cup sour cream
¼ cup raspberry preserves
3 tablespoons red wine vinegar
⅛ teaspoon Dijon mustard
4 firm, ripe pears
2 tablespoons lemon juice
1 head Bibb lettuce, torn
1 small head romaine lettuce, torn
½ cup freshly grated Parmesan cheese
6 bacon slices, cooked and crumbled
½ cup fresh raspberries

1. Whisk together first 4 ingredients. Set dressing aside.
2. Peel pears, if desired; quarter pears. Brush with lemon juice.
3. Arrange lettuce on 4 plates. Arrange pear quarters over lettuce. Drizzle with dressing; sprinkle with cheese, bacon, and raspberries. **Makes** 4 servings.

Honey-Spinach Salad

PREP: 10 MIN., OTHER: 2 HR.

¼ teaspoon salt
1 garlic clove, crushed
⅓ cup honey
⅓ cup olive oil
1 tablespoon lemon juice
2 (6-ounce) packages fresh baby spinach
1 (11-ounce) can mandarin oranges, drained
¾ cup coarsely chopped walnuts, toasted

1. Sprinkle salt in a large bowl; add garlic. Mash garlic and salt to a paste, using the back of a spoon. Combine honey, olive oil, and lemon juice in a jar. Cover tightly, and shake vigorously. Add honey mixture to the garlic mixture; stir well. Cover and chill at least 2 hours.
2. Remove stems from spinach; wash leaves thoroughly, and pat dry. Tear leaves into bite-size pieces. Combine spinach, oranges, and walnuts in a large bowl; toss well. Pour honey mixture over salad, tossing to coat. Serve immediately. **Makes** 6 servings.

FAMILY FAVORITE, QUICK
Greek Salad

Tangy Greek olives and crumbled feta cheese spread lively and intense flavor onto this popular salad.

PREP: 15 MIN.

6 cups torn iceberg lettuce
4 cups torn romaine lettuce
1 cup pitted ripe olives
2 medium tomatoes, cut into wedges
1 large cucumber, sliced
½ cup olive oil
3 tablespoons red wine vinegar
1 teaspoon dried oregano
½ teaspoon freshly ground pepper
1 cup crumbled feta cheese

1. Combine first 5 ingredients in a large bowl; toss well.
2. Combine olive oil and next 3 ingredients in a jar. Cover tightly, and shake vigorously. Pour dressing over salad, tossing to coat. Sprinkle with feta cheese. Serve immediately. **Makes** 10 servings.

QUICK
Spinach-and-Cranberry Salad With Warm Chutney Dressing

PREP: 20 MIN., COOK: 3 MIN.

2 tablespoons butter
1½ cups coarsely chopped pecans
1 teaspoon salt
1 teaspoon freshly ground pepper
2 (6-ounce) packages fresh baby spinach
6 bacon slices, cooked and crumbled
1 cup dried cranberries
2 hard-cooked eggs, finely chopped
Warm Chutney Dressing

1. Melt butter in a nonstick skillet over medium-high heat; add pecans, and cook, stirring constantly, 2 minutes or until toasted. Remove from heat; add salt and pepper, tossing to coat. Drain pecans on paper towels.
2. Toss together pecans, spinach, bacon, and next 2 ingredients. Drizzle with Warm Chutney Dressing, gently tossing to coat. Serve immediately. **Makes** 8 servings.

Warm Chutney Dressing

PREP: 5 MIN., COOK: 4 MIN.

6 tablespoons balsamic vinegar
⅓ cup bottled mango chutney
2 tablespoons Dijon mustard
2 tablespoons honey
2 garlic cloves, minced
¼ cup olive oil

1. Cook first 5 ingredients in a saucepan over medium heat, stirring constantly, 3 minutes. Stir in olive oil, blending well; cook 1 minute. **Makes** 1 cup.

Citrus-Blue Cheese Salad

Any combination of lettuces—curly leaf, romaine, Bibb, or fresh spinach—will work well in this salad.

PREP: 18 MIN., OTHER: 3 HR.

2 medium-size pink grapefruit
1 (0.7-ounce) envelope Italian dressing mix
½ cup vegetable oil
2 tablespoons water
10 cups mixed salad greens
2 oranges, peeled, seeded, and sectioned
1 (4-ounce) package crumbled blue cheese

1. Peel and section grapefruit, catching juice in a bowl. Reserve ¼ cup juice; set grapefruit sections aside. Combine reserved juice, dressing mix, oil, and water in a jar. Cover tightly, and shake vigorously. Chill at least 3 hours.
2. Layer half each of salad greens, grapefruit sections, and orange sections in a large salad bowl. Repeat procedure with remaining greens and fruit sections. Sprinkle with blue cheese. Cover and chill at least 3 hours. Pour dressing over salad, tossing to coat. Serve immediately. **Makes** 10 servings.

Orange-Walnut Spinach Salad

Sweet-and Sour Dressing ties the flavors together for this recipe.

PREP: 20 MIN., COOK: 3 MIN.

1 pound fresh spinach, torn into bite-size pieces
2 small heads Bibb lettuce, torn into bite-size pieces
2 oranges, peeled, seeded, and sectioned
1 small red onion, sliced and separated into rings
½ cup walnut or pecan pieces
2 teaspoons butter, melted
Sweet-and-Sour Dressing

1. Place first 4 ingredients in a large bowl. Sauté walnuts in butter until lightly browned; add to lettuce mixture. Toss with Sweet-and-Sour Dressing. Serve immediately. **Makes** 10 servings.

Sweet-and-Sour Dressing

PREP: 5 MIN., OTHER: 2 HR.

½ teaspoon paprika
½ teaspoon celery seeds
½ teaspoon dry mustard
½ teaspoon salt
½ teaspoon grated onion
¼ cup sugar
½ cup vegetable oil
¼ cup white vinegar

1. Combine all ingredients in a jar. Cover tightly, and shake vigorously. Chill at least 2 hours. Shake again before serving over salad. **Makes** 1 cup.

Curly Endive, Bacon, and Pecan Salad

Curly endive leaves have frilly edges and a slightly bitter taste. A sweet dressing and Parmesan shavings complement this colorful salad.

PREP: 12 MIN., COOK: 8 MIN.

3 cups loosely packed curly endive
3 cups loosely packed Boston lettuce
1 small red onion, thinly sliced
¾ cup pecan halves, toasted
6 bacon slices
¼ cup red wine vinegar
2 teaspoons brown sugar
¼ teaspoon salt
¼ teaspoon pepper
Shaved Parmesan cheese

1. Combine first 4 ingredients in a large bowl; set aside.
2. Cook bacon in a large skillet until crisp; remove bacon, reserving 2 tablespoons drippings in skillet. Coarsely crumble bacon; set aside. Add vinegar and next 3 ingredients to skillet; cook over low heat until thoroughly heated. Pour over greens; toss gently. Sprinkle with bacon, and top with cheese. Serve immediately. **Makes** 4 servings.

Curly Endive, Bacon,
and Pecan Salad

Baby Blue Salad

This salad is a popular item on Chef Franklin Biggs's menu at Homewood Gourmet in Birmingham.

PREP: 10 MIN.

¾ pound mixed salad greens
Balsamic Vinaigrette
4 ounces blue cheese, crumbled
2 oranges, peeled, sectioned, and
     quartered
1 pint strawberries, quartered
Sweet-and-Spicy Pecans (opposite page)

1. Toss greens with desired amount of Balsamic Vinaigrette. Toss in blue cheese and remaining ingredients. Serve immediately. **Makes** 6 servings.

Balsamic Vinaigrette

PREP: 10 MIN.

½ cup balsamic vinegar
3 tablespoons Dijon mustard
2 tablespoons honey
2 garlic cloves, minced
2 small shallots, minced
¼ teaspoon salt
¼ teaspoon pepper
1 cup olive oil

1. Whisk together first 7 ingredients until blended. Gradually whisk in olive oil. **Makes** 1⅔ cups.

Sweet-and-Spicy Pecans

PREP: 5 MIN., COOK: 10 MIN., OTHER: 10 MIN.

¼ cup sugar
1 cup warm water
1 cup pecan halves
2 tablespoons sugar
1 tablespoon chili powder
⅛ teaspoon ground red pepper

1. Stir together ¼ cup sugar and 1 cup warm water until sugar dissolves. Add pecans; soak 10 minutes. Drain, discarding syrup.
2. Combine 2 tablespoons sugar, chili powder, and red pepper. Add pecans, tossing to coat. Place pecans on a lightly greased baking sheet.
3. Bake at 350° for 10 minutes or until golden brown, stirring once. **Makes** 1 cup.

QUICK
Walnut-Goat Cheese Salad

PREP: 15 MIN.

¼ cup orange juice
3 tablespoons white wine vinegar
⅛ teaspoon salt
⅛ teaspoon ground white pepper
½ cup vegetable oil
¼ cup olive oil
6 cups mixed salad greens
½ cup chopped walnuts, toasted
6 ounces goat cheese, cut into
    ¼-inch-thick slices

1. Combine first 4 ingredients in container of a blender. With blender on high, gradually add oils in a slow, steady stream, processing until blended.
2. Arrange salad greens, walnuts, and goat cheese slices on individual salad plates. Serve dressing with salad. **Makes** 6 servings.

QUICK
Green Salad Vinaigrette

The combination of bacon, onion, and roasted pecans gives this salad its appeal. The pecans roast in a spicy cinnamon mixture—they're so good you'll be tempted to just nibble them alone. If you're so inclined, we suggest doubling the pecan recipe.

PREP: 10 MIN.

6 cups mixed salad greens
4 bacon slices, cooked and crumbled
1 small red onion, thinly sliced
Roasted Pecans
¼ cup olive oil
2 tablespoons raspberry vinegar
1½ teaspoons sugar
⅛ teaspoon salt
Freshly ground pepper

1. Combine first 4 ingredients in a large bowl, and toss well. Combine olive oil and remaining 4 ingredients in a jar. Cover tightly, and shake vigorously. Pour dressing over salad, tossing to coat. Serve immediately. **Makes** 6 servings.

Roasted Pecans

PREP: 10 MIN., COOK: 18 MIN.

1 tablespoon butter
2 tablespoons sugar
1 tablespoon orange juice
¼ teaspoon ground cinnamon
⅛ teaspoon ground red pepper
1 cup pecan halves

1. Melt butter in a large skillet over medium heat; stir in sugar and next 3 ingredients, Add pecans to skillet, stirring to coat. Spread pecans on a lightly greased baking sheet. Bake at 325° for 15 minutes, stirring every 5 minutes. Cool completely. Store in an airtight container. **Makes** 1 cup.

Bacon-Blue Cheese
Salad With White
Wine Vinaigrette

Bacon-Blue Cheese Salad With White Wine Vinaigrette

Serving this salad in cucumber rings makes it extra special.

PREP: 35 MIN., COOK: 8 MIN., OTHER: 30 MIN.

2 tablespoons chopped pecans
2 medium cucumbers, peeled
3 cups mixed baby greens
2 cooked thick-cut bacon slices, halved
⅓ cup shredded or matchstick carrots
¼ cup crumbled blue cheese
Salt and freshly ground pepper to taste
White Wine Vinaigrette

1. Place chopped pecans in a single layer in a shallow pan. Bake at 350° for 8 minutes or until lightly toasted, stirring occasionally. Let cool 30 minutes or until completely cool.
2. Using a Y-shaped vegetable peeler, cut cucumbers lengthwise into very thin strips just until seeds are visible. Discard cucumber core.
3. Shape largest cucumber slices into 4 (2½- to 2¾-inch-wide) rings. Wrap evenly with remaining cucumber slices. Stand rings upright on 4 serving plates.

4. Fill each cucumber ring evenly with mixed greens, next 3 ingredients, and toasted pecans. Sprinkle with salt and pepper to taste. Drizzle each salad with 1 tablespoon White Wine Vinaigrette, and serve with remaining vinaigrette. **Makes** 4 servings.
Note: Y-shaped vegetable peelers range in price from $6.99 to $19.95 and can be found at most kitchen, home goods, and discount stores.

White Wine Vinaigrette

PREP: 5 MIN.

¼ cup white wine vinegar
1 tablespoon Dijon mustard
1 garlic clove, minced
1 teaspoon sugar
½ cup olive oil
Salt and freshly ground pepper
        to taste

1. Whisk together first 4 ingredients until blended. Add oil in a slow, steady stream, whisking constantly until smooth. Whisk in salt and pepper to taste. Store in the refrigerator in an airtight container for up to 1 week. **Makes** about ⅔ cup.

Cucumber Ring Containers

Impress guests by serving the Bacon-Blue Cheese Salad With White Wine Vinaigrette in these clever containers.

1. Use a Y-shaped vegetable peeler to cut cucumbers into long, thin strips.

2. Shape the largest cucumber slices into 4 rings. Wrap them evenly with remaining cucumber slices.

QUICK
Fresh Pear Salad With Asian Sesame Dressing

PREP: 15 MIN.

2 cups shredded romaine lettuce
2 cups shredded red cabbage
3 red Bartlett pears, sliced
2 medium carrots, shredded (about 1 cup)
1 green onion, chopped
Asian Sesame Dressing
2 teaspoons sesame seeds, toasted (optional)

1. Toss together first 5 ingredients in a large bowl, and drizzle with Asian Sesame Dressing, tossing gently to coat. Sprinkle with sesame seeds, if desired. Serve immediately. **Makes** 4 to 6 servings.

Asian Sesame Dressing

PREP: 5 MIN.

¼ cup vegetable oil
2 tablespoons white wine vinegar
1 tablespoon soy sauce
2 teaspoons sugar
½ teaspoon sesame oil
¼ teaspoon dried crushed red pepper

1. Whisk together all ingredients. **Makes** ½ cup.

Orange Salad With Honey Dressing

This is a wonderful citrus salad for the holiday season when a bag of oranges is often on hand. A sweet-and-sour dressing blends the flavors beautifully.

PREP: 15 MIN.

¼ cup honey
2½ tablespoons lemon juice
2 tablespoons white vinegar
½ teaspoon dry mustard
⅛ teaspoon salt
⅛ teaspoon celery seeds
½ cup vegetable oil
1 medium-size head romaine lettuce, torn
5 oranges, peeled and sliced
½ small red onion, thinly sliced

1. Process first 6 ingredients in container of a blender until smooth, stopping once to scrape down sides. With blender on high, gradually add oil in a slow, steady stream; blend until thickened. Cover and chill.
2. Line individual salad plates with lettuce. Arrange orange and onion slices on lettuce; drizzle dressing over top. Serve immediately. **Makes** 6 servings.

Bibb Salad With Raspberry Maple Dressing

PREP: 15 MIN.

⅔ cup vegetable oil
¼ cup raspberry vinegar
2 tablespoons maple syrup
5 heads Bibb lettuce, torn
2 small red onions, sliced and separated into rings
2 cups crumbled blue cheese
½ cup pine nuts, toasted

1. Combine first 3 ingredients in a jar. Cover tightly, and shake vigorously.
2. Arrange lettuce and onion rings on individual salad plates. Sprinkle each salad with blue cheese and pine nuts, and drizzle with dressing. **Makes** 12 servings.

Mixed Green Salad With Cilantro-Lime Vinaigrette

Add extra jicama to coleslaw for a crunchier texture, or serve it with other fresh vegetables for dipping in your favorite dressing.

PREP: 15 MIN.

1 (5-ounce) bag mixed salad greens,
   thoroughly washed
2 oranges, peeled and sectioned
1 avocado, sliced
¼ cup peeled, cubed jicama
   (about ½-inch cubes)
6 tablespoons Cilantro-Lime Vinaigrette

1. Toss together first 4 ingredients in a large bowl. Serve immediately with Cilantro-Lime Vinaigrette. **Makes** 4 servings.

Cilantro-Lime Vinaigrette:
Use extra vinaigrette on salads or as a poultry marinade.

PREP: 10 MIN.

½ cup cider vinegar
2 tablespoons chopped fresh cilantro
1 teaspoon lime zest
2 tablespoons lime juice
1 tablespoon honey
¼ teaspoon salt
¼ cup olive oil

1. Whisk together first 6 ingredients; add oil in a slow, steady stream, whisking constantly until smooth. Whisk well before serving. **Makes** ¾ cup.

Summer Fruit Salad With Blueberry Vinaigrette

If you don't have nectarines, use peaches or chopped cantaloupe.

PREP: 26 MIN., OTHER: 1 HR.

8 cups mixed salad greens
1 pint fresh or frozen blueberries,
    thawed
1 pint fresh strawberries, halved
2 nectarines, sliced
Blueberry Vinaigrette
½ cup sliced almonds, toasted

1. Combine first 4 ingredients in a large bowl. Cover and chill 1 hour.
2. Drizzle with ⅓ cup Blueberry Vinaigrette, tossing to coat. Sprinkle with almonds. **Makes** 6 servings.

Blueberry Vinaigrette

PREP: 4 MIN.

¼ cup Blueberry Chutney (opposite page) or
    store-bought blueberry fruit spread
¼ cup minced onion
⅓ cup balsamic vinegar
1 teaspoon salt
½ teaspoon pepper
⅔ cup vegetable oil

1. Whisk together first 5 ingredients. Gradually whisk in oil until blended. Refrigerate leftover vinaigrette up to 2 weeks. **Makes** 1½ cups.

Summer Fruit Salad With
Blueberry Vinaigrette

Blueberry Chutney

PREP: 6 MIN.; COOK: 1 HR., 15 MIN.

1 large Granny Smith apple, peeled and diced
½ cup sugar
½ cup orange juice
1 tablespoon orange zest
1 teaspoon ground ginger
¼ to ½ teaspoon dried crushed red pepper
¼ teaspoon ground black pepper
4 cups fresh or frozen blueberries
3 tablespoons balsamic vinegar

1. Bring first 7 ingredients to a boil in a medium saucepan. Reduce heat to low; simmer, stirring occasionally, 15 minutes or until apple is tender. Stir in blueberries and vinegar; bring to a boil. Reduce heat to medium; cook, stirring occasionally, 1 hour or until thickened. **Makes** 3 cups.

QUICK
Fruit Salad With Blackberry-Basil Vinaigrette

PREP: 10 MIN.

8 cups gourmet mixed salad greens
1½ cups sliced mango
1½ cups pink grapefruit segments
1½ cups sliced fresh strawberries
1 cup fresh blackberries
1 large avocado, sliced
Blackberry-Basil Vinaigrette

1. Place salad greens and next 5 ingredients in a large bowl, and gently toss. Serve immediately with Blackberry-Basil Vinaigrette. **Makes** 6 servings.

Blackberry-Basil Vinaigrette

PREP: 5 MIN.

½ (10-ounce) jar seedless blackberry preserves
¼ cup red wine vinegar
6 fresh basil leaves
1 garlic clove, sliced
½ teaspoon salt
½ teaspoon seasoned pepper
¾ cup vegetable oil

1. Pulse blackberry preserves, red wine vinegar, and next 4 ingredients in a blender 2 or 3 times until blended. With blender running, pour vegetable oil through food chute in a slow, steady stream; process until smooth. **Makes** 1 cup.

QUICK
Citrus-Avocado Salad

Since grapefruit are available year-round, you can make this tangy salad anytime. The heavier the grapefruit, the juicier it will be. Be sure to section fruit over a bowl to catch the juices.

PREP: 15 MIN.

3 pink grapefruit, peeled and sectioned
3 oranges, peeled and sectioned
2 avocados, peeled and sliced
2 heads Bibb lettuce
Orange French Dressing
⅓ cup coarsely chopped walnuts

1. Combine first 3 ingredients; toss gently. Arrange fruit over lettuce, and top with Orange French Dressing. Sprinkle with walnuts. Serve immediately. **Makes** 8 servings.

Orange French Dressing

PREP: 5 MIN., OTHER: 1 HR.

1 (6-ounce) can frozen orange juice concentrate, thawed and undiluted
½ cup olive oil
¼ cup cider vinegar
3 to 4 tablespoons sugar
½ teaspoon dry mustard
¼ teaspoon salt

1. Combine all ingredients, stirring well. Cover and chill 1 hour. **Makes** 1½ cups.

"This salad has a really unexpected flavor combination. The acid from the tomatoes and the sweet watermelon are well balanced—really different and delicious."

REBECCA KRACKE GORDON, ASSISTANT TEST KITCHENS DIRECTOR

Tomato-and-
Watermelon Salad

Tomato-and-Watermelon Salad

This refreshing dish is adapted from Seasoned in the South:
Recipes From Crook's Corner *and* From Home *by*
Bill Smith, who has a passion for fresh, seasonal produce.
The salad is juicy, so use a slotted spoon if placing it on
lettuce. If serving without lettuce, offer guests a fork
and a spoon so they can enjoy the refreshing liquid.

PREP: 20 MIN.; OTHER: 2 HR., 15 MIN.

5 cups (¾-inch) seeded watermelon
    cubes
1½ pounds ripe tomatoes, cut into
    ¾-inch cubes
3 teaspoons sugar
½ teaspoon salt
1 small red onion, quartered and
    thinly sliced
½ cup red wine vinegar
¼ cup extra-virgin olive oil
Romaine lettuce leaves (optional)
Cracked black pepper to taste

1. Combine watermelon and tomato in a large bowl;
sprinkle with sugar and salt, tossing to coat. Let stand
15 minutes.
2. Stir in onion, vinegar, and oil. Cover and chill
2 hours. Serve chilled with lettuce leaves, if desired.
Sprinkle with cracked black pepper to taste. **Makes**
4 to 6 servings.

Fresh Fruit Salad

PREP: 25 MIN.

2 oranges, peeled and sectioned
1 medium pineapple, peeled and cut into
    chunks (about 6 cups)
1 small cantaloupe, cut into balls (3 cups)
1 cup sliced strawberries
1 cup seedless red grapes
2 medium bananas, sliced
1 ripe pear, sliced
1 tablespoon lemon juice
Fruit Dressing

1. Combine first 5 ingredients in a large bowl. Sprinkle
banana and pear with lemon juice; add to fruit mixture, and toss gently. Cover and chill up to 2 hours.
Pour Fruit Dressing over fruit, and toss gently before
serving. **Makes** 14 servings.

Fruit Dressing

PREP: 5 MIN.

½ cup orange juice
¼ cup vegetable oil
1 tablespoon sugar
½ teaspoon salt
¼ teaspoon paprika
¼ teaspoon celery seed
1 small garlic clove, crushed

1. Combine all ingredients in a small jar; cover and
shake gently to blend. Chill until ready to serve.
Remove garlic before serving. **Makes** ¾ cup.

White Bean-and-
Asparagus Salad

White Bean-and-Asparagus Salad
*After cooking the asparagus, this is practically
a dump-and-stir recipe.*

PREP: 20 MIN., COOK: 4 MIN., OTHER: 1 HR.

½ pound fresh asparagus, trimmed
7 dried tomatoes
1 garlic clove, minced
1 tablespoon brown sugar
2 tablespoons extra-virgin olive oil
2 tablespoons white wine vinegar
1 tablespoon water
1 teaspoon spicy brown mustard
¼ teaspoon dried rubbed sage
¼ teaspoon salt
¼ teaspoon pepper
1 (19-ounce) can cannellini beans, rinsed
    and drained
¼ cup chopped red onion
2 teaspoons drained capers
1 (5-ounce) bag gourmet mixed salad greens
1 tablespoon shredded Parmesan cheese

1. Arrange asparagus and dried tomatoes in a steamer
basket over boiling water. Cover and steam 2 to
4 minutes or until asparagus is crisp-tender. Set
tomatoes aside. Plunge asparagus into ice water to stop
the cooking process; drain. Cut asparagus into 1-inch
pieces, and chill until ready to use. Chop tomatoes.
2. Whisk together garlic and next 8 ingredients in a
medium bowl; add asparagus, tomatoes, beans, onion,
and capers, tossing to coat. Cover and chill 1 hour.
Serve asparagus mixture over salad greens; sprinkle
with cheese. **Makes** 6 servings.

Black Bean Salad
*Serve this fresh, hearty salad as a side dish with burgers when
you want a change from the usual potato salad and slaw.*

PREP: 15 MIN., COOK: 5 MIN., OTHER: 2 HR.

3 fresh ears corn
3 to 4 tablespoons lime juice
2 tablespoons olive oil
1 tablespoon red wine vinegar
1 teaspoon salt
½ teaspoon freshly ground pepper
2 (15-ounce) cans black beans, rinsed and drained
2 large tomatoes, seeded and chopped
3 jalapeño peppers, seeded and chopped
1 small red onion, chopped
1 avocado, chopped
¼ cup chopped fresh cilantro

1. Cook corn in boiling water to cover 5 minutes;
drain and cool. Cut corn from cob.
2. Whisk together lime juice and next 4 ingredients
in a large bowl. Add corn, black beans, and remaining ingredients; toss to coat. Cover and chill 2 hours.
Makes 6 to 8 servings.

Carrot-Raisin Salad
PREP: 10 MIN.

¾ pound carrots, scraped and shredded
½ cup raisins
½ cup chopped walnuts
½ cup mayonnaise
1 tablespoon sugar
1½ tablespoons cider vinegar
⅛ teaspoon lemon juice

1. Combine carrot, raisins, and walnuts in a bowl.
Combine mayonnaise and remaining 3 ingredients,
stirring well; add to carrot mixture. Toss gently. Cover
and chill. **Makes** 4 servings.

Chilled Vegetable Salad

PREP: 20 MIN.; COOK: 5 MIN.; OTHER: 8 HR., 30 MIN.

1 cup sugar
¾ cup cider vinegar
½ cup vegetable oil
1 medium-size green bell pepper,
    chopped
1 medium onion, chopped
3 celery ribs, sliced
1 (7-ounce) jar diced pimiento,
    undrained
1 (15¼-ounce) can small sweet
    green peas, drained
1 (14½-ounce) can French-cut green
    beans, drained
1 (11-ounce) can white shoepeg
    corn, drained
½ teaspoon salt
¼ teaspoon pepper

1. Bring first 3 ingredients to a boil in small saucepan over medium heat; cook, stirring often, 5 minutes or until sugar dissolves. Remove dressing from heat, and cool 30 minutes.
2. Stir together chopped bell pepper and next 8 ingredients in a large bowl; gently stir in dressing. Cover and chill salad 8 hours. Serve with a slotted spoon. **Makes** 8 cups.
Note: Salad may be stored in an airtight container in the refrigerator for several days.

Salad Savvy

- Chilling your salad plates or serving bowl will keep salad greens crisp longer.
- The best salads have a balance of textures, colors, and flavors. Contrast crunchy ingredients with smooth dressings, vibrant colors with muted hues, and mellow flavors with spicy bold ones.
- Dress for success: Resist heavy dressings that weigh down ingredients; a lighter dressing lets the freshness shine through.

> **I love this salad for a light meal served alongside baked chicken or steak. The blue cheese is a nice counterpart to the sweet onions and lends the salad body.**

DONNA FLORIO, SENIOR WRITER

(EDITOR'S CHOICE)
Roasted Onion Salad

PREP: 15 MIN., COOK: 15 MIN., OTHER: 5 MIN.

5 medium onions, cut into ½-inch-thick
    slices
¼ cup olive oil
8 cups gourmet mixed salad greens
½ cup chopped walnuts, toasted
1 (4-ounce) package crumbled blue cheese
Garlic Vinaigrette

1. Arrange onion slices in a lightly greased roasting pan. Drizzle evenly with olive oil.
2. Bake at 450° for 12 to 15 minutes or until onion slices are lightly charred. Cool 5 minutes.
3. Combine salad greens, walnuts, and blue cheese; toss gently. Top with onion slices; drizzle with Garlic Vinaigrette. **Makes** 8 servings.

Garlic Vinaigrette

PREP: 10 MIN.

3 garlic cloves
2 shallots
¼ cup chopped fresh parsley
2 tablespoons white wine vinegar
½ teaspoon dried crushed red pepper
½ teaspoon salt
½ teaspoon freshly ground black pepper
⅔ cup olive oil

1. Pulse garlic and shallots in a food processor 3 or 4 times. Add parsley and next 4 ingredients; process 20 seconds, stopping once to scrape down sides. With processor running, gradually pour olive oil in a slow, steady stream through food chute until blended. **Makes** 1 cup.

Bok Choy Salad

QUICK
Bok Choy Salad

PREP: 15 MIN., COOK: 10 MIN.

2 (3-ounce) packages ramen noodle
    soup mix
½ cup sunflower seeds
3 tablespoons slivered almonds, chopped
½ cup sugar
¼ cup olive oil
¼ cup cider vinegar
2 tablespoons soy sauce
1 bok choy, shredded
6 green onions, chopped

1. Remove flavor packets from soup mix; reserve for another use. Crumble noodles.
2. Combine noodles, sunflower seeds, and almonds. Spread on a 15- x 10-inch jelly-roll pan.
3. Bake at 350° for 8 to 10 minutes or until golden brown; set aside.
4. Bring sugar and next 3 ingredients to a boil in a saucepan over medium heat. Remove from heat; cool.
5. Place bok choy and green onions in a large bowl. Drizzle with sugar mixture. Add ramen noodle mixture, tossing well. Serve immediately. **Makes** 6 to 8 servings.

Crunchy Cabbage Slaw

PREP: 30 MIN., COOK: 10 MIN., OTHER: 1 HR.

1 (3-ounce) package ramen noodle
    soup mix
¼ cup sliced almonds
⅓ cup canola oil
¼ cup cider vinegar
2½ tablespoons sugar
1 small green cabbage, shredded
1 small carrot, grated
3 green onions, sliced

1. Remove flavor packet from soup mix, and reserve. Break ramen noodles into pieces, and place on a lightly greased baking sheet. Add sliced almonds.
2. Bake at 350°, stirring occasionally, 5 to 10 minutes or until toasted. Set aside.
3. Whisk together reserved flavor packet, oil, vinegar, and sugar in a bowl until blended. Chill 1 hour.
4. Toss together cabbage, carrot, onions, and dressing in a large bowl. Place noodles around outside edge of cabbage mixture, and top with almonds. **Makes** 6 to 8 servings.

Creamy Dill Salad

PREP: 10 MIN., OTHER: 8 HR.

4 green onions, sliced
1 (8-ounce) container sour cream*
1 cup mayonnaise*
2 tablespoons sugar
2 tablespoons chopped fresh dill
2 tablespoons white vinegar
1 teaspoon salt
½ teaspoon pepper
1 (16-ounce) package shredded coleslaw mix
1 (10-ounce) package finely shredded cabbage
Garnish: chopped fresh dill

1. Stir together first 8 ingredients in a large bowl until mixture is blended; stir in coleslaw mix and cabbage. Cover and chill 8 hours. Garnish, if desired. **Makes** 8 servings.
*Substitute 1 (8-ounce) container light sour cream and 1 cup light mayonnaise, if desired.

Best Barbecue Coleslaw

PREP: 10 MIN., OTHER: 2 HR.

½ cup sugar
½ cup mayonnaise
¼ cup milk
¼ cup buttermilk
2½ tablespoons lemon juice
1½ tablespoons white vinegar
½ teaspoon salt
⅛ teaspoon pepper
2 (10-ounce) packages finely shredded
    cabbage
1 carrot, shredded

1. Whisk together first 8 ingredients in a large bowl; add vegetables, tossing to coat. Cover and chill at least 2 hours. **Makes** 8 to 10 servings.

Broccoli-Squash Slaw

PREP: 20 MIN., OTHER: 2 HR.

¼ cup mayonnaise
¼ cup honey
2 tablespoons fresh lemon juice
1 teaspoon salt
½ teaspoon black pepper
⅛ to ¼ teaspoon ground red pepper
1 (12-ounce) package broccoli slaw
2 medium-size yellow squash, cut in half
    lengthwise and thinly sliced
1 red bell pepper, chopped
½ cup chopped pecans, toasted

1. Whisk together first 6 ingredients in a small bowl. Combine broccoli slaw, squash, and bell pepper in a large bowl. Add half of mayonnaise mixture (about ¼ cup), tossing to coat.
2. Cover and chill both slaw mixture and remaining mayonnaise mixture at least 2 hours or up to 24 hours before serving. Just before serving, drain slaw mixture and discard excess liquid; return to bowl. Add reserved half of mayonnaise mixture and pecans, tossing to coat. **Makes** 4 servings.

Broccoli Slaw

Broccoli Slaw

We enjoyed this picnic slaw a bit on the sweet side. If you'd like, reduce the sugar to ½ cup.

PREP: 6 MIN., COOK: 4 MIN., OTHER: 3 HR.

½ cup cider vinegar
¾ cup sugar
½ teaspoon salt
½ teaspoon mustard seeds
3 tablespoons vegetable oil
1 (16-ounce) package broccoli slaw
2 small Gala apples, chopped
½ cup raisins

1. Combine first 4 ingredients in a small saucepan. Bring to a boil. Boil until sugar dissolves. Remove from heat. Cool. Gradually whisk in oil.
2. Combine broccoli slaw, apple, and raisins in a large bowl; add vinaigrette, and toss well. Cover and chill 3 hours. **Makes** 8 servings.

Roasted New Potato Salad

If you like your potatoes crispier, bake about 10 minutes longer, stirring once.
Don't forget to schedule the extra time when planning your meal.

PREP: 15 MIN., COOK: 35 MIN.

2 tablespoons olive oil
2 pounds small red potatoes, diced
½ medium-size sweet onion, chopped
2 teaspoons minced garlic
1 teaspoon coarse salt
½ teaspoon freshly ground pepper
8 to 10 cooked crisp bacon slices, crumbled
1 bunch green onions, chopped
¾ cup prepared Ranch dressing
Salt and pepper to taste

1. Place oil in a 15- x 10-inch jelly-roll pan; add potatoes and next 4 ingredients, tossing to coat. Arrange potato mixture in a single layer.

2. Bake at 425° for 30 to 35 minutes or until potatoes are tender, stirring occasionally. Transfer potatoes to a large bowl.

3. Toss together potatoes, bacon, green onions, and dressing. Add salt and pepper to taste. Serve immediately, or cover and chill until ready to serve. **Makes** 4 to 6 servings.

Roasted New Potato Salad

Potato Cobb Salad

PREP: 30 MIN., COOK: 30 MIN., OTHER: 2 HR.

3 pounds Yukon gold potatoes
¾ teaspoon salt
1 (16-ounce) bottle olive oil-and-vinegar
    dressing, divided
8 cups mixed salad greens
2 large avocados
1 tablespoon fresh lemon juice
3 large tomatoes, seeded and diced
12 small green onions, sliced
2 cups (8 ounces) shredded sharp Cheddar cheese
4 ounces crumbled blue cheese
6 to 8 bacon slices, cooked and crumbled
Freshly ground pepper to taste

1. Cook potatoes in boiling salted water to cover
30 minutes or until tender. Drain and cool slightly.
Peel and cut into cubes.
2. Sprinkle potatoes evenly with ¾ teaspoon salt. Pour
1 cup dressing over potatoes; gently toss. Set aside
remaining dressing. Cover potato mixture; chill at
least 2 hours or overnight.
3. Arrange salad greens evenly on a large serving platter. Peel and chop avocados; toss with lemon juice.
4. Arrange potatoes, avocado, tomato, and next
4 ingredients in rows over salad greens. Sprinkle
with pepper. Serve with remaining dressing. **Makes**
8 to 10 servings.

Green Bean-Potato Salad

PREP: 20 MIN., COOK: 20 MIN., OTHER: 2 HR.

2 pounds red potatoes
1 pound fresh green beans, trimmed
¼ cup red wine vinegar
4 green onions, sliced
2 tablespoons chopped fresh tarragon
2 tablespoons Dijon mustard
2 tablespoons olive oil
2 teaspoons salt
1 teaspoon pepper
Garnish: fresh tarragon sprig

1. Combine potatoes and water to cover in a large
saucepan; bring to a boil over medium heat, and cook
for 13 minutes. Add green beans, and cook 7 minutes
or until potatoes are tender. Drain and rinse with cold
water. Cut each potato into 8 wedges.
2. Whisk together vinegar and next 6 ingredients in a
large bowl; add potato wedges and green beans, tossing gently to coat. Cover and chill 2 hours. Garnish,
if desired. **Makes** 8 servings.

MAKE AHEAD, QUICK
Lentil-and-Orzo Salad

PREP: 15 MIN., OTHER: 2 HR.

¼ cup vinaigrette dressing
2 tablespoons fresh lemon juice
½ teaspoon ground cumin
½ teaspoon salt
½ teaspoon ground black pepper
¼ teaspoon dried crushed red pepper
2 cups cooked lentils
1 cup cooked orzo
½ red bell pepper, diced
½ small red onion, diced
1½ tablespoons chopped fresh cilantro

1. Whisk together first 6 ingredients in a large bowl;
add lentils and remaining ingredients, tossing gently
to coat.
2. Cover and chill 2 hours. **Makes** 4 servings.

Wild Rice Salad

PREP: 10 MIN., COOK: 10 MIN., OTHER: 8 HR.

1 (6-ounce) package quick-cooking
       long-grain and wild rice mix
2 cups chopped cooked chicken
½ cup dried cranberries
1 Granny Smith apple, peeled and diced
1 medium carrot, grated
⅓ cup white balsamic vinegar*
¼ cup olive oil
¼ teaspoon salt
¼ teaspoon pepper
2 green onions, chopped
1 (2.25-ounce) package sliced almonds, toasted

1. Cook rice according to package directions; cool.
2. Stir together chicken, next 8 ingredients, and rice in a large bowl. Cover and chill 8 hours. Sprinkle with almonds just before serving. **Makes** 6 servings.
*Red wine vinegar may be substituted for white balsamic vinegar.
Note: For testing purposes only, we used Uncle Ben's Quick Cooking Long-Grain and Wild Rice Mix.

Curry Rice Salad

Curry dressing makes this rice salad memorable. Serve it warm or cold. Add some chopped cooked chicken, too, if you'd like to turn it into a main dish.

PREP: 10 MIN., COOK: 25 MIN., OTHER: 10 MIN.

1 (6-ounce) package long-grain and wild rice mix
2 cups chicken broth
1 cup raisins
1 cup hot water
½ cup sliced green onions
1 cup chopped pecans, toasted
1 (16-ounce) can garbanzo beans, drained
Lettuce leaves
Curry Dressing

1. Combine rice mix with seasoning packet and broth in a saucepan. Bring to a boil; cover, reduce heat, and simmer 20 to 25 minutes or until liquid is absorbed and rice is tender.

2. Combine raisins and water; let stand 10 minutes. Drain. Stir raisins, green onions, pecans, and beans into rice mixture. Serve on lettuce leaves. Drizzle with Curry Dressing. **Makes** 8 servings.

Curry Dressing

PREP: 5 MIN.

⅔ cup mayonnaise
1 tablespoon curry powder
1 tablespoon honey
1 tablespoon cider vinegar
⅛ teaspoon ground red pepper
2 teaspoons prepared mustard
1 teaspoon Worcestershire sauce

1. Combine all ingredients in a bowl; cover and chill. **Makes** ¾ cup.

Pasta Salad With Italian Vinaigrette

PREP: 35 MIN.

1 pound uncooked fusilli
¼ cup white wine vinegar
2 tablespoons chopped fresh parsley
1½ teaspoons dried Italian seasoning
1 teaspoon salt
½ teaspoon garlic powder
½ teaspoon pepper
¾ cup olive oil
1 cup grated Parmesan cheese
⅓ cup diced onion
1 (4-ounce) jar chopped pimiento,
       drained
1 (2¼-ounce) can sliced ripe olives,
       drained

1. Cook pasta according to package directions; drain.
2. Whisk together vinegar and next 5 ingredients in a large bowl. Add olive oil in a slow, steady stream, whisking constantly until blended. Add pasta, cheese, and remaining ingredients, tossing to coat. Serve immediately, or cover and chill 8 hours. **Makes** 10 cups.

Italian Pasta Salad

Italian Pasta Salad
Artichokes, salami, ripe olives, roasted red pepper, and basil turn pasta into an Italian feast.

PREP: 20 MIN.

2 (6-ounce) jars marinated artichokes, undrained
1 (12-ounce) package fusilli, cooked
2 (4½-ounce) cans sliced ripe olives, drained,
    or 1 cup whole kalamatas, pitted
1 (7-ounce) jar roasted red peppers, drained
    and sliced
8 ounces mozzarella cheese, cubed
¼ pound hard salami, cut into ¼-inch strips
½ cup shaved fresh Parmesan cheese
¼ cup finely chopped onion
½ cup chopped fresh flat-leaf parsley
½ cup chopped fresh basil
½ cup zesty Italian dressing

1. Drain artichokes, reserving liquid. Cut artichokes into fourths. Set aside.
2. Combine pasta, artichokes, reserved artichoke liquid, olives, and remaining ingredients in a large bowl; toss gently. Serve at room temperature, or cover and chill. **Makes** 6 servings.

pasta salads   **311**

Southwestern Cornbread Salad

PREP: 30 MIN., COOK: 15 MIN., OTHER: 2 HR.

1 (6-ounce) package Mexican cornbread mix
1 (1-ounce) envelope buttermilk Ranch salad
    dressing mix
1 small head romaine lettuce, shredded
2 large tomatoes, chopped
1 (15-ounce) can black beans, rinsed
    and drained
1 (15-ounce) can whole kernel corn with
    red and green peppers, drained
1 (8-ounce) package shredded Mexican
    four-cheese blend
6 bacon slices, cooked and crumbled
5 green onions, chopped

1. Prepare cornbread according to package directions; cool and crumble. Set aside.
2. Prepare salad dressing according to package directions.
3. Layer a large bowl with half each of cornbread, lettuce, and next 6 ingredients; spoon half of dressing evenly over top. Repeat layers with remaining ingredients and dressing. Cover and chill at least 2 hours. **Makes** 10 to 12 servings.

"This salad's a great choice for a covered-dish dinner. It's attractive, it travels well, and it always has folks asking for the recipe."

SHANNON SLITER SATTERWHITE, FOOD EDITOR

Southwestern
Cornbread Salad

Salad Niçoise

PREP: 20 MIN., COOK: 18 MIN., OTHER: 30 MIN.

2 pounds unpeeled small red potatoes
1½ pounds fresh green beans, trimmed
Herb Dressing
2 heads romaine lettuce
6 (3-ounce) packages albacore tuna, flaked
1 (2-ounce) can anchovy fillets, drained
    (optional)
5 hard-cooked eggs, quartered
5 plum tomatoes, cut into wedges or 1 (8-ounce)
    container grape tomatoes
1 cup sliced ripe olives

1. Cook potatoes in boiling water to cover 15 minutes or until tender; drain. Cool slightly; cut into slices. Set aside.
2. Cook green beans in boiling water to cover 3 minutes; drain. Plunge into ice water to stop the cooking process.
3. Toss together potato slices, green beans, and ½ cup Herb Dressing in a large bowl. Chill at least 30 minutes.
4. Tear 1 head romaine lettuce into bite-size pieces. Line a platter with leaves of remaining head of romaine lettuce. Arrange potato mixture over lettuce leaves. Top with torn lettuce pieces.
5. Mound tuna in center of greens. Arrange anchovies around tuna, if desired. Place eggs and tomato wedges on salad. Sprinkle with sliced olives. Serve with remaining Herb Dressing. **Makes** 8 servings.

Herb Dressing

PREP: 10 MIN.

1 cup olive oil
½ cup red wine vinegar
¼ cup drained capers
2 green onions, chopped
2 teaspoons dried basil
2 teaspoons dried marjoram
2 teaspoons dried oregano
2 teaspoons dried thyme
½ teaspoon dry mustard
½ teaspoon salt
½ teaspoon freshly ground pepper

1. Whisk together all ingredients. **Makes** 1½ cups.

Spicy Beef Salad

Lemongrass is an essential herb in Thai cooking. It tastes like fresh citrus; has long, gray-green leaves; and looks like a stiff green onion.

PREP: 15 MIN.; COOK: 12 MIN.; Other: 1 HR., 5 MIN.

1 large tomato, cut into thin wedges
1 large sweet onion, cut in half and
    thinly sliced
1 cucumber, diced
2 green onions, chopped
1 pound flank steak
1½ teaspoons salt, divided
2 teaspoons ground coriander, divided
2 small fresh Thai peppers or serrano peppers
1 stalk lemongrass, coarsely chopped*
2 garlic cloves
1 tablespoon chopped fresh ginger
2 tablespoons fresh lemon juice
1 tablespoon rice wine vinegar
¼ cup fish sauce
1 tablespoon olive oil
1 teaspoon sugar
Mixed salad greens
Garnish: sliced green onions

1. Combine first 4 ingredients; set aside.
2. Rub steak with ½ teaspoon salt and 1 teaspoon coriander.
3. Process remaining 1 teaspoon salt, remaining 1 teaspoon coriander, and next 9 ingredients in a food processor or blender until smooth. Chill dressing 1 hour.
4. Grill steak, covered with grill lid, over medium-high heat (350° to 400°) 6 minutes on each side or to desired degree of doneness. Let stand 5 minutes. Thinly slice steak.
5. Place steak and vegetable mixture in a large bowl, and drizzle with dressing, tossing to coat. Serve over salad greens; garnish, if desired. **Makes** 4 to 6 servings.
*2 teaspoons lemon zest may be substituted.

Cabbage-Onion-Sweet Pepper Medley

PREP: 15 MIN., COOK: 8 MIN.

½ small sweet red pepper
½ small sweet yellow pepper
½ small green pepper
2 slices bacon
1 onion, chopped
2 cups shredded cabbage
3 tablespoons white vinegar
1 tablespoon vegetable oil
1 tablespoon water
1½ teaspoons brown sugar
1½ teaspoons Dijon mustard
½ teaspoon salt
½ teaspoon pepper

1. Cut peppers into 2-inch-long thin strips; cut bacon into 1-inch pieces.
2. Cook bacon in a large skillet until crisp. Add pepper strips, onion, and cabbage, tossing gently.
3. Combine vinegar and remaining 6 ingredients in a jar; cover tightly, and shake vigorously. Add to vegetable mixture in skillet, stirring gently.
4. Bring to a boil; cover, reduce heat, and simmer 8 minutes or until cabbage is tender, stirring occasionally. Serve immediately. **Makes** 3 servings.

Brussels Sprouts and Baby Carrots
Serve this easy dish as part of a holiday feast

PREP: 8 MIN., COOK: 12 MIN.

1 (8-ounce) package frozen Brussels sprouts
1 (9-ounce) package frozen baby carrots
2 tablespoons brown sugar
1 teaspoon orange zest
2 tablespoons fresh orange juice

1. Cook Brussels sprouts and carrots according to package directions; drain vegetables.
2. Bring brown sugar, orange zest, and orange juice to a boil in a saucepan over medium heat, stirring until sugar dissolves. Toss with vegetables. Serve warm. **Makes** 4 servings.

Carrot Soufflé
A sprinkle of cinnamon sweetly spices this simple soufflé.

PREP: 10 MIN.; COOK: 1 HR., 25 MIN.

2 pounds carrots, chopped
½ cup butter, softened
1 cup sugar
3 large eggs, lightly beaten
2 tablespoons all-purpose flour
1 teaspoon baking powder
Ground cinnamon

1. Cook carrot in boiling water to cover 20 to 25 minutes or until tender; drain. Mash carrot and butter with a potato masher. Add sugar and egg, and beat at medium speed with an electric mixer 2 minutes.
2. Stir in flour and baking powder. Pour into a greased 11- x 7-inch baking dish. Sprinkle with cinnamon. Bake, uncovered, at 350° for 1 hour or until set. **Makes** 8 servings.

Carrots With Country Bacon

Carrots With Country Bacon

Country bacon in this recipe refers to thick-sliced or wood-smoked bacon. To partially make ahead, peel and slice carrots up to a day ahead. Store in a zip-top plastic freezer bag in refrigerator.

PREP: 19 MIN., COOK: 35 MIN.

4 thick bacon slices
2 pounds carrots, peeled and diagonally
    sliced into 1-inch pieces
2 cups water
¼ cup firmly packed light brown sugar
2 tablespoons butter
2 teaspoons chopped fresh thyme

1. Cook bacon in a large skillet over medium heat until crisp. Drain, reserving 1 tablespoon drippings in skillet. Crumble bacon, and set aside. Add carrots and next 3 ingredients to skillet. Bring to a boil. Cook over medium-high heat 30 to 35 minutes or until liquid is reduced to a glaze and carrots are tender. Sprinkle with thyme and reserved bacon. **Makes** 6 to 8 servings.

Carrot-Pecan Casserole
PREP: 15 MIN.; COOK: 1 HR., 5 MIN.

3 pounds baby carrots, sliced
⅔ cup sugar
½ cup butter, softened
½ cup chopped pecans, toasted
¼ cup milk
2 large eggs, lightly beaten
3 tablespoons all-purpose flour
1 tablespoon orange zest
1 teaspoon vanilla extract
¼ teaspoon ground nutmeg

1. Cook carrots in boiling water to cover in a saucepan 25 minutes or until tender; drain, let cool slightly, and process in a food processor until smooth.
2. Transfer carrots to a large mixing bowl; stir in sugar and remaining ingredients. Spoon into a lightly greased 11- x 7-inch baking dish. Cover and chill 8 hours, if desired.
3. Bake casserole, uncovered, at 350° for 40 minutes. **Makes** 6 to 8 servings.

Carrot-Sweet Potato Purée
PREP: 20 MIN., COOK: 17 MIN.

5 carrots, sliced
¾ cup water
¼ cup butter
1 (29-ounce) can sweet potatoes, drained
1 (16-ounce) can sweet potatoes, drained
1 (8-ounce) container sour cream
1 tablespoon sugar
1 teaspoon lemon zest
½ teaspoon ground nutmeg
¼ teaspoon salt
¼ teaspoon ground black pepper
⅛ teaspoon ground red pepper

1. Microwave carrot and ¾ cup water in a glass bowl at HIGH 10 to 12 minutes or until tender. Drain.
2. Process carrot and butter in a food processor until mixture is smooth, stopping to scrape down sides. Transfer to a large bowl.
3. Process sweet potatoes until smooth, stopping to scrape down sides. Add to carrot mixture.
4. Stir together sweet potato mixture, sour cream, and remaining ingredients. Spoon into a 1½-quart glass dish. (Cover and chill up to 2 days, if desired; let stand at room temperature 30 minutes.) Microwave at HIGH 4 to 5 minutes or until thoroughly heated. **Makes** 4 servings.

(EDITOR'S CHOICE)
Skillet Creamed Corn
PREP: 20 MIN., COOK: 27 MIN.

6 bacon slices
½ Vidalia onion, finely chopped
1 garlic clove, finely chopped
3 cups fresh corn kernels (about 6 ears)
¼ cup all-purpose flour
1½ cups half-and-half
½ teaspoon salt
¼ teaspoon pepper
1 tablespoon butter or margarine
1 tablespoon chopped fresh basil
Garnish: fresh basil sprigs

1. Cook bacon in a large skillet until crisp; remove bacon, and drain on paper towels, reserving 2 tablespoons drippings in skillet. Crumble bacon, and set aside.
2. Sauté onion and garlic in hot drippings 5 minutes or until tender. Stir in corn; cook 5 to 7 minutes or until golden. Remove from heat.
3. Cook flour in a large clean skillet over medium heat, stirring occasionally, about 5 minutes or until golden. Gradually whisk in half-and-half until smooth. Add corn mixture, salt, and pepper; cook 5 minutes or until thickened. Remove from heat; stir in butter and basil. Sprinkle each serving with bacon, and garnish, if desired. **Makes** 4 to 6 servings.

"This recipe is super easy to make, and I love the basil—it adds an unexpected flavor to corn."

MARY ALLEN PERRY, ASSOCIATE FOOD EDITOR

Skillet Creamed Corn

Creamy Fried Confetti Corn

Creamy Fried Confetti Corn

PREP: 15 MIN., COOK: 22 MIN.

8 bacon slices, chopped
4 cups fresh sweet corn kernels (about 8 ears)
1 medium-size white onion, chopped
⅓ cup chopped red bell pepper
⅓ cup chopped green bell pepper
1 (8-ounce) package cream cheese, cubed
½ cup half-and-half
1 teaspoon sugar
1 teaspoon salt
1 teaspoon pepper

1. Cook chopped bacon in a large skillet until crisp; remove bacon, and drain on paper towels, reserving 2 tablespoons drippings in skillet. Set bacon aside.
2. Sauté corn, onion, and bell peppers in hot drippings in skillet over medium-high heat 6 minutes or until tender. Add cream cheese and half-and-half, stirring until cream cheese melts. Stir in sugar, salt, and pepper. Top with bacon. **Makes** 6 to 8 servings.

Creamy Baked Corn

PREP: 10 MIN., COOK: 40 MIN.

2 to 4 bacon slices
1 tablespoon butter
2 tablespoons chopped onion
2 tablespoons all-purpose flour
1 teaspoon salt
1 cup sour cream
1 (16-ounce) package frozen corn, thawed

1. Cook bacon in a large skillet until crisp; remove bacon, and drain on paper towels, reserving 1 tablespoon drippings in skillet. Crumble bacon, and set aside.
2. Melt butter in hot drippings over medium heat; add onion, and sauté until tender.
3. Whisk in flour and salt until smooth and bubbly. Whisk in sour cream until smooth; cook, whisking often, 3 minutes. Stir in corn, and cook until thoroughly heated. Spoon into a lightly greased 8-inch baking dish; top with crumbled bacon.
4. Bake at 350° for 15 to 20 minutes or until bubbly. **Makes** 4 to 6 servings.

Batter-Fried Eggplant

If you buy a small, very fresh eggplant you won't need to peel it. Older eggplants should be peeled.

PREP: 15 MIN., COOK: 5 MIN. PER BATCH, OTHER: 30 MIN.

1 medium eggplant (about 1 pound)
2 teaspoons salt, divided
1 cup all-purpose flour
1 teaspoon baking powder
2 teaspoons Italian seasoning
1 teaspoon onion powder
⅛ teaspoon ground pepper
⅛ teaspoon garlic powder
⅔ cup milk
1 tablespoon olive oil or vegetable oil
2 large eggs, lightly beaten
Vegetable oil

1. Peel eggplant, if desired, and cut into finger-sized strips. To extract the bitterness, sprinkle 1 teaspoon salt on eggplant strips; let stand 30 minutes. Rinse and pat dry with paper towels.
2. Combine flour, remaining 1 teaspoon salt, baking powder, and next 7 ingredients in a bowl; stir until blended and smooth.
3. Pour oil to a depth of 2 to 3 inches into a Dutch oven; heat to 375°. Dip eggplant strips, one at a time, into batter, coating well. Fry eggplant strips, a few at a time, 3 to 5 minutes or until golden. Drain well on paper towels. Serve immediately. Serve with marinara sauce, if desired. **Makes** 4 servings.

Okra Creole

Okra Creole

PREP: 15 MIN., COOK: 25 MIN.

3 bacon slices
1 (16-ounce) package frozen sliced okra
1 (14½-ounce) can diced tomatoes
1 cup frozen onion seasoning blend
1 cup frozen corn kernels
½ cup water
1 teaspoon Creole seasoning
¼ teaspoon pepper
Hot cooked rice (optional)

1. Cook bacon in a Dutch oven until crisp; remove bacon, and drain on paper towels, reserving drippings. Crumble bacon, and set aside.
2. Cook okra and next 6 ingredients in hot drippings in Dutch oven over medium-high heat, stirring occasionally, 5 minutes. Reduce heat to low, cover, and simmer 15 minutes or until vegetables are tender. Top with crumbled bacon. Serve over rice, if desired. **Makes** 4 servings.

Simple Stir-Fried Okra

We prepared this recipe with frozen whole okra. The results were consistently tender, fragrant, and fresh-tasting.

PREP: 10 MIN., COOK: 20 MIN.

1 medium-size sweet onion, chopped
1 teaspoon mustard seeds*
½ teaspoon ground cumin
¼ teaspoon dried crushed red pepper
2 tablespoons vegetable oil
1 (16-ounce) package frozen okra, thawed,
    or 1 pound fresh okra
¾ teaspoon salt

1. Sauté first 4 ingredients in hot oil in a large skillet over medium-high heat 5 minutes or until onion is tender.
2. Add okra; sauté 15 minutes or until okra is lightly browned. Stir in salt. **Makes** 4 to 6 servings.
*Substitute ½ teaspoon dry mustard for 1 teaspoon mustard seeds, if desired.

Beer-Battered Onion Rings

PREP: 40 MIN., COOK: 20 MIN., OTHER: 30 MIN.

3 large Vidalia, Spanish, or Bermuda onions
2¼ cups all-purpose flour
2 teaspoons baking powder
1 teaspoon salt
¼ cup yellow cornmeal
2 cups beer
1 large egg, lightly beaten
Vegetable oil

1. Peel onions; cut into ½-inch-thick slices, and separate into rings. Place rings in a large bowl of ice water; let stand 30 minutes. Drain on paper towels.
2. Combine flour and next 3 ingredients; stir well. Add beer and egg, stirring until thoroughly blended and smooth. Chill batter 15 minutes.
3. Dip onion rings into batter, coating both sides well. Pour oil to a depth of 2 to 3 inches into a Dutch oven; heat to 375°. Fry onion rings, a few at a time, 3 to 5 minutes or until golden on both sides. Drain well on paper towels. Serve immediately. **Makes** 8 servings.

> **Cooking the rings in oil for a short time gives them a fried flavor without the calories.**
>
> HOLLEY JOHNSON, ASSOCIATE FOOD EDITOR

(EDITOR'S CHOICE)
Crispy "Fried" Onion Rings

PREP: 20 MIN., COOK: 12 MIN.

1 large sweet onion
½ cup low-fat buttermilk
1 egg white
½ cup all-purpose flour
2 tablespoons olive oil
Vegetable cooking spray
½ teaspoon coarse kosher salt

1. Cut onion into ¼-inch-thick slices, and separate into rings. Select largest 12 rings, reserving remaining onion slices for another use.
2. Whisk together buttermilk and egg white in a small bowl until blended.
3. Dredge onion rings in flour; dip into buttermilk mixture, coating well. Dredge again in flour, and place on a baking sheet.
4. Heat 2 teaspoons oil in a 10-inch skillet over medium-high heat. Tilt pan to coat bottom of skillet. Add 4 onion rings to skillet, and cook 1 minute on each side or until golden. Wipe skillet clean. Repeat procedure twice with remaining onion rings and oil. Place fried onion rings on an aluminum foil-lined baking sheet coated with cooking spray.
5. Bake at 400° for 3 minutes. Turn onion rings, and bake 3 more minutes. Remove from oven, and sprinkle with salt. Serve immediately. **Makes** 3 servings.

Beer-Battered "Fried" Onion Rings: Prepare as directed through Step 1. Reduce buttermilk to ¼ cup, and whisk together with ¼ cup light beer and 1 egg white. Proceed with Steps 3, 4, and 5 as directed.

Peppery Peas O' Plenty

PREP: 15 MIN., COOK: 40 MIN.

4 hickory-smoked bacon slices
1 large onion, chopped
1 cup frozen black-eyed peas
1 cup frozen purple hull peas
1 cup frozen crowder peas
1 cup frozen butter peas
1 cup frozen field peas with
    snaps
1 (32-ounce) container chicken
    broth
¾ to 1 teaspoon salt
1 tablespoon freshly ground pepper
1 tablespoon Asian garlic-chili sauce

1. Cook bacon in a Dutch oven until crisp; remove bacon, and drain on paper towels, reserving drippings in pan. Crumble bacon.
2. Sauté onion in drippings over medium-high heat 8 minutes or until translucent. Add black-eyed peas and next 8 ingredients; cook 20 minutes, uncovered. Top with bacon. **Makes** 4 to 6 servings.
Note: For testing purposes only, we used Bryan Sweet Hickory Smoked Bacon and A Taste of Thai Garlic Chili Pepper Sauce.

Cheesy Scalloped Potatoes

These potatoes are great for either a family supper or when company's coming for dinner.

PREP: 10 MIN.; COOK: 1 HR., 2 MIN.; OTHER: 15 MIN.

2½ pounds red potatoes, unpeeled
3 tablespoons butter
⅓ cup chopped green onions
⅓ cup chopped red bell pepper
1 garlic clove, minced
¼ teaspoon ground red pepper
2 cups whipping cream
¾ cup milk
¾ teaspoon salt
¼ teaspoon freshly ground pepper
1 cup (4 ounces) shredded Swiss cheese
¼ cup grated Parmesan cheese

1. Cut potatoes into ⅛-inch-thick slices; set aside.
2. Melt butter in a Dutch oven over medium-high heat; add green onions and next 3 ingredients. Cook, stirring constantly, 2 minutes. Add whipping cream and next 3 ingredients, stirring well.
3. Add potato slices; bring to a boil over medium heat, and cook, stirring gently, 15 minutes or until potato slices are tender. Spoon into a lightly greased 11- x 7-inch baking dish; sprinkle with cheeses.
4. Bake at 350° for 45 minutes or until bubbly and golden brown. Let stand 15 minutes before serving. **Makes** 8 servings.

FAMILY FAVORITE, QUICK
Lemon-Buttered New Potatoes
Peel a strip of skin from the potatoes for a striking presentation.

PREP: 20 MIN, COOK: 10 MIN.

2 pounds new potatoes
¼ cup butter
2 tablespoons chopped fresh parsley
1 teaspoon lemon zest
2 tablespoons fresh lemon juice
½ teaspoon salt
¼ teaspoon pepper
⅛ teaspoon ground nutmeg
Garnish: fresh parsley

1. Peel a thick strip around middle of each potato, using a vegetable peeler. Cover and cook potatoes in boiling water to cover 10 minutes or just until tender; drain.

2. Combine butter and next 6 ingredients in a small saucepan; cook over medium heat, stirring until butter melts. Pour butter mixture over potatoes; toss gently to coat. Garnish, if desired. **Makes** 6 servings.

vegetables **335**

Three-Cheese Mashed Potato Casserole

PREP: 35 MIN., COOK: 35 MIN.

4 large potatoes, peeled and cubed*
1 cup sour cream
1 (3-ounce) package cream cheese, softened
¼ cup butter, softened
⅔ cup milk
½ cup (2 ounces) shredded Cheddar cheese
½ cup (2 ounces) shredded Muenster cheese
1½ teaspoons salt
½ teaspoon pepper

1. Cook potatoes in boiling water to cover 15 minutes or until tender. Drain. Beat potatoes and next 3 ingredients at medium speed with an electric mixer until smooth. Stir in milk and remaining ingredients. Spoon into a lightly greased 2-quart baking dish. (Cover and chill 8 hours, if desired; let stand at room temperature 30 minutes before baking.)
2. Bake, uncovered, at 400° for 15 to 20 minutes or until thoroughly heated. **Makes** 4 servings.
*Substitute frozen mashed potatoes for cubed potatoes, if desired. Prepare according to package directions for 4 servings. For testing purposes only, we used Ore Ida Mashed Potatoes.

Baked Sweet 'n' Savory Mashed Potatoes

Sweet potatoes add a hint of flavor and a blush of color to traditional mashed potatoes. Reduced-fat cream cheese and chicken broth instead of cream keep the spuds mostly guilt free.

PREP: 20 MIN., COOK: 50 MIN.

3½ pounds baking potatoes, peeled and cut into 1-inch pieces
1 tablespoon salt, divided
1 (29-ounce) can sweet potatoes in syrup, drained and mashed
1 (8-ounce) package ⅓-less-fat cream cheese, softened
6 bacon slices, cooked and crumbled
¾ cup light sour cream
⅔ cup chicken broth
½ teaspoon pepper

1. Bring potatoes, 1 teaspoon salt, and water to cover to a boil in a Dutch oven; cook 30 minutes or until tender. Drain.
2. Return potatoes to Dutch oven. Add sweet potatoes and cream cheese; mash until smooth with a potato masher. Stir in bacon, next 3 ingredients, and remaining 2 teaspoons salt. Spoon mixture into a lightly greased 11- x 7-inch baking dish. Bake, uncovered, at 350° for 20 minutes. **Makes** 6 to 8 servings.

Sweet Potato Casserole

Sweet Potato Casserole

This golden baked favorite is sure to please your holiday guests. Make two recipes for a larger crowd.

PREP: 20 MIN.; COOK: 1 HR., 15 MIN.

8 medium-size sweet potatoes (6 pounds)
1 cup milk
¼ cup butter
3 tablespoons sugar
1 teaspoon vanilla extract
1 tablespoon orange juice
¼ teaspoon ground cinnamon
¼ teaspoon ground nutmeg
¼ teaspoon salt
1 (10.5-ounce) package miniature marshmallows

1. Bring sweet potatoes and water to cover to a boil, and cook 20 to 30 minutes or until tender; drain. Peel potatoes, and place in a mixing bowl.

2. Heat milk and next 3 ingredients in a saucepan over medium heat, stirring until butter melts and sugar dissolves. (Do not boil.) Stir in orange juice, spices, and salt.

3. Beat potatoes at medium speed with an electric mixer until mashed. Add milk mixture, beating until smooth. Spoon half of mashed sweet potatoes into a lightly greased 13- x 9-inch baking dish; top evenly with half of marshmallows. Spread remaining mashed potatoes over marshmallows.

4. Bake at 350° for 25 minutes. Top with remaining half of marshmallows, and bake 8 to 10 more minutes or until marshmallows are golden. **Makes** 8 to 10 servings.

Butternut Squash Soufflé
PREP: 15 MIN., COOK: 1 HR.

½ cup butter
½ cup all-purpose flour
1½ cups half-and-half
6 large eggs, separated
2 cups cooked, mashed butternut or acorn squash
½ teaspoon salt
½ teaspoon ground nutmeg

1. Melt butter in a heavy saucepan over low heat; add flour, whisking until smooth. Cook 1 minute, whisking constantly. Gradually add half-and-half; cook over medium heat, whisking constantly, until thickened and bubbly.
2. Whisk egg yolks until thick and pale. Gradually stir about one-fourth of hot mixture into yolks; stir into remaining hot mixture. Stir mashed squash, salt, and nutmeg.
3. Beat egg whites at high speed with an electric mixer until stiff peaks form; fold one-fourth of egg whites into squash mixture. Fold in remaining egg whites, and pour into a lightly buttered 2-quart soufflé dish.
4. Bake at 350° for 1 hour or until puffed and brown. Serve immediately. **Makes** 6 servings.

FAMILY FAVORITE
Yellow Squash Casserole
Made with Cheddar cheese, bacon, and buttery cracker crumbs, squash casserole beckons you to a second helping.

PREP: 20 MIN., COOK: 1 HR.

2 pounds yellow squash, sliced
1 cup water
2 small onions, minced
2 tablespoons butter, melted
1½ cups (6 ounces) shredded Cheddar cheese
1¼ cups round buttery cracker crumbs, divided
¼ teaspoon salt
¼ teaspoon pepper
4 slices bacon, cooked and crumbled
2 large eggs, lightly beaten

1. Combine squash and water in a large saucepan; bring to a boil. Cover, reduce heat, and simmer 15 minutes or until squash is tender. Drain well, and mash. Drain again, and set aside.
2. Sauté onion in butter in a large skillet over medium-high heat until tender. Combine squash, onion, cheese, ¾ cup cracker crumbs, salt, and remaining 3 ingredients; stir well.
3. Spoon mixture into a lightly greased 2-quart casserole; sprinkle with remaining ½ cup cracker crumbs. Bake, uncovered, at 350° for 40 to 45 minutes or until thoroughly heated. **Makes** 6 servings.

Spinach-Stuffed Squash
PREP: 15 MIN., COOK: 29 MIN.

4 large yellow squash
1½ teaspoons salt, divided
¼ cup butter, melted and divided
½ cup grated Parmesan cheese, divided
¼ teaspoon pepper
1 small onion, chopped
2 (10-ounce) packages frozen chopped spinach, cooked and well drained
1 cup sour cream
2 teaspoons red wine vinegar
¼ cup fine, dry breadcrumbs
1 tablespoon cold butter, cut up

1. Combine squash, ½ teaspoon salt, and water to cover in a Dutch oven. Bring to a boil, and cook 10 minutes or until tender. Cool.
2. Cut squash in half lengthwise, and remove seeds. Drizzle cut sides of squash evenly with 2 tablespoons melted butter; sprinkle evenly with 2 tablespoons cheese, ½ teaspoon salt, and pepper.
3. Pour remaining 2 tablespoons melted butter in a large skillet over medium-high heat, and add onion; sauté 4 minutes or until tender. Stir in cooked spinach, sour cream, red wine vinegar, and remaining ½ teaspoon salt. Spoon spinach mixture evenly into squash halves. Place squash in a 13- x 9-inch baking dish. Sprinkle with breadcrumbs and remaining 6 tablespoons cheese, and dot with cold butter.
4. Bake at 350° for 15 minutes or until thoroughly heated. **Makes** 6 to 8 servings.

Garden-Stuffed Yellow Squash

The curvy shape of crookneck squash makes an interesting presentation for stuffed shells.

PREP: 15 MIN., COOK: 29 MIN.

6 medium-size yellow squash
1 cup chopped onion
1 cup chopped tomato
½ cup finely chopped green pepper
1 tablespoon chopped fresh basil
¼ teaspoon salt
Dash of freshly ground pepper
1 cup (4 ounces) shredded Cheddar cheese
2 tablespoons butter
3 slices bacon, cooked and crumbled

1. Wash squash thoroughly; cover with water, and bring to a boil. Cover, reduce heat, and simmer 8 to 9 minutes or until squash is tender but still firm. Drain and cool slightly. Cut squash in half lengthwise; remove and discard seeds, leaving a firm shell. Combine onion, tomato, green pepper, basil, salt, and pepper in a bowl. Stir in cheese. Place squash shells in a 13- x 9-inch baking dish. Spoon vegetable mixture into shells; dot with butter. Sprinkle with bacon. Bake, uncovered, at 400° for 20 minutes. **Makes** 6 servings.

Two-Cheese Squash Casserole

Two-Cheese Squash Casserole

This begs to be taken to a potluck or family reunion.

PREP: 30 MIN., COOK: 1 HR.

4 pounds yellow squash, sliced
4 tablespoons butter, divided
1 large sweet onion, finely chopped
2 garlic cloves, minced
2½ cups soft breadcrumbs, divided
1¼ cups shredded Parmesan cheese,
    divided
1 cup (4 ounces) shredded Cheddar
    cheese
½ cup chopped fresh chives
½ cup minced fresh parsley
1 (8-ounce) container sour cream
1 teaspoon salt
1 teaspoon freshly ground pepper
2 large eggs, lightly beaten
¼ teaspoon garlic salt

1. Cook squash in boiling water to cover in a large skillet 8 to 10 minutes or just until tender. Drain well, gently pressing between paper towels.
2. Melt 2 tablespoons butter in a skillet over medium-high heat; add onion and garlic, and sauté 2 to 3 minutes or until tender. Remove skillet from heat; stir in squash, 1 cup breadcrumbs, ¾ cup Parmesan cheese, 1 cup Cheddar cheese, and next 6 ingredients. Spoon into a lightly greased 13- x 9-inch baking dish.
3. Melt remaining 2 tablespoons butter. Stir together melted butter, garlic salt, remaining 1½ cups soft breadcrumbs, and remaining ½ cup Parmesan cheese. Sprinkle mixture evenly over top of casserole.
4. Bake at 350° for 35 to 40 minutes or until set.
Makes 8 to 10 servings.

Italian Squash Pie

A thin layer of Dijon mustard on the crust seals it and prevents the pie from becoming soggy.

PREP: 20 MIN., COOK: 38 MIN.

1 (8-ounce) can refrigerated crescent rolls
2 teaspoons Dijon mustard
¼ cup butter or margarine
1½ pounds yellow squash (about 4 cups),
    thinly sliced*
1 medium onion, chopped
1 garlic clove, pressed
¼ cup chopped fresh parsley
1 tablespoon chopped fresh or ½ teaspoon
    dried basil
2 teaspoons chopped fresh or ½ teaspoon
    dried oregano
2 teaspoons chopped fresh or ½ teaspoon
    dried thyme
½ teaspoon salt
½ teaspoon pepper
2 large eggs
¼ cup milk
2 cups (8 ounces) shredded mozzarella cheese
Garnishes: fresh oregano sprigs, sliced yellow squash

1. Unroll crescent rolls; press dough on bottom and up sides of a 10-inch tart pan, pressing to seal perforations.
2. Bake at 375° for 6 minutes or until lightly browned. Gently press crust down with a wooden spoon. Spread crust with mustard, and set aside.
3. Melt butter in a large skillet over medium-high heat. Add squash, onion, and garlic; sauté 7 minutes or until tender. Remove from heat; stir in parsley and next 5 ingredients.
4. Whisk together eggs and milk in a large bowl; stir in cheese and vegetable mixture. Pour over crust.
5. Bake at 375° for 20 to 25 minutes or until a knife inserted in center comes out clean. Garnish, if desired.
Makes 6 servings.
*Substitute 1½ pounds zucchini for yellow squash, if desired.

Feta-Stuffed Tomatoes

You may use other cheeses of similar texture, such as goat cheese, in this easy side dish. (also pictured on cover)

PREP: 15 MIN., BAKE: 15 MIN.

4 large red tomatoes
4 ounces crumbled feta cheese
¼ cup fine, dry breadcrumbs
2 tablespoons chopped green onions
2 tablespoons chopped fresh parsley
2 tablespoons olive oil
¼ teaspoon salt
¼ teaspoon pepper
Garnish: flat-leaf parsley sprig

1. Cut tomatoes in half horizontally. Scoop out pulp from each tomato half, leaving shells intact; discard seeds, and coarsely chop pulp.

2. Stir together pulp, feta cheese, and next 6 ingredients. Spoon mixture evenly into tomato shells, and place in a 13- x 9-inch baking dish.

3. Bake at 350° for 15 minutes. Transfer to a serving dish. Garnish, if desired. **Makes** 8 servings.

Marinated Zucchini

PREP: 15 MIN., OTHER: 8 HR.

3 medium zucchini, thinly sliced
(about 1¼ pounds)
¼ cup chopped onion
¼ cup chopped green pepper
¼ cup chopped celery
1 tablespoon chopped pimiento
⅓ cup cider vinegar
¼ cup sugar
¼ cup vegetable oil
1 tablespoon white wine vinegar
½ teaspoon salt
¼ teaspoon pepper
⅛ teaspoon hot sauce

1. Combine first 5 ingredients in a large bowl;
toss lightly.
2. Combine cider vinegar and remaining 6 ingredients;
pour over zucchini mixture. Cover and marinate in
refrigerator at least 8 hours, stirring occasionally.
Serve with a slotted spoon. **Makes** 4 servings.

Zucchini Toss

*Here's a simple side dish that will go with
just about any entrée.*

PREP: 12 MIN., COOK: 5 MIN., OTHER: 5 MIN.

1 pound medium zucchini, cut into
¼-inch-thick slices
1½ teaspoons olive oil
1 tablespoon freshly grated Parmesan cheese
¼ teaspoon lemon zest
¼ teaspoon salt
¼ teaspoon pepper

1. Sauté zucchini in hot oil in a large skillet over
medium-high heat 5 minutes or until crisp-tender.
Remove from heat; cover and let stand 5 minutes.
2. Combine cheese and remaining 3 ingredients.
Spoon zucchini into a serving dish, and sprinkle
with cheese mixture; toss gently. Serve immediately.
Makes 3 servings.

Vegetable Kabobs

*Red pepper and zucchini get a brief grilling on
short skewers. Pair them with chicken,
pork, or beef for dinner.*

PREP: 10 MIN., COOK: 12 MIN.

4 medium-sized sweet red peppers, seeded
and cut into ½-inch strips
4 small zucchini, cut into ½-inch-thick
slices
½ cup vegetable oil
¼ cup lemon juice
¼ cup white wine vinegar
1 tablespoon plus 1 teaspoon Worcestershire
sauce
2 teaspoons dried Italian seasoning
1 teaspoon salt

1. Thread pepper strips and zucchini slices into
eight 6-inch bamboo skewers. Place kabobs in a
large shallow dish
2. Combine oil and remaining 5 ingredients; pour
over kabobs. Cover and marinate in refrigerator
8 hours, turning once.
3. Remove kabobs from marinade, reserving marinade.
Grill kabobs, covered with grill lid, over medium-
hot coals (350° to 400°) 10 to 12 minutes or until
vegetables are crips-tender, turning and brushing
with marinade occasionally. **Makes** 4 servings.

Southern Turnip Greens
and Ham Hocks

Southern Turnip Greens and Ham Hocks

We simmered the ham hocks for about 2 hours until the meat easily pulled away from the bones. If you want to save time, just simmer 30 to 45 minutes to release the flavor.

PREP: 30 MIN., COOK: 3 HR.

1¾ pounds ham hocks, rinsed
2 quarts water
2 bunches fresh turnip greens with roots
   (about 10 pounds)
1 tablespoon sugar

1. Bring ham hocks and 2 quarts water to a boil in an 8-quart Dutch oven. Reduce heat, and simmer 1½ to 2 hours or until meat is tender.
2. Remove and discard stems and discolored spots from greens. Chop greens, and rinse thoroughly; drain. Peel turnip roots, and cut in half.
3. Add greens, roots, and sugar to Dutch oven; bring to a boil. Reduce heat; cover and simmer 45 to 60 minutes or until greens and roots are tender. **Makes** 10 servings.

FAMILY FAVORITE
Pineapple Casserole

PREP: 12 MIN., COOK: 20 MIN.

1 (20-ounce) can pineapple chunks in juice,
   undrained
½ cup sugar
3 tablespoons all-purpose flour
1 cup (4 ounces) shredded Cheddar
   cheese
1 cup buttery cracker crumbs
3 tablespoons butter, melted

1. Drain pineapple, reserving 3 tablespoons juice. Combine sugar and flour; stir in reserved pineapple juice. Stir in cheese and pineapple chunks. Spoon mixture into a greased 1-quart baking dish.
2. Combine cracker crumbs and butter, stirring well; sprinkle over pineapple mixture. Bake, uncovered at 350° for 20 minutes or until browned. Serve hot. **Makes** 4 servings.

Roasted Pears With Gorgonzola Cream

PREP: 12 MIN., COOK: 17 MIN.

3 large ripe Bosc pears, peeled
   and halved
2 tablespoons butter, melted
1 (3-ounce) package cream
   cheese, softened
3 ounces Gorgonzola cheese,
   softened
2 tablespoons whipping cream
¼ cup walnuts, finely chopped

1. Scoop out core from each pear half with a melon baller, leaving at least a 1-inch-thick shell. Slice about ¼ inch from rounded sides to make pear halves sit flat, if necessary.
2. Brush cut side of each pear half with melted butter, and place cored side up on a greased baking sheet. Bake, uncovered, at 450° for 15 minutes.
3. Process cheeses and cream in a food processor until creamy. Spoon mixture into center of each warm pear half.
4. Broil pears 3 inches from heat 1 to 2 minutes or until lightly browned. Place on serving plates. Sprinkle with walnuts. Serve warm. **Makes** 6 servings.

Fiesta Chowder, page 353

everyday
soups 'n'
sandwiches

Hot Brown Soup

Here's a quick and easy way to use Thanksgiving leftovers.

PREP: 10 MIN., COOK: 15 MIN.

¼ cup butter
¼ cup minced onion
¼ cup all-purpose flour
½ teaspoon garlic salt
⅛ teaspoon hot sauce
4 cups milk
1 cup (4 ounces) shredded sharp Cheddar
    cheese
½ cup chopped cooked ham
½ cup chopped cooked turkey
Toppings: crumbled bacon, chopped tomato,
    chopped fresh parsley

1. Melt butter in a Dutch oven over medium heat. Add onion; sauté until tender. Add flour, garlic salt, and hot sauce; cook, stirring constantly, 1 minute. Gradually stir in milk; cook until thickened and bubbly. Reduce heat; stir in cheese until melted. Add ham and turkey; cook, stirring occasionally, until heated (do not boil). Serve with desired toppings. **Makes** 3 to 4 servings.

Chunky Italian Soup

PREP: 20 MIN., COOK: 45 MIN.

1 pound lean ground beef or beef tips
1 medium onion, chopped
2 (14½-ounce) cans Italian-style stewed
    tomatoes
1 (11-ounce) can cream of tomato bisque soup,
    undiluted
4 cups water
2 garlic cloves, minced
2 teaspoons dried basil
2 teaspoons dried oregano
1 teaspoon salt
½ teaspoon pepper
1 tablespoon chili powder (optional)
1 (16-ounce) can kidney beans, drained
1 (16-ounce) can Italian-style green beans,
    drained
1 carrot, chopped
1 zucchini, chopped
8 ounces rotini noodles, cooked
Grated Parmesan cheese

1. Cook beef and onion in a Dutch oven over medium heat, stirring until beef crumbles and is no longer pink; drain. Return mixture to pan. Stir in tomatoes, next 7 ingredients, and, if desired, chili powder; bring to a boil. Reduce heat; simmer, stirring occasionally, 30 minutes. Stir in kidney beans and next 3 ingredients; simmer, stirring occasionally, 15 minutes. Stir in pasta. Sprinkle each serving with cheese. **Makes** 6 servings.

Chunky Italian Soup

Tortilla Soup

Tortilla Soup

Grilled chicken gives this soup smoky flavor, but chopped
rotisserie chicken makes a fine shortcut

PREP: 25 MIN.; COOK: 1 HR., 15 MIN.

5 skinned and boned chicken breasts
2 tablespoons olive oil
1 teaspoon salt
½ teaspoon pepper
4 corn tortillas, cut into 1-inch pieces
1 large onion, chopped
5 garlic cloves, minced
3 tablespoons vegetable oil
8 cups chicken broth
1 (14½-ounce) can stewed tomatoes, undrained
    and chopped
1 (10-ounce) can diced tomatoes and green chiles
2 tablespoons chopped fresh cilantro or parsley
1 tablespoon ground cumin
½ teaspoon pepper
1 bay leaf
6 corn tortillas, cut into ¼-inch strips
½ cup vegetable oil
2 cups (8 ounces) shredded Monterey Jack cheese
    with peppers, or mozzarella cheese
Avocado slices (optional)

1. Drizzle chicken with olive oil; sprinkle with salt
and ½ teaspoon pepper. Grill chicken, covered with
grill lid, over medium-high heat (350° to 400°)
6 to 8 minutes on each side or until done. Cool and
coarsely chop chicken.
2. Sauté tortilla pieces, onion, and garlic in 3 tablespoons
hot oil in a Dutch oven over medium-high heat
5 minutes or until onion is tender. Add chicken,
broth, and next 6 ingredients. Bring to a boil; reduce
heat, and simmer 30 minutes. Discard bay leaf.
3. Fry tortilla strips in ½ cup hot oil in a large
skillet until crisp. Drain on paper towels. Sprinkle
fried tortilla strips and cheese over each serving. Top
with avocado, if desired. **Makes** 8 to 10 servings.

Mexican Chicken-Corn Chowder

PREP: 20 MIN., COOK: 30 MIN.

3 tablespoons butter
4 skinned and boned chicken breasts, cut into
    bite-size pieces (1½ pounds)
1 small onion, chopped
2 garlic cloves, minced
2 cups half-and-half
2 cups (8 ounces) shredded Monterey Jack cheese
2 (14¾-ounce) cans cream-style corn
1 (4.5-ounce) can chopped green chiles,
    undrained
½ teaspoon hot sauce
¼ teaspoon salt
½ to 1 teaspoon ground cumin
2 tablespoons chopped fresh cilantro
Garnishes: chopped fresh cilantro, Anaheim chile

1. Melt butter in a Dutch oven over medium-high heat;
add chicken, onion, and garlic, and sauté 10 minutes.
Stir in next 7 ingredients; cook over low heat, stirring
often, 15 minutes. Stir in 2 tablespoons cilantro.
Garnish, if desired. **Makes** 5 to 6 servings.

Easy Chili

Top each serving with shredded Cheddar cheese and corn chips. If you want to thicken this saucy chili, stir in finely crushed saltine crackers until you achieve the desired thickness. Complete the meal with sliced apples and grapes.

PREP: 15 MIN., COOK: 6 HR.

1½ pounds lean ground beef
1 onion, chopped
1 small green bell pepper,
    chopped
2 garlic cloves, minced
2 (16-ounce) cans red kidney beans,
    rinsed and drained
2 (14½-ounce) cans diced tomatoes
2 to 3 tablespoons chili powder
1 teaspoon salt
1 teaspoon pepper
1 teaspoon ground cumin

1. Cook first 4 ingredients in a large skillet over medium-high heat, stirring until beef crumbles and is no longer pink; drain. Place mixture in a 5-quart slow cooker; stir in beans and remaining ingredients. Cook at HIGH 3 to 4 hours or at LOW 5 to 6 hours. **Makes** 6 to 8 servings.

She-Crab Soup

PREP: 10 MIN.; COOK: 1 HR., 20 MIN.

1 quart whipping cream
⅛ teaspoon salt
⅛ teaspoon pepper
2 fish bouillon cubes
2 cups boiling water
¼ cup unsalted butter
⅓ cup all-purpose flour
2 tablespoons lemon juice
¼ teaspoon ground nutmeg
1 pound fresh crabmeat
Garnish: chopped parsley
⅓ cup sherry (optional)

1. Combine first 3 ingredients in a heavy saucepan; bring to a boil over medium heat. Reduce heat, and simmer 1 hour. Set aside. Stir together fish bouillon cubes and 2 cups boiling water until bouillon dissolves.
2. Melt butter in a large heavy saucepan over low heat; add flour, stirring until smooth. Cook 1 minute, stirring constantly. Gradually add hot fish broth; cook over medium heat until thickened. Stir in cream mixture, and cook until thoroughly heated. Add lemon juice, nutmeg, and crabmeat. Ladle into individual serving bowls. Garnish, if desired. Add a spoonful of sherry to each serving, if desired. **Makes** about 4 to 5 servings.
Note: For testing purposes only, we used Knorr Fish Bouillon Cubes. It is important to use good-quality sherry, not cooking sherry, for this soup.

Fiesta Chowder

PREP: 15 MIN., COOK: 15 MIN.

3 tablespoons all-purpose flour
1 (1.4-ounce) package fajita seasoning, divided
4 skinned and boned chicken breasts, cubed
3 tablespoons vegetable oil
1 medium onion, chopped
1 teaspoon minced garlic
1 (15¼-ounce) can whole kernel corn with red
    and green peppers, drained
1 (15-ounce) can black beans, rinsed and drained
1 (14½-ounce) can Mexican-style stewed
    tomatoes
1 (4.5-ounce) can chopped green chiles
3 cups water
1 cup uncooked instant brown rice
1 (2¼-ounce) can sliced ripe olives (optional)
1 (10¾-ounce) can condensed nacho cheese soup

3 tablespoons chopped fresh cilantro
1 tablespoon lime juice
Garnish: chopped fresh cilantro
Breadsticks (optional)

1. Combine flour and 2 tablespoons fajita seasoning in a zip-top plastic freezer bag; add chicken. Seal and shake to coat.
2. Cook chicken in hot oil in a large Dutch oven over high heat, stirring often, 4 minutes or until browned. Reduce heat to medium-high; add onion and garlic. Sauté 5 minutes. Stir in remaining fajita seasoning, corn, next 5 ingredients, and, if desired, olives. Bring mixture to a boil; reduce heat to medium-low, cover, and simmer 5 minutes. Remove lid, and stir in nacho cheese soup, 3 tablespoons chopped cilantro, and lime juice. Garnish, if desired, and serve with breadsticks, if desired. **Makes** 8 to 10 servings.

Fiesta Chowder

Hot Ham-and-Cheese Rollups

*To enjoy for lunch, reheat a rollup in the microwave
at HIGH 1 minute or until thoroughly heated.*

PREP: 20 MIN., COOK: 25 MIN., OTHER: 5 MIN.

1 (13.8-ounce) refrigerated pizza crust
    dough
2 tablespoons chopped fresh or 2 teaspoons
    dried basil
6 ounces thinly sliced maple-glazed ham
1 cup (4 ounces) shredded part-skim
    mozzarella cheese
Pasta sauce or mustard (optional)

1. Roll out dough to a 12-inch square. Sprinkle with
basil to ½ inch from edges. Top with ham slices, and
sprinkle with cheese to ½ inch from edges.
2. Roll up dough, beginning at 1 end; place, seam
side down, on an aluminum foil-lined baking sheet
coated with cooking spray.
3. Bake at 400° for 20 to 25 minutes or until golden
brown. Cool 5 minutes. Cut into 1½-inch slices.
Serve rollups with pasta sauce or mustard, if desired.
Makes 4 servings.

Club Wraps

*Sandwiches are often the answer for suppers
on-the-go. Wrap these individually in plastic wrap
for after the game or an impromptu picnic.
If you leave out certain ingredients
for picky eaters, mark the plastic wrap
with a permanent marker.*

PREP: 20 MIN.

½ cup creamy mustard-mayonnaise
    blend
4 (10-inch) flour tortillas
½ pound thinly sliced smoked
    turkey
½ pound thinly sliced honey ham
2 cups shredded iceberg lettuce
1 cup (4 oz.) shredded mozzarella or
    smoked provolone cheese
2 medium tomatoes, seeded and
    chopped
½ small red onion, diced
8 fully cooked bacon slices
½ teaspoon pepper

1. Spread mustard-mayonnaise blend evenly over
1 side of each tortilla, leaving a ½-inch border.
2. Layer turkey and next 6 ingredients evenly over
tortillas; sprinkle with pepper. Roll up tortillas;
secure with wooden picks, and cut in half diagonally.
Makes 4 servings.

Club Wraps

Turkey, Bacon, and
Havarti Sandwich

Turkey, Bacon, and Havarti Sandwich

Use precooked bacon to save time. Microwave according to package directions to crisp
before you assemble the sandwich. Havarti is a Danish cheese that's semisoft with small
irregular holes and a mild flavor; substitute Muenster if you can't find it. Strawberries,
apple slices, or cantaloupe will pair nicely with these flavors. (also pictured on back cover)

PREP: 20 MIN., OTHER: 1 HR.

1 (7-inch) round sourdough bread
    loaf
¼ cup balsamic vinaigrette
½ pound thinly sliced smoked
    deli turkey
1 (12-ounce) jar roasted red bell
    peppers, drained and sliced
6 (1-ounce) slices Havarti cheese
4 fully-cooked bacon slices
Garnish: dill pickle spears

1. Cut top 2 inches off sourdough loaf, reserving top; hollow out loaf, leaving a 1-inch-thick shell. (Reserve soft center of bread loaf for other uses, if desired.)
2. Drizzle 2 tablespoons vinaigrette evenly in bottom bread shell; layer with half of turkey, peppers, and cheese. Repeat layers, and top with bacon. Drizzle evenly with remaining 2 tablespoons vinaigrette, and cover with reserved bread top; press down firmly. Wrap in plastic wrap, and chill at least 1 hour or up to 8 hours before serving. Cut into 4 wedges. Garnish, if desired. **Makes** 4 servings.
Note: For testing purposes only, we used Newman's Own Balsamic Vinaigrette salad dressing.

> **One bite of this muffuletta, and you'll know why these large, round sandwiches remain enduring standards of the New Orleans food scene.**

LYDA JONES BURNETTE, TEST KITCHENS DIRECTOR

(EDITOR'S CHOICE)
Muffuletta

PREP: 10 MIN.

1 (10-inch) round Italian bread loaf
2 cups Olive Salad
½ pound sliced hard salami
½ pound sliced cooked ham
6 Swiss cheese slices
6 thin provolone cheese slices

1. Cut bread loaf in half horizontally; scoop out soft bread from both halves, leaving a 1-inch-thick shell. Reserve soft bread centers for another use, if desired.
2. Spoon 1 cup Olive Salad evenly into bottom bread shell; top with salami, ham, cheeses, and remaining 1 cup Olive Salad. Cover with bread top, and cut crosswise into wedges or quarters. **Makes** 4 servings.

Olive Salad

PREP: 15 MIN., OTHER: 8 HR.

1 (1-quart) jar mixed pickled vegetables
1 red onion, quartered
1 (16-ounce) jar pitted green olives, drained
1 (6-ounce) can medium pitted ripe olives,
    drained
¼ cup sliced pepperoncini salad peppers
2 tablespoons capers
1 tablespoon minced garlic
½ cup olive oil
1½ teaspoons dried parsley flakes
1 teaspoon dried oregano
1 teaspoon dried basil
½ teaspoon ground black pepper
1 (7.25-ounce) jar roasted red bell peppers,
    drained and coarsely chopped (optional)

1. Drain pickled vegetables, reserving ¼ cup liquid.
2. Pulse pickled vegetables 4 times in a food processor or until coarsely chopped; pour into a large bowl. Pulse onion 4 times in food processor or until coarsely chopped; add to pickled vegetables in bowl. Pulse olives and salad peppers in food processor 4 times or until coarsely chopped; add to vegetable mixture. Stir in capers, next 6 ingredients, reserved ¼ cup pickled vegetable liquid, and, if desired, chopped red bell peppers. Cover and chill 8 hours. Chill leftover mixture up to 2 weeks. **Makes** 6 cups.
Note: We used mixed pickled vegetables that contained cauliflower, onions, carrots, peppers, and celery.

QUICK
Smoked Chicken and Fontina Panini
Pick up a smoked chicken from the deli or your local barbecue joint, or use rotisserie chicken for this sandwich.

PREP: 7 MIN., COOK: 4 MIN.

1 (8-ounce) loaf ciabatta bread, cut in half
    lengthwise
3 tablespoons jarred pesto
2 plum tomatoes, sliced
1 cup shredded smoked chicken
2 ounces fontina cheese, sliced

1. Preheat panini press according to manufacturer's instructions.
2. Spread bottom half of bread with pesto. Top with tomatoes, chicken, and cheese. Top with bread.
3. Place sandwich in panini press; cook 3 to 4 minutes or until cheese melts and bread is toasted. Cut in half, and serve hot. **Makes** 2 servings.

Caramelized Onion BLT

Caramelized Onion BLT

PREP: 8 MIN., COOK: 7 MIN.

12 bacon slices
2 medium tomatoes
Olive oil
8 sourdough bread slices
½ cup mayonnaise
1 tablespoon chopped fresh basil
8 sourdough bread slices, toasted
4 curly leaf lettuce leaves
Caramelized Onions
4 (½-ounce) Swiss cheese slices
Salt and pepper to taste

1. Cook bacon in a large skillet until crisp; remove bacon, and drain on paper towels, reserving 1 tablespoon drippings for Caramelized Onions. Cut each tomato into 4 slices

2. Brush 1 side of each bread slice lightly with olive oil. Grill bread 45 seconds or until toasted.

3. Stir together mayonnaise and basil; spread mixture on 1 side of each bread slice. Top 4 bread slices with lettuce, 2 tomato slices, Caramelized Onions, cheese, and 3 bacon slices; sprinkle with salt and pepper to taste. Top with remaining bread slices. **Makes** 4 servings.

Caramelized Onions

PREP: 5 MIN., COOK: 30 MIN.

2 tablespoons butter
1 tablespoon bacon drippings
2 sweet onions, sliced
½ teaspoon salt
¼ teaspoon freshly ground black pepper

1. Melt butter with bacon drippings in a skillet over medium heat. Add onion, salt, and pepper; cook 20 to 30 minutes or until caramelized, stirring often. **Makes** about 1½ cups.

Philly Firecrackers

*The snappy dressing makes this wrap very tasty.
It's quick and very convenient.*

PREP: 20 MIN., OTHER: 8 HR.

½ cup sour cream*
½ cup mayonnaise*
1 green onion, chopped
2 tablespoons prepared horseradish
½ teaspoon salt
½ teaspoon pepper
8 (12-inch) flour tortillas
1 pound roast beef, cut into
    24 thin slices
2 (6-ounce) packages deli-style sharp Cheddar
    cheese slices (optional)
2 cups shredded iceberg lettuce

1. Stir together first 6 ingredients until blended. Spread evenly on 1 side of each tortilla; top each with 3 beef slices and, if desired, 2 cheese slices. Sprinkle evenly with shredded lettuce.
2. Roll up tortillas tightly; wrap in parchment paper or plastic wrap. Chill 8 hours. **Makes** 8 servings.
Note: For testing purposes only, we used Sargento Deli Style Sharp Cheddar Cheese slices.
*Substitute ½ cup light sour cream and ½ cup light mayonnaise, if desired.

Debate Barbecue Sandwiches

*Roast some frozen steak fries to turn these sandwiches
into a quick and easy weeknight supper.*

PREP: 15 MIN., COOK: 8 HR.

1 (3-pound) boneless pork loin roast,
    trimmed
1 cup water
1 (18-ounce) bottle barbecue sauce
¼ cup firmly packed brown sugar
2 tablespoons Worcestershire sauce
1 to 2 tablespoons hot sauce
1 teaspoon salt
1 teaspoon pepper
Hamburger buns
Coleslaw

1. Place roast in a 4-quart electric slow cooker; add 1 cup water.
2. Cover and cook at HIGH 7 hours or until meat is tender; stir with a fork, shredding meat. Add barbecue sauce and next 5 ingredients; reduce setting to LOW, and cook, covered, 1 hour. Serve barbecue on buns with coleslaw. **Makes** 20 servings.

Grilled-Shrimp Gyros With Herbed Yogurt Spread
Chill wraps until ready to serve.

PREP: 25 MIN., COOK: 10 MIN., OTHER: 30 MIN.

1½ pounds unpeeled, medium-size raw shrimp
2 tablespoons Greek seasoning
2 tablespoons olive oil
6 (12-inch) wooden skewers
4 (8-inch) pita rounds or gyro rounds
Herbed Yogurt Spread
½ cup crumbled feta cheese
1 large tomato, chopped
1 cucumber, thinly sliced

1. Peel shrimp, and devein, if desired.
2. Combine seasoning and olive oil in a zip-top plastic freezer bag; add shrimp. Seal and chill 30 minutes.
3. Soak skewers in water 30 minutes while shrimp marinate; thread shrimp onto skewers.
4. Grill, covered with grill lid, over medium heat (300° to 350°) about 5 minutes on each side or just until shrimp turn pink.

5. Wrap each pita round in a damp cloth; microwave at HIGH 10 to 15 seconds or until soft. Spread 1 side of each pita round with Herbed Yogurt Spread. Top evenly with shrimp, cheese, tomato, and cucumber; roll up. **Makes** 4 servings.

Herbed Yogurt Spread
PREP: 5 MIN.

½ cup low-fat yogurt
1 garlic clove, minced
1 tablespoon chopped fresh or ¾ teaspoon dried oregano
1 teaspoon chopped fresh mint
2 teaspoons lemon juice
¼ teaspoon pepper

1. Whisk together all ingredients; chill until ready to serve or up to 8 hours. **Makes** about ½ cup.

Grilled-Shrimp Gyros With
Herbed Yogurt Spread

> I love shrimp, and this sandwich is one of my favorites. The recipe is quick and easy, and the crispy tender shrimp have a great flavor.
>
> ASHLEY ARTHUR, ASSISTANT RECIPE EDITOR

Shrimp Po'boys

(EDITOR'S CHOICE)

Shrimp Po'boys

PREP: 32 MIN., COOK: 16 MIN.

2 pounds unpeeled, large raw shrimp
1¼ cups all-purpose flour
½ teaspoon salt
½ teaspoon pepper
½ cup milk
1 large egg
Peanut oil
⅓ cup butter
1 teaspoon minced garlic
4 French bread rolls, split
Rémoulade Sauce
1 cup shredded lettuce

1. Peel shrimp, and devein, if desired.
2. Combine flour, salt, and pepper. Stir together milk and egg until smooth. Toss shrimp in milk mixture; dredge in flour mixture.
3. Pour oil to a depth of 2 inches into a Dutch oven; heat to 375°. Fry shrimp, in batches, 1 to 2 minutes or until golden; drain on wire racks.
4. Melt butter; add garlic. Spread cut sides of rolls evenly with butter mixture; place on a large baking sheet.
5. Bake at 450° for 8 minutes. Spread cut sides of rolls evenly with Rémoulade Sauce. Place shrimp and lettuce on bottom halves of rolls; cover with roll tops. **Makes** 4 sandwiches.

Rémoulade Sauce

PREP: 5 MIN.

1 cup mayonnaise
3 green onions, sliced
2 tablespoons Creole mustard
2 garlic cloves, pressed
1 tablespoon chopped fresh parsley
¼ teaspoon ground red pepper
Garnish: sliced green onions

1. Stir together first 6 ingredients in a small bowl until well blended. Garnish, if desired. **Makes** about 1¼ cups.

Chunky Apple Cake With Cream Cheese Frosting

PREP: 25 MIN., COOK: 45 MIN.

½ cup butter, melted
2 cups sugar
2 large eggs
1 teaspoon vanilla extract
2 cups all-purpose flour
1 teaspoon baking soda
1 teaspoon salt
2 teaspoons ground cinnamon
4 Granny Smith apples, peeled and
    sliced
1 cup chopped walnuts, toasted
Cream Cheese Frosting
Chopped walnuts, toasted (optional)

1. Stir together first 4 ingredients in a large bowl until blended. Combine flour and next 3 ingredients; add to butter mixture, stirring until blended. Stir in apple slices and 1 cup walnuts. Spread into a greased 13- x 9-inch baking pan.
2. Bake at 350° for 45 minutes or until a wooden pick inserted in center comes out clean. Cool completely in pan on a wire rack. Spread with Cream Cheese Frosting; sprinkle with walnuts, if desired. Cover and store in refrigerator. **Makes** 12 to 15 servings.

Cream Cheese Frosting

PREP: 10 MIN.

1 (8-ounce) package cream cheese,
    softened
3 tablespoons butter, softened
1½ cups powdered sugar
⅛ teaspoon salt
1 teaspoon vanilla extract

1. Beat cream cheese and butter at medium speed with an electric mixer until creamy. Gradually add sugar and salt, beating until blended. Stir in vanilla. **Makes** 1⅔ cups.

Coconut Sheet Cake

PREP: 15 MIN., COOK: 45 MIN., OTHER: 30 MIN.

3 large eggs
1 (8-ounce) container sour cream
⅓ cup water
1 (8.5-ounce) can cream of coconut
½ teaspoon vanilla extract
1 (18.25-ounce) package white cake mix
Coconut-Cream Cheese Frosting

1. Beat eggs at high speed with an electric mixer 2 minutes. Add sour cream, ⅓ cup water, and next 2 ingredients, beating well after each addition. Add cake mix, beating at low speed just until blended. Beat at high speed 2 minutes. Pour batter into a greased and floured 13- x 9-inch baking pan.
2. Bake at 325° for 40 to 45 minutes or until a wooden pick inserted in center comes out clean. Cool cake in pan on a wire rack. Cover pan with plastic wrap, and freeze cake 30 minutes. Remove cake from freezer.
3. Spread Coconut-Cream Cheese Frosting on top of chilled cake. Cover and store in refrigerator. **Makes** 12 servings.
Note: If desired, cake can be baked in 1 greased and floured 15- x 10-inch jelly-roll pan for 30 to 32 minutes or until a wooden pick inserted in center comes out clean. **Makes** 15 servings.

Coconut-Cream Cheese Frosting
This delectable frosting is very rich and thick.

PREP: 10 MIN.

1 (8-ounce) package cream cheese,
    softened
½ cup butter, softened
3 tablespoons milk
1 teaspoon vanilla extract
1 (16-ounce) package powdered sugar
1 (7-ounce) package sweetened flaked
    coconut

1. Beat cream cheese and butter at medium speed with an electric mixer until creamy; add milk and vanilla, beating well. Gradually add sugar, beating until smooth. Stir in coconut. **Makes** 4 cups.

Mississippi Mud Cake

The women of Huffman United Methodist Church in Birmingham, Alabama, used this recipe for the church's 125th anniversary celebration. Of the 100 cakes made, none were left over.

PREP: 20 MIN., COOK: 30 MIN.

1 cup butter, melted
2 cups sugar
½ cup unsweetened cocoa
4 large eggs, lightly beaten
1 teaspoon vanilla extract
⅛ teaspoon salt
1½ cups all-purpose flour
1½ cups coarsely chopped pecans, toasted
1 (10.5-ounce) bag miniature marshmallows
Chocolate Frosting

1. Whisk together melted butter and next 5 ingredients in a large bowl. Stir in flour and chopped pecans. Pour batter into a greased and floured 15- x 10-inch jelly-roll pan.
2. Bake at 350° for 20 to 25 minutes or until a wooden pick inserted in center comes out clean. Remove from oven; top warm cake evenly with marshmallows.

Return to oven, and bake 5 more minutes.
3. Drizzle Chocolate Frosting over warm cake. Cool completely. **Makes** 15 servings.
Note: Substitute 2 (19.5-ounce) packages brownie mix, prepared according to package directions, for first 7 ingredients, if desired. Stir in chopped pecans. Bake at 350° for 30 minutes. Proceed with marshmallows and frosting as directed.

Chocolate Frosting

PREP: 10 MIN.

1 (16-ounce) package powdered
    sugar
½ cup milk
¼ cup butter, softened
⅓ cup unsweetened cocoa

1. Beat all ingredients at medium speed with an electric mixer until smooth. **Makes** 2 cups.

Dark Chocolate Bundt Cake

"This divine cake is a must for my chocolate-loving family. My pan is a little smaller than what the recipe calls for, so I fill it halfway and bake the extra batter in disposable aluminum foil pans to give out to family and friends during the holidays."

ASHLEY LEATH, ASSISTANT RECIPE EDITOR

(EDITOR'S CHOICE)

Dark Chocolate Bundt Cake

This cake is so simple to make you won't believe
you started from scratch. (also pictured on cover)

PREP: 20 MIN.; COOK: 1 HR., 20 MIN.; OTHER: 45 MIN.

8 ounces semisweet chocolate,
    coarsely chopped
1 (16-ounce) can chocolate syrup
1 cup butter, softened
2 cups sugar
4 large eggs
2½ cups all-purpose flour
½ teaspoon baking soda
¼ teaspoon salt
1 cup buttermilk
1 teaspoon vanilla extract
Garnishes: Wintry-White Icing, strawberry slices

1. Melt chocolate in a microwave-safe bowl at HIGH for 30-second intervals until melted (about 1½ minutes total). Stir in chocolate syrup until smooth.
2. Beat butter at medium speed with an electric mixer until creamy. Gradually add sugar, beating at medium speed until light and fluffy. Add eggs, 1 at a time, beating just until blended after each addition.
3. Sift together flour, baking soda, and salt. Add to butter mixture alternately with buttermilk, beginning and ending with flour mixture. Beat at low speed just until blended after each addition. Stir in vanilla and melted chocolate just until blended. Pour batter into a greased and floured 14-cup Bundt pan.
4. Bake at 325° for 1 hour and 20 minutes or until a long wooden pick inserted in center comes out clean. Cool cake in pan on a wire rack 15 minutes; remove from pan to wire rack, and let cool 30 minutes or until completely cool. Garnish, if desired. **Makes** 12 servings.

Wintry-White Icing

PREP: 5 MIN.

2 cups powdered sugar
3 to 4 tablespoons milk
1 teaspoon vanilla extract

1. Stir together all ingredients in a medium bowl until smooth. **Makes** about ¾ cup.

Milk Chocolate Pound Cake

Melted candy bars make this pound cake super moist.

PREP: 15 MIN.; COOK: 1HR., 5 MIN.; OTHER: 15 MIN.

1 cup butter, softened
1½ cups sugar
4 large eggs
6 (1.55-ounce) milk chocolate candy
    bars, melted
2½ cups all-purpose flour
¼ teaspoon baking soda
⅛ teaspoon salt
1 cup buttermilk
1 cup chopped pecans
½ cup chocolate syrup
2 teaspoons vanilla extract
Powdered sugar (optional)

1. Beat butter at medium speed with an electric mixer 2 minutes or until creamy. Gradually add sugar, beating 5 to 7 minutes. Add eggs, 1 at a time, beating after each addition just until yellow disappears. Add melted candy bars, stirring well.
2. Combine flour, baking soda, and salt; add to butter mixure alternately with buttermilk, beginning and ending with flour mixture. Mix at low speed after each addition just until blended. Stir in pecans, chocolate syrup, and vanilla.
3. Pour batter into a greased and floured 10-inch tube pan or 12-cup Bundt pan. Bake at 325° for 1 hour and 5 minutes or until a wooden pick inserted in center comes out clean. Cool in pan on a wire rack 10 to 15 minutes; remove from pan, and cool completely on wire rack. Sprinkle with powdered sugar, if desired. **Makes** 12 servings.
Note: For testing purposes only, we used Hershey's Milk Chocolate Candy Bars.

Chocolate Italian Cake

This wonderful cake is a chocolate version of the classic Italian Cream Cake.

PREP: 30 MIN., COOK: 30 MIN., OTHER: 10 MIN.

5 large eggs, separated
½ cup butter, softened
½ cup shortening
2 cups sugar
2¼ cups all-purpose flour
¼ cup unsweetened cocoa
1 teaspoon baking soda
1 cup buttermilk
1 cup sweetened flaked coconut
⅔ cup finely chopped pecans
2 teaspoons vanilla extract
Chocolate-Cream Cheese Frosting
        (opposite page)
Garnish: pecan halves

1. Beat egg whites at high speed with an electric mixer until stiff peaks form; set aside.

2. Beat butter and shortening until creamy; gradually add sugar, beating well. Add egg yolks, 1 at a time, beating until blended after each addition.

3. Combine flour, cocoa, and baking soda; add to butter mixture alternately with buttermilk, beginning and ending with flour mixture. Beat at low speed until blended after each addition. Stir in coconut, chopped pecans, and vanilla. Fold in egg whites. Pour batter into 3 greased and floured 8-inch round cake pans.

4. Bake at 325° for 25 to 30 minutes or until a wooden pick inserted in center comes out clean. Cool in pans 10 minutes. Remove cake layers to wire racks, and cool completely.

5. Spread Chocolate-Cream Cheese Frosting between layers and on top and sides of cake. Garnish, if desired. Store in refrigerator. **Makes** 1 (3-layer) cake.

Buttered F
With Bana

PREP: 30 MI

1 cup bu
2½ cups
6 large e
3 cups all
¼ teaspo
1 (8-ounc
1 teaspo
1 teaspo
½ cup sug
Buttered F
Bananas F
Vanilla ice

1. Beat but
mixer unti
4 to 5 min
time, beati

Chocolate Italian
Cake

Chocolate-Cream Cheese Frosting

PREP: 10 MIN.

1 (8-ounce) package cream cheese,
    softened
½ cup butter, softened
2 teaspoons vanilla extract
¼ teaspoon ground cinnamon
1 (16-ounce) package powdered
    sugar
¼ cup unsweetened cocoa
¼ cup buttermilk
⅔ cup finely chopped pecans

1. Beat first 4 ingredients at medium speed with an electric mixer until creamy.
2. Combine powdered sugar and cocoa; gradually add to butter mixture alternately with buttermilk, beginning and ending with powdered sugar mixture. Beat at low speed until blended after each addition. Stir in pecans. **Makes** 4 cups.

Hummingbird Cake

This recipe originally ran in the magazine in 1978, and the stream of letters from readers requesting the recipe has never stopped.

PREP: 36 MIN., COOK: 23 MIN.

3 cups all-purpose flour
2 cups sugar
1 teaspoon baking soda
½ teaspoon salt
1 teaspoon ground cinnamon
3 large eggs, lightly beaten
¾ cup vegetable oil
1½ teaspoons vanilla extract
1 (8-ounce) can crushed pineapple,
    undrained
1 cup chopped pecans
1¾ cups mashed ripe banana
    (about 4 large)
Cream Cheese Frosting

1. Combine first 5 ingredients in a large bowl; add eggs and oil, stirring just until dry ingredients are moistened. Add vanilla, pineapple, pecans, and bananas, stirring just until combined.
2. Pour batter into 3 greased and floured 9-inch round cake pans.
3. Bake at 350° for 23 minutes or until a wooden pick inserted in center comes out clean. Cool in pans on wire racks 10 minutes; remove from pans, and cool completely on wire racks.
4. Spread Cream Cheese Frosting between layers and on top and sides of cake. Store in refrigerator. **Makes** 1 (3-layer) cake.

Cream Cheese Frosting

PREP: 5 MIN.

½ cup butter, softened
1 (8-ounce) package cream cheese,
    softened
1 (16-ounce) package powdered sugar,
    sifted
1 teaspoon vanilla extract
½ cup chopped pecans

1. Beat butter and cream cheese at medium speed with an electric mixer until creamy. Gradually add powdered sugar, beating at low speed until blended. Beat at high speed until smooth; stir in vanilla and pecans. **Makes** 3¼ cups.

> **"Who can resist a handheld cake swathed in creamy frosting? We call for using a mixer, but you can stir together by hand with great results. Because the mixer adds more air to the batter, you'll end up with 17 cakes rather than 24 when you stir by hand."**

MARIAN COOPER CAIRNS, TEST KITCHENS PROFESSIONAL

(EDITOR'S CHOICE)

Chocolate-Mint Cupcakes

PREP: 10 MIN.; COOK: 25 MIN.; OTHER: 1 HR., 10 MIN.

1 (18.25-ounce) package German chocolate
    cake mix
1 (16-ounce) container sour cream
¼ cup butter, melted
2 large eggs
1 teaspoon vanilla extract
Chocolate Buttercream
¼ cup finely chopped thin crème de menthe
    chocolate mints
Garnish: shaved or chopped thin crème de menthe
    chocolate mints (optional)

1. Beat first 5 ingredients at low speed with an electric mixer just until dry ingredients are moistened. Increase speed to medium, and beat 3 to 4 minutes or until smooth, stopping to scrape bowl as needed.
2. Place paper baking cups in muffin pans, and coat with cooking spray; spoon batter evenly into baking cups, filling each two-thirds full.
3. Bake at 350° for 25 minutes or until a wooden pick inserted in center comes out clean. Cool in pans on wire racks 10 minutes; remove cupcakes from pans to wire racks, and cool 1 hour or until completely cool.
4. Prepare Chocolate Buttercream as directed, stirring in ¼ cup finely chopped thin crème de menthe chocolate mints. Spread cupcakes evenly with Chocolate Buttercream. Garnish with shaved or chopped thin crème de menthe chocolate mints, if desired. Store in refrigerator. **Makes** 2 dozen.
Note: For testing purposes only, we used Andes Créme de Menthe Thins.

Chocolate Buttercream

PREP: 10 MIN.

½ cup butter, softened
1 (3-ounce) package cream
    cheese
1 (16-ounce) package powdered
    sugar
¼ cup milk
1 teaspoon vanilla extract
1 cup dark chocolate morsels

1. Beat butter and cream cheese at medium speed with an electric mixer until creamy. Gradually add powdered sugar, beating at low speed until blended. Increase speed to medium, and slowly add milk and vanilla, beating until smooth.
2. Microwave dark chocolate morsels in a microwave-safe bowl at MEDIUM 1½ to 2 minutes or until melted and smooth, stirring at 30-second intervals. Gradually add melted chocolate to butter mixture; beat until blended and smooth. **Makes** 3 cups.
Note: For testing purposes only, we used Nestlé Chocolatier Dark Chocolate Morsels.

Coconut Cupcakes

PREP: 15 MIN.; COOK: 25 MIN.; OTHER: 1 HR., 10 MIN.

1 (18.25-ounce) package white cake mix
    with pudding
1¼ cups buttermilk
¼ cup butter, melted
2 large eggs
2 teaspoons vanilla extract
½ teaspoon almond extract
Coconut Buttercream (opposite page)
Sweetened flaked coconut

1. Beat first 6 ingredients at low speed with an electric mixer just until dry ingredients are moistened. Increase speed to medium, and beat 2 minutes or until batter is smooth, stopping to scrape bowl as needed.

Coconut Cupcakes

2. Place paper baking cups in muffin pans, and coat with cooking spray; spoon batter evenly into baking cups, filling each two-thirds full.

3. Bake at 350° for 25 minutes or until a wooden pick inserted in center comes out clean. Cool in pans on wire racks 10 minutes; remove cupcakes from pans to wire racks, and cool 1 hour or until completely cool.

4. Spread cupcakes evenly with Coconut Buttercream, and sprinkle with sweetened flaked coconut.
Makes 2 dozen.
Note: For testing purposes only, we used Pillsbury Moist Supreme Classic White Cake Mix.

Coconut Buttercream

PREP: 10 MIN.

½ cup butter, softened
1 (3-ounce) package cream cheese
1 (16-ounce) package powdered sugar
¼ cup cream of coconut
1 teaspoon vanilla extract

1. Beat butter and cream cheese at medium speed with an electric mixer until creamy. Gradually add powdered sugar, beating at low speed until blended. Increase speed to medium, and slowly add cream of coconut and vanilla, beating until smooth. **Makes** 3 cups.

Heavenly Angel Food Cake

You may also bake this in an ungreased angel food cake pan for 30 to 35 minutes or in three ungreased (9-inch) round pans for 15 to 18 minutes or until a wooden pick inserted in center comes out clean. (also pictured on back cover)

PREP: 15 MIN., COOK: 35 MIN., OTHER: 1 HR.

2½ cups sugar
1½ cups all-purpose flour
¼ teaspoon salt
2½ cups egg whites
1 teaspoon cream of tartar
1 teaspoon vanilla extract
1 teaspoon fresh lemon juice
Lemon-Cream Cheese Frosting (opposite page)
Garnishes: fresh mint leaves

1. Line bottom and sides of a 13- x 9-inch baking pan with aluminum foil, allowing 2 to 3 inches to extend over sides of pan. (Do not grease pan or foil.) Sift together first 3 ingredients.

2. Beat egg whites and cream of tartar at high speed with a heavy-duty electric stand mixer until stiff peaks form. Gradually fold in sugar mixture, ⅓ cup at a time, folding just until blended after each addition. Fold in vanilla and lemon juice. Spoon batter into prepared pan. (Pan will be very full. The batter will reach almost to the top of the pan.)

Heavenly Angel Food Cake

3. Bake at 375° on an oven rack one-third up from bottom of oven 30 to 35 minutes or until a wooden pick inserted in center of cake comes out clean. Invert cake onto a lightly greased wire rack; let cool, with pan over cake, 1 hour or until completely cool. Remove pan; peel foil off cake. Transfer cake to a serving platter. Spread Lemon-Cream Cheese Frosting evenly over top of cake. Garnish, if desired. Store in refrigerator. **Makes** 15 servings.

Lemon-Cream Cheese Frosting

This is a very soft frosting, perfect for spreading over a sheet cake. If you use it for a layer cake, reduce the lemon juice to 1 Tablespoon.

PREP: 10 MIN.

1½ (8-ounce) packages cream cheese,
    softened
¼ cup butter, softened
¼ cup fresh lemon juice
1 (16-ounce) package powdered sugar
2 teaspoons lemon zest

1. Beat cream cheese and butter at medium speed with an electric mixer until creamy; add lemon juice, beating just until blended. Gradually add powdered sugar, beating at low speed until blended; stir in lemon zest. **Makes** about 3½ cups.

> **Though I'm not a big fan of angel food cake, I just love this recipe. It's a snap to put together, and the wonderful texture of the cake is perfectly complimented by the fluffy lemon frosting.**
>
> ASHLEY LEATH, ASSISTANT RECIPE EDITOR

Warm Fudge-Filled Cheesecake

PREP: 20 MIN.; COOK: 1 HR., 15 MIN.; OTHER: 1 HR.

½ cup butter, softened
⅓ cup sugar
1 cup all-purpose flour
1 tablespoon vanilla, divided
⅔ cup chopped pistachios
4 (8-ounce) packages cream cheese,
    softened
1½ cups sugar
4 large eggs
1 (12-ounce) package semisweet chocolate
    mini-morsels
Sweetened whipped cream (optional)
Garnish: chocolate shavings

1. Beat butter at medium speed with an electric mixer until creamy; add ⅓ cup sugar, beating well. Gradually add flour, beating at low speed until blended. Stir in 1 teaspoon vanilla and pistachios. Press into bottom and 1½ inches up sides of a 9-inch springform pan.
2. Bake at 350° for 12 to 15 minutes or until golden. Cool on a wire rack.
3. Beat cream cheese at medium speed with an electric mixer until light and fluffy; gradually add 1½ cups sugar, beating well. Add eggs, 1 at a time, beating just until yellow disappears. Stir in remaining 2 teaspoons vanilla (do not overmix).
4. Pour half of batter into crust, and sprinkle with chocolate morsels to within ¾ inch of edge. Pour in remaining batter, starting at outer edge and working toward center. Place cheesecake on a baking sheet.
5. Bake at 350° for 1 hour or until set. Cool on a wire rack 1 hour. Serve slightly warm with sweetened whipped cream, if desired. Garnish, if desired. Store in refrigerator. **Makes** 12 servings.

MAKE AHEAD
Key Lime Cheesecake With Strawberry Sauce

PREP: 20 MIN.; COOK: 1 HR., 13 MIN.; OTHER: 8 HR., 15 MIN.

2 cups graham cracker crumbs
¼ cup sugar
½ cup butter, melted
3 (8-ounce) packages cream cheese, softened
1¼ cups sugar
3 large eggs
1 (8-ounce) container sour cream
1½ teaspoons lime zest
½ cup Key lime juice
Garnishes: strawberry halves, lime slice,
    lime zest
Strawberry Sauce

1. Stir together first 3 ingredients; press on bottom and 1 inch up sides of a greased 9-inch springform pan. Bake at 350° for 8 minutes; cool.
2. Beat cream cheese at medium speed with an electric mixer until fluffy; gradually add 1¼ cups sugar, beating until blended. Add eggs, 1 at a time, beating well after each addition. Stir in sour cream, lime zest, and juice. Pour batter into crust.
3. Bake at 325° for 1 hour and 5 minutes; turn oven off. Partially open oven door; let stand in oven 15 minutes. Remove from oven, and immediately run a knife around edge of pan, releasing sides.
4. Cool completely in pan on a wire rack; cover and chill 8 hours. Garnish, if desired, and serve with Strawberry Sauce. Store in refrigerator. **Makes** 10 to 12 servings.

Strawberry Sauce

PREP: 5 MIN.

1¼ cups fresh strawberries
¼ cup sugar
1½ teaspoons grated lime rind

1. Process all ingredients in a food processor until smooth, stopping to scrape down sides. **Makes** 1 cup.

384 sweet endings

Pecan Praline Cheesecake
PREP: 30 MIN.; COOK: 1 HR., 10 MIN.; OTHER: 9 HR.

1½ cups crushed gingersnaps (about 24 cookies)
½ cup butter, melted and divided
3 (8-ounce) packages cream cheese, softened
1 cup granulated sugar
6 tablespoons all-purpose flour, divided
3 large eggs
1 teaspoon vanilla extract
¼ teaspoon salt
¼ cup firmly packed light brown sugar
½ cup chopped pecans, toasted
15 caramels (optional)
2 tablespoons heavy whipping cream (optional)

1. Stir together gingersnaps and ¼ cup melted butter; press mixture into bottom and 2 inches up sides of a 9-inch springform pan.
2. Beat cream cheese, granulated sugar, and 2 tablespoons flour at medium speed with an electric mixer 2 minutes. Add eggs, vanilla, and salt; beat 3 minutes. Pour batter into prepared crust. Set aside.
3. Stir together brown sugar, pecans, remaining ¼ cup flour, and remaining ¼ cup melted butter until crumbly. Sprinkle around edge of cream cheese mixture.
4. Bake at 300° for 1 hour and 10 minutes or until center is firm. Turn off oven. Leave cheesecake in oven 30 minutes. Remove cheesecake from oven; cool in pan on a wire rack 30 minutes.
5. Cover and chill 8 hours. Drizzle caramel topping on edge of chilled cheesecake, if desired. To make caramel topping, place caramels and whipping cream in a 1-cup microwave-safe bowl. Microwave at HIGH 30 seconds to 1 minute, stirring halfway through cooking time, until melted. Store in refrigerator.
Makes 10 to 12 servings.
Note: Substitute commercial caramel ice-cream topping for caramel topping, if desired.

Sour Cream Cheesecake
PREP: 25 MIN.; COOK: 1 HR., 5 MIN.; OTHER: 8 HR., 20 MIN.

1 cup graham cracker crumbs
¼ cup finely chopped pecans
1 tablespoon brown sugar
3 tablespoons butter, melted
3 (8-ounce) packages cream cheese, softened
1 cup sugar
4 large eggs
2 teaspoons vanilla extract
1 (16-ounce) carton sour cream
⅓ cup red currant jelly
1 pint fresh strawberries, sliced

1. Combine first 4 ingredients; press mixture into bottom of a 9-inch springform pan. Bake at 325° for 10 minutes. Cool on a wire rack.
2. Beat cream cheese at medium speed with an electric mixer until creamy; gradually add 1 cup sugar, beating until smooth. Add eggs, 1 at a time, beating until blended after each addition. Stir in vanilla. Gently stir sour cream into cream cheese mixture. Pour into prepared crust.
3. Bake at 325° for 50 to 55 minutes or until center is almost set. Turn oven off. Carefully run a knife around edge of pan to loosen cheesecake. Let cheesecake stand in oven with door closed 20 minutes. Remove from oven. Cool on a wire rack; cover and chill at least 8 hours.
4. Heat currant jelly in a small saucepan over low heat until melted; cool. Arrange sliced strawberries on top of cheesecake. Brush melted jelly evenly over strawberries. Remove sides of pan before serving. Store in refrigerator. **Makes** 10 to 12 servings.

White Chocolate-Raspberry Cheesecake

Raspberry preserves make a luscious layer within this cheesecake. (pictured on cover)

PREP: 22 MIN., COOK: 58 MIN., OTHER: 8 HR.

2 cups graham cracker crumbs
3 tablespoons sugar
½ cup butter, melted
5 (8-ounce) packages cream cheese, softened
1 cup sugar
2 large eggs
1 tablespoon vanilla extract
12 ounces white chocolate, melted and
    cooled slightly
¾ cup raspberry preserves
Garnish: fresh raspberries

1. Preheat oven to 350°. Combine first 3 ingredients; press crumb mixture into bottom of a lightly greased 9-inch springform pan. Bake at 350° for 8 minutes; cool slightly.
2. Beat cream cheese at medium speed with an electric mixer until creamy; gradually add 1 cup sugar, beating well. Add eggs, 1 at a time, beating after each addition. Stir in vanilla. Add melted white chocolate, beating well.
3. Microwave raspberry preserves in a small microwave-safe bowl at HIGH 30 seconds to 1 minute or until melted; stir well.
4. Spoon half of cream cheese batter into prepared crust; spread a little more than half of melted preserves over batter, leaving a ¾-inch border. Spoon remaining cream cheese batter around edges of pan, spreading toward the center. Cover remaining raspberry preserves, and chill.
5. Bake at 350° for 50 minutes or until cheesecake is just set and slightly browned. Remove from oven; cool completely on a wire rack. Cover and chill at least 8 hours.
6. Run a knife around edge of pan, and release sides. Reheat remaining preserves briefly in microwave to melt. Pour preserves over top of cheesecake, leaving a 1-inch border. Remove sides of pan. Garnish each serving, if desired. Store in refrigerator. **Makes** 12 servings.
Note: To remove seeds from raspberry preserves, press preserves through a fine sieve using the back of a spoon, if desired.

Chocolate-Cherry Tart

This rich, dense dessert is a great choice for easy entertaining.

PREP: 25 MIN.; COOK: 1 HR., 10 MIN.; OTHER: 8 HR.

1½ cups chocolate cookie crumbs
2 tablespoons sugar
¼ cup butter, melted
1 cup sugar
½ cup butter, melted
2 large eggs
½ teaspoon vanilla extract
¼ teaspoon almond extract
⅔ cups all-purpose flour
1 teaspoon baking powder
3 tablespoons cocoa
1 (16-ounce) can pitted tart water-packed
    red cherries, well drained
½ cup chopped pecans, toasted
1 cup whipping cream
2 tablespoons powdered sugar
2 tablespoons cherry liqueur (optional)

1. Combine first 3 ingredients; press firmly into bottom and 1 inch up sides of a greased and floured 9-inch springform pan. Set crust aside.
2. Beat 1 cup sugar and ½ cup melted butter at medium speed with an electric mixer until smooth. Add eggs and flavorings, beating well.
3. Combine flour, baking powder, and cocoa; add to egg mixture, beating until well blended. Stir in cherries and pecans; pour into prepared crust.
4. Bake at 325° for 1 hour and 10 minutes or until center springs back when touched. Cool on a wire rack.
5. Cover tart, and chill 8 hours.
6. Beat whipping cream until foamy; gradually add powdered sugar, beating until soft peaks form. Gently fold in liqueur, if desired.
7. Remove sides of springform pan; slice tart into wedges. Serve whipped cream mixture with tart. Store leftovers in refrigerator. **Makes** 1 (9-inch) tart.

Cream Cheese Flan

You can invert this pretty flan onto any flat dish with a rim.

PREP: 15 MIN.; COOK: 1 HR., 25 MIN.; OTHER: 3 HR., 5 MIN.

1½ cups sugar, divided

7 egg yolks

1 (14-ounce) can sweetened condensed milk

1 (12-ounce) can evaporated milk

¾ cup milk

1½ teaspoons vanilla extract

⅛ teaspoon salt

4 egg whites

1 (8-ounce) package cream cheese

1. Sprinkle 1 cup sugar in a medium-size heavy saucepan; place over medium heat, and cook, stirring constantly, 5 minutes or until sugar melts and turns a light golden brown. Quickly pour hot caramelized sugar into a 9-inch cake pan. Using oven mitts, tilt dish to evenly coat bottom and sides. Let stand 5 minutes (sugar will harden).

2. Whisk together egg yolks and next 5 ingredients in a large bowl.

3. Process egg whites, cream cheese, and remaining ½ cup sugar in blender until smooth. Stir egg white mixture into egg yolk mixture. Pour custard mixture through a wire-mesh strainer into a large bowl; pour custard over caramelized sugar.

4. Place dish in a large shallow pan. Add hot water to pan to a depth of one-third up sides of pan.

5. Bake at 350º for 1 hour and 20 minutes. Carefully remove cake pan from water bath; cool completely on a wire rack. Cover and chill at least 3 hours.

6. Run a knife around edge of flan to loosen; invert onto a serving plate. Store leftovers in refrigerator. **Makes** 6 to 8 servings.

Fudge Pie

Fudge Pie

PREP: 12 MIN., COOK: 40 MIN.

¾ cup butter
3 (1-ounce) unsweetened chocolate baking
    squares
3 large eggs
1½ cups sugar
¾ cup all-purpose flour
1 teaspoon vanilla extract
¾ cup chopped pecans, toasted and divided
Toppings: vanilla ice cream, chocolate syrup

1. Cook butter and chocolate in a small saucepan over low heat, stirring often until melted.
2. Beat eggs at medium speed with an electric mixer 5 minutes. Gradually add sugar, beating until blended. Gradually add chocolate mixture, flour, and vanilla, beating until blended. Stir in ½ cup pecans.
3. Pour mixture into a lightly greased 9-inch pie plate.
4. Bake at 350° for 35 to 40 minutes or until center is firm. Cool. Top each serving with vanilla ice cream and chocolate syrup; sprinkle with remaining chopped pecans. **Makes** 1 (9-inch) pie.

Fudgy Chocolate Malt-Peppermint Pie
PREP: 45 MIN., COOK: 40 MIN., OTHER: 8 HR.

½ cup butter
2 (1-ounce) unsweetened chocolate
   baking squares
1 (1-ounce) semisweet chocolate
   baking square
1 cup granulated sugar
2 large eggs
1 teaspoon vanilla extract
¼ cup all-purpose flour
¼ cup chocolate malt mix
¼ teaspoon salt
¼ teaspoon ground cinnamon
1 cup coarsely chopped pecans
1 pint peppermint ice cream, softened
1 cup whipping cream
¼ cup powdered sugar
¼ cup crushed peppermint candy

1. Melt first 3 ingredients in a heavy saucepan over low heat, stirring occasionally until smooth. Remove from heat; cool.
2. Beat chocolate mixture and granulated sugar at medium speed with an electric mixer until blended. Add eggs and vanilla, beating until smooth. Add flour and next 3 ingredients, beating until blended. Stir in pecans. Pour into a lightly greased 9-inch pie plate.
3. Bake at 325° for 40 minutes. Remove from oven; cool completely on wire rack.
4. Press down center of crust gently. Spread ice cream over crust. Cover and freeze 8 hours.
5. Beat whipping cream and powdered sugar at medium speed with electric mixer until soft peaks form. Spread over ice cream. Sprinkle with crushed candy. Store in freezer. **Makes** 1 (9-inch) pie.
Note: For testing purposes only, we used Ovaltine Chocolate Malt Mix.

Coffee Ice Cream Pie
PREP: 20 MIN., COOK: 12 MIN.

1 (7-ounce) can flaked coconut
½ cup butter, melted
½ cup chopped pecans
2 tablespoons all-purpose flour
½ gallon coffee ice cream, softened
1 cup whipping cream
¼ cup sifted powdered sugar
Chocolate curls
¼ cup Kahlúa or other coffee-flavored
   liqueur (optional)

1. Combine first 4 ingredients; press mixture in bottom and up sides of a 10-inch pie plate. Bake at 375° for 10 to 12 minutes or until lightly browned; cool completely on a wire rack. Spoon ice cream into prepared crust, and freeze until firm.
2. Beat whipping cream until foamy; gradually add powdered sugar, beating until soft peaks form. Spread whipped cream over ice cream layer; top with chocolate curls. Cut into wedges; drizzle each serving with 1 tablespoon Kahlúa, if desired. Store leftovers in freezer. **Makes** 1 (10-inch) pie.

Luscious Lemon Pie

A chilled lemon (or lime) pie is a refreshing dessert after a grilled fish dinner. Substitute fresh lime juice and zest for a lime pie.

PREP: 15 MIN., COOK: 8 MIN., OTHER: 3 HR.

1 cup sugar
3 tablespoons cornstarch
1 tablespoon lemon zest
¼ cup butter
¼ cup fresh lemon juice
1 cup milk
3 egg yolks, lightly beaten
1 (8-ounce) container sour cream
1 baked 9-inch pastry shell
Whipped cream
Garnish: lemon zest

1. Combine first 7 ingredients in a heavy saucepan. Cook over medium heat 7 to 8 minutes or until smooth and thickened, stirring constantly. Remove from heat.
2. Fold sour cream into filling, and pour into pastry shell; cover and chill at least 3 hours before serving. Top pie with whipped cream, and garnish, if desired. Store in refrigerator. **Makes** 1 (9-inch) pie.

Coconut Cream Pie

Look for cream of coconut near the piña colada and margarita mixes.

PREP: 25 MIN., COOK: 8 MIN., OTHER: 2 HR.

1⅔ cups graham cracker crumbs
¼ cup sugar
⅓ cup butter, melted
1 (8-ounce) package cream cheese, softened
1 cup cream of coconut
1 (3.4-ounce) package cheesecake instant pudding mix
1 (6-ounce) package frozen sweetened flaked coconut, thawed
1 (8-ounce) container frozen whipped topping, thawed
1 cup whipping cream
Garnish: sweetened flaked coconut

1. Stir together first 3 ingredients; press mixture evenly in bottom and up sides of a 9-inch pie plate.
2. Bake at 350° for 8 minutes; remove to a wire rack, and cool completely.
3. Beat cream cheese and cream of coconut at medium speed with an electric mixer until smooth. Add pudding mix, beating until blended.
4. Stir in coconut; fold in whipped topping. Spread cream cheese mixture evenly into prepared crust; cover and chill 2 hours or until set.
5. Beat whipping cream with an electric mixer until soft peaks form, and spread evenly over top of pie. Garnish, if desired. Store in refrigerator. **Makes** 1 (9-inch) pie.
Note: For testing purposes only, we used Jell-O Instant Pudding Cheesecake Flavor.

Key Lime Pie

PREP: 30 MIN., COOK: 38 MIN., OTHER: 8 HR.

1¼ cups graham cracker crumbs
¼ cup firmly packed light brown sugar
⅓ cup butter, melted
2 (14-ounce) cans sweetened
    condensed milk
1 cup fresh Key lime juice
2 egg whites
¼ teaspoon cream of tartar
2 tablespoons sugar
Garnish: lime slices

1. Combine first 3 ingredients. Press into a 9-inch pie plate. Bake at 350° for 10 minutes; cool. Stir together milk and lime juice until blended. Pour into crust.

2. Beat egg whites and cream of tartar at high speed with an electric mixer just until foamy. Add sugar, 1 tablespoon at a time, beating until soft peaks form and sugar dissolves (2 to 4 minutes). Spread meringue over filling.

3. Bake at 325° for 25 to 28 minutes. Chill 8 hours. Garnish, if desired. Store in refrigerator. **Makes** 8 servings.

Key Lime Pie

Lemon-Blueberry Cream Pie

PREP: 25 MIN., COOK: 8 MIN., OTHER: 2 HR.

1⅔ cups graham cracker crumbs
¼ cup granulated sugar
⅓ cup butter, melted
1 (8-ounce) package cream cheese, softened
1 (14-ounce) can sweetened condensed milk
¼ cup powdered sugar
1 (3.4-ounce) package lemon instant
   pudding mix
2 teaspoons lemon zest
½ cup fresh lemon juice
1 pint fresh blueberries
2 tablespoons blueberry preserves
1 cup whipping cream
Garnishes: lemon slices, fresh blueberries

1. Stir together first 3 ingredients; press evenly in bottom and up sides of a 9-inch pie plate.
2. Bake piecrust at 350° for 8 minutes; remove piecrust to a wire rack, and cool completely.
3. Beat cheese, milk, and powdered sugar at medium speed with an electric mixer until creamy. Add pudding mix, zest, and juice; beat until blended. Spread half of lemon mixture evenly into prepared crust.
4. Stir together blueberries and preserves; spread evenly over lemon mixture. Spread remaining lemon mixture over blueberry mixture; cover and chill 2 hours or until set.
5. Beat whipping cream with an electric mixer until soft peaks form, and spread around outer edge of pie, forming a 3-inch border. Store in refrigerator. Garnish, if desired. **Makes** 1 (9-inch) pie.

Lemon-Blueberry Cream Pie

Fresh Blackberry Pie

Though this pie should be assembled and served the same day, you can get a head start by combining the berries and sugar and chilling them the night before.

PREP: 30 MIN.; COOK: 17 MIN.; OTHER: 10 HR., 30 MIN.

1½ cups fresh blackberries
1¼ cups sugar, divided
½ (15-ounce) package refrigerated piecrusts
3 tablespoons cornstarch
1¼ cups water
½ teaspoon vanilla extract
1 (3-ounce) package raspberry gelatin
4 drops blue liquid food coloring
Sweetened whipped cream (optional)

1. Gently toss berries and ¼ cup sugar in a large bowl; cover and chill 8 hours. Drain.
2. Fit piecrust into a 9-inch pie plate according to package directions; fold edges under, and crimp. Prick bottom and sides of piecrust with a fork.
3. Bake at 450° for 7 to 9 minutes or until lightly browned.
4. Stir together cornstarch and remaining 1 cup sugar in a small saucepan; slowly whisk in 1¼ cups water and vanilla. Cook over medium heat, whisking constantly, 7 to 8 minutes or until mixture thickens.
5. Stir together raspberry gelatin and blue liquid food coloring in a small bowl; whisk into the warm cornstarch mixture.
6. Spoon blackberries into piecrust. Pour glaze evenly over berries, pressing down gently with a spoon to be sure all berries are coated. Chill 2½ hours. Serve with whipped cream, if desired. **Makes** 1 (9-inch) pie.

Granny Smith Apple Pie

PREP: 30 MIN., COOK: 50 MIN.

1½ (15-ounce) packages refrigerated piecrusts, divided
6 medium Granny Smith apples, peeled and sliced
1½ tablespoons lemon juice
¾ cup brown sugar
½ cup granulated sugar
⅓ cup all-purpose flour
1 teaspoon ground cinnamon
½ teaspoon ground nutmeg

1. Unroll and stack 2 piecrusts; gently roll or press together. Fit into a 9-inch deep-dish pie plate.
2. Toss together apple and lemon juice in a large bowl. Combine brown sugar and next 4 ingredients; sprinkle over apple mixture, and toss to coat. Spoon into prepared piecrust.
3. Unroll remaining piecrust; place over filling. Fold edges under, and crimp; cut slits in top for steam to escape.
4. Bake at 450° for 15 minutes. Reduce oven temperature to 350°, and bake 35 more minutes. **Makes** 1 (9-inch) pie.

Sweet Potato Pie

Sweet Potato Pie

PREP: 10 MIN., COOK: 45 MIN.

1 (14½-ounce) can mashed sweet potatoes
¾ cup milk
¾ cup firmly packed brown sugar
2 large eggs
1 tablespoon butter, melted
½ teaspoon salt
½ teaspoon ground cinnamon
1 unbaked (9-inch) pastry shell
Sweetened whipped cream
Garnish: ground cinnamon

1. Process first 7 ingredients in a blender until smooth, stopping once to scrape down sides. Pour into pastry shell.
2. Bake at 400° for 10 minutes. Reduce oven temperature to 350°, and bake 35 minutes or until a knife inserted in center comes out clean, shielding edges with aluminum foil after 20 minutes to prevent excessive browning. Let cool completely. Serve with whipped cream. Garnish, if desired. **Makes** 1 (9-inch) pie.

Simmie's Pecan Pie

PREP: 5 MIN., COOK: 1 HR.

3 large eggs
¾ cup sugar
1 cup dark corn syrup
3 tablespoons butter, melted
⅛ teaspoon salt
1 teaspoon vanilla extract
1½ cups chopped pecans
1 unbaked 9-inch pastry shell

1. Stir together eggs and sugar until blended. Stir in corn syrup and next 3 ingredients. Stir in chopped pecans. Pour mixture into pastry shell. Place pie on a baking sheet.
2. Bake at 400° on lower oven rack for 15 minutes. Reduce oven temperature to 325°, and bake 40 to 45 more minutes, shielding with aluminum foil to prevent excessive browning, if necessary. **Makes** 1 (9-inch) pie.

Mystery Pecan Pie

Taste pecan pie and cheesecake together in this recipe, and the only mystery will be "Where'd it all go?"

PREP: 15 MIN., COOK: 55 MIN.

1 (15-ounce) package refrigerated
    piecrusts
1 (8-ounce) package cream cheese,
    softened
4 large eggs
¾ cup sugar, divided
2 teaspoons vanilla extract,
    divided
¼ teaspoon salt
1 cup chopped pecans
1 cup light corn syrup

1. Unroll and stack 2 piecrusts; gently roll or press together. Fit into a 9-inch pie plate according to package directions; fold edges under, and crimp.
2. Beat cream cheese, 1 egg, ½ cup sugar, 1 teaspoon vanilla, and salt at medium speed with an electric mixer until smooth. Pour into piecrust. Sprinkle with pecans.
3. Stir together corn syrup, remaining 3 eggs, remaining ¼ cup sugar, and remaining 1 teaspoon vanilla; pour mixture over pecans.
4. Bake at 350° for 50 to 55 minutes or until set. **Makes** 1 (9-inch) pie.

Fudge Swirl Soufflé

*A rich swirl of chocolate and vanilla awaits
under the puffed hat of this showy soufflé.*

PREP: 25 MIN.; COOK: 1 HR., 25 MIN.

¾ cup sugar
½ cup all-purpose flour
¾ teaspoon salt
1⅓ cups milk
1 teaspoon vanilla extract
1 cup semisweet chocolate morsels
6 large eggs, separated
¼ teaspoon cream of tartar
Garnish: chocolate curls
Crème Anglaise (optional)

1. Combine first 3 ingredients in a saucepan. Combine milk and vanilla; gradually stir into sugar mixture. Cook over medium heat, stirring constantly, 15 minutes or until mixture thickens. Remove from heat.
2. Transfer half of mixture to a bowl. Add chocolate morsels to remaining mixture in saucepan; stir until melted.
3. Beat egg yolks at medium speed with an electric mixer until thick and pale. In another bowl, beat egg whites and cream of tartar at high speed until stiff peaks form, using clean, dry beaters. Stir half of egg yolks and whites into vanilla custard mixture and half into chocolate custard mixture.
4. Pour mixtures alternately in a zig-zag pattern into an ungreased 3-quart soufflé dish or casserole. Cut through mixture with a knife to create a swirl.
5. Bake at 325° for 65 to 70 minutes or until set. Serve immediately. Garnish soufflé, and serve with Crème Anglaise, if desired. **Makes** 8 servings.

Crème Anglaise

PREP: 5 MIN., COOK: 15 MIN.

2 cups milk
½ cup sugar, divided
5 egg yolks
½ teaspoon vanilla extract

Combine milk and ¼ cup sugar in a heavy non-aluminum saucepan. Bring to a simmer over medium heat. Beat remaining ¼ cup sugar and egg yolks at high speed until pale and mixture forms a ribbon.
6. Gradually add hot milk mixture to egg mixture, whisking until blended; return to saucepan. Cook over medium-low heat, stirring constantly, until custard thickens slightly and coats a spoon. Remove from heat; strain, if necessary. Stir in vanilla. Cover and chill. **Makes** 2 cups.

QUICK
Cranberries Jubilee

*These scarlet jewels are a takeoff on cherries jubilee
and are perfect for a Christmas dessert.*

PREP: 10 MIN., COOK: 10 MIN.

1 cup sugar
1 cup water
⅛ teaspoon ground cinnamon
2 cups fresh cranberries
⅓ cup chopped pecans
3 tablespoons rum
Vanilla ice cream

1. Combine first 3 ingredients in a large saucepan. Bring to a boil over medium heat, stirring occasionally; boil 5 minutes. Add cranberries, and return to a boil; cook 5 minutes, stirring occasionally. Stir in pecans. Remove from heat.
2. Place rum in a long-handled, small saucepan; heat just until warm (do not boil). Remove from heat. Ignite with a long match; pour over cranberries. When flames die down, spoon over ice cream. **Makes** 1½ cups.

Tiramisù

You can also toast the ladyfingers for a crunchier texture.

PREP: 25 MIN., COOK: 20 MIN., OTHER: 2 HR.

⅔ cup granulated sugar
3 cups whipping cream, divided
2 large eggs
2 egg yolks
1 tablespoon all-purpose flour
½ vanilla bean, split
1 (16-ounce) package mascarpone cheese
3 tablespoons Marsala (optional)
¾ cup brewed espresso*
1 (7-ounce) package ladyfingers
3 tablespoons powdered sugar
1 tablespoon unsweetened cocoa

1. Stir together granulated sugar, 2 cups whipping cream, and next 4 ingredients in a heavy saucepan. Cook over medium heat, stirring constantly, 20 minutes or until thickened. Cool mixture completely. Discard vanilla bean. Whisk in mascarpone.

2. Stir Marsala into espresso, if desired. Dip each ladyfinger in espresso mixture, and arrange on bottom and up sides of a 13- x 9-inch baking dish. Pour mascarpone mixture over ladyfingers.

3. Beat remaining 1 cup whipping cream at high speed with an electric mixer until foamy; gradually add powdered sugar, beating until soft peaks form. Spoon over mascarpone mixture, and sprinkle with cocoa. Cover and chill 2 hours. Store in refrigerator. **Makes** 10 servings.

*Espresso can be prepared by stirring together 1 cup hot water and ½ cup ground espresso coffee. Let stand 5 minutes; pour through a wire-mesh strainer lined with a coffee filter into a glass measuring cup, discarding grounds.

Note: For testing purposes only, we used Bellino Savoiardi ladyfingers.

Lemon Bars

Lemon bars never go out of style, and this version is one of our favorites. The bars have a thick shortbread crust and just the right amount of lemon in the chess-like filling.

PREP: 20 MIN., COOK: 50 MIN.

2½ cups all-purpose flour, divided
¾ cup sifted powdered sugar, divided
1 cup cold butter, cut up
½ teaspoon baking powder
4 large eggs, beaten
2 cups sugar
⅓ cup lemon juice

1. Combine 2 cups flour and ½ cup powdered sugar. Cut butter into flour mixture with a pastry blender until mixture is crumbly.
2. Spoon flour mixture into a 13- x 9-inch pan; press into pan evenly and firmly, using fingertips. Bake at 350° for 20 to 25 minutes or until lightly browned.
3. Combine ½ cup flour and baking powder; set aside. Combine eggs, 2 cups sugar, and lemon juice; beat well. Stir dry ingredients into egg mixture, and pour over crust.
4. Bake at 350° for 22 to 25 minutes or until lightly browned and set. Cool on a wire rack. Sprinkle with ¼ cup powdered sugar, and cut into bars.
Makes 2 dozen.

Double Chocolate Brownies

Two kinds of chocolate distinguish these brownies from the typical box variety. They sport a white chocolate base laced with chunks of dark chocolate.

PREP: 20 MIN., COOK: 35 MIN.

1 cup butter
8 (2-ounce) white chocolate baking bars, coarsely chopped
4 large eggs
¼ teaspoon salt
1 cup sugar
1 tablespoon vanilla extract
2 cups all-purpose flour
1 (8-ounce) package semisweet chocolate squares, coarsely chopped
1 cup macadamia nuts or pecans, coarsely chopped

1. Melt butter in a heavy saucepan over low heat; remove from heat. Add half of white chocolate (do not stir).
2. Beat eggs and salt at high speed with an electric mixer until mixture is slightly thickened. Add sugar; beat 2 to 3 minutes or until fluffy. Add butter mixture, vanilla, and flour, beating until smooth.
3. Fold in remaining chopped white chocolate, semisweet chocolate, and nuts. Spoon batter into a lightly greased 15- x 10-inch jelly-roll pan.
4. Bake at 350° for 30 to 35 minutes or until lightly browned. Cool in pan on wire rack. Cut into squares.
Makes 2½ dozen.

Double Chocolate
Chunk-Peanut Cookies

Double Chocolate Chunk-Peanut Cookies

PREP: 20 MIN., COOK: 15 MIN. PER BATCH

½ cup butter, softened
½ cup shortening
1 cup chunky peanut butter
1 cup granulated sugar
1 cup firmly packed brown sugar
2 large eggs
2 cups all-purpose flour
⅓ cup unsweetened cocoa, sifted
1½ teaspoons baking soda
1 teaspoon baking powder
1 teaspoon ground cinnamon
½ teaspoon salt
1 cup unsalted dry-roasted peanuts
1 (11.5-ounce) bag chocolate chunks

1. Beat butter and shortening at medium speed with an electric mixer until creamy; add chunky peanut butter and sugars, beating well. Add eggs, beating until blended.
2. Combine flour and next 5 ingredients. Add to butter mixture, beating well.
3. Stir in peanuts and chocolate chunks.
4. Shape dough into 2-inch balls (about 2 tablespoons for each cookie). Flatten slightly, and place on ungreased baking sheets.
5. Bake at 375° for 12 to 15 minutes or until lightly browned. Cool on pan 2 minutes; remove to wire racks to cool completely. **Makes** about 2 dozen.

Chocolate Chunk-Peanut Cookies: Increase flour to 2½ cups; omit ⅓ cup unsweetened cocoa. Proceed as directed.

White Chocolate Chip-Oatmeal Cookies

PREP: 15 MIN., COOK: 12 MIN. PER BATCH

1 cup butter, softened
1 cup firmly packed light brown sugar
1 cup granulated sugar
2 large eggs
2 teaspoons vanilla extract
3 cups all-purpose flour
1 teaspoon baking soda
1 teaspoon baking powder
1 teaspoon salt
1½ cups uncooked regular oats
1 (12-ounce) package white
    chocolate morsels
1 cup coarsely chopped pecans

1. Beat butter at medium speed with an electric mixer until creamy; gradually add sugars, beating well. Add eggs, 1 at a time, beating just until yellow disappears after each addition. Stir in vanilla.
2. Combine flour and next 3 ingredients; gradually add to butter mixture, beating until blended. Stir in oats, morsels, and pecans. Drop by tablespoonfuls onto greased baking sheets.
3. Bake at 350° for 12 minutes. Cool on baking sheets 3 minutes; remove to wire racks to cool completely.
Makes about 5 dozen.

Giant Oatmeal-Spice Cookies

If you like these cookies spicier, increase the ginger, allspice, and cloves.

PREP: 20 MIN., COOK: 14 MIN. PER BATCH

1½ cups all-purpose flour
1 teaspoon ground cinnamon
½ teaspoon salt
½ teaspoon baking soda
½ teaspoon ground ginger
¼ teaspoon ground allspice
⅛ teaspoon ground cloves
1 cup butter, softened
1 (16-ounce) package dark brown sugar
2 large eggs
1 teaspoon vanilla extract
3 cups quick-cooking oats
1 cup chopped pecans, toasted
½ cup raisins (optional)

1. Stir together first 7 ingredients.
2. Beat butter and sugar at medium speed with an electric mixer until fluffy. Add eggs and vanilla, beating until blended. Gradually add flour mixture, beating at low speed until blended.
3. Stir in oats, chopped pecans, and if desired, raisins.
4. Drop dough by ¼ cupfuls onto lightly greased baking sheets; lightly press down dough.
5. Bake, in batches, at 350° for 12 to 14 minutes (cookies should not be brown around the edges, and centers will not look quite done). Cool slightly on baking sheets. Remove to wire racks; cool completely.
Makes about 2½ dozen.

Soft Coconut Macaroons

Soft Coconut Macaroons

Using clear vanilla extract will keep the macaroons pearly white,
but if you don't have it, regular vanilla will work fine.

PREP: 10 MIN., COOK: 20 MIN. PER BATCH

4 egg whites
2⅔ cups sweetened flaked coconut
⅔ cup sugar
¼ cup all-purpose flour or matzo meal
½ teaspoon clear vanilla extract
¼ teaspoon salt
¼ to ½ teaspoon almond extract

1. Stir together all ingredients in a large bowl, blending well. Drop dough by teaspoonfuls onto lightly greased baking sheets.
2. Bake at 325° for 18 to 20 minutes or until golden. Remove to wire racks to cool completely. **Makes** about 3 dozen.

Raspberry Shortbread

PREP: 15 MIN., COOK: 40 MIN.

1 cup butter, softened
⅔ cup granulated sugar
2½ cups all-purpose flour
1 (10-ounce) jar seedless raspberry jam,
    divided
1½ cups powdered sugar
3½ tablespoons water
½ teaspoon almond extract

1. Beat butter and granulated sugar at medium speed with an electric mixer until light and fluffy. Gradually add flour, beating at low speed until blended. Divide dough into 6 equal portions; roll each portion into a 12- x 1-inch strip. Place strips on lightly greased baking sheets.
2. Make a ½-inch-wide x ¼-inch-deep indentation down the center of each strip using the handle of a wooden spoon. Spoon half of jam evenly into indentations.
3. Bake at 350° for 15 minutes. Remove from oven; spoon remaining jam into indentations. Bake 5 more minutes or until lightly browned.
4. Whisk together powdered sugar, water, and extract; drizzle over warm shortbread. Cut each strip diagonally into 1-inch slices. Cool in pans on wire racks.
Makes 6 dozen.

FAMILY FAVORITE
Sweetheart Jamwiches

PREP: 45 MIN., COOK: 17 MIN.

1 (15-ounce) package refrigerated
    piecrusts
1 egg white, lightly beaten
2 tablespoons granulated sugar
1 (3-ounce) package cream cheese,
    softened
¼ cup powdered sugar
2 tablespoons butter, softened
½ teaspoon almond extract
½ (10-ounce) jar seedless raspberry preserves
    or strawberry jam
½ cup white chocolate morsels
1 tablespoon butter
Red sparkling sugar (optional)

1. Unroll piecrusts on a lightly floured surface. Cut with a 2-inch heart-shaped cookie cutter. Reroll remaining dough, and repeat procedure (there should be a total of 46 pastry hearts). Brush 1 side of each pastry heart with egg white, and sprinkle evenly with granulated sugar. Place pastry hearts on 2 ungreased baking sheets.
2. Bake at 400° for 7 to 8 minutes or until lightly browned. Remove hearts to wire racks, and let cool.
3. Stir together cream cheese, powdered sugar, 2 tablespoons butter, and almond extract until blended.
4. Spread cream cheese mixture evenly on unsugared sides of half the hearts; spread about ½ teaspoon preserves over mixture on each heart. Top with remaining hearts, unsugared sides down.
5. Microwave white chocolate morsels and 1 tablespoon butter in a glass bowl at HIGH 1 minute or until melted. Stir until smooth. Place mixture in a small zip-top plastic freezer bag; seal bag. Snip a tiny hole in 1 corner of bag, and drizzle over tarts. Let cool completely; sprinkle with red sparkling sugar, if desired. Place in candy boxes, if desired.
Makes 23 tarts.

Lemon-Raspberry Tartlets

*Seasonal berries, fresh herbs, and lemon twists add
an array of color to these time-saving tartlets.*

PREP: 10 MIN

1 (10-ounce) jar lemon curd
1 (2.1-ounce) package frozen mini phyllo pastry
    shells, thawed
60 to 75 fresh raspberries (about ¾ pint)*
Garnishes: 15 small fresh mint leaves, lemon rind curls

1. Spoon lemon curd evenly into 15 mini pastry
shells; top each with 4 to 5 fresh berries. Garnish,
if desired. **Makes** 15 tartlets.
*60 to 75 fresh blueberries may be substituted.
Note: For testing purposes only, we used Athens
Mini Fillo Shells.

index